Bridges Between Psychology and Linguistics:
A Swarthmore Festschrift for Lila Gleitman

Bridges Between Psychology and Linguistics:
A Swarthmore Festschrift for Lila Gleitman

Edited by

Donna Jo Napoli
Swarthmore College

Judy Anne Kegl
*Swarthmore College
and Rutgers University*

LEA LAWRENCE ERLBAUM ASSOCIATES, PUBLISHERS
1991   Hillsdale, New Jersey   Hove and London

Lawrence Erlbaum Associates, Inc., Publishers
365 Broadway
Hillsdale, New Jersey 07642

Library of Congress Cataloging-in-Publication Data

Bridges between psychology and linguistics : a Swarthmore festschrift
for Lila Gleitman / edited by Donna Jo Napoli, Judy Anne Kegl.
   p.   cm.
   Includes bibliographical references and index.
   ISBN 0-8058-0783-7
   1. Psycholinguistics. I. Gleitman, Lila R. II. Napoli, Donna
Jo., 1948-   III. Kegl, Judy Anne.
   P37.B75 1991
   401'.9--dc20   90-43394
                                                 CIP

Printed in the United States of America
10   9   8   7   6   5   4   3   2   1

Contents

Introduction

Lila Gleitman taught linguistics and psycholinguistics at Swarthmore College from 1968 to 1972. In just those 4 years, Lila instilled a passion for linguistic inquiry in dozens of students. Furthermore, she founded linguistic studies at the college. Several of the articles in this volume are written by people who studied with her during those years.

Lila's influence on Swarthmore students and alumni extends well beyond those 4 years. As a psychologist of language, Lila has dedicated herself to the study of the language of one of our most unempowered groups—children, particularly blind and deaf children. She has been a pioneer in first-language acquisition and reading studies, and her work has helped to establish the legitimacy of these fields. Researchers in child language, in reading, and in the acquisition, processing, and production of language in alternate modalities are all, directly or indirectly, Lila's students. It is in this spirit that other Swarthmore alumni contributed to this volume.

Lila spans the gap from developmental psychology to theoretical linguistics in multiple ways. She has provided strong evidence that structure can influence the acquisition of language's syntactic and semantic rules. Her work serves as a model to any scholar brave enough to attempt such a bridge. Lila's work with Feldman and Goldin-Meadow in 1978 on children from whom linguistic communication was withheld offers persuasive evidence that the language mechanism is innate in the human brain. Precisely this kind of work forms the foundation upon which theories of universal grammar stand. Lila has made the balancing act of universal grammarians less precarious. And in the desire to laud Lila for this work, still other alumni contributed to this volume.

There are 14 articles here, ranging from those that fall squarely in the area of cognitive psychology to ones that concentrate on issues in psycholinguistics; in particular, to those that fall squarely in theoretical core linguistics. We therefore present this volume as one more bridge from psychology to linguistics, honoring Lila, without whose work this bridge would not be easy to discern.

We begin the volume with cognitive psychology. Emily Bushnell (class of 1972) looks at the developmental course of visually guided reaching, showing that following its emergence at about 4 months of age and a period of intense practice, visually guided reaching actually declines in practice. Bushnell attributes this decline to skill mastery, where visually elicited reaches exhibited after the decline are distinguished from those of very young infants. This decline entails a release of attention, which may be an important factor in infants' cognitive development.

David Rosenbaum (class of 1970) argues that one of the bridges between psychology and linguistics is the system that allows intentions to be physically expressed. The motor system allows for the realization of intentions, both linguistic and nonlinguistic. Movements of the body, like the segments of a sentence, must be ordered according to one's wishes. But how is the ordering achieved? What sorts of representations govern production of voluntary motor acts? How are the representations structured, executed, and formed? What happens to the representations after they have been executed? The studies described in Rosenbaum's paper provide some answers. They will look surprisingly familiar to students of linguistics and branches of psychology that, historically, have paid little attention to the cognitive substrates of motor performance.

Lance Rips (class of 1970) takes a hard look at the role of similarity in judging category membership and offers further experimental evidence in support of Armstrong, Gleitman, and Gleitman's claim that there is no way to reduce category membership to similarity among instances. He discusses several experiments in which subjects were asked to decide about the similarity of instances with respect to certain categories, the typicality of instances with respect to the same categories, or the likelihood that instances are actually members of these categories. By examining these three types of judgment as a function of the properties of the instances, he identifies factors that affect similarity but don't affect categorizing. He then examines criticisms of these results and their impact upon resemblance theory.

Thomas F. Shipley (class of 1982) discusses some of the properties of objects in our environment and the consequences for the visual system of these properties. The relative smoothness of objects may allow the visual system to identify the boundaries of objects using discontinuities in various factors, such as luminance, motion, and stereoscopic disparity. He discusses a number of domains including brightness illusions, texture grouping, stereoscopic depth perception, and structure from optic flow. The chapter also explores recent extensions of the usefulness of discontinuities into other domains such as unit formation, apparent motion, and intermodal interactions. In each domain, the use of discontinuities appears to minimize the computational requirements for perception of objects or surfaces.

D. D. Hilke (class of 1973) offers this volume's first chapter that enters the arena of psycholinguistics. Hilke examines the relationship between infant vocalizations and significant changes in experience. The changes in facial expressions of 8-month-old infants were recorded and used as indicators of corresponding changes in subjective experience. The amount of vocalization correlated directly to the amount of subjective experience. Hilke proposes that many infant vocalizations are initially meaningful from the infant's perspective, suggesting that vocal occurrence develops from being personally expressive into being more conventionally expressive. There is the possibility that the infant's evolving capacity to structure vocalizations may be related to the corresponding evolution of the capacity to structure subjective experiences.

Gary Dell (class of 1972) collaborated with Paula Brown (who is one of two contributors to this volume who is not a Swarthmore alumnus) on approaching the question of what mechanisms are involved as a speaker adapts the verbal message to the listener's comprehension needs. They distinguish particular listener adaptations from generic listener adaptations. The first type are adaptive to variations in the circumstances of characteristics of the listener(s) (are they children, are they distant, are they less competent in some way?) and are created by consulting a model of the listener in the speaker's beliefs. The second type is a bias toward making content, structure, and manner of production easy to comprehend for the average listener, and this adaptation occurs through devices inherent in the speech production (such as exaggerated articulation). It relies on the intimate relationship between information processing during production and that during comprehension.

Margaret B. Rawson (class of 1923 and the recipient of an honorary doctorate from Swarthmore College in 1983) looks at the interrelationships between the study of dyslexia and the study of linguistics as a science, showing that they are increasingly interacting and mutually beneficial. Their differing angles of approach and competence give perspective to their common interest in language acquisition. Linguistics probes toward the mind of man, the symbol user, while linguistics itself explores the language route. Dyslexia researchers study the mind's organ, the brain, as well as other components of human nature, to learn how human beings function or fall short in the acquisition of language and how problems in this area can best be alleviated. Rawson argues that verbal language as a human attribute has been achieved through evolutionary time and has become so firmly a part of the human genetic equipment that one childhood now suffices for establishing speech well, generally with relatively little awareness of teaching. The alphabetic principle of phonologic coding from speech to print is the necessary next step in the learning of a language like English. An indispensable coin of the linguistics–dyslexia realm, it is fundamental to the later stages in achievement of literacy and in the full use of language as a major resource for enrichment of the human mind.

Ray Jackendoff (class of 1965) and Barbara Landau (the second contributor who is not a Swarthmore alumnus) explore how language encodes objects and spatial relationships, starting from the premise that any aspect of spatial understanding that can be expressed in language must also be present in spatial representations. However, language imposes constraints on the expression of these spatial relationships that do not follow from the spatial representational system itself, but rather (at least partially) from a property of language design. They discuss in detail the differences between the way object shapes are represented when they are being named and the way they are represented when they play the role of figure or ground object in a locational expression. They argue that these differences follow from a neurological separation of spatial cognition into "what" and "where." Thus, linguistic evidence offers a new source of insight into the nature of spatial representation in the brain.

Elizabeth F. Shipley (class of 1951) looks at the English familiar form of address used today only by a few linguistically conservative Quakers. Years ago, she participated in a study of the pattern of the use of familiar (T) and formal (V) second person pronouns in Quaker families, and found that most children addressed with T by their parents consistently used V. This paper reports on a follow-up study of some of the same families, where the use of T is found to have declined still further. One conclusion of the original is supported by the follow-up results: Children's initial mastery of second person pronouns is based upon observation of speech not addressed to the child. The relevant conversations for pronoun mastery are not, then, primarily conversations between members of the child's immediate family. In addition, individuals who received T within the family as children but used only V were found in adulthood to have some residual competency with T forms. The data here suggest evidence for children's role in language change.

Thomas Hun-tak Lee (class of 1973) analyzes the factors relevant to the interpretation of scope in Mandarin. His evidence comes from first-language acquisition. He designed experiments in which children in the ages of 3 to 8 years were asked to act out their interpretation of two sentences, where one showed a scope ambiguity and the other did not. Linearity and hierarchical superiority were among the potential factors in scope interpretation tested here. He compared his findings to the interpretations assigned to those sentences by adult speakers. The findings show that although younger children may apply a variety of strategies that are not necessarily consistent from one speaker to the next, by the age of 6 years, Chinese speakers have established a strong tendency to interpret wide or narrow scope on the basis of linear order. By the age of 7 years, this tendency is a firm rule. In addition, ambiguity in scope interpretation can be linked to a thematic hierarchy, wherein sensitivity to this interpretation principle does not arise until after the age of 7 years.

Ann Reed (class of 1965) gives us the first purely theoretical linguistic chapter. She discusses the interpretation of English partitive constructions like "one of the boys" and argues that this interpretation requires that the matrix NP evoke a discourse entity which is a subgroup of the embedded NP and that the embedded NP (e.g. "the boys") access a discourse entity. The requirement of discourse reference accounts for several distributional idiosyncrasies of partitive expressions, including the Partitive Constraint: the apparent preference for a definite NP in the embedded NP, and the Definite Head Constraint: the necessity for an explicit restrictive modifier when the determiner is "the."

Geoffrey Coulter's (class of 1972) chapter is a study of American Sign Language of the Deaf, ASL, the gestural language used by the Deaf in the United States and parts of Canada. Although ASL has been recognized as a natural human language for some time now (rather than a makeshift system of communication used by deaf people), it has not been clear to many phonologists whether the abstract patterns of articulation of ASL should properly be considered phonological patterns. Here Coulter suggests that three characteristics define a system of articulation as a phonology: (a) having a limited set of arbitrary, discrete components, (b) having linear structure organized hierarchically (into segments, syllables, feet, words, phrases), (c) having a modular system of context-sensitive rules. Because ASL exhibits all these characteristics, we must conclude that ASL has phonological structure of the usual kind, and therefore that at least certain properties of phonological structure are characteristic of language in general, regardless of the peripheral apparatus through which a language expresses itself.

John Goldsmith (class of 1972) argues that the principles that govern phonology give us information about human thought and intelligence; phonology is a cognitive system that organizes information and for which, importantly, is the system of sound contrasts and constructs within the grammar. Goal-directed behavior is manifest in phonology in so-called conspiracies (for example, the fact that the bulk of vowel epenthesis and deletion rules are sensitive to the syllable structure of the output of the rule[s]). Another example of goal-directed behavior is found in spreading rules, which aim to create structures that are as saturated as possible (for example, each vowel getting a tone). Well-formedness conditions and phonological rules interact in mutually supportive ways: Phonological rules apply just in case their output better satisfies the phonotactics than their input. Goldsmith names this view of the system harmonic phonology and suggests that such a dynamic view of phonology might justify a radical reorganization of phonological theory, more in keeping with models of parallel distributed processing.

One last chapter is by Robert May (class of 1973). In this paper, May explores the relationship of Logical Form, as developed in contemporary linguistic theory, to notions of logical form found in philosophical and logical inquiries. The view presented is that this linguistic level embeds a logical form, in the sense that Logical Form represents the information required for the proper application of the rules of the truth definition. The relation of the syntax and semantics of quantification is discussed as a central case in point, and two matters are addressed in this context. Is it a necessary condition that Logical Form be a disambiguated level in order to qualify as a logical form? The second matter is a formal development of the theory of Logical Form intended to capture the generalization that prior syntactic movement is tied to the scope possibilities observed for sentences of multiple generalization.

The bridge is here. We invite you to cross it.

Donna Jo Napoli
Judy Anne Kegl

The *Decline* of Visually Guided Reaching During Infancy*

Emily W. Bushnell
Tufts University

The emergence of visually guided reaching and grasping has long been recognized as an important occurrence during infancy. The origins of this perceptual–motor skill and the precise nature of its precursors are matters currently under investigation and debate by developmental psychologists (for recent discussions, see Bower, 1974; Bushnell, 1981; Lockman & Ashmead, 1983; McDonnell, 1979; von Hofsten, 1982). In this commentary, these popular issues are avoided, and a later phase in the development of eye–hand coordination is focused on instead. The plan is to document that following its emergence and a period of intense exercise, visually guided reaching *declines* in practice and is replaced by reaching of a more visually elicited style in most circumstances. The nature of this decline is then discussed, and in the end, it is suggested that the decline may be of particular significance for infants' cognitive development.

There is general agreement in the literature that visually guided reaching is first exhibited sometime between 3 and 5 months of age (cf., Bower, 1974; Bruner, 1969; Halverson, 1931; McDonnell, 1979; Piaget, 1952; White, Castle, & Held, 1964). At younger ages, infants have been observed to exhibit behaviors that indicate eye–hand coordination (Bower, Broughton, & Moore, 1970; Bruner, 1970; DiFranco, Muir, & Dodwell, 1978; McDonnell, 1979; Rader & Stern, 1982; von Hofsten, 1982; White et al., 1964), but these are not considered to be visually guided reaches. The behaviors have been vari-

*Reprinted with stylistic changes only, with the permission of the publisher from *Infant Behavior and Development*, *8*, (1985), pp. 139–155.

ously identified as intentional reaches (Bower, et al., 1970), swiping (White, et al., 1964), "preadaptations" for reaching (Bruner, 1973), "prefunctional" reaches (von Hofsten, 1982), reaching-like arm movements (Rader & Stern, 1982), and "prereaching" (Trevarthen, 1975). In what follows, the last term is used for brevity's sake, and it should be noted that this early eye–hand coordination is a matter for some debate. The very existence of prereaching has even been questioned (Ruff & Halton, 1978), but von Hofsten's (1982) precise observations of newborns' arm movements seem to authenticate the behavior. However, the continuity of prereaching and later forms of eye–hand behavior is uncertain. Von Hofsten (1984) recently reported that the amount of prereaching decreases abruptly at 7 weeks of age, at which time the form of the behavior changes, too. This break at 7 weeks is then followed by a period of practically no eye–hand behavior, after which reaching activity that can be described as visually guided begins to appear. Also at issue are whether prereaching is sensitive to spatial dimensions such as three-dimensionality (see Bower, 1972; Bower, Dunkeld, & Wishart, 1979; DiFranco, Muir, & Dodwell, 1978; Dodwell, Muir, & DiFranco, 1979) and whether it indexes the intention to touch or grasp the target object (see Bower et al., 1970; von Hofsten, 1982). Amidst the controversies about it, though, there seems to be consensus that prereaching differs from the reaching that emerges at about 4 months in at least three respects. Because these distinctions also figure in the analysis of the development of reaching during the second half of the first year, they are discussed next at some length.

The most obvious distinction between prereaching and later reaching is that prereaching is much less accurate. Bower (1974) reported that the arm extensions of very young infants result in contact with the target object only 40% of the time, whereas those of infants over 20 weeks old result in contact at least 80% of the time. Other researchers have found prereaching to be even less accurate than Bower noted; von Hofsten (1982) reported that his neonatal subjects touched the object on only 22 out of 232 reaches or 9% of the time, Ruff and Halton (1978) reported a hit rate of 7%, and Dodwell, Muir, & DiFranco (1976) reported one of just 3%.

A second distinction between prereaching and the reaching that emerges at about 4 months is that prereaching has been characterized as ballistic, or visually *elicited,* whereas the later reaching is visually *guided.* That is, in prereaching, the arm movement is preprogrammed or fully aimed at the target object before or at the moment the movement is launched. An arm movement with a trajectory that consists of a single movement element would by definition be ballistic, but arm movements with trajectories that consist of several elements at different angles or otherwise distinguished might also be ballistic. In either case, the critical property is that the course of the movement is not purposefully altered during its performance or upon its completion. In contrast, the reaches of infants beginning at about 4 months involve a continuous feedback process; the arm's approach to the target object is monitored and may be adjusted throughout the reach.[1]

The evidence that prereaching arm movements are ballistic is not as strong as that regarding their other properties. The clearest proof would derive from comparing prereaches toward stationary objects to those toward objects whose locations were changed after the initiation of the arm movement; however, this comparison has not yet been made. The evidence that does exist consists first of all of subjective descriptions of very young infants' arm movements as "swipes" (White et al., 1964), "flings" (Bower et al., 1970), and "explosive" (Bruner, 1973). These observations that prereaches are very rapidly executed and therefore unlikely to incorporate constant vigilance and adjustments are substantiated by analyses of their spatiotemporal qualities. Von Hofsten (1982) found that the forward extensions of neonates came closest to the target object on the average just 1.04 seconds after their start. Under similar experimental conditions, the approach time for the (guided) reaches of infants 18 and 21 weeks old averaged about 1.8 seconds (von Hofsten, 1979). The inaccuracy of prereaching in a sense supports that it is ballistic, too. None of the researchers cited earlier for reporting that very young infants' arm movements usually terminate without contacting the object has noted that such misses are followed by corrective actions. The results of two studies in which infants reached while wearing prism glasses also support the notion that prereaching is ballistic; these and the considerable evidence that the reaching that follows prereaching is guided are presented after the third distinction between the two is introduced.

The third distinction between prereaching and the reaching first exhibited at about 4 months has to do with the basis on which each sort of reach is accomplished. For eye–hand coordination, there are actually three variables that may be involved—the visually localized target (the seen target), the visually localized hand (the seen hand), and the proprioceptively or kinesthetically localized hand (the felt hand). Under normal circumstances, reaching can be successful (i.e., be related to the position of the target) if either the seen target and the felt hand *or* the seen target and the seen hand map onto one another

---

[1]It is important to note that identifying the reaching that emerges at about 4 months as visually guided rather than ballistic does not preclude that it may be "predictive." That is, "ballistic" and "predictive" are not synonymous. Von Hofsten and Lindhagen (1979) studied the prehensile responses of infants to moving objects and found that infants can successfully "catch" moving objects at about the same age that they first consistently reach for and successfully grasp stationary ones, namely, at about 4 months. With more detailed analyses of these reaches for moving targets, von Hofsten (1980) showed that such reaches, even by infants of 4 and 5 months, were "predictive," meaning that the hand was aimed at a point where the moving object would be when the reach was completed, rather than at the point where the object was seen when the reach was initiated. Thus, that a reach is "predictive" implies that a future position of the seen object (however perceived or calculated) is used as the goal location rather than the immediate position of the object. The hand may, however, approach that identified goal location either ballistically or with guided control.

or "match." The available evidence (to be reviewed later) indicates that prereaching makes use of the former matching mechanism, whereas the reaching emergent at about 4 months utilizes the latter. That is, the eye–hand coordination of newborns and very young infants seems to be based on some sort of prewired visuoproprioceptive or visuomotor spatial coordination. The eye–hand coordination of somewhat older babies, though, is accomplished otherwise, by their monitoring and progressively reducing the "gap" between the seen target and the seen hand. Thus, for this later sort of reaching, the seen hand must be attended to and localized, but for prereaching, the seen hand is irrelevant.

The idea that eye–hand coordination changes early in life from using the felt hand to using the seen hand is strongly supported by the results of several studies in which the perception of the seen hand was interfered with. Lasky (1977) observed the reaching of infants under normal circumstances and in a mirror condition where they could see the target object but could not see their hands as they reached for it. Infants 3½ 'and 4½ months old reached equally well in the two conditions, indicating that they do not utilize the sight of the hand during reaching. In contrast, infants 5½ and 6½ months old reached more "clumsily" in the mirror condition than otherwise, which suggests that they do rely on the sight of the hand when reaching. The older infants also often aborted reaches and became upset in the mirror condition, presumably because they were "looking for" their hands, which did not appear.

Bower (1976) observed infants reaching for objects while they were wearing prism glasses that laterally displaced the seen object and the seen hand. Under such circumstances, seen target–seen hand reaching will still be successful, but seen target–felt hand reaching will result in a "miss." Bower reported that infants younger than 24 weeks of age routinely missed the object and, following the miss, pulled their hands back and reached erroneously again. Infants older than 24 weeks started their reaches off in the inappropriate direction, but corrected the trajectory as soon as their hands came into view. These "mid-reach" corrective actions reveal not only that the seen hand was attended to by the older infants, but also that their reaches were guided rather than ballistic. Conversely, the younger infants' failure to remedy their misses either within or between reaches supports the claim that prereaching is ballistic. McDonnell (1975) also observed infants who were wearing prism glasses. He reported that infants ranging in age from 4 to 10 months all corrected the trajectories of their reaches, thereby evidencing both use of the seen hand and guidance. However, the youngest infants' trajectories were the most deviant and seemed to reflect an abrupt switch to visual control after a substantial misaimed component. Thus, McDonnell's results, like Bower's, indicate that reliance on visual feedback of the hand during reaching increases between 4 and 6 months.

Finally, the observations of von Hofsten (1979) add to the evidence that, starting at about 4 months, reaching is guided rather than ballistic. He found that 4- and 5-month-old infants' approaches to targets were relatively slow and devious (i.e., made up of zigzag and roundabout movements), consisted of several elements each of about the same duration, and often contained elements directed away from the target. Though such features do not necessarily mean that the reaches were guided, ballistic approaches would ordinarily be more rapid and direct. The infants also generally fixated the target throughout the reach, as is characteristic of guided reaching. Whether the apparent guidance involved the seen hand or the felt hand is not indicated by von Hofsten's data; though the target rather than the hand was fixated, the hand was undoubtedly within the visual field during most of each approach.

The case has been presented that the eye–hand behavior evident during the earliest months of life is inaccurate, ballistic, and based on a mapping of vision and proprioception, whereas the reaching that emerges at about 4 months is more accurate, guided, and based on matching the seen target and the seen hand. It should be noted at this juncture that the second and third distinctions that have been discussed are logically independent; a reach based on matching the seen target and the felt hand, for instance, could be either ballistically aimed or involve continuous monitoring and adjustment (see Hay, 1979). Empirically, however, these two distinctions are often blurred, as techniques for studying one of them often provide information concerning the other, too (as when prism glasses are employed, e.g.). Furthermore, it seems that in practice a ballistic reach could rarely involve the seen hand, because the latter would often be unavailable when the reach was initiated. In what follows, where the term "prereaching" is no longer appropriate, the term "visually elicited" will be used to refer to reaches that are both ballistic and based on a visuoproprioceptive mapping, and the term "visually guided" will be used to refer to reaches that are not ballistic and that are based on reducing the gap between the seen target and the seen hand.

It should also be acknowledged at this point that the particular age at which prereaching is succeeded by the later form is identified somewhat differently by the several investigators whose work has been cited. Thus, Lasky (1977) and Bower (1976) located the transition between 4½ and 6 months, whereas von Hofsten's several studies (1979, 1982, 1984) considered together indicate that it occurs between 2 and 4 months. McDonnell (1975) found that reaching was sensitive to visual feedback of the hand by 4 months, but also noted that it became more so between 4 and 6 months. These differences most likely derive from differences in the subject selection procedures, stimulus conditions, and constraints on posture and vision employed in the various studies. Although the effects of such variables are interesting, what is important for the purposes of this commentary is that by all accounts, guidance and the seen hand become more and more integral aspects of reaching over the first half-year of life.

Eye–hand behavior during the second half-year of life has also been of in-

terest to developmental psychologists. Observations of older infants have generally focused on manual sensitivity to various object properties (e.g., Lockman,
Ashmead, & Bushnell, 1984; Pieraut-le Bonniec, 1985), on handedness (e.g.,
Ramsey, 1980), or on responses in special situations such as those involving
multiple objects or those demanding detour reaching (e.g., Bruner, 1970; Lockman, 1984). However, some evidence concerning the status of visually guided
reaching after its initial appearance has accumulated. McDonnell and Abraham (1979) studied perceptual adaptation in infants who repeatedly reached
for objects while wearing laterally displacing prism glasses. They reasoned that
adaptation should be minimal when reaching is visually guided, because no
intercue discrepancy exists to motivate it; with prism glasses, closing on the
seen target with the seen hand still results in a successful reach, because these
are not displaced relative to one another. McDonnell and Abraham generally
observed aftereffects indicating that adaptation had occurred, but they noted
that the magnitude of adaptation decreased between 5 and 7 months of age.
This finding implies that the seen hand is relied on increasingly over this age
period, as discussed earlier. Interestingly, though, McDonnell and Abraham
found that, after dropping off at 7 months of age, the magnitude of adaptation
then *increased* again by 9 months. McDonnell (1979) interpreted this pattern
of results as evidence that visually guided reaching "peaks" at around 7 months
of age and is then gradually replaced by a more ballistic style of reaching. He
cited Halverson's (1931) descriptions of the target approaches of infants of different ages as further support for this return to visually elicited reaching.

McDonnell's suggestion that reaching becomes *less* visually guided toward
the ¾ mark of the first year is supported by the secondary results of several
recent investigations. Bushnell (1982) studied 8-, 9½-, and 11-month-olds as
they reached for an object that appeared to be located under a little shelf. The
shelf was actually a half-silvered mirror that reflected the image of an object
hidden above the shelf. The reaching situation was therefore similar to that
studied by Lasky (1977); although the hand did not disappear entirely as it
passed under the shelf, its appearance became somewhat transparent and
"ghostly." Although the purpose of the study was to observe the infants' reactions when the object actually located under the shelf differed from the object
seen, a number of main effects of age were found in addition to the condition
effects of major interest. The 8-month-olds looked at the mirror image for shorter durations than the 9½- and 11-month-olds did, they touched the object under the shelf for shorter durations, and they looked and touched simultaneously for shorter durations. Basically, the younger infants were rather reluctant
to interact with the apparatus. Bushnell speculated that the strange appearance of their hands was noticed by the 8-month-olds and disrupted their reaching, as the hand's absence interfered with the reaching of 5½- and 6½-month-
olds in Lasky's study. The 9½- and 11-month-olds, though, did not seem to
be as concerned with the appearance of their hands.

In another task in the same study, Bushnell (1982) compared the behavior of the infants as they reached for an ordinary, palpable object and for an optically created, nonpalpable image of the same object. Both the 9½-month-olds and the 11-month-olds accompanied greater percentages of their touching with looking on the unusual, virtual-object trials (86% and 89%, respectively) than they did on the control trials (69% and 73%, respectively). The 8-month-olds, however, did not exhibit this difference. They showed a ceiling effect, accompanying the same high percentage (84%) of their touching with looking on *both* sorts of trials. Evidently, 8-month-olds visually monitor their prehensile activities intently in most situations, even routine ones, but older infants do not; they monitor their prehensile activities intently only in special circumstances.

Further evidence that the role of visual guidance during reaching becomes less important toward the end of the first year was reported by Lockman, Ashmead, and Bushnell (1984). They observed the hand positioning and looking behavior of 5- and 9-month-old infants as they reached for horizontally and vertically oriented dowels. Infants of both ages usually looked at the dowel throughout the reach, at least until they had touched the target. Sometimes, however, infants stopped looking at the dowel before they touched it, even though they continued the reach and grasped the dowel. Such instances of "looking away" while reaching were significantly more frequent among the 9-month-olds than among the 5-month-olds. The 9-month-olds' reaches with looking away were just as accurate as those with looking throughout, though—that is, they involved no less anticipatory hand orientation.

Thus, in each of the three instances described, infants 9 months and older paid less attention to the seen hand and the seen target as they reached than did younger infants, as would be expected if visually guided reaching declines toward the end of the first year. Von Hofsten's (1979) quantitative analyses of the approach phase of 4- to 9-month-old infants' reaches provide additional support for this same development trend. He found that the patterns for a number of different parameters were all consistent with the notion that reaching becomes more and more preprogrammed as the infant approaches 9 months of age. For instance, the number of distinct movement elements within a given approach decreased between 18 and 36 weeks of age. At 18 weeks, over 60% of the reaches consisted of three or more movement elements, but by 36 weeks, over 75% of the reaches consisted of just one or two movement elements. Furthermore, over the same age period, greater and greater proportions of the duration, the distance, and the force of the reach were lodged within the first movement element as opposed to within subsequent ones.

It seems, then, that the developmental course of visually guided reaching during infancy may be represented by an inverted "U"-shaped curve. Although infants between the ages of about 4 and 8 months make trajectory adjustments and visually attend to the target and to their hands throughout their reaches, infants both younger and older do not. Rather, their reaches are substantially preprogrammed (ballistic) and are accomplished with less attention to the target and the hand. As shown earlier, this general pattern of a developmental rise and then fall of visually guided reaching is well grounded in the empirical literature on infants' eye–hand behavior, though the specific ages at which the successions occur may vary according to the reaching situation and surely vary from infant to infant. Explanations for the rise and subsequent fall of visually guided reaching are not so firmly established, however.

A number of factors have been supposed to be involved in the emergence of visually guided reaching. Bower (1974) suggested that visually guided reaching arises mainly because it is so much more accurate than the prereaching that preceeds it. The visually elicited arm movements of very young infants, it may be recalled, rarely result in contact with the seen object. Prereaching may be inaccurate because the visuoproprioceptive mapping on which it is based is not very precise or because young infants' motor control is relatively poor or both. The important point is that erroneous arm movements resulting from whatever source of imprecision *cannot* be compensated for with visually elicited reaching. An inherent feature of such reaching is that errors are not informative. Upon extending the arm in a direction presumed to be appropriate and then missing the target, there is no way to perceive to what extent and in what direction the arm should be moved to obtain the object after all. The situation is analogous to when one fails to pinpoint an object on top of a table with the hand pointing underneath the table. With visually guided reaching, however, imprecise movements of the arm *can* be compensated for, because the extent and direction of the "miss" are perceivable. As the "gap" between the seen target and the seen hand either shrinks or grows, one knows that the current movement is more or less appropriate. Hence, attending to the seen hand may be a reaching strategy that young infants adopt over prereaching because they discover that it leads more consistently to their contacting and obtaining the reached-for object.

The suggestion that infants adopt the strategy of visual guidance over prereaching because it is more successful presupposes that contacting the seen target is a "desired" or reinforcing consequence of eye–hand behavior. That this motivational circumstance may not pertain prior to 4 months could explain why visually guided reaching does not emerge any earlier than it does. Bower (1974) also argued that during the first months of life, the infant's processing capacity is so limited that he or she cannot attend to the seen target and the seen hand simultaneously. Thus, the discovery that the gap between the target and the hand is informative would be precluded until processing capacity became sufficiently mature at about 4 months.

Neurophysiological maturation may also be a factor in determining the onset of visually guided reaching. Lockman and Ashmead (1983) and von Hofsten (1984) both made reference to Kuyper's work on the primate motor system; this work established that gross movements of the upper limb are effected by a subcortical system (the "proximal" system) that is functional at birth, whereas fine movements of the hand and fingers are effected by a later developing cortical system (the "distal" system). It seems likely that prereaching might reflect the operation of the proximal system, whereas visually guided reaching would require the integrated functioning of both systems. Such a sequence of a simply organized, reflexive behavior being superseded by a more complex, but more adaptive response system is not uncommon in development. By this account, the rise of visually guided reaching would be contingent on the "kicking in" of the distal system at about 4 months.

Probably the motivational, attentional, and neurophysiological considerations mentioned all play a role in the evolution of visually guided reaching during the first 6 months of life. The subsequent decline of visually guided reaching is no doubt also multiply determined, but because it has not been focused on heretofore, specific factors have not been identified. In the following, an explanation for the decline of visually guided reaching that draws primarily on concepts from the fields of learning and information processing is proposed. The account is admittedly speculative, but it is plausible and it leads to some intriguing conclusions involving cognitive development during infancy.

The analysis that is offered to explain the decline of visually guided reaching hinges on the fact that once such reaching emerges at about 4 months, it is for a time employed assiduously. Though the prereaching of newborns and very young infants may only be observed with precise techniques and under certain conditions, parents and developmental psychologists alike know that a typical 6-month-old will reach for (and obtain) any and all objects within arm's length. Indeed, infants from about 5 months on can be counted on to reach for seen objects to such an extent that reaching is used as a dependent variable in many investigations of infant development (see, for example, Bryant, Jones, Claxton, & Perkins, 1972; Yonas & Granrud, 1985). The frequent execution of visually guided reaching constitutes nothing other than practice of a sensorimotor skill, and it naturally leads to first perfection and then overlearning of that skill. It is exactly this repetition and consequent mastery of visually guided reaching that may bring about its eventual decline.

Consider that an unskilled visually guided reach may be thought of as a sequence of discrete responses. The gap between the target and the hand is assessed and a movement made, the gap is reassessed and another movement made, and so on. Von Hofsten's (1979) quantitative descriptions of individual reaches by 15- and 18-week-olds substantiate this characterization, as do McDonnell's (1975) trajectory plots of the reaches of infants wearing prism goggles. According to traditional learning theory (see Mandler, 1962), when such a goal-oriented sequence of responses is executed again and again, response errors are reduced and ultimately eliminated. For example, rats repeatedly placed in a maze with a food reward in the goal box take fewer and fewer wrong turns and finally none. Similarly, infants repeatedly reaching under visual guidance make fewer and fewer overshoots and undershoots and finally none— in the end, the seen target–seen hand gap never widens during a particular reach, but only progressively narrows. Once errorless performance of a sequence of responses has been achieved, further repetitions of the sequence ("overlearning") result in what has been called response "integration" (Mandler, 1962). That is, with repeated errorless executions of a sequence, the transitions or interruptions between the discrete components are smoothed, reduced, and finally eliminated, so that the whole sequence functions as and may be evoked as a unit. This phenomenon of integration apparently occurs at the level of neurophysiology, as is illustrated by Lashley's (1951) classic case of the piano student who, after extensive practice but not initially, can play an arpeggio at a rate faster than that at which the finger movements could be individually programmed. In the case of visually guided reaching during infancy, the process of first error reduction and then response integration is vividly portrayed in von Hofsten's (1979) work on infants' prehensile approaches. His various analyses showed that although the reaches of 4- and 5-month-olds are slow and consist of many "zigs and zags" and "stops and starts," the reaches of 9-month-olds are relatively rapid, direct, and unitary. Bruner (1973) also discussed the integration process specifically with respect to visually guided reaching, albeit in somewhat different terms. He noted that repetition results in the coordination of "feed-forward" or "efferent copy" discharges with the actual feedback received from the effectors as the sequence is executed. He furthermore equated these feed-forward discharges with the "intention" to execute the sequence. Thus, once the feed-forward–feedback coordination is achieved, the whole completed action sequence is in a sense represented in the initially formed intention.

Whether phrased in Mandler's stimulus–response terms or Bruner's sensorimotor terms, the integration resulting from constant practice has the same implication so far as getting the hand to a particular seen location is concerned. Response integration means that the entire sequence of discrete movements required to reduce any given seen target–seen hand gap to nothing can be "unleashed" from an initial assessment of the relative positions of the target and the hand, *with no additional, intermediate assessments being taken.* Such intermediate assessments have been eliminated from the sequence through practice, and the "sequence" is in effect a single, once-aimed movement. Hence, after initiating the one movement, the infant can, without sacrificing accuracy, ignore the hand and look away from the target. It is just such indiscretions— ignoring the hand and looking away from the target—that have been taken as evidence for the reduced role of visual guidance in reaching after about 9 months. Thus, the developmental decline of visually guided reaching may be accounted for by the overlearning of the behavior itself.

The analysis of the decline of visually guided reaching offered above might be verified by studying the eye–hand behavior of infants prevented from practicing or overlearning visually guided reaching after its emergence. One could observe, for example, the consequent reaching behavior of infants who for medical reasons were unable to use their hands for some time between 4 and 8 months of age. Alternatively, one could observe the consequent reaching behavior of infants whose experience had been modified so as to accelerate the emergence and practice of visually guided reaching (see White, 1967; White & Held, 1966). If the mastery of visually guided reaching is responsible for its decline, then the decline should occur later than normal for the "deprived" infants and earlier than normal for the infants in the "enrichment" experiment. The relative amount of motor exercise and the developmental status of other factors involved in reaching tasks would somewhat confound the interpretation of such comparisons, though. The surest way in theory to test the proposed account would be to study the reaching behavior of infants who were able to practice and succeed at visually guided reaching as usual, but who were not able to overlearn it. Imagine, for example, that infants constantly wore prism glasses whose displacement was randomly varied from moment to moment. This kind of experiment is, of course, neither feasible nor ethical, but one would predict that for such subjects, reliance on feedback of the seen hand would not decline as they neared the end of the first year.

An important implication of the proposed explanation for the decline of visually guided reaching is that the nonguided reaches of infants older than 9 months are not equivalent to those of infants younger than 4 months. As is often the case with such nonlinear developmental patterns (Strauss, 1982), the behaviors of either end of the U-shaped curve are only superficially similar. The "visually elicited" reaches after 9 months are not really visually elicited reaches at all, but are actually very skilled, overlearned visually guided reaches. They are still essentially based on matching the positions of the seen hand and the seen target; however, the infant now *knows* so well how to get the seen hand to a seen target in any given location that he or she needn't constantly monitor the gap between them to glean and make use of its information. Another way of characterizing the later reaches is to note that the practice of previous months has led to a perfect coordination between various positions of the seen hand and positions of the felt hand. This perfect coordination means that a seen target–seen hand reach can be accomplished by substituting the felt hand for the seen hand. Such substitution may be involved in the adeptness with which older infants as compared to 4- and 5-month-olds "chase down" a rapidly moving target without directly looking at their hands (von Hofsten, 1980). This sort of seen target–felt hand matching, in which the felt hand in a sense represents the seen hand, is quite different from the visuoproprioceptive mapping on which prereaching is based, in which the seen hand is not a factor of any sort.

The difference between the early visually elicited reaches (prereaching) and those that follow the peak period of visually guided reaching may be fully appreciated if yet another consequence of practice is considered. When a sequence of responses is overlearned, along with the responses becoming integrated, the behavior becomes routinized or "automatic," meaning that the act can be accomplished unconsciously, with little or no drain on the individual's attentional resources (Lachman, Lachman, & Butterfield, 1979; Norman, 1976). This automaticity is indeed often the very goal of practice. Mandler (1975) pointed out that a characteristic of behaviors that initially were executed with considerable attention but have become automatic through extensive practice is that they may be "brought back into consciousness, particularly when they are defective in their particular function" (p. 245). This "return to consciousness" allows the actor to deal with the difficulty that effected the return. Mandler noted, however, that automatic behaviors that have never been under the control of conscious processes (such as reflexes) cannot similarly be brought back to consciousness. If they go awry for some reason, the errors cannot be rectified. The two sorts of visually elicited reaches under discussion typify Mandler's "once conscious" and "never conscious" automatic behaviors. As has already been noted, when their visually elicited reaches fail to obtain an object, older infants increase the extent of visual monitoring (Bushnell, 1982). Similarly, 9- and 10-month-olds readily revert to genuine visually guided reaching to obtain prismatically displaced targets (McDonnell, 1975). When the very young infant's visually elicited prereaches fail, however, there is no such fallback. The reaching is not overlearned, visually guided reaching that can be returned to conscious control for correction. Rather, it is based on a rudimentary visuo-proprioceptive mapping that is hard-wired and never was (nor will be) conscious. When this system fails (as with virtual images and prism glasses), the infant is somewhat in the position of Sperry's (1956) frogs for whom left and right were surgically reversed. He or she is remedyless, and either repeatedly reaches and misses or becomes frustrated and upset (Bower, 1974, 1976; Bower, Broughton, & Moore, 1970).

In most circumstances, of course, the "return" to visually guided reaching that is possible for the older infant is not called for. Except when the perceived location of the target is interfered with, the infant of 9 months or older reaches smoothly and directly to the target without having to think about it. Although the decline of visually guided reaching is an important phenomenon in and of itself and furthermore serves as a prime example of skill mastery, it is in particular the automaticity entailed by the decline that could be of major developmental significance. As is elaborated in the remaining remarks, the automaticity of reaching may facilitate certain key aspects of cognitive development.

The conjecture just introduced rests on the widely accepted notion that consciousness (or focal attention, working space, etc.) is of limited capacity. Hence, when executing an act requires a lot of attention, as in the early stages of skill development, there is little attention available for other purposes. When the

act is overlearned and has become automatic, though, the attention it former-
ly commanded is "released." Bruner (1970, 1973) has emphasized this advantage of mastering a skill. He noted that the released attention may be uti-
lized for embedding the overlearned act as a component itself in a higher-order
act or conversely for analyzing the act and reordering the components to construct a new behavior.

In the case of reaching at about 9 months, an important consequence of
automatization may be that the released attention effectively lengthens the time
that can be spanned by the infant's awareness. Mandler (1975) used the term
"frame of consciousness" to emphasize the limited capacity aspect of attention. Only a certain amount of information regarding past, present, or future
interactions with the environment can be processed ("thought about") at one
time—can "fit" within a single frame of consciousness. Furthermore, cognitive psychologists have suggested that in order for two bits of information
(memories, perceptions, or whatever) to be encoded together and meaningfully related to one another, they must be attended to simultaneously—they must
fit within a single frame of consciousness. For example, Triesman (Triesman
& Gelade, 1980; Triesman & Schmidt, 1982; Triesman, Sykes, & Gelade, 1977)
demonstrated that for two visual features to be conjoined and perceived as forming a single worldly object, they must be present in the same "fixation" (frame)
of attention. Thus, to the extent that a given memory, perception, or activity
demands most of one's attention, other memories, perceptions, or activities
cannot simultaneously be attended to and therefore cannot be related to the
given one. Similarly, if two memories, perceptions, et cetera are separated in
time by a third which demands most of one's attention, the separated items
cannot be related to one another.

Instances of preclusion as just described must often be the case during the
developmental "peak" of visually guided reaching. It has been argued that
between the ages of 4 and 8 months, the act of executing an accurate reach
demands a great deal of the infant's attention. The target and the hand are
concentrated on throughout the act, which may be said to fill a whole frame
of consciousness. Hence, it would not be possible for memories, perceptions,
or activities attended to prior to or after the reach to be meaningfully connected with the reach nor with one another. This restriction would naturally inter-
fere with the encoding of many cause–effect, means–end, or other such sequences of events. For example, the reappearance of an object could not be
related to the reach for the cloth with which it was covered, nor to the memory
of its prior disappearance. Similarly, the reach for an object on which a second object rests could not be related to the subsequent retrieval of the second
object. When the bridging act of reaching no longer fully occupies the infant's
attention, though, the before and after states or the actions and consequences
in such instances can be encoded together. By this reasoning, the automatization of reaching may be considered prerequisite to the attainment of these
familiar cognitive milestones.

To investigate whether the development of visually guided reaching and cognitive development are related in the way that has been proposed, one could first of all examine the correlation between the developmental status of an individual infant's reaching and his or her performance on certain cognitive tasks. The absence of a relationship between the mastery of reaching and success on tasks such as object permanence tasks would comprise evidence against the analysis that has been presented. Alternatively, a direct relationship between reaching and cognitive development would be consistent with the proffered analysis. Such a relationship could, of course, be accounted for in other ways, too; to more clearly identify the mastery of reaching as a determinant of cognitive development, one might examine the cognitive abilities of those infants referred to earlier, whose histories regarding visually guided reaching had been artificially slowed, hastened, or otherwise manipulated. Finally, one could assess the validity of the account that has been presented by focusing on the presumed availability of attention during mature reaching as opposed to during reaching before it has been overlearned. For example, infants could be confronted with left/right discrimination problems in an operant conditioning paradigm, with sometimes head turning and sometimes reaching as the mode of response. The difference in how readily the two sorts of problems were solved could be determined for mature reachers and for infants whose reaching had not yet been overlearned. According to the argument that has been presented, the problems with reaching should be easier relative to the "standard" provided by the problems with head turning for the mature reachers than for the infants whose reaching had not yet been overlearned; for the latter infants, the full attention demanded by the act of reaching would disrupt the connection between the choice of which position to reach toward and whether or not reinforcement ensued.

Researchers have yet to carry out the procedures just mentioned or others that likewise could specifically confirm or disprove the proposed relationship between the decline of visually guided reaching and cognitive development. It is noteworthy, though, that a number of psychologists have perceived "discontinuities" or substantial advances in cognitive development at the ¾ mark of the first year. Foremost among these, of course, is Piaget (1952, 1954), who observed that infants first search for concealed objects and exploit cause–effect or spatial relationships as means to distinct ends at about 8 to 9 months. McCall (1979) similarly marked 8 months as the onset of a distinct stage of cognitive development, characterized by the separation of means from ends. Kagan (1979) and Zelazo and Kearsley (1980) have also argued that a "major cognitive transition" occurs between 9½ and 11½ months, characterized by the emergence of the ability to "activate hypotheses" and evidenced, for example, by the use of objects in functionally appropriate rather than stereotypical ways.

That a qualitative leap forward in cognitive abilities occurs just when reaching has become overlearned is probably not coincidental. The intelligent behaviors referred to by the cited authors—searching for objects, using tools, and so on—almost always involve an act of prehension. To reiterate the argument that has been presented, it seems that the 4- to 8-month-old infant pays full attention to the seen target and the seen hand while reaching for an object. The infant of that age may therefore suffer from a sort of temporal "disconnection syndrome," which would prohibit the apprehension of various relationships critical for the construction of reality. Accordingly, visually guided reaching may serve as a kind of "brake" on cognitive development (Harris, 1983). This brake would be released as visually guided reaching is mastered and no longer requires the infant's conscious control. Only then would the reaching infant have sufficient attentional resources to, in Gratch's (1979) words, "step out of the stream of conduct" and reflect upon what he or she is doing, as opposed to concentrating on just doing it. Thus, it might be that the *decline* of visually guided reaching plays a more direct role in cognitive development than does its emergence.

ACKNOWLEDGMENTS

Preparation of this manuscript was supported in part by Grant HD 18093 from the National Institutes of Health. I wish to thank Jeffrey Lockman, Herb Pick, Beverly Roder, and two anonymous reviewers for their helpful comments on an earlier draft.

Lila—
   Whenever anyone asks me how I came to be an experimental psychologist, I have a very precise answer. It was all on account of you. I remember distinctly the afternoon we chanced to meet in the mimeograph room in Parrish Annex. You asked me what I was going to do after graduating, and when I said I didn't really know, you encouraged me to continue on in psychology. I remember being flattered, and also finding the idea appealing. Your Language and Thought seminar that semester was so challenging and exciting and fun, and well, if my work life (life work?) could be like that, that would be pretty good. I voiced my 60's-shaped objection, though, that academics as a profession seemed rather selfish and irrelevant in view of all the problems in the real world, and you countered with some deep philosophical–historical reasoning about the importance of pursuing knowledge and inspiring the next generation to do the same. I don't recall the details of your argument anymore, but it must have been persuasive, for here I am a psychology professor. As a researcher, I guess I have become my own mentor, but as a teacher, I think often of your example and I aspire to someday excite and influence my students as you did me.
—Emily

REFERENCES

Bower, T. G. R. (1972). Object perception in infants. *Perception, 1,* 15–30.

Bower, T. G. R. (1974). *Development in infancy.* San Francisco: Freeman.

Bower, T. G. R. (1976). Repetitive processes in child development. *Scientific American, 235,* 38–47.

Bower, T. G. R., Broughton, J. M., & Moore, M. K. (1970). Demonstration of intention in the reaching behavior of neonate humans. *Nature, 228,* 679–681.

Bower, T. G. R., Dunkeld, J., & Wishart, J. G. (1979). Infant perception of visually presented objects. *Science, 203,* 1137–1138.

Bruner, J. S. (1968). *Processes of cognitive growth: Infancy.* Worcester, MA: Clark University Press.

Bruner, J. S. (1969). Eye, hand, and mind. In D. Elkind & J. Flavell (Eds.), *Studies in cognitive development* (pp. 223–235). New York: Oxford University Press.

Bruner, J. S. (1970). The growth and structure of skill. In K. Connolly (Ed.), *Mechanism of motor skill development* (pp. 63–94). New York: Academic Press.

Bruner, J. S. (1973). Organization of early skilled action. *Child Development, 44,* 1–11.

Bryant, P. E., Jones, P., Claxton, V., & Perkins, G. M. (1972). Recognition of shapes across modalities by infants. *Nature, 240,* 303–304.

Bushnell, E. W. (1981). The ontogeny of intermodal relations: Vision and touch in infancy. In H. L. Pick, Jr. & R. D. Walk (Eds.), *Intersensory perception and sensory integration* (pp. 5–36). New York: Plenum Press.

Bushnell, E. W. (1982). Visual–tactual knowledge in 8-, 9½-, and 11-month-old infants. *Infant Behavior and Development, 5,* 63–75.

DiFranco, D., Muir, D. W., & Dodwell, P. C. (1978). Reaching in very young infants. *Perception, 7,* 385–392.

Dodwell, P. C., Muir, D. W., & DiFranco, D. (1976). Responses of infants to visually presented objects. *Science, 194,* 209–211.

Dodwell, P. C., Muir, D. W., & DiFranco, D. (1979). Infant perception of visually presented objects. *Science, 203,* 1138–1139.

Gratch, G. (1979). The development of thought and language in infancy. In J. D. Osofsky (Ed.), *Handbook of infant development* (pp. 439–461). New York: Wiley.

Halverson, H. (1931). An experimental study of prehension in infants by means of systematic cinema records. *Genetic Psychology Monographs, 10,* 107–287.

Harris, P. L. (1983). Infant cognition. In P. H. Mussen (Ed.), *Handbook of child psychology: Vol. 2. Infancy and developmental psychobiology* (pp. 689–782). New York: Wiley.

Hay, L. (1979). Spatial–temporal analysis of movements in children: Motor programs versus feedback in the development of reaching. *Journal of Motor Behavior, 11,* 189–200.

Hofsten, C. von. (1979). Development of visually directed reaching: The approach phase. *Journal of Human Movement Studies, 5,* 160–178.

Hofsten, C. von. (1980). Predictive reaching for moving objects by human infants. *Journal of Experimental Child Psychology, 30,* 369–382.

Hofsten, C. von. (1982). Eye–hand coordination in the newborn. *Developmental Psychology, 18,* 450–461.

Hofsten, C. von. (1984). Developmental changes in the organization of prereaching movements. *Developmental Psychology, 20,* 378–388.

Kagan, J. (1979). Structure and process in the human infant: The ontogeny of mental representation. In M. H. Bornstein & W. Kessen (Eds.), *Psychological development from infancy* (pp. 159–182). Hillsdale, NJ: Lawrence Erlbaum Associates.

Lachman, R., Lachman, J. L., & Butterfield, E. C. (1979). *Cognitive psychology and information processing: An introduction.* Hillsdale, NJ: Lawrence Erlbaum Associates.

Lashley, K. S. (1951). The problem of serial order in behavior. In L. A. Jeffress (Ed.), *Cerebral mechanisms in behavior: The Hixon Symposium* (pp. 112–146). New York: Wiley.

Lasky, R. E. (1977). The effect of visual feedback of the hand on the reaching and retrieval behavior of young infants. *Child Development, 48,* 112–117.

Lockman, J. J. (1984). The development of detour ability during infancy. *Child Development, 55,* 482–491.

Lockman, J. J., & Ashmead, D. H. (1983). Discontinuities in the development of manual behavior. In L. P. Lipsitt & C. K. Rovee-Collier (Eds.), *Advances in infancy research* (Vol. 2, pp. 113–136). Norwood, NJ: Ablex.

Lockman, J. J., Ashmead, D. H., & Bushnell, E. W. (1984). The development of anticipatory hand orientation during infancy. *Journal of Experimental Child Psychology, 37,* 176–186.

Mandler, G. (1962). From association to structure. *Psychological Review, 69,* 415–427.

Mandler, G. (1975). Consciousness: Respectable, useful, and probably necessary. In R. L. Solso (Ed.), *Information processing and cognition: The Loyola Symposium* (pp. 229–254). Hillsdale, NJ: Lawrence Erlbaum Associates.

McCall, R. B. (1979). The development of intellectual functioning in infancy and the prediction of later IQ. In J. D. Osofsky (Ed.), *Handbook of infant development* (pp. 707–741). New York: Wiley.

McDonnell, P. M. (1975). The development of visually guided reaching. *Perception and Psychophysics, 19,* 181–185.

McDonnell, P. M. (1979). Patterns of eye–hand coordination in the first year of life. *Canadian Journal of Psychology, 33,* 253–267.

McDonnell, P. M., & Abraham, W. C. (1979). Adaptation to displacing prisms in human infants. *Perception, 8,* 175–185.

Norman, D. A. (1976). *Memory and attention: An introduction to human information processing.* New York: Wiley.

Piaget, J. (1952). *The origins of intelligence in children.* New York: W. W. Norton.

Piaget, J. (1954). *The construction of reality in the child.* New York: Basic Books.

Pieraut-le Bonniec, G. (1985). Hand–eye coordination and infants' constructing convexity and concavity properties. *British Journal of Developmental Psychology, 3,* 273–280.

Rader, N., & Stern, J. D. (1982). Visually elicited reaching in neonates. *Child Development, 53,* 1004–1007.

Ramsey, D. S. (1980). Onset of unimanual handedness in infants. *Infant Behavior and Development, 3,* 377–385.

Ruff, H. A., & Halton, A. (1978). Is there directed reaching in the neonate? *Developmental Psychology, 14,* 425–426.

Sperry, R. W. (1956). The eye and the brain. In R. Held & W. Richards (Eds.), *Perception: Mechanisms and models* (pp. 362–366). San Francisco: Freeman.

Strauss, S. (Ed.). (1982). *U-shaped behavioral growth.* New York: Academic Press.

Trevarthen, C. (1975). Growth of visuomotor coordination in infants. *Journal of Human Movement Studies, 1,* 57.

Treisman, A. M., & Gelade, G. (1980). A feature-integration theory of attention. *Cognitive Psychology, 12,* 97–136.

Treisman, A. M., & Schmidt, H. (1982). Illusory conjunctions in the perception of objects. *Cognitive Psychology, 14,* 107–141.

Treisman, A. M., Sykes, M., & Gelade, G. (1977). Selective attention and stimulus integration. In S. Dornic (Ed.), *Attention and performance VI* (pp. 333–361). Hillsdale, NJ: Lawrence Erlbaum Associates.

von Hofsten, C., & Lindhagen, K. (1979). Observations on the development of reaching for moving objects. *Journal of Experimental Child Psychology, 28,* 158–173.

White, B. L. (1967). An experimental approach to the effects of experience on early human behavior. In J. P. Hill (Ed.), *Child psychology* (Vol. 1, pp. 201–226). Minneapolis, MN: University of Minnesota Press.

White, B. L., Castle, P., & Held, R. (1964). Observations on the development of visually directed reaching. *Child Development, 35,* 349–364.

White, B. L., & Held, R. (1966). Plasticity of sensorimotor development in the human infant. In J. Rosenblith & W. Allinsmith (Eds.), *The causes of behavior.* Boston: Allyn & Bacon.

Yonas, A., & Granrud, C. (1985). Reaching as a measure of visual development. In G. Gottlieb & N. Krasnegor (Eds.), *The measurement of audition and vision during the first year of life: A methodological overview* (pp. 301–322). Norwood, NJ: Ablex.

Zelazo, P. R., & Kearsley, R. B. (1980). The emergence of functional play in infants: Evidence for a major cognitive transition. *Journal of Applied Developmental Psychology, 1,* 95–117.

Programs for
Movement Sequences

David A. Rosenbaum
University of Massachusetts, Amherst

A central aim of the behavioral sciences is to understand how behavioral sequences are centrally controlled. When we talk, type, or engage in other voluntary activities, we rely on a complex set of internal events to activate the appropriate muscles at the appropriate times. These events can be studied at different levels—the mechanical level, the physiological level, and the psychological level. An advantage of working at the psychological level is that one can investigate the functional characteristics of the behavior system as a whole. Another advantage is that for many practical purposes it is less critical to have a detailed understanding of the physical substrates of behavior than to have a general appreciation of the factors that affect how behaviors are selected and in turn carried out. For example, the design of effective training procedures for typewriting can proceed without detailed analyses of the musculature and innervation of the hand, though it can benefit from such analyses.

One of the first psychological analyses of the sequencing of behavior was offered by the American neurophysiologist Karl Lashley (1951). He argued that movement sequences are controlled by central programs. As an alternative, he considered the possibility that the elements of a movement sequence are triggered by feedback from the elements that immediately precede them. The latter view was called *reflex chaining;* it was held by many American behavioral scientists in Lashley's era. Lashley argued against the reflex chain hypothesis on the grounds that sensory feedback is not strictly required for movement sequences to be performed successfully. He observed that if normal feedback pathways are disrupted, humans and animals can still perform the sequences correctly, provided they were once able to do so. In the same vein, he noted that practiced movement sequences, such as well-learned piano arpeggios, can be performed at high rates, too quickly for each keystroke to await feedback from the one before it. To support the program hypothesis directly, Lashley suggested that errors made in everyday performance demonstrate that information about forthcoming movements is available well before the movements are performed. If someone says "the queer old dean" rather than "the dear old queen," for example, it is reasonable that the initial consonants in "dear" and "queen" were available before either consonant was produced (Fromkin, 1980).

If central programs underlie the production of movement sequences, several questions come to mind: (a) How are the programs structured? (b) How are they executed? (c) How are they constructed before being executed? (d) What happens to them after they have been executed? The research that my colleagues have done, in conjunction with work by others, has turned up some promising, though still preliminary, answers to these questions. The research suggests that programs for movement sequences are: (a) structured hierarchically; (b) executed in a way that depends directly on hierarchical organization; (c) constructed by specifying abstract movement features in hierarchical framework; and (d) preserved after being executed. In this chapter I explain how these principles were arrived at and why I think they reflect efficient strategies for movement control. I also argue that because these principles are similar to principles of memory for nonmotoric information, the results support the hypothesis that memory for symbols originates in cognitive representations for perceptual–motor skills (e.g., Piaget, 1952).

STRUCTURE AND EXECUTION

Consider the first two questions raised earlier: How are motor programs structured, and how are they executed? My colleagues and I addressed these questions by studying performance of keyboard sequences (Rosenbaum, Kenny, & Derr, 1983). Keyboard sequences can be performed rapidly and with few errors once they have been well learned. In addition, they are important for practical purposes and are easy to record in the laboratory. Each keyboard sequence we studied (see Fig. 2.1) was supposed to be performed from memory as quickly as possible, six times consecutively, with no stops between renditions, and with a minimum time between keystrokes of 20 msec. A computer recorded the responses and sounded a tone when six renditions were completed (or when a mistake was made). Subjects could stop responding any time after the tone sounded. The experiment took place over a 3-day period.

Figure 2.1 shows the mean latencies and errors from the second and third days of the experiment. (The data from the first day were essentially the same, except that the responses were performed more slowly and less accurately.) As seen in Figure 2.1, the mean latencies and errors changed systematically with serial position in the sequence. Both measures had the largest values for responses 1 and 5, intermediate values for responses 3 and 7, and smallest values for responses 2, 4, 6, and 8.

Of the models we considered to account for these results, the one we found most satisfying assumes that motor programs are both structured and executed in a hierarchical fashion. As seen in Fig. 2.2, we visualized the motor program as a tree, the nodes of which correspond to instructions to be read out or "decoded" for the needed sequence to be produced. We assumed that the program is executed through a *tree traversal* process, the defining characteristic of which is that any given node must be traversed before any node below it or to the right is traversed. A tree traversal process provides a graphic metaphor for the retrieval of information defined by a phrase structure grammar. The key property of the process is that each constituent of the grammar must be defined before any constituent below it or to its right can be defined.

The way we tested the tree traversal model was to assume that each decoding operation takes time and is subject to error. Based on this assumption, the latency and number of errors associated with a response should increase with the number of decoding operations that immediately precede it. By

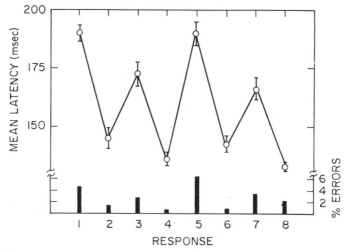

FIG. 2.1 Mean latencies and errors for individual responses in memorized sequences depend on the serial position of the responses within the sequences. In this experiment, people performed button-pressing sequences with the right index finger (I), left index finger (i), right middle finger (M), and left middle finger (m). The sequences were IiIiMmMm, MmMmIiIi, ImImMiMi, and MiMiI-mIm, as well as their mirror images. The latencies for response 1 are the times for the first response after the eighth response of the previous rendition. The data come from the second and third days of the study and are averaged over the sequences and subjects who performed them. The estimates of ± SE are based on between-subject differences. [Reproduced from Rosenbaum, Kenny, & Derr, 1983.]

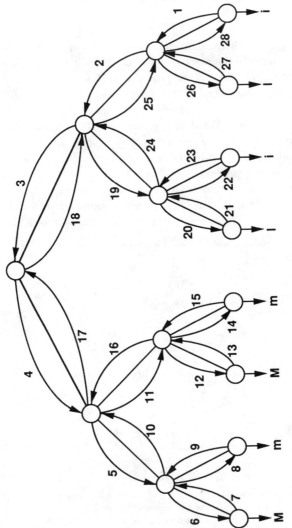

FIG. 2.2. A tree-traversal model can account for the results of the finger-tapping experiment of Rosenbaum, Kenny, and Derr (1983). The terminal nodes contain instructions for individual finger taps. Higher-level nodes contain information about the partitioning of the sequence into segments. Numbers indicate how the nodes are traversed, in this case after the final response is produced and the sequence is produced again. M, m, I, and i denote responses made with the right middle finger, left middle finger, right index finger, and left index finger, respectively. [Based on Rosenbaum, Kenny, & Derr, 1983.]

hypothesis, responses 1 and 5 should require the most decoding operations, responses 3 and 7 should require an intermediate number, and responses 2, 4, 6, and 8 should require the smallest number. The results confirmed these predictions, as seen in Figure 1. Another result that supported the tree traversal model was that the response substitutions that subjects committed were just the sort that would be expected if "wrong turns" were made in the tree. In fact, if a theoretical distribution of response substitutions is generated by assuming a fixed probability of making a wrong turn at any node (where all nodes are assumed to have the same wrong-turn probability), the predicted substitution pattern is remarkably similar to the pattern that was observed.

Because the sequences in the experiment of Rosenbaum et al. (1983) had a transparent hierarchical organization, it is perhaps not surprising that the results supported the hierarchical model. We used such sequences to allow for the possibility of strongly rejecting the tree traversal model: If the model were not supported for these sequences, it would be hard to imagine that it could be supported for any. Having found evidence for the model, the crucial question was whether the model could be supported for sequences whose organization was not obviously hierarchical.

One way to address this question was to consider data that characterize a much larger number of sequences. A relevant set of data came from a study in which typists typed short words after the presentation of a reaction signal (Sternberg, Monsell, Knoll, & Wright, 1978). On each trial, the word to be typed was presented before the reaction signal appeared, so subjects could become highly prepared to type the word ahead of time. Sternberg et al. (1978) found that the time between keystrokes within the word, as well as the time for the first keystroke after the reaction signal, increased with word length (the *length* effect). They also found that keystroke latencies were longer in the middle of the word than at the ends (the *serial position* effect). Sternberg and his colleagues suggested that the length effect reflected the operation of a memory search process, where the time to retrieve a motor subprogram corresponding to any given keystroke increased with the number of subprograms to be executed (i.e., the number of keystrokes in the word being typed). This model accounted for the length effect and, with additional assumptions, could be shown to account for the serial position effect.

The tree traversal model can also account for the length effect and serial position effect of Sternberg and his colleagues. Suppose that before initiating each to-be-typed sequence, typists constructed a hierarchically organized program for the sequence to be typed. Suppose in addition that they spontaneously organized programs for words of a given length into all possible binary tree representations. That is, they did not necessarily represent a sequence with the same binary tree. It is then possible to predict the mean number of nodes to be traversed just before the response in each serial position for a sequence of any given length. The mean is the number of nodes for that response, averaged over all possible binary tree representations. The number of nodes for the first response is the number of nodes between the root of the tree and the leftmost terminal node (again averaged over all possible binary tree representations for a sequence of given length). As seen in Table 2.1, the mean number of nodes before the *first* response increases with sequence length (because more complex trees are associated with longer sequences), the mean number of nodes *between* responses increases with sequence length (for the same reason), and the mean number of nodes in the middle of the sequence is longer than at the ends (because large chunk boundaries tend to occur in mid-sequence). Because more time is needed for each additional node traversal, the tree traversal model accounts for the qualitative features of the results of Sternberg and his colleagues. It is noteworthy that Sternberg and his colleagues also obtained the length effect and serial position effect for speech. Thus, to a first approximation, the tree traversal model also accounts for the timing of speech (Cooper & Paccia-Cooper, 1980; but see Gee & Grosjean, 1983).

What implications can be drawn from the apparent generality of the tree traversal process? One is that motor programs are not simply read from memory the way a tape is read from a tape head. Instead, they are executed nonlinearly, through the decoding of information from high to low levels. This means that for movement sequences to be performed as rapidly as they are, the decoding must occur at high rates. (Based on the data reviewed above, each decoding operation appears to take only 13 msec.)

Another implication is that motor programs are executed in a way that reflects the way they are built. Many students of skilled behavior have argued that motor programs are constructed from elementary, prepackaged routines (e.g., Miller, Galanter, & Pribram, 1960). This method of program construction allows for flexibility and rapidity of performance. If programs are executed via tree traversal, the components of the program can be decoded in much the same way as they were initially assembled.

TABLE 2.1

Mean Number of Steps Predicted by the Tree-Traversal Model for Responses 1 Through n in Sequences of Length $n = 2$ Through $n = 6$.

	Response						
Length	*1*	*2*	*3*	*4*	*5*	*6*	*Mean (2 through n)*
2	2.0	2.0	—	—	—	—	2.0
3	2.5	2.5	2.5	—	—	—	2.5
4	3.0	2.0	4.0	2.0	—	—	2.7
5	3.3	2.3	3.5	3.5	2.3	—	2.9
6	3.5	2.3	3.5	3.6	3.5	2.3	3.0

CONSTRUCTION

Let us now turn directly to the question of how motor programs are constructed before being executed. My colleagues and I addressed this question by conducting experiments in which people choose between possible motor sequences. In one series of experiments (Rosenbaum, Inhoff, & Gordon, 1984) different finger sequences were performed in response to different visual signals (typically an X or an O in the center of a computer screen). On a given trial, the identity of the sequence to be performed was unknown until the choice signal appeared, at which time the subject was supposed to perform the designated sequence as quickly as possible.

Table 2.2 illustrates one such experiment (Rosenbaum et al., 1984, Experiment 4). Each of two finger sequences was performed with the right or left hand and was paired with the mirror image or non-mirror-image of the sequence, performed with the other hand. For example, in one condition, the choice was between iim and IIM, where i denotes a left index finger response, m denotes a left middle finger response, I denotes a right index finger response, and M denotes a right middle finger response. The sequences iim and IIM are mirror images. In another condition the choice was between iim and IMM, which are not mirror images. Two other choices, tested in other blocks of trials, completed the pairing of left- and right-hand sequences: imm versus IMM (a mirror image pair), and imm versus IIM (a non-mirror-image pair). The question was whether the time to perform a given sequence, such as iim, would be affected by its relation to the other possible sequence. If there were such an effect, the interaction could be attributed to the program *construction* process, because execution of a sequence and perception of its corresponding reaction signal are presumably unaffected by choice context.

There was a marked effect of choice context on the time to initiate each sequence. Choice reaction times were shorter in the mirror-image condition than in the non-mirror-image condition. An explanation of this result is based on the idea that motor programs may be like mathematical functions in that they consist of arguments as well as operators that can be applied to those arguments. The operators, for present purposes, can be thought of as *parameters,*

TABLE 2.2
Choice Conditions and Mean Choice Reaction Times (in msec) ± SE

	Performed Finger Sequence	
Relation to other possible sequence	*Index–Index–Middle*	*Index–Middle–Middle*
Mirror	434 ± 15	441 ± 15
Non-Mirror	492 ± 10	491 ± 7

From an experiment of Rosenbaum, Inhoff, and Gordon (1984).

and the arguments can be thought of as *subprograms*. When a person prepares to choose between mirror-image sequences, he or she can ready a list of subprograms with instructions for different finger *types* (e.g., index, index, middle) to which a single "hand parameter" applies. The corresponding function might be written: *hand* (index, index, middle). When the reaction signal appears, the value of *hand* can be specified as *left* or *right* and the entire sequence can then be fully defined. However, when a choice must be made between non-mirror-image sequences, not only must a hand parameter be specified, but the finger identity (index or middle) of the second subprogram must also be defined. The longer initiation time for the non-mirror condition can be explained by assuming that this extra step takes extra time.

From this account one can speculate that, in general, motor programs are constructed by applying parameters to motor subprograms. If this idea is correct, one should find evidence for it in another domain. Figure 2.3 presents confirming evidence from speech production (Rosenbaum, Gordon, Stillings, & Feinstein, 1987). Subjects in this experiment made simple utterances consisting of one, two, or three syllables, where the two possible utterances in each condition differed with respect to a single vowel. In one condition subjects chose

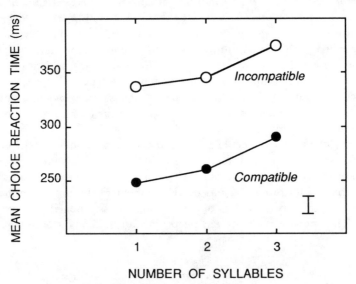

NUMBER OF SYLLABLES

FIG. 2.3   The mean choice reaction time to begin one of two possible utterances of one syllable (/gi/ vs. /gu/), two syllables (/gibi/ vs. /gubu/), or three syllables (/gibidi/ vs. /gubudu/) increases with the number of syllables to be said, and is longer by a roughly constant amount when the signal designating the required utterance is *compatible* with its distinguishing vowel than when the signal designating the required utterance is *incompatible* with its distinguishing vowel. The estimate of ± SE is based on between-subject variability. [Based on Rosenbaum, Gordon, Stillings, & Feinstein, 1987.]

between /gi/ and /gu/, in another condition they chose between /gibi/ and /gubu/, and in another condition they chose between /gibidi/ and /gubudu/. We were interested in the possibility that the vowel distinguishing the two possible sequences could be chosen in a single step, and that the chosen vowel could then be applied in a distributive fashion to the entire set of consonant subprograms. To test this hypothesis, we introduced an experimental manipulation that we thought would affect the time to choose the vowel. In half the conditions, the sequence containing the /i/ vowel was signalled by a high-pitched tone, and the sequence containing the /u/ vowel was signalled by a low-pitched tone. In the other conditions, the mapping of signals to responses was reversed. We determined in an informal pilot study that people perceived /i/ as higher than /u/, so we hypothesized that mapping the high tone to /i/ and the low tone to /u/ would be more compatible than mapping the low tone to /i/ and the high tone to /u/. Furthermore, provided that selection of the vowel occurs only once, the effect of the mapping relation on choice reaction tim·e would be statistically independent of the effect of the number of syllables to be pronounced.

The results confirmed the prediction. As subjects were asked to say more syllables, the time to begin saying them increased, as the tree-traversal model predicted. In addition, choice reaction times were longer in the incompatible mapping condition than in the compatible mapping condition, again as expected, and replicating earlier results (Gordon & Meyer, 1984). Most importantly, there was no interaction between sequence length and stimulus–response compatibility, confirming what would be expected if the vowel for the entire syllable sequence were specified in a single stage of processing. Results of other experiments from this study (Rosenbaum et al., 1987) showed that the vowel was in fact distributively applied to all the consonants before the utterance was initiated, not just to the first syllable.

Another set of experiments (Inhoff, Rosenbaum, Gordon, & Campbell, 1984) showed that choices between right- and left-hand *finger* sequences can also be achieved through the distributive assignment method. In these experiments, subjects chose between finger sequences consisting of 1, 2, or 3 finger presses made with either hand, and where the reaction signal appeared either on the same side of the screen as the responding hand (the compatible condition) or on the opposite side (the incompatible condition). Choice reaction times increased with the number of finger presses in the sequence to be produced, and were longer in the incompatible condition than in the compatible condition. However, there was no interaction between sequence length and compatibility. Thus as in the speech experiment, a single parameter (left or right hand) could be applied distributively to an entire set of subprograms.

Collectively, these results suggest that motor programs are constructed, in part, by specifying values of abstract parameters describing ordered sets of subprograms (e.g., specifying a vowel for a consonant–vowel–consonant–vowel sequence, or determining the hand for a finger sequence). An advantage of this programming method is that only a small number of programs needs to be stored in long-term memory. Supplying different parameters to a small set of stored programs allows those programs to be tuned adaptively depending on the task at hand (Schmidt, 1975). The capacity for distributive parameter assignment also fits with a hierarchical model, for superordinate nodes can be viewed both as ''feature sites,'' where parametric information about nodes below them is represented, and ''segmentation sites,'' where boundaries concerning serial order are established.

THE FATE OF MOTOR PROGRAMS

Having considered how motor programs are constructed before being executed, let us now ask what happens to motor programs after they have been carried out. One possibility is that they are immediately lost from working memory. Another is that they are maintained. The latter method has an advantage. If a program remains in working memory after it has been executed, just those aspects of the program that distinguish it from the next program can be edited (Rosenbaum, 1980). By contrast, if the program were lost from working memory, the next program would have to be constructed de novo. Recognizing this point provides an added reason for embracing a parametric conception of motor programming: Because it is efficient to make as few changes as possible when modifying a program, it is convenient to decompose the program into just those components that distinguish it from its successors.

If motor programs are in fact constructed by modifying programs that were recently performed, the time to prepare motor programs should depend on their similarity to programs that were just executed. This prediction was confirmed in a study by Rosenbaum, Weber, Hazelett, and Hindorff (1986). One of the tasks was to recite the first few letters of the alphabet over and over again, as quickly as possible, for 10 sec. A special instruction was always to alternate between stressed and unstressed pronunciations. Given this instruction, there was a *fixed* mapping between stress and letter identity when the list to be recited had an even number of letters (e.g., AbCdAbCd . . .), but there was a *variable* mapping between stress and letter identity when the list had an odd number of letters (e.g., AbCdEaBcDe . . .). If the program for production of a letter is preserved after the letter has been produced, and if the stress of the letter is an independent program component, it should be possible to speak more quickly when repeating an even number of letters than when repeating an odd number of letters under the alternating-stress instruction.

As seen in Figure 2.4, this is just what happened. The mean number of letters recited, and the accuracy of recitation, were higher when the number of letters was even than when it was odd. In addition, the odd–even difference

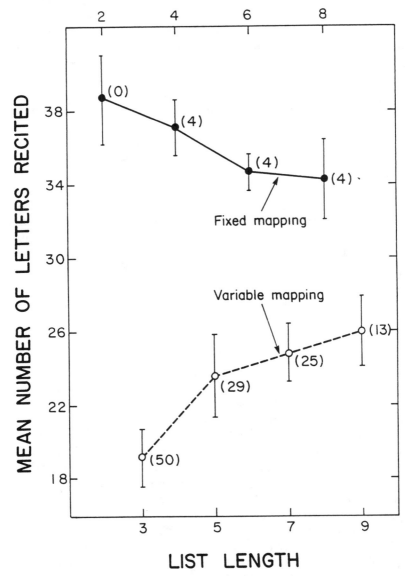

FIG. 2.4. The mean number of letters spoken during 10 sec. of repeated recitation of the first *n* letters of the alphabet is lower when *n* is odd than when *n* is even, provided subjects always alternate between stressed and unstressed pronunciations. Percentage of errors (in parentheses) is lower when *n* is even. The difference can be attributed to the fixed mapping of stresses to letters in the even-*n* condition and the variable mapping of stresses to letters in the odd-*n* condition. Estimates of ±SE are based on between-subject differences. [Reproduced from Rosenbaum, Weber, Hazelett, & Hindorff, 1986.]

got smaller as the number of letters increased. The convergence of the odd and even curves accords with the expectation that as successive productions of a program are separated by longer delays, it should matter less whether all the parameters remain the same (since the parameter information becomes less available over time). My colleagues and I referred to the slowing of performance accompanying the need to change movement parameters as the *parameter remapping* effect.

The parameter remapping effect extends to other speech parameters and other domains of motor performance. In keyboard tasks, response rates are slower than when a given finger makes different numbers of repeated keystrokes in successive productions than when the same finger makes the same number of repeated keystrokes in successive productions (Rosenbaum et al., 1986). In another domain, violin bowing, skilled amateur players are less successful at performing series of bowstrokes when there is a variable mapping of number of bow stops to bowing directions than when there is a fixed mapping of bow stops to bowing directions. Such an impairment would only be expected if associations between or among movement parameters were preserved after their corresponding programs were executed.

MOTOR PROGRAMS AND MEMORY

As I mentioned earlier, our work not only sheds light on the control of movement sequences; it also illuminates the relation between motor control and memory. An important similarity between motor programming and memory emerging from our research is reliance on hierarchies. Motor programs appear to be structured hierarchically and executed in a way that depends directly on this form of organization. Hierarchical organization is also well established for memory of semantic categories such as fruits, birds, and furniture (Johnson, 1978). When people are asked to recall lists of semantically categorized materials, the errors they make and the delays between the recalled items are well described by tree-traversal processes (Chase & Simon, 1973; Reitman & Rueter, 1980). Because this process is used for motor control as well as verbal, symbolic recall, it appears that serial recall is achieved in the same way, regardless of the type of material being recalled.

Another similarity between motor programming and memory is the presence of interference. When two items (A and B) are associated to a common item (e.g., A-C, B-C), they are usually remembered more poorly than when they are associated to different items (e.g., A-C, B-D). It is as if the bond between A and C and the bond between B and C are mutually interfering. Interference effects have been observed in a wide range of situations, including the learning of paired associates (Ceraso, 1967), sentence verification (Anderson, 1983), and perceptual recognition (Schneider & Shiffrin, 1977). The parameter remapping effect can also be viewed as an instance of memory interference because the same putative program is effectively weakened by taking different parameter values on different occasions. Finding that memory interference applies to motor performance points again to reliance on common principles in the motor and memory systems. This outcome may in turn indicate that the functional properties of memory at higher cognitive levels are based ontogenetically (Piaget, 1952) and/or phylogenetically (Kimura, 1979; Lieberman, 1984) on motor programs. One reason why this conjecture is appealing is that skillful movement demands memory retrieval; motor programming after all is, a kind of recall. It would be surprising if memory for higher functions did not capitalize on the retrieval schemes that presumably were established earlier in evolution or in individual development.

A final important similarity between motor control and memory revealed by our studies is reliance on autonomous parameters or features. The breakdown of information into features is a familiar idea in perception and memory, where many lines of research indicate that percepts (Treisman, 1986) and memories (Bower, 1967) are featurally organized. Saying that actions are constructed from basic parameters is consistent with this broad generalization. The clear advantage of a parametric system for movement is that the same motor "schemas" can be flexibly applied to any of a wide range of situations by choosing appropriate parameter values (Arbib, 1981). Once one knows how to tie one's shoes, for example, one can tie laces of string or leather, with one's shoes in a wide range of orientations, and so on. The capacity to generalize over performance domains—so central for the expression of skill—may therefore depend on the ability to adjust parameters for programs guiding behavior.

ACKNOWLEDGMENTS

Supported in part by National Science Foundation grants BNS–8710933 and BNS–9008665 a Research Career Development Award from the National Institutes of Health. The chapter was completed while the author was a Fellow at the Netherlands Institute for Advanced Study, Wassenaar, The Netherlands.

REFERENCES

Anderson, J. R. (1983). *The architecture of cognition.* Harvard University Press.
Arbib, M. A. (1981). Perceptual structures and distributed motor control. In V. B. Brooks (Ed.), *Handbook of physiology—The nervous system II.* Bethesda, MD: American Physiological Society.
Bower, G. H. (1967). A multi-component theory of the memory trace. In K. W. Spence & J. T. Spence (Eds.), *The psychology of learning and motivation, Vol. 1.* New York: Academic Press.

Ceraso, J. (1967). The interference theory of memory. *Scientific American, 217*(4), 117–124.

Chase, W. G., & Simon, H. A. (1973). The mind's eye in chess. In W. G. Chase (Ed.), *Visual information processing.* New York: Academic Press.

Cooper, W. E., & Paccia-Cooper, J. (1980). *Syntax and speech.* Cambridge: Harvard University Press.

Fromkin, V. A. (Ed.). (1980). *Errors in linguistic performance.* New York: Academic Press.

Gee, J., & Grosjean, F. (1983). Performance structures: A psycholinguistic and linguistic appraisal. *Cognitive Psychology, 15,* 411–458.

Gordon, P. C., & Meyer, D. E. (1984). Perceptual–motor processing of phonetic features in speech. *Journal of Experimental Psychology: Human Perception and Performance, 10,* 153–178.

Inhoff, A. W., Rosenbaum, D. A., Gordon, A. M., & Campbell, J. A. (1984). Stimulus–response compatibility and motor programming of manual response sequences. *Journal of Experimental Psychology: Human Perception and Performance, 10,* 724–733.

Johnson, N. F. (1978). Coding processes in memory. In W. K. Estes (Ed.), *Handbook of learning and cognitive processes* (pp. 87–129). Hillsdale, NJ: Lawrence Erlbaum Associates.

Kimura, D. (1979). Neuromotor mechanisms in the evolution of human communication. In H. D. Steklis & M. J. Raleigh (Eds.), *Neurobiology of social communication in primates.* New York: Academic Press.

Lashley, K. S. (1951). The problem of serial order in behavior. In L. A. Jeffress (Ed.), *Cerebral mechanisms in behavior* (pp. 112–131). New York: Wiley.

Lieberman, P. (1984). *The biology and evolution of language.* Cambridge, MA: Harvard.

Miller, G. A., Galanter, E., & Pribram, K. H. (1960). *Plans and the structure of behavior.* New York: Holt, Rinehart, & Winston.

Piaget, J. (1952). *The origins of intelligence in children.* (2nd ed.). (M. Cook, Trans.). New York: International Universities Press.

Reitman, J. S., & Rueter, H. H. (1980). Organization revealed by recall orders and confirmed by pauses. *Cognitive Psychology, 12,* 554–581.

Rosenbaum, D. A. (1980). Human movement initiation: Specification of arm, direction, and extent. *Journal of Experimental Psychology: General, 109,* 444–474.

Rosenbaum, D. A., Gordon, A. M., Stillings, N. A., & Feinstein, M. H. (1987). Stimulus–response compatibility in the programming of speech. *Memory and Cognition, 15,* 217–224.

Rosenbaum, D. A., Inhoff, A. W., & Gordon, A. M. (1984). Choosing between movement sequences: A hierarchical editor model. *Journal of Experimental Psychology: General, 113,* 372–393.

Rosenbaum, D. A., Kenny, S., & Derr, M. A. (1983). Hierarchical control of rapid movement sequences. *Journal of Experimental Psychology: Human Perception and Performance, 9,* 86–102.

Rosenbaum, D. A., Weber, R. J., Hazelett, W. M., & Hindorff, V. (1986). The parameter remapping effect in human performance: Evidence from tongue twisters and finger fumblers. *Journal of Memory and Language, 25,* 710–725.

Schmidt, R. A. (1975). A schema theory of discrete motor skill learning. *Psychological Review, 82,* 225–260.

Schneider, W., & Shiffrin, R. M. (1977). Controlled and automatic human information processing: I. Detection, search, and attention. *Psychological Review, 84,* 1–66.

Sternberg, S., Monsell, S., Knoll, R. L., & Wright, C. E. (1978). The latency and duration of rapid movement sequences: Comparisons of speech and typewriting. In G. E. Stelmach (Ed.), *Information processing in motor control and learning* (pp. 117–152). New York: Academic Press.

Treisman, A. M. (1986). Properties, parts, and objects. In K. R. Boff, L. Kaufman, & J. P. Thomas (Eds.), *Handbook of perception and human performance, Vol. II.* New York: John Wiley.

Similarity and the Structure of Categories

Lance J. Rips
University of Chicago

Life used to be a lot easier in the categorization business. In the 1970s and early 1980s, we thought we had the right line on human categories. The general idea was that an item is a member of a category if it is sufficiently typical of that category. For example, an apple is a fruit because it's typical of fruit (or more typical of fruit than of other categories, such as vegetable). An item is typical of a category if it bears some (family) resemblance to a sample of category members or resembles a prototypical member. Apples, after all, share lots of properties with members of the fruit category and are probably quite similar to a prototype fruit. The higher this degree of resemblance, the greater the degree of typicality. Hence, the greater the resemblance, the more likely it is that the instance is itself a category member.

Quite a bit of experimental evidence supported this view (as summarized in Smith & Medin, 1981). For instance, in several studies, reaction times and errors in verifying class inclusion sentences turned out to be a function of rated typicality (e.g., Rips, Shoben, & Smith, 1973; Rosch, 1973; Smith, Shoben, & Rips, 1974). Apples, for example, are extremely typical fruit, olives extremely atypical fruit; and subjects are correspondingly faster and more accurate in answering the question *Is an apple a fruit?* than *Is an olive a fruit?* This typicality effect seemed to be reducible, in turn, to an effect of resemblance. The more typical instances were those that subjects judged more similar to the category (Rips, et al., 1973). If similarity begets typicality begets probability of being in a category, then all that remained in order to explain categorization was to give an account of how subjects calculate similarity. After Tversky's (1977) paper on features of similarity, such an account seemed at hand.

Lila Gleitman deserves credit for deflating this optimistic mood. If typicality is what explains category membership, then you might expect membership to be a graded function of degree of typicality. Apples are more typical fruit than cantaloupes are more typical than olives are more typical than tennis balls, with many levels of typicality in between. We might therefore suppose that apples are better fruit than cantaloupes are better fruit than . . . than tennis balls. Armstrong, Gleitman, and Gleitman (1983) showed, however, that this doesn't correctly reflect subjects' beliefs about categories. Subjects will rate instances as varying in typicality, alright; but at the same time they'll swear that category membership is not a continuous or a fuzzy matter, but crisply all-or-none. Apples and cantaloupes are fruit and tennis balls aren't. As for olives, search me. They're either one or the other, though I'm not sure which. The Law of Excluded Middle applies to category membership in a way that it doesn't apply to category typicality or similarity.

The moral from Armstrong and colleagues is that we were too hasty in running together similarity, typicality, and degree of membership. To rectify this mistake, we might therefore take a more careful look at how these properties vary over the instances in a category's domain. If we're lucky, we might find differences in the shape of these functions that will give us clues to where the resemblance theory of categorizing went wrong. In the first section of this chapter, I mention some attempts of this sort to look at similarity, typicality, and probability of category membership for some very simple concepts, and I argue that the results of these studies tend to support the Armstrong–Gleitman thesis: There is no way to reduce category membership to similarity among instances. We're dealing with notoriously slippery notions, though, and it's possible that the "similarity" our subjects judged is the wrong kind of similarity. At least, that's the reaction of some critics of these results. The second part of the chapter examines these criticisms to see how much of the resemblance theory they are able to salvage.

SOME EMPIRICAL RESULTS
ON SIMILARITY AND CATEGORIZING

The experiments that I describe all have approximately the same structure. In each of them, we ask subjects to think about instances whose properties vary in systematic ways and about a category (or categories) they might belong to. Subjects then decide, in separate conditions, about the similarity of the instances with respect to the categories, the typicality of the instances with respect to the same categories, or the likelihood that the instances are actually members of these categories. By examining these three types of judgment as a function of the instances' properties, we may be able to identify factors that affect similarity (or typicality) but don't affect categorizing. If this is true, then we have some evidence that similarity isn't a necessary part of categorizing. Details about these experiments appear in Rips (1989) and Collins and Rips (1989); I cover just the basics here.

Lessons from Armstrong

We can think of the Armstrong–Gleitman study (their Experiment 3) as an example of this sort of endeavor. When subjects evaluate the typicality of instances in a category like even number, their responses tend to be continuous. Some instances are better examples than others. But the same subjects believe that category membership is discrete. No matter what the relative typicality or exemplariness of an instance, it's either an even number or not. So the typicality profile of instances must be very different from the membership profile of the same instances in these sorts of categories. The conclusion would seem to be that there's more to belonging to a category than being typical. Strictly speaking, this isn't Armstrong and colleagues' conclusion: Their official position is skepticism about the *evidence* for graded category membership. (If graded reaction times and typicality ratings are evidence that category membership is graduated, then one should *not* find such evidence for well-defined categories like even number, which are obviously all-or-none. Since Armstrong and colleagues *do* find grades of typicality for even numbers and similar categories, then the evidence isn't any good.) Nevertheless, the contrast between continuous typicality and discrete membership suggests that people think about these properties in distinct ways.

One reaction to this difference between typicality and membership, however, is that it may reflect a difference in the way the questions are put. In the first place, ratings of typicality are likely to encourage graded responses in a way that a yes/no question about membership is not. Subjects may feel an obligation to spread their ratings over the response categories (Parducci & Perrett, 1971; Poulton, 1989, chap. 4), and this will tend to make the typicality ratings look graded. Of course, this is perfectly fine for Armstrong and colleagues' skeptical point—it's really part of the issue they were raising—but it provides a way out of the conclusion I'd like to draw. Second, you might suppose that the Armstrong–Gleitman typicality ratings and membership questions appeal to different levels of thought about categories. The question "Does it make sense to rate items in this category for *degree of membership* in the category?" requires subjects to reflect on their beliefs about categories in a way that "How typical (how good an example) is Instance i of Category C?" does not. Answers to the first question could be due to professors, encyclopedia salesmen, and other unsavory types persuading the poor subjects to defer to authority on such matters, convincing them that there are experts with true answers about membership. But it's less likely that the typicality question calls for this sort of indirect reasoning about the nature of categories.

For my purposes it seems important to ask the categorization question in a way that parallels the similarity and typicality questions. So instead of asking for yes/no answers about category membership, I asked the subjects for the likelihood that an instance was a member. This allows use of the same response setup for the three question types. Moreover, subjects are free to interpret likelihood as a subjective matter, something they can evaluate directly, just as they can similarity or typicality. If we find differences in subjects' responses under these circumstances, we can dismiss the obvious criticisms just mentioned. One might object that evaluating likelihood of membership isn't the same as evaluating degree of membership. Although this is correct, if similarity and likelihood of membership diverge in our experiments, it seems highly improbable that similarity and degree of membership will converge. On the face of it, similarity and category likelihood seem much more compatible than similarity and category membership; hence, if we can drive a wedge between the former pair, we will be in a good position to argue for a distinction between the latter.

Warm Ups

These experiments got their start in a simple demonstration concerning pairs of everyday categories, such as teapots and tennis balls or U.S. quarters and pizzas (Rips, 1989, Experiment 1). We picked these pairs so that the items in them varied on a given physical dimension. Teapots and tennis balls vary in volume; quarters and pizzas in diameter. However, one item in each pair had relatively fixed values on this dimension (tennis balls, quarters), while the other item (teapots, pizzas) varied much more widely. There were 36 pairs in all, ranging over a variety of dimensions.

On each trial of the experiment, subjects considered one of these pairs, and they estimated the boundary points of the categories on the relevant dimension. In the case of teapots and tennis balls, for instance, they estimated the volume of the smallest teapot they could remember and the volume of the largest tennis ball. Let's suppose, in this example, that a particular subject said that the largest tennis ball had a volume of x cm³ and the smallest teapot a volume of y cm³. We then told the subject that we were thinking of an object with a volume of $(x + y)/2$ cm³ but whose other properties were unknown. Subjects in one condition then had to decide whether this intermediate object was more similar to a teapot or a tennis ball, subjects in a second condition had to decide whether it was more typical of a teapot or a tennis ball, and subjects in a third condition whether it was more likely to be a teapot or a tennis ball.

The main outcome of this study was that subjects tended to choose the more variable member of the pair when asked about category likelihood, but choose the fixed member when asked about similarity. The typicality subjects split the difference. Choices favored the variable item on 63% of trials in the likelihood condition, 46% of trials in the typicality condition, and 31% of trials in the similarity condition. What appears to be happening is that constraints on the size of the fixed category make it unlikely to accommodate the intermediate object. "Tennis balls have to be the same size," as one of the subjects said; so the intermediate object must be a member of the opposite category, teapots. However, these constraints seem to be irrelevant for similarity judgments. Suppose instead that the closer the intermediate object is to the size of an average category member, the more similar it is to that category (see the next section of this chapter for more evidence in favor of this assumption). This will tend to mean that the intermediate object is more similar to the fixed category, given the way we chose the value of the intermediate item. For example, suppose a subject thinks that tennis balls have a fixed volume of 150 cm³ and that teapots range in size from 250 to 2500 cm³, with a usual size of 1250. In this case, we would have picked 200 cm³ as the intermediate value [i.e., (150 + 250)/2]. Because this is much closer in absolute terms to the usual size of tennis balls (150) than to the usual size of teapots (1250), the intermediate object should seem more similar to tennis balls.

In this situation, then, subjects believe that an instance is more likely to belong to one category than a second, even though they judge the same instance more similar to the second than the first. Other findings (Rips, 1989, Experiments 3, 4) provide further evidence for this flip-flop. In these experiments, subjects read paragraphs describing a creature or an artifact whose properties changed and then rated the similarity, typicality, and category likelihood of the instance with respect to a pair of contrast categories. For example, they might read about a creature with fish-like properties who comes to have reptilian properties as the result of a nuclear accident. Such a creature tends to be rated more likely to be a fish but more similar to a reptile. In a related study, subject were to imagine immature creatures who grew into altered adult forms—for instance, a creature with fish-like properties who metamorphoses into one with reptile-like properties. This time subjects consider the immature form more likely to be, but not more similar to, a reptile than a fish. (In these experiments, typicality ratings were usually closer to similarity ratings than to category likelihood.)

Perhaps the simplest way to summarize these results is to say that when subjects evaluate the similarity of an instance with respect to a category, they take into account characteristics like visual appearance, disregarding inner, relational, or theoretical properties. In deciding on category membership, however, they make use of the latter properties and ignore mere appearance. Viewed in this way, these findings are consistent with developmental work by Gelman and Markman (1986) and Keil (1989) showing that school-aged children—maybe even preschoolers—realize that it's possible to override perceptual commonalities in establishing what species an instance belongs to.

Whether or not this interpretation is correct, however, the reversals in sub-jects' responses between conditions indicate that they view similarity and category likelihood as distinct issues. It may therefore be profitable to pinpoint the distinction by studying categories whose key properties we can vary more precisely.

Studies of Frequency and Distance

Allan Collins and I (Collins & Rips, 1989) used a slightly different paradigm to study the resemblance theory. In this procedure, subjects inspect frequency histograms for ad hoc categories that vary along some quantitative dimension like weight or temperature. They're then asked to rate a series of items whose values range over this dimension, with separate groups again rating similari-ty, typicality, and category likelihood. The idea is that differences in the shape of the ratings over these continua can provide information about factors that influence these decisions.

Bimodal categories. Figure 3.1 shows what one of these histograms was like. We asked subjects to suppose that a meteorologist was studying a group of daily high temperatures in the Chicago area, half from the month of Febru-ary and half from August. The histogram gives the distribution of these tem-peratures. We then mentioned a particular temperature value—say, 76°F— and asked the subject to rate either the similarity, typicality, or category likeli-hood of this temperature with respect to the category defined by the histogram. The test values varied across trials so that we swept out the range of the x-axis in 8°F increments. (The values were at the center of the intervals marked on the axis: 4°F, 12°F, etc.) In our first experiment, the histograms always had

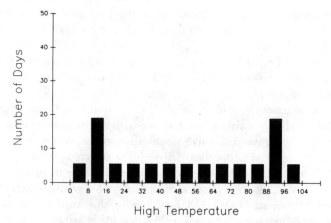

FIG. 3.1.   Stimulus histogram from Collins & Rips (1989, Experiment 1) il-lustrating a sample of 100 daily high temperatures from February and August.

a bimodal form with peaks in the position shown in Figure 3.1, and the frequency of the nonpeak intervals was equal. However, the ratio of peak to nonpeak frequencies varied over trials. In addition to the problems about temperatures, we used a second cover story concerning the weight of a group of boys, half 8-year-olds and half 13-year-olds. The form of the histograms for these weight problems, however, was exactly the same as for the temperature problems. Only the axis labeling differed.

Our use of bimodal histograms in this experiment was prompted by a conjecture about the role of frequency in category versus similarity judgments. It's reasonable to suppose that the relative frequency in Fig. 3.1 should determine judged likelihood that a particular value would be in the category, given the close relationship between likelihood and frequency.[1] Thus, we would expect the category likelihood judgments to follow the contours of the histogram. But what about the similarity judgments? I suggested earlier, in discussing the teapot/tennis ball results, that the similarity of an instance to a category may depend on how close the instance is to the average category member. In a situation like this where we know the entire category distribution, an average member might have the distribution's mean or median value, both of which happen to be 52°F in Fig. 3.1. The greater the absolute distance between the test value and this central value, the lower the subjective similarity. Bimodal histograms have the advantage that the frequencies associated with the intervals are not strongly correlated with the distance of the intervals from the mean or median, over the range with which we are concerned. Thus, bimodal graphs allow us to separate the effects of frequency and distance in a clear-cut way.

The results from this experiment accord very well with the idea that frequency dominates likelihood judgments, whereas distance dominates similarity. The basic findings appear in Fig. 3.2, where mean ratings (from the subjects' 0 to 10 scale) are plotted as a function of the ordinal position of the test value within the histogram. The histograms' peaks were always at positions 2 and 12, as in Fig. 3.1. Figure 3.2 shows that the category likelihood ratings (labeled with squares) are at their maxima at just these positions and are relatively flat elsewhere. However, the similarity function (labeled with triangles) has an entirely different shape: highest at the mean or median and declining monotonically on both sides. Thus, as we expected, similarity falls off steadily with distance from the center of the distribution. Finally, rated typicality seems a compromise between similarity and likelihood, just as it was in the teapot

---

[1]This isn't quite so obvious from a statistical point of view. We asked subjects to estimate the likelihood that an instance was in a category, given that it had a certain value. We could express this as a conditional probability, $P(c|v)$. But the frequency information in the histogram actually gives (something close to) the converse probability: the probability that an instance has a certain value, given that it's in the category, $P(v|c)$. However, these two probabilities are related via Bayes Theorem, and one will be a linear function of the other if the prior probabilities $P(v)$ and $P(c)$ are constant.

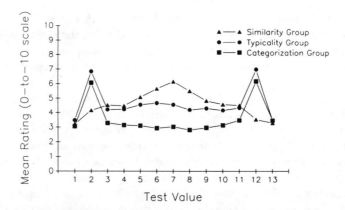

FIG. 3.2.   Mean ratings from Collins & Rips (1989, Experiment 1), for similarity, typicality, and category likelihood as a function of the position of the test value within the histogram. X-axis values from temperature and weights problems have been linearly transformed to the same scale.

experiment. The most typical points are at the peaks of the histograms, but among the nonpeak positions the central values in the histogram are more typical than the peripheral ones. Frequency at positions 1 and 13 was always the same as at positions 3–11 (see Fig. 3.1); however, subjects rated the latter positions as more typical than the former.

Unimodal categories.   The similarity and category-likelihood curves in Fig. 3.2 could hardly be more distinct, thanks to the bimodal form of the histograms. One problem, however, is that bimodal categories may be fairly rare, and the way we defined these categories may have struck subjects as odd. To get multiple peaks, we relied on mixtures of items (e.g., temperatures from August or from February) that seem to be rather arbitrary disjunctions, rather than everyday categories. To some extent, the data cited in the previous section provide some comfort here, because they suggest that we can get related findings with ordinary items like pizzas and teapots. Still, it would be of interest if the differential effects of distance and frequency also hold for unimodal distributions. We wouldn't expect as dramatic differences as in the bimodal case, for the reasons we have discussed; but a careful look at judgments for unimodal histograms could turn up confirming evidence.

For purposes of generality, then, Collins and I repeated our experiment with four single-peaked distributions. Figure 3.3 contains the histograms, one with a short central peak, a second with a taller central peak, a third with a peak at the extreme right of the distribution, and a final, skewed distribution. (The superimposed curves are data that are discussed shortly.) As in the previous experiment, we told subjects that these graphs represented temperatures or boys' weights, but this time there was no indication that the categories were mixtures of heterogeneous elements. The procedure was the same as before: Sub-

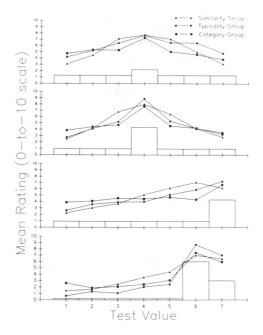

FIG. 3.3. Mean ratings from Collins & Rips (1989, Experiment 3) as a function of position of the test value. Each pair of axes corresponds to a different stimulus histogram, whose outline is superimposed.

jects saw on each trial one of the histograms and a single test value marked on the x-axis. Separate groups of subjects rated how similar the test value is to the set of items represented by the graph, how typical it is of the set, or how likely it is to be from the set. The pairs of graphs and test values appeared in a random sequence in the subjects' booklets. They might see, for example, test value 4 with the short central-peaked graph, followed by test value 7 with the skewed graph, and so on.

Figure 3.3 plots the mean ratings from the three conditions over the corresponding histograms. The similarity, typicality, and likelihood curves are obviously much more alike than in Fig. 3.2. This is because distance and frequency are closely correlated in the stimulus distributions. Nevertheless, you can see some qualitative differences in shape that reflect the contributions of these two factors. First, the likelihood curve (square symbols) is flatter than the similarity (triangles) or the typicality (circle) curves over the nonpeak values. This is what we would expect on the supposition that likelihood depends on frequency but similarity (and, to some extent, typicality) on distance to the mean or median. Frequency is uniform over the nonpeaks in these histograms so likelihood ratings should be uniform too. However, distance decreases continuously from the mean/median, hence similarity ratings should slope in the same way. Second, consider the histogram whose peak is at the extreme right. The maximum value

of the similarity curve for this condition is at position 6, whereas the maximum
of the likelihood curve is at 7. A probable reason for this difference is that position 6 is closer to the mean or median of the histogram than is position 7.
Hence, if the similarity subjects are relying on distance to the mean or median
and likelihood subjects on raw frequencies, then we should find exactly this
shift in the position of the maxima.[2]

We can get a more systematic look at the differences among the similarity,
typicality, and category-likelihood judgments using multiple regression. In this
analysis, we use frequency and distance of the test values as independent variables in order to discern their effects on the three types of ratings. For a given
test value, the associated frequency is simply the height of the histobar above
that value. As the distance measure, we used the absolute value of the difference between the test value and the median of the distribution. We performed
separate regressions of the ratings for each subject and problem type (i.e., temperatures versus weights) and then calculated the standardized regression coefficients (β weights) for the two variables. (The standardized weights allow us
to compare the relative effects of distance and frequency, because they don't
depend on the arbitrary units with which these two variables were measured.)
It helps in understanding these results if we switch the sign of the distance coefficients, so that larger values of both independent variables imply higher ratings. In other words, in place of distance to the median, we can look at the
effect of closeness to the median—roughly speaking, the "centrality" of the
test value in the distribution.

The regression results support the impression from Fig. 3.3 that category
likelihood depends mainly on frequency and similarity on centrality (or distance). For the category ratings, the average frequency coefficient (mean β)
is 0.55 and the average centrality coefficient is 0.21. In the similarity ratings,
however, the average frequency coefficient is essentially zero (-0.04), but the
coefficient for centrality is 0.73. Typicality ratings are again intermediate: 0.41
for frequency and 0.37 for centrality. An analysis of the individual coefficients
confirms a significant interaction between the predictor (frequency versus centrality) and type of rating (similarity, typicality, or category likelihood).

In short, we get the same conclusion from unimodal categories as from bimodal ones. On one hand, subjects attend to frequency when they have to determine how likely it is that an instance with a given value is a member of
the category in question. On the other hand, they turn to distance to the median

---

[2]In the remaining histograms, the mean and median coincide with the mode or peak, so they
can't discriminate the two hypothetical strategies. It's also worth noticing that in the histogram
with the peak at the right, the midrange of the graph is at position 4, the mean at approximately
position 5, the median approximately at 6, and the mode at 7. If the similarity subjects are computing distance to the most representative or central value, then the median rather than the midrange,
mean, or mode would seem to be subjectively most central. Caution is necessary, however, because
the effect is small, the only significant difference being between positions 4 and 6.

(or some closely related measure of central tendency) when judging how similar the same instance is to the category. For bimodal categories, this difference leads to radically different response profiles, as we saw in Fig. 3.2. But even with unimodal categories, we find both qualitative and quantitative differences in the shape of the curves. These differences, along with those for the more naturalistic categories that we discussed in the previous section, make it difficult to contend that category likelihood is reducible to similarity, at least if this similarity is the sort that our subjects had in mind.

CONCLUSIONS AND CRITICISMS

> The most difficult problem of all is to explain *how far* one may depart, whether in scientific or logical definitions, from the correct use in the language of the terms one is defining, for the sake of simplicity.
>
> E. J. Lemmon (1959)

According to the old, comforting resemblance story, the more similar instance i to the members of category C, the more typical i to C; and the more typical i to C, the more likely i is a C. This is supposed to be a theoretical story about how categorization works; but you might naturally suppose that if it's true, subjects' judgments about similarity, typicality, and category likelihood would follow suit. The problem is that they don't. It's easy to arrange experiments in which the judged similarity of instances to a category goes up, while their likelihood of being in the category goes down. The divergence of the curves in Fig. 3.2 illustrates this uncoupling of rated similarity and categorization.

Still, someone who's inclined to accept the resemblance story has some room to maneuver, as the theoretical description may not map directly onto the empirical one. There may be reasons to think that subjects' ratings aren't a proper measure of what resemblance theory posits. Why should we take subjects' similarity judgments at face value, knowing what we do about the biases that affect them? Perhaps if we fix things so that what subjects are rating coincides with what resemblance theory means by "similarity," then the results will fall in place. Of course, some fixes are more interesting than others. If we're free to define "similarity" however we like, then we can always gerrymander the definition so that the predictions hold; but this would be a purely terminological matter without any substantive interest for psychology (Goodman, 1970; Murphy & Medin, 1985). The resemblance theory is only salvageable if the kind of "similarity" it uses can be related in a fairly natural way to its "correct use in the language."

So resemblance theory has a dilemma: On one hand, if "similarity" means similarity in the sense that our subjects understand it, then the resemblance theory is wrong, given the results we've reviewed. On the other hand, if "similarity" is whatever function we need to make the theory work, then resemblance theory is utterly trivial. In what follows, some possible ways to avoid this dilemma are considered in order to get a better grip on our findings.

Why Bother?

One reason for thinking that there might be a solution to resemblance theory's problem is that in some studies similarity or typicality has been a good predictor of categorization. For example, Shoben, Smith, and I showed that rated similarity (Rips et al., 1973) and rated typicality (Smith et al., 1974) of a subordinate (e.g., robin) to a superordinate category (bird) predicts the amount of time people take and the errors they make in answering class-inclusion questions *(Is a robin a bird?)*. More recent experiments with artificial categories also claim that similarity predicts the likelihood that a particular instance will be classified as a member of a category (e.g., Hintzman, 1986; Medin & Schaffer, 1978; Nosofsky, 1986). If similarity and categorization are different beasts, then why should all this research point at a close relationship between them?

Naturalistic categories.   In the case of natural categories, it's not hard to understand why similarity sometimes predicts category behavior. Consider Fig. 3.3 once again. The three curves within each of the panels are obviously highly correlated, despite the differences that we observed. According to the hypothesis developed earlier, this is because frequency and distance from the median are themselves highly correlated for unimodal categories. Because distance heavily influences similarity and frequency heavily influences category likelihood, the two types of ratings look much the same on first glance. If natural categories are mostly unimodal over the properties that are salient to people (as seems reasonable), then we should expect similarity–likelihood correlations for these categories too. Furthermore, we'd expect natural categories to have smoother contours than the ones in Fig. 3.3—something more like a normal distribution or similar function rather than the step functions we employed in the experiments. With a normally-distributed category, frequency and distance from the median will be even more closely correlated; one is a strictly monotonic transformation of the other. This suggests that we could take similarity as a proxy for frequency in situations where the exact distribution of a category is unknown. Similarity can serve as a heuristic for category likelihood in just the same way that representativeness serves as a heuristic for probability in the well-known theory of Kahneman and Tversky (1972). Indeed, they may be exactly the same heuristic.

Artificial categories.   It's more difficult to understand why similarity should predict categorization probabilities in experiments with artificial categories. These studies have employed categories that are far from normal and still find evidence that aggregate similarity between a target item and previously learned category members is an excellent predictor of the category to which subjects will assign the item. One possibility is that subjects carry over a similarity heuristic from naturalistic situations to these artificial categories. Notice, too, that these experiments often use only a small number of training instances as exemplars of the to-be-learned categories, and in some studies (e.g., Nosofsky, 1986) subjects receive thousands of preliminary trials on these exemplars. The presence of well-learned exemplars and the absence of other clues to category membership may make similarity to the exemplars the only reasonable strategy when the transfer test rolls around.

There is a prior question, however. We need to ask whether the "similarity" defined in these studies has anything to do with its natural-language counterpart. Certainly, there's no reason to insist that "similarity" (the theoretical concept) exactly matches the ordinary meaning of the term. But "similarity" can't be entirely free-floating without risk of circularity. Consider Nosofsky's (1986) model as an example. In this theory, there seem to be three levels of analysis that are related to similarity. First, there is a multidimensional representation in which stimulus elements correspond to points. At the middle level, there are "similarities" that are calculated from the distances in the dimensional structure, but that are also affected by attention: "Similarities" change as attention gives greater weight to some dimensions over others. In Nosofsky's research relating identification to categorization, there are several sets of "similarity" parameters at this level—one set to model identification performance and four others specific to individual categories (and that differ in the weights assigned to component dimensions). Finally, there is a third level of similarity judgments, particular responses to questions about similarity. These judgments are a function of "similarity" as well as other task-specific factors. Nosofsky's (1985, 1986) experiment, however, never descended to this third level, as subjects never had to decide on the similarity of the stimulus items.

Within this framework, the claim that similarity predicts categorization means that there is some set of "similarity" parameters that can be used to model the probability that subjects will classify an instance as a member of Category A rather than B. However, to claim that similarity predicts categorization also requires that the "similarity" parameters be grounded to similarity in a non-question-begging way. There is a special problem about this that Nosofsky's results pose. In order to predict the categorization data, Nosofsky (like Medin & Schaffer, 1978) assumes that the probability of classifying instance i as a C depends on the summed "similarity" of i to C exemplars, divided by the summed "similarity" of i to all exemplars. In order to get satisfactory fits, however, Nosofsky found that he needed to consider not just "similarity" to the C exemplars that subjects had learned during training trials, but also "similarity" to other test stimuli that the subjects also considered to be members of C. In other words, the predictions assume that subjects have already classified the test items as members of one of the categories and use that information to make their classification response on any given test trial. This may well be a reasonable assumption in an experiment like this in which subjects classify the same small set of stimuli (16 of them) over many different trials. But it raises the question of whether similarity is predicting categorization or categorization predicting similarity and makes it difficult to see how we can give "similarity" a well-grounded interpretation.

Maybe there's a way to slip between the horns of our dilemma—to exhibit a notion of similarity that predicts category judgments, corresponds in some recognizable way to our usual understanding of similarity, but isn't so closely tied that it runs into the problems posed by the results of the previous section. Nosofsky's framework, for example, allows for an abstract type of similarity (or family of similarity concepts) that might satisfy these requirements. However, the empirical results on similarity and categorizing don't provide much reason to be optimistic. With naturalistic categories, it's difficult to tease apart the contribution of similarity from other important factors. With artificial categories, it's hard to find something that answers to similarity that doesn't presuppose the category membership it is supposed to predict. Maybe this situation shouldn't be surprising. Theories of similarity (e.g., Shepard, 1987; Tversky, 1977) generally assume that category structure affects subjective similarity. If this is true, then the resemblance theory's assertion that similarity affects categorizing is likely to sound rather hollow.

Deep Similarity

A common response to the evidence in the first part of this chapter is that it shows only that similarity based on superficial properties is unable to account for categorizing. Perhaps what really matters to categorizing is similarity based on deeper features of the instance and category (Medin & Ortony, 1989). This response is tempting because subjects in the experiments I've described do seem to be neglecting more "theoretical" properties such as variability (in the teapot study), base rate frequency (in the histogram studies), or underlying biological properties (in the studies about animals) in making their similarity judgments. As these latter characteristics are exactly what they seem to rely on when making category judgments, maybe subjects use similarity in both conditions, but similarity calculated over different dimensions of the instances.

A variation on this objection is that the instances subjects were considering in the different conditions might not be the same. It's possible, for example, that when subjects have to determine whether a 200 cm³ object is a teapot or a tennis ball they conceive of this intermediate object in a different way from the situation in which they must decide whether it's more similar to a teapot or a tennis ball. If the objects imagined in the two cases are different, then it's not surprising that the decisions flip-flop the way they do. In the case of the mutant animal study, subjects may be comparing the test instance to two different standards. When they're asked about the similarity of the fish-like animal who turns reptile-like, they compare the test instance to exemplars that have a typical fish or reptile appearance; when asked about category membership, however, they may compare the instance to the sorts of mutant exemplars they've seen in Japanese monster movies (as John Anderson has suggested in conversation). Again, similarity may be at work in both cases, but a similarity based on a different subset of properties. If we could somehow hold constant the objects and standards that the subjects are imagining, then we'd get the same responses in the two key conditions.

This objection tends to ignore the question of why subjects' similarity judgments diverge from the hypothetical deep-similarity metric that's supposed to be responsible for category likelihood. The subjects were certainly not under instructions to attend to surface properties and ignore more theoretical ones, and there doesn't seem to be any other obvious aspect of the experiments that would push subjects in this direction. You can imagine Gricean reasons why subjects might differentiate similarity and category decisions if they had to make both judgments in a single session. But except for the studies about animals, separate groups of subjects made the similarity and category ratings; so Gricean pressures shouldn't move these ratings around. Another possibility is that similarity via surface properties is easier to assess, perhaps because deeper attributes take longer to retrieve. Therefore, when subjects rate similarity, they take the easy way out and stick to surface features, resorting to deeper properties only when they must in categorizing. But is it really true that the "deeper" properties are more difficult to handle? In the histogram studies, subjects had frequency information staring them in the face; they could read it off the y-axis directly, as in Fig. 3.1. Distance to the median, however, must have required at least as much computational work, especially for the unimodal histograms in which the median wasn't at the midrange of the distribution (the two bottom histograms in Fig. 3.3). Yet it's frequency that affected category ratings, and distance that affected similarity. If similarity ratings are determined by properties that take least effort to extract, then the results ought to have come out the other way around.

It seems much more plausible to take subjects' ratings at face value: Similarity just doesn't depend very much on the "deeper" properties that sometimes determine category membership. The deep similarity idea entails second-guessing subjects about what "similarity" means, and we've already glimpsed the dangers of doing this in the previous section. Deep similarity, like theoretical similarity, begins to seem vacuous once we cut it loose from the intuitions to which it is moored. What lies behind the deep similarity hypothesis seems to be the notion that any mental comparison can be viewed as a sort of similarity computation. And because it's probably true that category ratings in our experiments depend on some sort of comparison—one that takes into account "deep" properties of the instance and the category—this leads psychologists to conclude that similarity must be at work here. But there's no good reason to suppose that every comparison involves similarity. When a program checks a certain position in Register 7 to see if a 0 is stored there, it's doing a kind of comparison. Yet it's peculiar to insist that the program is calculating the similarity between what's in that position and a 0. Likewise, checking the frequency of a distribution at a particular point may involve comparison, but it can hardly be said to involve similarity. In short, pumping up the notion of similarity to cover all comparisons leaves it too bloated for interesting psychological explanation.

The troubles that attend deep similarity also afflict the idea that subjects are attending to different instances or different standards in the similarity and category conditions. Even if we grant that different instances or standards are involved, we're still left with the problem of explaining why it is that subjects choose one type of instance or standard when they're asked to assess similarity and another when asked to assess category likelihood. The motivation for the different standards idea (like the motivation for "deep" similarity) is to be able to point to common processes that come into play in both sorts of judgment. But although these common processes may exist and although we might want to use "similarity" in a technical sense to denote them, it doesn't follow that category likelihood is just a matter of "similarity." For by using "similarity" in this way, we've left out a critical component that determines the likelihood judgments. The resemblance theory is no better off than before, because we now have to supplement the "similarity" mechanism with a theory about choice of standards in the critical conditions.

Categorizing Versus Sentence Understanding

Some of the tensions in the literature on categorization come from a clash between two goals. One goal is to explain how it is that people can recognize instances as members of simple categories, particularly in a perceptual context. Given a perceptual representation of a certain sort, how do we know that what's represented is a haddock rather than a perch? The other goal is to explain how our knowledge of these simple categories relates to our knowledge of more complex ones. How is it that we can determine the meaning of *fried haddock* based on our knowledge of *haddock?* Investigators who feel most comfortable with the resemblance theory are usually those who attend to the first of these goals (e.g., Hintzman, 1986; Medin & Schaffer, 1978; Nosofsky, 1986), whereas investigators who are least comfortable with resemblance theory are those mainly concerned with the second (e.g., Armstrong et al., 1983; Fodor, 1981; Osherson & Smith, 1981). This isn't an accident. It's easiest to see how similarity might apply when we're sorting things into simple categories. It's much more difficult to tell a convincing story about how similarity handles more complex categories that we get by combining elementary ones. For example, many models of categorization assume that our knowledge of haddocks consists of memories of specific haddocks that we've encountered, plus a similarity metric that allows us to tell new haddocks from nonhaddocks. But even given this information, we don't seem to have made much progress in understanding *fried haddock* and identifying its exemplars.

The problem this poses for resemblance theory is that there is no obvious way to get from the similarity metric for the component categories to the similarity metric for the composite one. We obviously use different criteria to classify haddocks and fried haddocks, but how do we figure out what the criteria of the latter are? Typically we can't use similarity to exemplars of the composite categories (e.g., similarity to remembered fried haddocks), because there are too many such composites to go around. For most of these categories, we have never seen an exemplar, and yet we seem to have some idea of what the category is like. A more probable alternative is that we compute similarity for the composite as a function of what we know about the components. This may not be impossible for some composite categories (see Smith, Osherson, Rips, & Keane, 1988, for one attempt to deal with simple adjective–noun combinations), but it's not clear that it can be solved with any generality (Fodor, 1981). (Murphy, 1988, discussed some of the difficulties). We may have to face the fact that for many composites there just isn't any similarity function that would reliably pick out exemplars from nonexemplars. This is especially clear for composites like *Mesozoic haddock* or *invisible haddock* or *mythical haddock*. I suppose one could say that a Mesozoic haddock is more similar to a haddock (a modern one) than to a perch, but this isn't the sort of similarity that will take us very far in recognizing exemplars of the composite category (e.g., distinguishing them from other haddocks).

Does this mean that we can't categorize instances as members of these composite categories? Not at all. There are lots of ways to classify instances besides measuring their similarity. If experts are around, we can use their advice to classify at second hand. Or we can use a variety of inferential strategies to the same end. If we happen to know the haddock came from the proper geological spot, we might be in a good position to suppose that what we've got is a Mesozoic one. Inferential classifications like these are the mainstay of scientific endeavor. In psychology if we classify a response in an experiment as exhibiting PI or mental rotation or conservation, we do it on the basis of an often lengthy chain of inferences. Calling this kind of inferencing "similarity" doesn't do justice to the complicated evidence-sifting that scientists typically perform.

I think it's not too farfetched to suppose that subjects in the experiments described in the first part of this chapter are quite capable of the same sorts of inferential classifications. On this story, similarity and category likelihood diverge in these experiments because subjects realize that establishing category membership takes the kind of detective work that can't be described in terms of similarity. Once we get beyond basic-level categories, classification begins to be less like semblance and more like science.

ACKNOWLEDGMENTS

The preparation of this chapter was supported by National Institute of Mental Health Grant MH39633 and by a fellowship from the James McKeen Cattell foundation. Thanks also to the Psychology Department at Stanford University for their hospitality while this chapter was being written.

I would like to thank Allan Collins, Evan Heit, David Rumelhart, and Edward Smith for their help in thinking about this research.

REFERENCES

Armstrong, S. L., Gleitman, L. R., & Gleitman, H. (1983). What some concepts might not be. *Cognition, 13,* 263–308.

Collins, A., & Rips, L. J. (1989). *Categories and resemblance.* Unpublished manuscript, University of Chicago, Psychology Department, Chicago.

Fodor, J. A. (1981). The present status of the innateness controversy. In *Representations: Philosophical essays on the foundations of cognitive science* (pp. 257–316). Cambridge, MA: MIT Press.

Gelman, S. A., & Markman, E. (1986). Categories and induction in young children. *Cognition, 23,* 183–209.

Goodman, N. (1970). Seven strictures on similarity. In L. Foster & J. W. Swanson (Eds.), *Experience and theory* (pp. 19–29). Amherst: University of Massachusetts Press.

Hintzman, D. L. (1986). "Schema abstraction" in a multiple-trace memory model. *Psychological Review, 93,* 411–428.

Kahneman, D., & Tversky, A. (1972). Subjective probability: a judgment of representativeness. *Cognitive Psychology, 3,* 430–454.

Keil, F. C. (1989). *Concepts, kinds, and cognitive development.* Cambridge, MA: MIT Press.

Lemmon, E. J. (1959). Is there only one correct system of modal logic? *Proceedings of the Aristotelian Society, 33,* 22–40.

Medin, D. L., & Ortony, A. (1989). Psychological essentialism. In S. Vosniadou & A. Ortony (Eds.), *Similarity and analogical reasoning* (pp. 179–195). Cambridge, England: Cambridge University Press.

Medin, D. L., & Schaffer, M. M. (1978). Context theory of classification learning. *Psychological Review, 85,* 207–238.

Murphy, G. L. (1988). Comprehending complex concepts. *Cognitive Science, 12,* 529–562.

Murphy, G. L., & Medin, D. L. (1985). The role of theories in conceptual coherence. *Psychological Review, 92,* 289–316.

Nosofsky, R. M. (1985). Overall similarity and the identification of separable-dimension stimuli: A choice model analysis. *Perception & Psychophysics, 38,* 415–432.

Nosofsky, R. M. (1986). Attention, similarity, and the identification–categorization relationship. *Journal of Experimental Psychology: General, 115,* 39–57.

Osherson, D. N., & Smith, E. E. (1981). On the adequacy of prototype theory as a theory of concepts. *Cognition, 9,* 35–58.

Parducci, A., & Perrett, L. F. (1971). Category rating scales: Effects of relative spacing and frequency of stimulus values. *Journal of Experimental Psychology, 89,* 427–452.

Poulton, E. C. (1989). *Bias in quantifying judgments.* Hillsdale, NJ: Lawrence Erlbaum Associates.

Rips, L. J. (1989), Similarity, typicality, and categorization. In S. Vosniadou & A. Ortony (Eds.), *Similarity and analogical reasoning* (pp. 21–59). Cambridge, England: Cambridge University Press.

Rips, L. J., Shoben, E. J., & Smith, E. E. (1973). Semantic distance and the verification of semantic relations. *Journal of Verbal Learning and Verbal Behavior, 12,* 1–20.

Rosch, E. (1973). On the internal structure of perceptual and semantic categories. In T. E. Moore (Ed.), *Cognitive development and the acquisition of language* (pp. 111–144). New York: Academic Press.

Shepard, R. N. (1987). Toward a universal law of generalization for psychological science. *Science, 237,* 1317–1323.

Smith, E. E., & Medin, D. L. (1981). *Categories and concepts.* Cambridge, MA: Harvard University Press.

Smith, E. E., Osherson, D. N., Rips, L. J., & Keane, M. (1988). Combining concepts: A selective modification model. *Cognitive Science, 12,* 485–528.

Smith, E. E., Shoben, E. J., & Rips, L. J. (1974). Structure and process in semantic memory: A featural model for semantic decisions. *Psychological Review, 81,* 214–241.

Tversky, A. (1977). Features of similarity. *Psychological Review, 84,* 327–352.

Perception of a Unified World: The Role of Discontinuities

Thomas F. Shipley
Swarthmore College

The ability of an impressionist painter, such as Monet, to capture a single moment on canvas lies in his skill in capturing the interaction of light and surfaces. What makes such a skill particularly impressive is the visual system of humans which extracts the *properties* of surfaces. Painters must ignore their own visual system, which provides them with information about objects, and try to reproduce the pattern of reflected light that the visual system uses to perceive the objects in a scene. This chapter discusses the relationship between reflected light and the mechanisms in the visual system responsible for perception of surfaces and objects. The general approach follows both Marr (1982) and Gibson (1979) in considering how light might be affected by objects in a scene and how the visual system could take advantage of the regularities in how light is affected when determining the boundaries of objects.

The task of the visual system is to locate and provide sufficient information to identify quickly and accurately all objects and surfaces in a scene. The information available to do this comes from the light projected from the scene to the observer. There are a number of sources of information for the presence and identity of objects in the way this light is structured. Although using all such sources might be the most accurate way to provide information about objects in an image, it would not be the most efficient. The visual system is presumably limited in the amount of information it can process and the time available for processing, so it probably does not use **all** possible sources of information. Which sources of information are used? In the following sections I focus on discontinuities as potential sources of information for both surface and object perception. In both cases the focus is on information resulting from the discrete nature of objects.

DISCONTINUITIES AND SURFACE PERCEPTION

Before the visual system can identify the objects present in any visual scene it must initially process that scene to determine the boundaries of surfaces. In the present paper the term "surface" is used to refer to the visible surfaces of a unit, and "object" refers to the whole unit. So, for example, partial occlusion of an object will result in a number of surfaces; the boundaries of each surface would be a combination of the boundaries of the occluded object and the occluding object.

Many models of surface localization are based on surface boundary localization (for example, Marr & Hildreth, 1980). The boundaries of surfaces could be identified using differences in a number of properties, including: luminance, texture, binocular disparity, and motion. This section focuses on boundary identification from these four sources of information. For each source I review the evidence for a general mechanism of surface identification based on: (a) using discontinuities in surface features to locate surface boundaries, and (b) interpolation of the internal surface features using the feature values at the boundary.

Consider the objects in our environment; they have some very important properties (Marr, 1982; Spelke, 1984). They are discrete and, relative to the volume of an object, there is a great deal of space that is not filled by a solid. In a world such as ours, where objects tend not to occupy the same space, this implies that objects are relatively smooth; in general two adjacent points on the same object will be close in depth whereas two points chosen from a scene at random will not be close. Furthermore, objects are relatively uniform in composition; two adjacent areas on the same object will tend to be the same material but two areas chosen from anywhere in a scene will tend not to be the same material. These properties of our world impose very important constraints on the way light will be structured by the objects in a visual scene. In particular, two-dimensional projections of a three-dimensional scene will have the following properties. Two points that are proximal in the projection will tend to have the same features if they were points projected from the same object *but* two points projected from different objects will tend *not* to have the same features. When smooth surfaces are projected onto a smooth surface, points that are close on the projected surface will be close in the projection. These points will also tend to have the same luminance and texture[1] because, as noted earlier, the reflectance and texture of nearby points on an object are similar. The discrete nature of objects implies that points from the same object will tend to move in the same manner in a projection. And, their relative

---

[1]The notion of the texture of a point may be confusing; texture cannot be determined by considering a single point because texture is the relationship of a number of points. Here, one may consider the texture of a point to refer to the relationship of that point to nearby points.

smoothness implies that objects will tend to have the same disparity in two projections (as in the case of two eyes). On the other hand, points from different objects will tend not to share these properties.

It is important to realize that these relationships between points in a projection are hardly deterministic. It will not always be the case that two adjacent points will be identical in luminance, texture, motion, and disparity; rather, the relationships can best be thought of as tendencies. There are two important implications of these tendencies. First, surface boundaries will tend to be marked by abrupt changes in luminance, texture, disparity, and motion. Second, the system could estimate feature values within a surface based on the features of the surface boundaries, and thereby avoid having to compute the feature values for all points on all surfaces. Abrupt changes, or discontinuities, in such features could serve to quickly and accurately identify the boundaries of surfaces. Interpolation of the properties within these boundaries would provide the system with an initial, fairly accurate, representation of the scene without requiring that the feature values at all points on a surface be assessed. If necessary, later processing could provide information about changes of features within surfaces.

Lightness

What evidence is there that we locate surface boundaries based on abrupt changes in luminance and use those values to fill in the surface lightness? There are a number of models of edge detection based on abrupt changes in luminance. Marr and Hildreth (1980) proposed one of the first such models; a more recent example is Grossberg and Mingolla (1985). There is little psychological evidence for models based on abrupt changes in luminance, but there is a great deal of evidence that the visual system interpolates the central regions of surfaces.

Two predictions follow from the claim that the perception of the internal features of a surface are based on the value of the features at the edge:

1. Observers should report, at least initially, that the internal features of a surface match the feature values at the edge, even when they do not physically match.

2. If the edge of a surface is removed, the area within the surface should match the area surrounding the surface in appearance, even when the two regions are physically different.

The Craik–O'Brien–Cornsweet (COC) illusion (Cornsweet, 1970; Craik, 1940; O'Brien, 1958) is an example of a case where the brightness of a figure appears to be influenced by the luminance at the edge of the figure. In the COC illusion the internal region of a central figure appears brighter even though

it matches the surrounding area in luminance. The illusion is produced by a
luminance ramp at the edge of the surface. A graph of the luminance of a cross
section of COC display is shown in Fig. 4.1a. The abrupt change in luminance
is seen as the edge of the figure and the central region appears brighter than
the outer region (as illustrated in Fig. 4.1b). The luminance values at the edge
appear to influence the perception of the brightness of the entire surface. This
brightness illusion does not occur when there is no abrupt change in luminance.
When no luminance discontinuity is present only the local luminance differences are reported (Cornsweet, 1970; Todorović, 1987). That the discontinuity in luminance appears to be necessary for this phenomenon indirectly supports the hypothesis that the visual system uses discontinuities to locate the
edge of a surface.

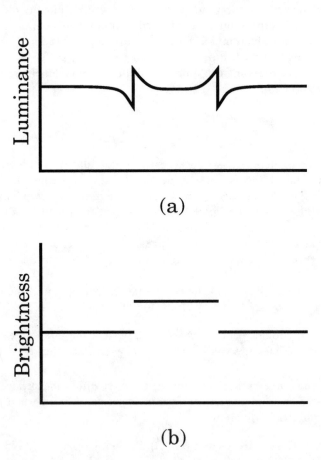

FIG. 4.1.   a) The luminance profile of a cross section of a COC display illustrating the luminance ramps. The discontinuity in luminance is generally seen
as the edge of a figure. b) The perceived brightness of a COC display.

Yarbus (1967) provided a number of cases that confirm the second prediction of an edge-based interpolation model. With the help of a special display system, he studied the effects of stabilizing, on the retina, the edge of one surface surrounded by a second. One effect of stabilizing an edge is that the visual system no longer treats it as an edge in a visual scene (in the same way that the blood vessels on our retinas are not seen as edges of surfaces in the world). When subjects are shown such displays, for example a black square on a larger grey circle with the edge of the internal surface (the black square) stabilized, the display appears as a uniform grey circle. This occurs even though the area within the square is reflecting less light than the other regions of the circle.

Support for a model of surface brightness based on abrupt changes in luminance and some sort of interpolation of lightness is strong, but there are a number of unanswered questions. Recent research on the COC illusion suggests that the luminance ramp outside the surface is more important in producing the illusion than the inner ramp (Todorović, 1987). This suggests that the simple model I have described is not sufficient.

Texture

The visual system appears to be able to use properties other than luminance to identify boundaries. For example, a "T" is clearly seen in Fig. 4.2a, yet there is no luminance difference between the inside and outside of the figure. The boundary of this figure results from the change in orientation of the elements, or texture, of the figure. Just as reflectance differs across surfaces so too does texture. Therefore, the visual system can also use changes in texture to identify surface boundaries. Accounts of how this is accomplished are difficult to provide given the large number of ways that texture elements can differ.

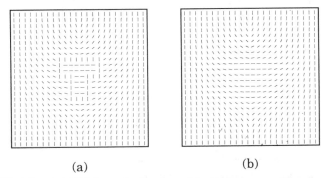

(a)   (b)

FIG. 4.2.   a) A "T" is seen in the center of the display presumably as a result of the discontinuity in texture element orientation. b) The discontinuity in orientation, present in (a), has been removed; as a result, no central figure is seen.

Difference in orientation of the elements, number of line ends, and shape, to name a few, are sufficient to produce a percept of separate surfaces (Beck, 1982). These changes in the properties of elements must be abrupt, as in Fig. 4.2a; when the change is not abrupt, as in Fig. 4.2b, no figure is seen. Such displays suggest that the visual system uses discontinuities in texture to localize surface boundaries. But what constitutes a discontinuity in a property, such as shape of the elements, which is not unidimensional, is not immediately clear. Regardless of whether it is conceptually useful to approach texture segregation as resulting from discontinuities in texture element's properties, one may ask whether the texture at the discontinuity is interpolated over other parts of the surface. No demonstration of a texture analog of the COC effect has been reported to my knowledge.

Stereoscopic Depth

Most current models of the perception of stereoscopic depth from two images assume that fusion of the images is sufficient (Marr & Poggio, 1976). Once a match between the parts of the left and right image has been achieved, computing the depth of the various parts is assumed to be a simple, straightforward procedure. It is not clear that computing the depth to each point on a surface from its relevant disparity value is the most efficient way to achieve depth perception or three dimensional shape perception. Perhaps a more efficient solution lies in the calculation of the depth of only part of the array and filling in the remaining areas by interpolation. But, which areas should be used as anchors for the interpolation processes? Because objects are discrete and relatively smooth the most useful parts of the array would be the boundaries of objects. The boundaries of objects that project to both images will result in disparity discontinuities in the fused image (Marr, 1982). Points within the areas bounded by disparity discontinuities will be approximately the same distance from the observer and therefore have about the same disparity. For surfaces whose edges are not the same distance from the observer the disparity will tend to vary continuously across the surface.

Gillam and her colleagues (Gillam, Flagg, & Findlay, 1984; Gillam, Chambers, & Russo, 1988) have provided some fairly compelling evidence that fusion and perception of depth are indeed independent processes. They have shown that discontinuities in disparity clearly influence the perception of depth in random dot stereograms. They suggest that disparity discontinuities are a stereoscopic primitive responsible for initial stereoscopic depth perception. They further hypothesize that the depth of an area is initially assigned on the basis of the disparity value at the discontinuity, and only later do the disparity values within such an area affect perceived depth.

Their evidence comes from a set of studies in which subjects were asked to report the orientation of surfaces seen in displays with discontinuities in disparities and displays without such discontinuities. The dependent measure they used was the amount of time after fusion (fusion occurs, on average, 2–3 seconds after presentation) necessary to distinguish the type of display. In Gillam, Chambers, and Russo (1988) three types of displays were used: whole field slant, twist, and hinge. These are illustrated in Fig. 4.3. Neither whole field slant nor hinge have disparity discontinuities. But, twist displays do have an area of discontinuity in disparity bisecting the display. For displays with a vertical axis of slant (such as those shown in Figure 4.3) subjects reported seeing a twist display after about 6 seconds, and reported whole field slants and hinges after 31 and 27 seconds respectively. The effect of discontinuity in disparity was also present when horizontal axis of slant was used but the differences between the three groups were smaller. All three displays contained the same maximum disparity values, but subjects only reported seeing large depth differences when a discontinuity in disparity was present.

Gillam's work shows that the perceived depth of points in a fused image is not necessarily related to the disparity of those points. The depth of any given point is not a direct function of its disparity, and the effect of disparity appears to be modulated by the presence of discontinuities. Consistent with this idea, there is some evidence that the perceived depth of a surface in a random dot stereogram is determined, in part, by the disparity of the points on the edge of the surface. Anstis, Howard, and Rogers (1978) reported a stereoscopic version of the Craik–O'Brien–Cornsweet effect. Just as the brightness of a surface appears to be affected by a luminance ramp at its edge, the depth of a surface appears to be influenced by a disparity ramp at its edge. When a random dot surface, shaped like the surface in Fig. 4.4, is presented stereoscopically, the side with the ramp tilted toward the observer (the left side in Fig. 4.4) appears to be closer.

In both Fig. 4.5a and 4.5b most people initially see flat circles, but after 10 to 15 seconds of viewing, Fig. 4.5a should resolve itself into a hemisphere.

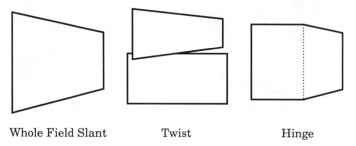

Whole Field Slant   Twist   Hinge

FIG. 4.3. Random dot arrays of three different types are illustrated here: one in which the entire field of dots was slanted, a second in which half the field of dots was slanted in one direction and the other half of the field slanted in the other, and a third where half the field was flat and half was tilted up from the flat area. [After Gillam, Chambers, and Russo, 1988.]

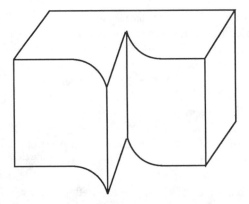

FIG. 4.4.   a) An illustration of the surface shape used to produce a stereoscopic analog of the Craik–O'Brien–Cornsweet effect. In such a display the left side will generally appear closer than the right side.

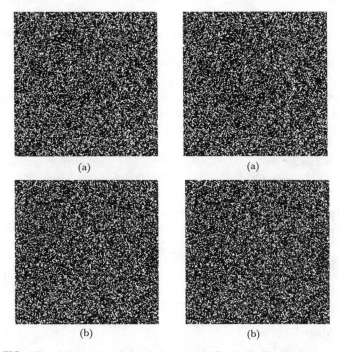

FIG. 4.5.   a) A stereoscopic hemisphere and b) flat circle. The hemisphere appears to some viewers, on initial viewing as a flat circle, suggesting that the central region is initially determined by disparity at the boundaries of the figure.

Initially the form appears to be determined by the disparity at the edges, but eventually the disparity in the middle affects the percept. Apparently the visual system can update the interpolated disparities, using the actual internal disparities, to provide a more accurate representation. Perhaps the system samples the internal disparities, and when the difference between actual and interpolated disparities is large the system uses the actual values.

Motion

The optical displacement of a surface can provide information about its form. Displacement may be the result of a moving object, or the parallax of objects at different depths due to motion of the observer. In some cases optical displacement alone is sufficient for perceiving the form of the surface. Consider two surfaces with identical reflectance and texture, for example, two surfaces made of random dots, one slightly in front of the other. The boundaries of the nearer surface can be clearly seen when the surfaces move relative to each other (Anderson & Cortese, 1989; Gibson, Kaplan, Reynolds, & Wheeler, 1969; Hildreth, 1983). Hildreth (1983) suggested that the visual system uses the discontinuities in motion to identify the boundaries of the near form. To support this claim Hildreth noted that we see boundaries along regions of motion discontinuities in displays that contain very complex motion patterns. An example of such a display is one generated by moving dots within the left half of an array so that dots that are close together move in similar but not identical directions, while the dots in the right half of the array move in the opposite directions (as if they were the mirror image of the dots in the left section). The vertical region where the dots move in opposite directions is a motion discontinuity that is clearly visible even though there is no clear impression of concerted motion in the left or right areas of the display.

The problem of determining the depth and orientation of surfaces from two views differing in horizontal offset is similar to the problem of determining the depth and orientation of surfaces from motion parallax. To see why these two problems are similar, imagine that the motion parallax was produced by moving a monocular observer 2 inches horizontally. The view of the scene at the start and end of the motion are identical to the input to the two eyes of a binocular observer. Although the information in the transition from right to left view may be important, one may still ask whether displays like the ones used by Gillam et al. (1988) presented over time would produce similar results. Surfaces oriented in depth may only appear in the displays with discontinuities in motion.

Although we do not know whether motion discontinuities are necessary for perceiving depth in motion parallax, there is some evidence that the depth of a surface is affected by the motion parallax at a motion discontinuity. Rogers and Graham (1983) reported a motion parallax version of the COC effect. A random dot surface shaped like the surface in Fig. 4.4 was shown to subjects moving their heads from side to side. The side with the ramp inclined toward the observer was reported as being closer. Again, the perceived depth of a surface appears to be influenced by the depth at its edges. Interestingly, the depth illusion, in both the stereoscopic case and the motion parallax case, only appears when the discontinuity in depth is oriented vertically (Rogers & Graham, 1983).

Combining Lightness, Texture, Stereoscopic Disparity, and Motion

How is the surface information from these different sources organized and combined? Integration of information from a number of sources requires some means by which the various source arrays can be aligned. If they were not aligned, information from one object might be applied to another object. Poggio, Gamble, and Little (1988) proposed that the information from different sources are organized by identifying discontinuities in each type of array (luminance, texture, motion, and stereoscopic disparity) and using these to coordinate the arrays. Discontinuities will tend to appear at surface edges, and this property supplies the system with a small number of features, common to the luminance, texture, motion, and stereoscopic disparity arrays, that can be used to establish correspondence between the arrays.

Integration of the arrays allows greater accuracy in the localization and identification of the edges of surfaces. Each source of information has its weakness: Shadows may obscure luminance discontinuities, objects of similar material are difficult to identify solely on the basis of texture, not all objects move, and distant objects will not produce discontinuities in disparity or motion parallax. So, although edges will usually result in discontinuities in a number of the arrays, sometimes only a part of any given edge may appear in each array. By combining the arrays the limitations inherent in each source of information can be overcome.

DISCONTINUITIES AND UNIT FORMATION

The processes discussed in the previous section provide detailed information about the layout of edges in the environment. The sheer amount of information appears to have prompted some to hypothesize that this information alone is sufficient for perception of objects. Poggio and colleagues (1988) suggested that object perception is the result of a recognition process applied to the surfaces defined by differences in luminance, texture, motion, and stereoscopic disparity. This recognition process searches for pieces of a familiar object.

Presumably such a process will fare better than object perception based on recognition of parts in only the luminance and texture domains. But such a model cannot account for the ability to perceive the unity of partially occluded *novel* objects. As some of the following figures (for example Figs. 4.8 and 4.11) demonstrate, there must be some, more general, unit formation process that proceeds along with or precedes recognition. Such a process would be responsible for the interpolation of contours between edges, resulting in the perception of whole objects. The following is a brief description of one such model, proposed by Kellman and Shipley (in press).

A Discontinuity Theory of Unit Formation

Discontinuities in motion, stereoscopic disparity, luminance, and texture may supply information about the layout of surface boundaries, but a general unit formation mechanism is necessary to form these multiple surfaces into the objects we perceive. Like the problem of identifying surface edges, the problem of identifying object boundaries cannot be solved efficiently by a mechanism that uses *all* possible sources of information in the array. The information to be considered must be constrained in some manner. Kellman and Shipley (in press) suggested that this information consists of the set of edges that contain discontinuities in their first derivative (or D1). A sharp bend in a contour is a D1 (see Fig. 4.6). The reason for choosing D1s as the basis for the constraint comes from projective geometry. Whenever two objects are projected onto a

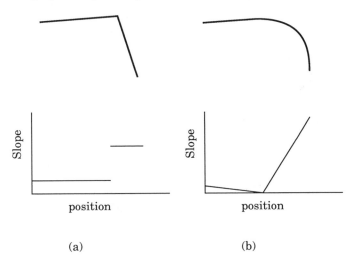

FIG. 4.6.   The upper figures illustrate two continuous functions. The lower figures provide graphs of the first derivative of each function. The function on the left (a) has a discontinuity in its first derivative whereas the one on the right (b) has a continuous first derivative.

surface in such a way that their boundaries overlap (Fig. 4.7), the intersection of their boundaries will form a discontinuity. Appendix A in Kellman and Shipley (in press) provides a formal proof, but for present purposes the following argument should be sufficient. Consider any of the intersections in Fig. 4.7: The boundaries of the two units will form a D1 *unless* they have the same orientation. Two edges will never have *exactly* the same orientation, so a D1 will *always* be formed at their intersection. Therefore, D1s will always be present in the boundaries of the visible parts of objects, and they may be used to limit the set of edges considered by any unit formation process. Note that the D1s are not necessary and sufficient for unit formation, as D1s can also occur on the boundaries of single objects. The issue of necessary *and* sufficient conditions for unit formation will be discussed later.

When one object occludes part of the boundary of another we perceive the further object as a whole object, not two or more incompletely bounded entities. Although partial occlusion of objects may be the most important it is not the only situation in which we perceive boundaries in the absence of local specification by luminance, texture, motion, or disparity. Figure 4.8 illustrates some other cases. Figure 4.8a is an example of partial occlusion: Although neither figure is familiar the four grey areas are clearly seen as part of a single figure. The occluded edges serve to unify the visible parts of the display but they are not perceived as a gradient of any kind (color, texture, motion, or disparity); in Michotte's terminology they are perceived *amodally*. Figure 4.8b and 4.8c

FIG. 4.7. Two randomly shaped figures whose projections onto the surface of the page overlap.

illustrate cases in which the interpolated edges do appear as gradients; they are perceived *modally*. In Fig. 4.8b the figure seen to be partially occluded in Fig. 4.8a appears as a subjective figure. The edges of the subjective figure seen between the black areas (inducing elements) are not defined in the luminance domain yet they appear as a brightness gradient. As we will see later, subjective edges may appear as other types of gradients. Figure 4.8c illustrates the case of spontaneously splitting figures. The homogeneous black area is generally seen as two black figures, one in front of the other. One of the figures resembles the occluding black figure in Fig. 4.8a, the other resembles the subjective figure in Fig. 4.8b. The depth relation of the two figures is unstable, meaning that over time, the two figures will alternate as to which is seen in front of the other. Note that regardless of which figure is seen in front, when it is seen in front it has modal edges. Finally, in Fig. 4.8d, a filmy or transparent figure is seen. Like the subjective figure the interpolated edges appear to be modal, yet the inducing elements can be seen through the figure.

Figure 4.8 serves to illustrate one of Kellman and Shipley's central claims, that perception of subjective figures is a special case of unit formation. In other words, perception of partially occluded objects and subjective figures is governed

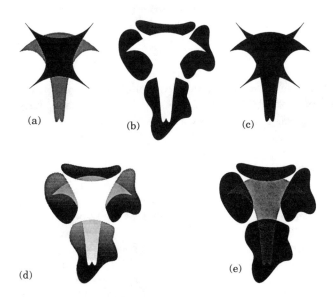

(a)

(b)

(c)

(d)

(e)

FIG. 4.8. Examples of figures whose boundaries are not entirely specified in the luminance domain. Note that the same central figure is seen in each of the five types of displays. a) A partially occluded figure, b) a subjective figure, c) a spontaneously splitting figure, d) a transparent subjective figure, and e) a standard transparent figure.

by the same process. Experimental investigation of the perception of unity in subjective figure displays and equivalent partially occluded figure displays appear to confirm this claim (Kellman & Shipley, 1987; Shipley & Kellman, 1989). The general strategy used in each experiment was to construct two sets of matched displays. One set contained a variety of subjective figures, the other contained matching partially occluded figures. Subjects were asked to rate the clarity of the subjective figure seen in the subjective figure displays and were asked to rate unity (how strongly the visible parts appeared to be part of a single figure) in the partially occluded figure displays. If perception of subjective figures and partially occluded figures results from the same process, then subjects' responses to the two ostensibly different tasks should be highly correlated. A subjective figure judged to be very clear would imply that the corresponding partially occluded figure would be judged to be a single figure, and conversely a weak or unclear subjective figure implies that the corresponding partially occluded figure will not appear to be a single figure.

A simple rule, which can be induced from Fig. 4.8, was used to match subjective figures and partially occluded figures. To create a subjective figure display that matches a particular partially occluded figure, inducing elements are placed in such a way that each visible boundary of the partially occluded figure is defined by the boundary of an inducing element (see Figs. 4.8a and 4.8b). Furthermore, the boundary removed from a complete figure to form each inducing element should be the boundary of the occluder in the partially occluded figure display. Interestingly, when the two figures are combined, as in Fig. 4.8e, the result may be a transparent figure or figures.

In one experiment, a set of figures, illusory and occluded, was generated by sampling from figures which varied along a single dimension (Kellman & Shipley, 1987). Subjects were asked to rate the clarity and unity of figures in which the alignment of the parts varied. Alignment varied from complete (Fig. 4.9a) to 40 minutes of misalignment (Fig. 4.9b). Subject's reports of unity and subjective contour clarity are shown in Fig. 4.10. The correlation between judgments was very high (r = .99), suggesting that alignment, or lack thereof, affects the two percepts in the same manner.

In a second experiment, the set of figures was generated by sampling from a much larger region of subjective-figure/partially-occluded-figure "space" (Shipley & Kellman, 1989). This was accomplished by constructing random occluded figures and random occluders. The algorithm used to construct these figures was constrained to produce figures that are both radially monotonic (any given radian only crosses the boundary once) and smooth. An example of a random occluded and a random occluding figure are shown in Fig. 4.11a. The matching set of subjective figure displays was constructed by applying the rule previously discussed. Figure 4.11b is the subjective figure displays corresponding to the partially occluded figure shown in Fig. 11a. Again the clarity judgments and the unity judgments were highly correlated (r = .95). Sub-

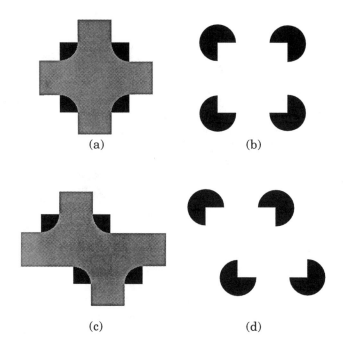

(a)   (b)

(c)   (d)

FIG. 4.9. Displays from an experiment in which the alignment of edges was varied in both partially occluded figures (a and c) and subjective figures (b and d). Misalignment varied from none (a and b) to 35 minutes (c and d).

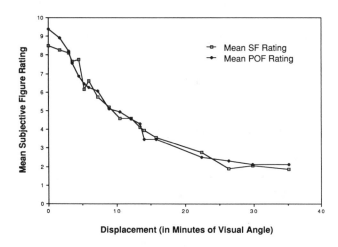

FIG. 4.10. A graph of the contour clarity ratings of subjective figures (SF ratings) and unity ratings of partially occluded figures (POF ratings) as a function of alignment. Figure 4.9 provides examples of the displays shown to subjects.

69

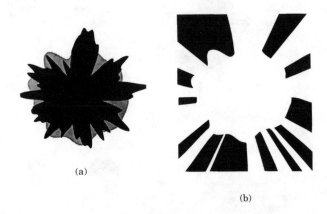

FIG. 4.11.   a) An example of a random partially occluded figure and b) its corresponding subjective figure display.

jects were also asked to make local judgments of unity and clarity. They were asked to indicate the adjacent parts of a partially occluded figure that appeared to be part of the same object, as well as the parts that did not appear to be part of the same object. In the subjective figure displays, they were asked to report the clearest and weakest subjective contours. Again the correlation between the two types of judgments was high (r = .87). Clear subjective contours tended to be reported between areas that were judged to be part of the same object in the partially occluded figure display, and the weakest subjective contours were reported in areas between parts that did not appear to be part of the same object.

The Discontinuity Model

The unit formation model proposed by Kellman and Shipley (in press) is based on D1s in the edges of optically specified regions (luminance, motion, texture, and stereoscopically defined edges). Perceived units are the combination of optically specified edges and edges interpolated between D1s. The appearance of the unit (modal or amodal) depends on the relative depth of that unit and the other units in the display.

Spatial D1s

D1s are used by the visual system to identify optically specified edges that may be parts of the boundary of a unit. Therefore D1s are necessary for the perception of units that are not completely optically specified. This implies that removing D1s from a display in which a unit is not completely specified should result in the loss of that unit. This appears to be the case for both partially occluded figures and subjective figures (Shipley & Kellman, 1990). In Fig. 4.12a, where D1s are present on the inducing elements, subjects were more likely to report seeing a subjective circle, and rated its clarity higher than the potential subjective circle in Fig. 4.12b, where the D1s have been removed. The same pattern of results was obtained when irregular subjective figures and inducing element were used; displays with D1s on the inducing elements were consistently rated higher than displays with the D1s absent. These differences could have been the result of an additive effect of D1s; for example, D1s could simply increase the strength or clarity of a subjective figure. This possibility was ruled out by demonstrating that parameters that affect the clarity of subjective figures, such as number of inducing elements, only have an effect when D1s are present. If D1s simply had an additive effect then the effect of number of inducing elements should have shown up both in displays with and displays without discontinuities, but this did not happen.

D1s also appear to influence the formation of units in partially occluded figure displays. Evidence for this comes from a recent series of studies on the effect of D1s on perceived depth. Subjects were shown displays like the one in Fig. 4.13a and asked to report whether they saw the grey or the black areas in front. If D1s were present in the boundaries of the black areas the subjects generally reported seeing the black in back of the grey figure, but if the D1s had been removed, as in Figure 4.13b, the black pieces were seen in front of the central figure.

D1s appear to be necessary for unit formation in both subjective figures and partially occluded figures. This provides further support for the hypothesis that unit formation in the two domains is the result of the same process. It also supports the hypothesis that discontinuities in the first derivative of an edge are instrumental in identifying the relevant edges for formation of units in general.

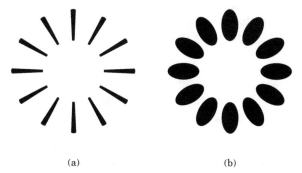

(a)   (b)

FIG. 4.12.   An illustration of the importance of discontinuities for the perception of subjective figures. Subjects report clear subjective figures in displays where the inducing elements have discontinuities (a), and no clear subjective figure in displays without discontinuities (b).

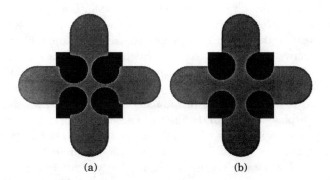

(a)   (b)

FIG. 4.13.   An illustration of the importance of discontinuities on interposi-
tion. a) The four black areas are seen as part of a square behind a grey figure
when discontinuities are present on the black areas. b) When the discontinuities
have been removed the four black areas appear to be in front of the grey figure.

Interpolation Between D1s

The presence of D1s is not sufficient for unit formation; any two edges with
D1s are not necessarily part of the same unit. Identifying which edges form
a unit requires the use of additional information in the form of the relative
position of the two edges. Kellman and Shipley called the necessary relative
position *relatability*. If two edges containing D1s are relatable, a contour is interpolated between them. For two edges to be relatable the potential contour
that joins them must meet two requirements. It must be monotonic and it must
not contain any D1s. Two edges can be related by a monotonic curve if the
linear extrapolation of both edges meet. Figures 4.14a and 4.14b are examples
of edges that are not monotonically relatable. The relationship between D1s
and relatability is crucial. D1s determine which edges are considered for relatability *and* which interpolated edges are acceptable. It may be helpful to think
of the unit formation process as trying to minimize the number of D1s in unit
boundaries.

The edges that serve as the input for the interpolation process may be defined by luminance, texture, stereoscopic, or motion differences. Either of the
last two processes will provide information about the three-dimensional orientation of the edge. This information is used by the unit formation process; the
relatability of edges is based on their position and orientation in three dimensions. Figure 4.15 provides an example of a three-dimensional subjective figure.
When the two images are fused, a helix passing through two elliptical holes
is seen. The helix is positioned so that its nearest points are in front of the
page and its farthest point behind the page. This figure illustrates a number
of important points. First, subjective contours clearly need not be two dimensional (Gregory & Harris, 1974). Second, the near parts of the helix which

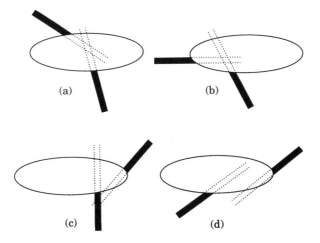

FIG. 4.14.   Two edges are relatable if lines extrapolated from the discontinuity intersect. a) and b) are examples of relatable edges, and c) and d) are examples of edges that are not relatable.

FIG. 4.15.   A stereogram of a subjective three-dimensional helix, parts of which appear in front of the page while other parts appear behind the page. Note that the subjective edges that appear in front of the page appear modal, whereas the edges that go behind the page appear amodal.

are not optically defined have modal contours whereas the far sections, the areas behind the surface of the page, appear amodal. The near and far sections of the helix differ only in their disparity suggesting that the difference between modal and amodal contours lies not in the unit formation process but in their depth placement relative to other surfaces (such as the surface of the page).

Spatiotemporal Discontinuities

The model as described so far deals only with the case of unit formation in static images. Yet objects in the world move and when an observer moves the projections from two objects may well change. Because D1s are projectively invariant and will always occur when one object occludes another, the spatial model could be used to identify units over time by being applied repeatedly to individual time slices. Such a simple model of unit formation can be rejected on the basis of a number of studies in which subjects report clear units when shown kinematic displays, yet do not perceive the same units when shown a set of static images selected from the motion sequence (Kellman & Cohen, 1984). Subjects shown displays in which a black triangle on a black background sequentially occludes parts of several irregular white figures report a robust subjective triangle. Yet when shown static frames from the motion sequence subjects report no triangle. Clearly the system is taking advantage of the fact that the relative motion of two units provides additional information on their boundaries. Kellman and Shipley (in press) suggested that the difference between static unit formation and unit formation over time lies in the presence of spatiotemporal discontinuities, and the visual system's ability to interpolate edges across gaps in both space and time.

Discontinuities in the shape of a curve serve as the initiating condition for unit formation in static displays. Kinematic unit formation may also be based on shape discontinuities, where the shape discontinuities are observed over time Kellman & Shipley, (in press). Alternatively, the system may take advantage of discontinuities resulting from the interaction of two units over time. One such discontinuity is the *change* in the projected shape of an edge over time. The projected shape of an object will not change discontinuously if it is rotated or translated, but will change discontinuously when occluded by another object. Figure 4.16a illustrates the case of a nondiscontinuous change and Fig. 4.16b shows a discontinuous change. Assessing the relative merits of these two models is very difficult using normal displays because shape discontinuities and change-in-shape discontinuities will almost always co-occur. But, displays can be designed that separate these two sources of information. Figure 4.17 provides an example of a sequence of images where the change in shape over time is discontinuous without introducing shape discontinuities. Informal reports of a moving square in such displays suggest that spatial D1s are not necessary for unit formation over time.

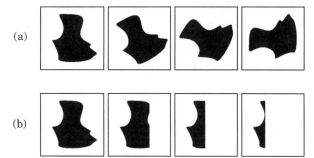

(a)

(b)

FIG. 4.16. A sequence of time slices illustrating two types of change. a) A spatiotemporally continuous change in the boundaries of a figure and b) a spatiotemporally discontinuous change.

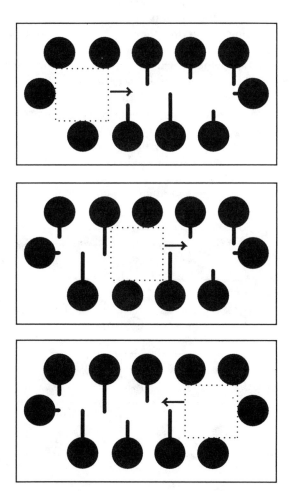

FIG. 4.17. Sequential views of a display in which the moving square is defined by spatiotemporal but not spatial discontinuities.

Spatiotemporal Relatability

Following Kellman and Cohen (1984) and Kellman and Loukides (1987), Kellman and Shipley (in press) defined spatiotemporal relatability as a situation in which the edges of a "unitary, rigid object translating at a constant velocity or rotating at a constant angular velocity" should be relatable. They do allow that relatability may include other types of motion, such as constant acceleration or certain types of nonrigid motion, but these have not been investigated.

Spatiotemporal relatability, like spatial relatability, is defined as the inverse of spatiotemporal discontinuity. Two edges are spatiotemporally relatable if for any given interval in time they can be connected by an edge that is monotonic, has no spatial discontinuities, and is not changing discontinuously. Spatiotemporal relatability can be distinguished from spatial relatability in two ways. First, the edges being related need not be present in the luminance domain at the same time. Although the edges in Fig. 4.18a defined at different points in time do not relate spatially, they do relate spatiotemporally as illustrated in Fig. 4.18b. The position of edges relevant for determining spatiotemporal relatability is not simply the position of each edge when it was defined in the luminance domain (where it last occluded an inducing element). It must be the position of one luminance-defined edge and the extrapolated position of an edge defined in the luminance domain at an earlier point in time. Strict

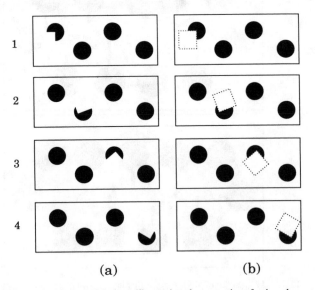

FIG. 4.18.   Sequential views illustrating the necessity of using the extrapolated position of an edge when relating edges to form a figure (b).

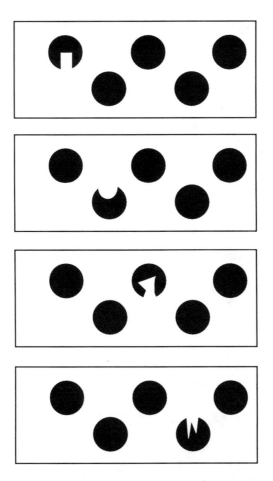

FIG. 4.19.   A sequence of views in which discontinuous changes in the boundary of the occluding object may block spatiotemporal relatability.

spatiotemporal relatability may require that such relationships be reciprocal;
in other words, the extrapolation of the luminance-defined edges both forward
and backward in time must be spatially relatable. The second difference between spatiotemporal relatability and spatial relatability is the requirement that
relatable edges not exhibit discontinuous changes in their shape over time.
Figure 4.19 provides an example of a display in which spatiotemporal relatability might fail because the edges of a translating unit would have to change
discontinuously with each frame.

Finally, the concept of spatiotemporal monotonicity is somewhat different
from that of spatial monotonicity. Spatiotemporal monotonicity entails spatial
monotonicity; two edges are spatiotemporally monotonic if their relative orien-

tation within a figure is such that a spatially monotonic edge can be interpolated between them. Spatiotemporal monotonicity requires any change in shape over time to progress in one direction—the change cannot reverse direction (e.g., if the radius of an interpolated curve is increasing it must continue to increase). Perhaps both the requirements of spatiotemporal relatability and spatiotemporal monotonicity as described here may be too stringent, not capturing all of the situations in which humans perceive units over time. But they should, at least, provide a concrete starting point for research on unit formation in the fourth dimension.

DISCONTINUITIES AND APPARENT MOTION

The notions of spatiotemporal discontinuities and spatiotemporal relatability were developed by Kellman and Shipley to deal with partial occlusion over time, providing an outline for how edges are interpolated across both space and time. Like partial occlusion in spatial arrays, the central focus is on specifying the conditions under which an entire edge will be seen when only parts of the edge are physically specified. Although there has been relatively little research done on kinematic unit formation, there has been a great deal of work done on a related issue, apparent motion. In a simple apparent motion display one figure will be shown (frame 1), followed by an interval in which no figure is shown (inter-stimulus interval or ISI), which is followed by the presentation of a second figure at a different location than the first figure (frame 2). Within a fairly wide range of ISI times observers will report seeing a figure move from one location to the other.

Why should we perceive motion in a display containing two stationary figures? Perhaps the mechanisms responsible for perception of apparent motion normally serve the purpose of keeping track of objects that are moving behind other objects, for example, a jaguar running on the other side of some trees. Given the similarity between partial occlusion over time and complete occlusion over time, perhaps the same constructs that were applied to partial occlusion over time can be extended to apparent motion.

In partial occlusion over time we were concerned with establishing the appropriate correspondence between two edges seen at different points in time. The result of successfully establishing correspondence is the perception of a connecting edge. In apparent motion the principle concern is establishing the correspondence between units present at different points in time. The result of successfully establishing correspondence in this case is the perception of motion, and the perception of unity across time. In other words, the object retains its identity across time and space; one object is seen to move.

Spatiotemporal discontinuities are present when an object undergoes partial occlusion *and* when an object undergoes complete occlusion or is revealed.

So spatiotemporal discontinuities will occur when the figure in frame 1 disappears and when the figure in frame 2 appears. Perhaps apparent motion will be seen when a unit undergoes changes that produce spatiotemporal discontinuities that are spatiotemporally relatable. This approach to apparent motion has a number of interesting implications which will be explored in the following sections.

The Relationship Between Spatiotemporal Relatability and Long-Range Apparent Motion

Braddick (1974) proposed that two separate processes are responsible for the perception of apparent motion. The two processes are the short-range process, which he believed is also responsible for perception of real motion, and the long-range process. The short and long refer to the fact that the two processes appear to detect motion over different spatial ranges. The short-range process appears to be sensitive to displacements of less than 15 ' arc and to be sensitive to change in position over very short periods of time (ISI < 20 ms). In contrast, the long-range process requires longer periods of time (50–500 ms) and can act over a much greater spatial range. The short range process appears to use point by point matching, enabling the perception of motion even in cases where part of a random dot field is shifted (Julesz, 1971). In contrast, the long range process is not sensitive to point by point relations, rather it appears to match contours or units. Ramachandran, Rao and Vidyasagar (1973) showed that motion is even seen in displays in which there is no correlation between the frames in the texture that defines the figure. In their displays, differences in texture defined a square in both frame 1 and 2, but the texture used in the two frames was different. Such experiments have led researchers to suggest that edges or figures are the basic units, or tokens, for the long range process.

The short-range process appears to correspond to the process responsible for detecting discontinuities in motion at surface edges (discussed earlier). The long-range process, on the other hand, may correspond to spatiotemporal relatability.

Discontinuities as an Efficient Solution to the Problem of Detecting Motion Over Long Periods of Time

One of the problems with current models of long range apparent motion (for example Ullman, 1979) is that most require that the system somehow keep track of all of the potential tokens in a scene for longer periods of time (up to at least ½ a second). Such storage is required by motion perception models based on the establishment of correspondence between tokens from two different times. But most everyday scenes contain hundreds if not thousands of potential tokens, and these tokens would have to be encoded and stored several times a second for a substantial part of a second. Certainly it is possible that some tokens are stored for long periods of time, but it seems unlikely that they could be stored in the quantities demanded by such models. The storage requirements for motion perception could be drastically reduced by storing only the units that change in a spatiotemporally discontinuous manner. Constraining the tokens to be considered to just those tokens that have recently disappeared or reappeared drastically reduces the memory required for motion perception. Reducing the number of tokens to be considered also greatly simplifies the establishment of correspondence between tokens.

Reducing the information load by discarding information has been reported in other aspects of motion perception; it is not unique to this hypothesis. Ramachandran (1985) reported that although motion in apparent motion is determined by the outer boundaries of a figure, the internal texture of that figure also appears to move. The internal texture is "captured" by the moving boundary. Interestingly, changes in the relationship of the texture to the boundary seem to be ignored—the system appears to interpolate the internal texture of a figure and discard this information about its change. The system loses little by discarding this information because the internal texture of an object is unlikely to change when its outer boundary moves. Discarding such information saves processing by not requiring the establishment of point by point correspondence.

Apparent Motion and Dynamic Occlusion

Conceptualizing apparent motion in terms of the relatability of spatiotemporally discontinuous units implies that apparent motion displays may appear as dynamic occlusion. Under certain circumstances the figures that are normally seen as moving may be seen as two stationary figures being successively occluded by a third unit. The existence of such a percept was demonstrated by Petersik and McDill (1981). They showed subjects a display sequence similar to the one shown in Fig. 4.20a. Such a display is bistable; at short ISIs subjects reported seeing a white unit moving in front of stationary black bars (Fig. 4.20b). At longer ISIs subjects reported seeing successive motion of the bars, as is illustrated in Fig. 4.20c.

Why is the occluding unit only seen under certain time intervals? Consider Figs. 4.21a and 4.21b which provide a graph of the spatiotemporal relationships in the displays with long and short ISI displays. In the short ISI displays the spatiotemporal discontinuities at the points labeled A and B are spatiotemporally close to each other. If the units at A and B are related, the bars will be seen to be stationary; in addition, A and C can be related, resulting in an occluding unit. The postulated relatability is indicated with dotted lines in

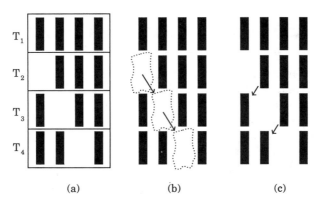

FIG. 4.20. a) Four frames (labeled T1 through T4) from an apparent motion
sequence. Two different percepts were reported by subjects. b) When short ISI
were used subjects reported an amphorous white figure passing in front of stationary bars. c) When long ISI were used the subjects reported seeing a bar shift
left illustrated with an arrow.

Figure 21a. As the ISI increases the length AB will increase faster than AC.
At some point the relatability between A and B, and A and C will become
weaker than the relatability between C and B (see Fig. 4.21b). At that point
the moving occluder will no longer be seen but a moving bar (C to B) will
be seen. Such an account would predict that, if relatability is affected by both
temporal and spatial gaps, one should be able to trade off an increase in ISI
by increasing the distance between bars.

The moving occluding figure seen at short ISIs did not have sharp edges,
and subjects generally described the figure as a "rectangular shadow." Andersen and Cortese (1989) reported a similar case when a figure with a clear,
well defined, boundary emerges. They found that subjects are able to discriminate among a set of four figures (star, diamond, square, and circle) in
displays where the boundary of the figures are only specified by the accretion
and deletion of texture. These displays simulated the accretion and deletion
pattern of a sparsely textured field as it moved behind a static figure. Deletion
and accretion of each texture element was all or none, like Petersik and McDill's
displays. Apparently spatiotemporal relatability can result in a unit with defined boundaries even in cases where the edges of such a unit are **not** defined
in the luminance domain at any point in time.

Spatial and Temporal Limits of Spatiotemporal
Relatability

Edges that are distant, either temporally or spatially, tend not to belong to
the same unit. While investigating the limits of spatial relatability we discovered a rather interesting law (Shipley & Kellman, 1988). There do not appear
to be any absolute limits on spatial relatability; it appears to be a function

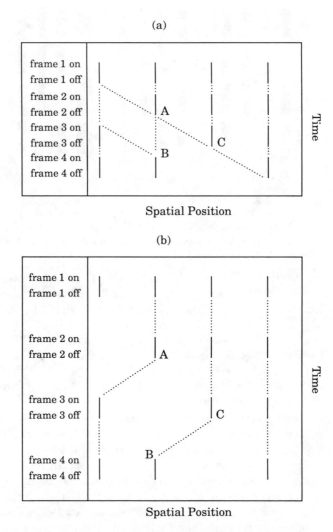

frame 1 on
frame 1 off
frame 2 on
frame 2 off
frame 3 on
frame 3 off
frame 4 on
frame 4 off

A

B

C

Time

Spatial Position

(b)

frame 1 on
frame 1 off

frame 2 on
frame 2 off

frame 3 on
frame 3 off

frame 4 on
frame 4 off

A

B

C

Time

Spatial Position

FIG. 4.21.   The spatiotemporal profile for the displays illustrated in Figure 4.20a
for a) short ISIs and b) long ISIs. Solid lines refer to the presence, over time,
of a solid figure. The end of each solid line is a spatiotemporal discontinuity.
The relatability between spatiotemporal discontinuities are illustrated with dotted lines. The switch from moving occluder to moving bars (see Figs. 4.20b and
4.20c) may be determined by the relative spatiotemporal position of points A,
B, C.

of both the distance to be interpolated **and** the amount of specified contour. The clarity of a subjective edge appears to be a ratio of the length of the subjective edge to the length of the entire figure's edge (subjective edge plus specified edge). Gillam (1981) found a similar ratio to hold for perceived unity in moving displays and suggested that the reason such a ratio holds is that it is invariant with viewing distance. Unity, in both cases, does not appear to be affected by viewing distance. Perhaps a similar spatiotemporal ratio may account for the finding that space and time can be traded off in apparent motion (for a review of the relevant literature see Neff, 1930).

Additional Issues for Spatiotemporal Discontinuity Account of Apparent Motion

This model is offered as a different perspective on apparent motion; it is not meant to account for all findings within the domain. If the model is to be developed into a full model of apparent motion the following two observations must be accounted for.

First, the tokens of motion appear to be more diverse than bounded figures. For example, alternation of the two displays labeled T1 and T2 shown in Fig. 4.22 results in a clear percept of parts of the single unit at T1 splitting into the two units at T2, and then reuniting. The tokens in this case appear, as Ullman (1979) has suggested to be edges and not units. For explanatory purposes I have presented the model as applying to units, but all of the important concepts would hold if edges were substituted for units. Perception of motion could be the result of *edges* interpolated between spatiotemporally discontinuous *edges*.

The second observation requires more substantial elaboration of the model. Sigman and Rock (1974) showed in a series of experiments that relative form of the units undergoing apparent motion is an important variable. In their displays both frames contain two figures—the two different figures in frame 1 are shown in reversed positions in frame 2. An example of such a display is shown in Fig. 4.23. There are a number of potential percepts in such a display. The subjects could report: (a) two figures which appear to switch places,

T₁   T₂

FIG. 4.22.   Two frames which produce the percept of an object splitting and recombining when shown in rapid alternation.

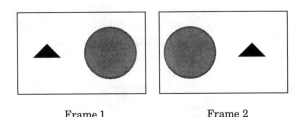

Frame 1   Frame 2

FIG. 4.23.   Two frames from an apparent motion sequence. Subjects generally report seeing a single circle alternately covering and uncovering two stationary triangles.

(b) one circle which appears to move back and forth in front of two stationary
triangles, (c) one triangle which appears to move back and forth in front of
two stationary circles, or (d) the circle appears to change nonrigidly into a triangle while the triangle changes into a circle. Sigman and Rock found that
subjects reported the second percept (b) almost exclusively. They argued that
this percept offered the most plausible "hypothesis" for the changes seen when
the two frames alternated. When the circle used in both frames was smaller,
or the triangle larger, so that the circle could not hide the triangle, subjects no
longer reported percept b, rather, they reported percept a. Using the spatiotemporal relatability to predict which of the percepts will predominate is not simple. The dominant percept would depend on the outcome of competition in
relatability between the two discontinuities present at the onset and offset of
the two frames. Nothing described so far would suggest that competition will
vary as a function of the relative sizes of the units. Exactly how such relationships might be incorporated into the rules of relatability is not clear.

DISCONTINUITIES AND EVENT PERCEPTION

Just as we can gain information about a surface from a number of different
sources, so too can we gain information about events from a number of different modalities. An event such as the catching of a ball will have, at least, visual,
auditory, and haptic consequences. How is the information from these modalities coordinated? One could imagine that the coordination is based on a three
or four dimensional map in which information about the location and motion
of objects comes from all three domains. Although such a map may be part
of the coordination it is not sufficient given the differences in spatial resolution
in the three domains. The auditory system may localize an object at a slightly
different location than the visual system locates that same object. In fact when
such a mismatch occurs, as with a ventriloquist's dummy or a television set,
we do not perceive two separate events but a single unified event generally

localized where the visual event occurs. How are the visual and auditory information combined to form a single event?

Consider the natural sound domain. Sound may result from either the passage of air over a surface, or the collision of two objects. In the latter case the physical interactions of the two objects that produces a sound will also have consequences on the motion of those objects. The collision of two objects tends to produce abrupt changes in both the acceleration and velocity of the objects. Just as the velocity change resulting from a collision will be abrupt so to will be the amplitude change in the sound produced by the collision. In other words, a collision will produce discontinuities in both the auditory and visual domains. Perhaps the discontinuities in the two domains can be used by the perceptual system to coordinate the information coming from each.

One example of such coordination is the ventriloquism effect. The perceived direction of a sound is influenced by visual events correlated with the sound. In the case of a ventriloquist's dummy, the sound appears to come from the dummy and not from the actual source, the ventriloquist. Perhaps the perceptual system is picking up the correspondence between the discontinuities in the motion of the dummy and the discontinuities in the speech stream. The results of a number of experiments reported by Spelke, Born, and Chu (1983) are consistent with the hypothesis that the integration of sight and sound is based on discontinuities in the two domains. Infants will look at a visual event that is correlated with a series of sounds (for example a ball bouncing and the sound of something hitting a surface), in preference to a visual event that is not correlated with sound. Spelke and colleagues used this looking preference to investigate the aspects of the visual events that are important in determining the preference. Apparently, changes in the direction of travel of a ball that are correlated with a sharp sound (stick hitting a tin) are looked at in preference to the same event where the changes in direction do not occur when the sound occurs. The change in direction need not be a result of a collision with a surface, in fact, babies show no preference when sudden changes at a surface and sudden changes in midair are compared. When continuous motions are used, as with an object traveling a circular path, no preference is shown toward an object that is always in the same place in space when the sound occurs. When the object reversed direction along the circle a preference was seen. They also showed adults each pair of displays, one on either side with the sound coming from the center, and asked them to report the direction of the sound source. The adults reported the largest shift in sound position away from the center with the displays in which the direction of travel changed. The direction of shift was always toward the object whose motion was correlated with the sound.

The position of objects in a visual scene does not appear to be as important for establishing visual–auditory correspondence as other aspects such as changes in motion. Although this is consistent with discontinuities being the basis for establishing correspondence it is hardly definitive. Many questions remain, for example, is any change in motion sufficient for establishing correspondence, or are discontinuous changes required?

CONCLUSION

The statistical properties of the distribution of objects in our environment has a number of interesting consequences for the way the visual system gathers information about objects. The relative smoothness of objects may allow the visual system to identify the boundaries of objects using discontinuities in various features. We have discussed a number of domains including: brightness illusions, texture grouping, stereoscopic depth perception, structure from optic flow, and boundary completion in partly occluded figures as well as subjective figures. In each domain the use of discontinuities appears to minimize the computational requirements for perception of objects or surfaces. In some of these domains, such as stereoscopic depth perception and boundary completion, there is fairly convincing evidence that discontinuities are necessary. Finally, discontinuities may be relevant to one of the major questions in event perception: How is information from different senses coordinated? Discontinuities in each domain may be used to establish correspondence between visual and auditory events. In sum, discontinuities may provide an important source of information for perceptual processing relevant to objects.

ACKNOWLEDGMENT

I believe that the study of object and surface perception is not as removed from the study of language as it may appear at first glance. Some of the work presented in this chapter is conceptually very similar to Lila Gleitman's own work on language learning. Both are concerned with analyzing the structure of the available information. Where I am interested in the way the physics of the world structures light and how that structure is reflected in the visual system, Lila is interested in how the structure of a language can influence the learning of its syntactic rules. I have no doubt that Lila's insights into the structure of language have influenced my own thinking about the importance of structured information in perception. That such influence can span such an ostensibly wide gap is, I believe, a credit to both Swarthmore and Lila's work.

REFERENCES

Andersen, G. J., & Cortese, J. M. (1989). 2-D contour perception resulting from kinetic occlusion. *Perception and Psychophysics, 46,* 49–55.

Anstis, S. M., Howard, I. P., & Rogers, B. J. (1978). A Craik-O'Brien-Cornsweet illusion for visual depth. *Vision Research, 18,* 217–312.

Beck, J. (1982). Textural segmentation. In J. Beck (Ed.), *Organization and representation in perception* (pp. 285–317). Hillsdale, NJ: Lawrence Erlbaum Associates.

Braddick, O. J. (1974). A short-range process in apparent motion. *Vision Research, 14,* 519–527.

Cornsweet, T. N. (1970). *Visual Perception.* New York: Academic Press.

Craik, K. J. W. (1940). *Visual Adaptation.* Unpublished Doctoral Thesis, Cambridge University.

Gibson, J. J. (1979). *The ecological approach to visual perception.* Boston: Houghton Mifflin.

Gibson, J. J., Kaplan, G. A., Reynolds, H. N., & Wheeler, K. (1969). The change from visible to invisible: A study of optical transitions. *Perception and Psychophysics, 5,* 113–116.

Gillam, B. (1981). Separation relative to length determines the organization of two lines into a unit. *Journal of Experimental Psychology: Human Perception and Performance, 7,* 884–889.

Gillam, B., Chambers, D., & Russo, T. (1988). Postfusional latency in stereoscopic slant perception and the primitives of stereopsis. *Journal of Experimental Psychology: Human Perception and Performance, 14,* 163–174.

Gillam, B., Flagg, T., & Findlay, D. (1984). Evidence for disparity changes as the primary stimulus for stereoscopic processing. *Perception and Psychophysics, 36,* 559–564.

Gregory, R. L., & Harris, J. (1974). Illusory contours and stereo depth. *Perception and Psychophysics, 15,* 411–416.

Grossberg, S., & Mingolla, E. (1985). Neural dynamics of form perception: Boundary completion, illusory figures, and neon color spreading. *Psychological Review, 92,* 173–211.

Hildreth, E. C. (1983). *The measurement of visual motion.* Cambridge: The MIT Press.

Julesz, B. (1971). *Foundations of cyclopean perception.* Chicago: The University of Chicago Press.

Kellman, P. J., & Cohen, H. (1984). Kinetic subjective contours. *Perception and Psychophysics, 35,* 237–244.

Kellman, P. J., & Loukides, M. (1987). An object perception approach to static and kinetic subjective contours. In S. Petry & G. E. Meyer (Eds.), *The Perception of Illusory Contours* (pp. 151–164). New York: NY: Springer-Verlag.

Kellman, P. J., & Shipley, T. F. (1987, November). *Interpolation processes in visual object perception: Evidence for a discontinuity theory.* Paper presented at the 28th Annual Meeting of The Psychonomic Society, Seattle.

Kellman, P. J., & Shipley, T. F. (in press). Visual interpolation in object perception. Cognitive Psychology.

Marr, D. (1982). *Vision.* San Francisco: Freeman.

Marr, D., & Hildreth, E. C. (1980). Theory of edge detection. *Proceedings of the Royal Society of London, B. 207,* 187–217.

Marr, D., & Poggio, T. (1976). Cooperative computation of stereo disparity. *Science, 194,* 283–287.

Neff, W. S. (1930). A critical investigation of the visual apprehension of movement. *American Journal of Psychology, 48,* 1–42.

O'Brien, V. (1958). Contour perception, illusion, and reality. *Journal of the Optical Society of America, 48,* 112–119.

Petersik, J. T., & McDill, M. (1981). A new bistable motion illusion based upon "kinetic optical occlusion." *Perception, 10,* 563–572.

Poggio, T., Gamble, E. B., & Little, J. J. (1988). Parallel integration of vision modules. *Science, 242,* 436–440.

Ramachandran, V. S. (1985). Apparent motion of subjective surfaces. *Perception, 14,* 127–134.

Ramachandran, V. S., Rao, V. M., & Vidyasagar, T. R. (1973). Apparent movement with subjective contours. *Vision Research, 13,* 1399–1401.

Rogers, B. J., & Graham, M. E. (1983). Anisotropies in the perception of three-dimensional surfaces. *Science, 221,* 1409–1411.

Shipley, T. F., & Kellman, P. J. (1988, November). *Discontinuity theory and the perception of illusory figures.* Paper presented at the 29th Annual Meeting of The Psychonomic Society, Chicago.

Shipley, T. F., & Kellman, P. J. (1989, November). *Visual interpolation in the third and fourth dimensions.* Paper presented at the 30th Annual Meeting of The Psychonomic Society, Atlanta.

Shipley, T. F., & Kellman, P. J. (1990). The role of discontinuities in the perception of subjective figures. *Perception and Psychophysics, 48*(3), 259–270.

Sigman, E., & Rock, I. (1974). Stroboscopic movement based on perceptual intelligence. *Perception, 3,* 9–28.

Spelke, E. (1984). Perception of unity, persistence, and identity: Thoughts on infants' conceptions of objects. In J. Mehler & E. Fox (Eds.), *Neonate Cognition: Beyond the blooming, buzzing confusion* (pp. 89–113). Hillsdale, NJ: Lawrence Erlbaum Associates.

Spelke, E. S., Born, W. S., & Chu, F. (1983). Perception of moving, sounding objects by 4-month-old infants. *Perception, 12,* 719–732.

Todorović, D. (1987). The Craik–O'Brien–Cornsweet effect: New varieties and their theoretical implications. *Perception and Psychophysics, 42,* 545–560.

Ullman, S. (1979). *The interpretation of visual motion.* Cambridge: The MIT Press.

Yarbus, A. L. (1967). *Eye movements and vision.* NY: Plenum Press.

Infant Vocalizations and Changes in Experience

D. D. Hilke
Cornell University and Smithsonian Institution

ABSTRACT

The possibility that infant vocalizations occur in conjunction with significant changes in experience was tested in a study of seven infants aged 0;8. Each infant was videotaped during an isolated freeplay session with each of three toys. Two indices of changing experience were used to identify portions of the tape where increased vocalizing was expected. The Place Index identified potentially significant changes in experience via major changes in locus of attention. The Reaction Index employed certain rapid changes in expression (e.g., smile, startle, brow change) as indicators of corresponding changes in subjective experience. As predicted, periods of the tape encompassed by either or both of these indices evidenced significantly more vocalizations than remaining portions of the tape. Implications of these results for theories of infant communicative competence and for infant language development are discussed.

INTRODUCTION

Researchers have recently proposed that a relationship exists between early linguistic vocalizations and changing attention. Greenfield (1982), for example, suggested that "the attentional system is geared to variability from the very beginning of life, and that a speaker's language use is coordinated with this system as it emerges." Lempert and Kinsbourne (1985) reviewed a number of studies in support of a more limited claim concerning the relationship of attention and vocalizations. They concluded that early naming may function as a component of selective orienting, a sort of verbalized perception

(Vygotsky, 1978) accompanying the orienting response. With the possible exception of Furrow and James (1985),[1] however, experiments that have specifically examined the correspondence between changes in attention and infant vocal behavior have failed to reveal a strong correlation (Kagan, 1971).

Under the joint assumptions that an infant's attentional system serves to direct the *acquisition* of information, and that an infant's vocal system serves to *emit* information, it is not surprising that the relationship between these systems is weak. The domains over which each system operates are not necessarily identical. The attentional system is focused on acquiring information from the environment. By contrast, the vocal system emits information concerning the infant. Only to the extent that perceived changes in the environment correspond closely with significant changes in the infant's current experience should one observe a correlation between attention and vocalization.

A bias towards investing in variability would be a functionally sound policy for both systems, however. A human infant that systematically directed its attention to less certain, and therefore more informative (Berlyne, 1974), aspects of the environment would increase its capacity to acquire information about that environment. Similarly, an infant who vocalized in conjunction with changes in experience would effectively highlight the more variable (and hence more informative) aspects of its own experience. Greenfield (1982) may be correct that "language is, from the beginning, used selectively where the speaker perceives variability . . ." However, it is more likely to be variability in the speaker's personal experience, rather than variability in the environment, and hence in the environment-oriented attentional system.

Over the last few years, my research (Hilke, 1983, 1985) has focused on a simple yet powerful hypothesis: that infant vocalizations are more likely to occur in conjunction with significant changes in the infant's current experience. My initial formulation of this hypothesis has been quite general. The term "vocalizations" is meant to encompass most vocal productions of the infant including grunts, sighs, squeals, laughs, calls, and cries, as well as the more frequently studied coos, babbles, and protowords. The phrase "significant changes in the infant's current experience" refers to discrete moments during which the infant's experience is in transition. This phrase has a broad interpretation which theoretically encompasses changes in the infant's activity, cognition, or physical state, whether due to social or nonsocial causes. The phrase "significant change" refers to fluctuations in that experience that are relatively more informative (Greenfield & Zukow, 1978), more salient, or in other ways more important to the infant. The phrase is meant to be theoretically

---

[1]Furrow and James (1985) compared the prevalence of "re-oriented" attention during vocalizing with the prevalence of "re-oriented" attention in a matched sample of nonvocal periods. As predicted, there were more instances of "re-oriented" attention during the vocal periods. However, Furrow and James did not comment on the fact that this pattern is apparently reversed during periods of more rapidly changing attention ("unfocused" periods).

neutral with respect to the manner in which such variability is represented by the infant, or the manner in which its importance is determined.

Seeking Empirical Support for the Hypothesis

While few researchers have explicitly examined the occurrence of vocalizations, there is extant evidence that infant vocalizations can be responsive to particular changes in experience. Bloom (1977) and Papoušek and Papoušek (1975) reported that the vocalizations of very young infants are differentially distributed depending on the nature and progress of conditioning sessions. Significant relationships have also been documented between vocal occurrence and the realization of a contingency relationship (Watson, 1972), the achievement of assimilation after some effort (Kagan, 1971; McCall, 1972), the realization of mastery (Shultz & Zigler, 1970), the experience of effort independent of success (Clark & Hilke, 1980), and various changes in the infant's social and/or verbal context throughout infancy (e.g., O'Conner, 1975; Ratner & Bruner, 1978; Schaffer, 1977).

While each author offers a distinct interpretation for these phenomena depending on the age and context of the infant, all of the interpretations given are consistent with the more general relationship proposed here. Each makes a specific claim that the infant is more likely to vocalize during some particular, and potentially significant, change in the infant's experience.

Nonetheless, while each of these studies demonstrates a relationship consistent with the hypothesis, there is no study which provides compelling support for it. Although the literature on social vocalizing demonstrates that infant vocalizations can by systematically related to short term changes in social context, the personally expressive nature of these vocalizations is mitigated by two possibilities: first, that the infant might be engaging in a well-learned social ritual (Bruner, 1983; Ninio & Bruner, 1978; Ratner & Bruner, 1978), and second, that the systematicity of the infant's vocal productions might be a direct result of responding to adult social stimuli which were themselves systematic (Bullowa, 1975; Fogel, 1977; Kay, 1977; Schaffer, Collis, & Parsons, 1977). While the nonsocial studies (Clark & Hilke, 1980; McCall, 1972; Shultz & Zigler, 1970; Watson, 1972) better assure that the observed vocalizations are closely related to the infant's personal experience, the depth of analysis used in these studies offers only limited assurance that the determining factors produced discrete short-term effects.

To avoid the ambiguities inherent in previous research, the present study incorporated the best features of both the social and nonsocial research. It emulated the social studies (e.g., Brazelton, Tronick, Adamson, Als, & Wise, 1975; Stern, Beebe, Jaffe, & Bennett, 1977) by making within-subject comparisons between momentary changes in an infant's experience and the occurrence of vocalizations. It emulated the more cognitively-oriented studies (Shultz & Zigler, 1970; Zelazo, Hopkins, Jacobson, & Kagan, 1974) by employing a nonsocial situation where infants alone determined the pattern that their vocalizations took with respect to their changing experience. In addition, a free play paradigm was chosen to assure that the experimental situation could not directly manipulate the infant's experience, the infant's vocal behavior, or the relationship between them. Given this paradigm, any relationship observed between momentary changes in experience and vocal occurrence should represent a natural part of the infant's behavioral repertoire.

METHOD

Subjects

Seven infants aged 0;8 served as subjects. There were four boys and three girls. All were from middle class, suburban homes where American English was spoken. Six were White; one was Black.

Procedure

After an initial period of familiarization with the home-like environment of the laboratory, each infant was secured into a highchair, and one of three toys was placed on the highchair tray within easy reach.

The principal toy used was a Fisher Price Turn and Learn Activity Center which consisted of a truncated plastic pyramid which spun on a circular base. There were four different slanted faces on the sides of the pyramid (including a phone dial and mirror), and a bright squeaky button was located on the top face. The second toy consisted of a circular metal tray with ten circular indentations around its perimeter. Brightly colored balls were placed into six of these indentations. Finally, each infant was given a colored plastic flower pot full of 1-inch alphabet blocks. The pot was always presented to the child inverted with most of the blocks, but not all, hidden beneath it.

Sessions varied in length depending on the child's interest in each of the toys presented. A total of 43 minutes of codable behavior was achieved from the sample of seven children.

Each session was videotaped and later copied through a machine which consecutively numbered each field of the tape. By referencing these numbers in all coding procedures, the location and duration of vocal and nonvocal behaviors could be determined.

Coding Procedures: Utterance Coding

With the picture portion of the tape obscured, each tape was reviewed in order to determine the onset, offset, and form of each utterance produced by the infant. For the purposes of coding, an utterance was defined as any audible vocal sound produced from a single breath that was not characteristic of simple respiration. Ultimately excluded from the data base were all coughs, hiccoughs, chokes and other utterances of apparently organic origin. The remaining utterances were termed "vocalizations" and included work-like utterances, babbles, grunts, coos, and squeals, as well as a few isolated laughs, sobs, and sighs.

Utterance coding was undertaken by a coder naive to the purposes of the experiment and was checked for reliability against randomly selected portions of the tape coded by the experimenter. Disagreements were resolved by multiple reviewings of the tape to determine the correct location of the utterance. Based on this sample, vocalizations were correctly detected 95% of the time, false alarms were quite low (5%), and the mean error in determining the moment of vocal onset was less than one thirtieth of a second. (See Hilke, 1985 for a more complete description of utterance coding procedures.)

Indices of Experience Change

In developing behavioral indices for major changes in subjective experience, two approaches seemed plausible. One could seek direct, nonvocal expressions associated with such changes (consider a smile, or a startle, for example); and/or one could attempt to interpret the sequential flow of an infant's activity over time and infer significant changes in subjective experience given the pattern of objective changes observable in the infant's actions. For this study, two indices of changing experience were used, each representing one of these two approaches.

The first index, the Reaction Index, consisted of a set of brief, but distinctive, changes (Transitions) in the infant's expression which have been traditionally associated with changes in experience. This set, called Reaction Transitions (see Table 5.1), included Smiles, Grimaces or Frowns, Sudden Glee, Brow Changes, Startles, and Freezes. (One additional type of reaction, the Double Take, was coded but excluded from the final data set when reliability checks revealed both a high number of "misses," and persistent misidentification of Double Takes as Other reactions.) In addition to being brief and distinctive, these behaviors all share the common quality of being primarily expressive, in that they are rarely functional to the infant's prior (or subsequent) behavior context.

The principal advantage of the Reaction Index in addressing the hypothesis is its diversity in the set of significant changes to which it corresponds. For example, smiles, glee, and grimaces correspond most closely to affective changes in experience. Brow changes appear to involve changes of a more cognitive nature. Freezes and startles probably express changes of a more systemic nature. Since the hypothesis has a broad scope of experience changes which it

TABLE 5.1
Reactions Used to Identify Significant Changes in Infant Experience

Type	Description
Sudden glee	An unexpected and quickly accomplished brightening of the entire face.
Sudden smile	Any of a number of unanticipated and quickly accomplished behavioral sequences commonly labelled as smiles.
Sudden pout or grimace	Any unexpected and quickly accomplished mouth or facial expression associated with negative affect.
Sudden brows	Any unexpected and quickly accomplished movement of the infant's eyelids and/or eyebrows so as to result in the eye or eyebrow areas quickly moving into a new position.
Startle/shudder	An unexpected and quickly accomplished movement of the infant's entire body in unison and to no apparent purpose other than withdrawal.
Freeze	An unexpected and complete halt in behavior.
Other	Any other marked, discontinuous, and unanticipated behavioral sequence which is not functionally related to the infant's immediately preceding or subsequent behaviors.

might address, using an index that encompasses a similarly broad spectrum of experience changes is an asset.

The second index, the Place Index, was developed by taking an alternative and complementary approach which makes inferences based on the flow of the infant's behavior independent of any nonvocal expressions which might accompany the infant's behavior. In preliminary observations, it was noted that the nature of the infant's activity depends critically on the place where his or her attention is focused. For example, objects and events close at hand (Here) offer a dramatically different set of behavioral options (e.g., touch, eat, throw) than those at a distance (There). While activity change is not mandated by major shifts in attention, activity change is frequently coincident with them. Thus, major shifts in attention can serve as an index of activity change, albeit an imperfect one. (A related argument was made by Greenfield (1978) who suggested that objects at a distance (There) are perceived as less certain than those close at hand (Here), implying yet another dimension of experience which may change as an infant's attention shifts between Here and There.)

Coding Procedures: Experience Coding

Each tape was coded twice, once for each index of experience change (i.e., change in place of attention, reactions). For each index, tapes were reviewed in order to identify instances of the index (transitions), to record the exact duration and location of each instance (transitional period), and to subclassify the observed transitions according to type (e.g., "Here to There" place transition; "sudden brow change" reaction transition).

The beginning of a place transition was defined as the first field during which any participating body part began withdrawing from the activity at the old place, immediately antecedent to a shift to the new place. The endpoint of the transition segment was defined as the moment when two or more body parts had begun active participation at the new place of attention. The body parts used in this determination of shifting attention consisted of the eyes, head, right hand/arm, and left hand/arm.

Consider the following example:

> The infant is looking at the pyramid toy as he gently turns it about with his right hand. As the last turn is being completed, the infant's head begins to pull back and turn aside. Immediately thereafter the infant's eyes begin to shift their gaze. As the infant's gaze shifts to his left, the right hand, having completed the last spin of the toy, returns to the neutral position next to the infant's body. Nearly simultaneously with the withdrawal of the right hand, the left hand and arm are moved slightly, rising about an inch off the tray but making no other movements. The eyes now focus on the highchair tray. The left hand beings to move downward to grasp the side of the tray. The head completes its orientation toward the tray.

In this example, the Transition segment begins with the frame during which the infant's head first begins to pull back. The head is the first participating body part to withdraw from the former locus of attention. The Transition periods ends with the precise frame during which the left arm/hand begins its downward movement towards the tray. The left arm/hand is the second body part to actively participate at the new place. The first actively participating body part at the tray is the eyes.

The beginning of a reaction transition was defined as the first field during which any of the reacting body parts deviated from their prereaction positions and began the brief sequence of behaviors comprising the Reaction. The endpoint of the reaction transition was defined as the last frame during which any part of the infant's body was participating in the reaction sequence.

All experience coding was undertaken by a second coder who was naive to the purposes of the experiment and unaware of the nature of coding procedures undertaken by the utterance coder. Experience coding was accomplished with the sound *off* and was judged for accuracy and reliability against a separate coding made by the experimenter of randomly selected portions of the tape.

Reliability

Accuracy in coding place transitions were quite high. Transitions were correctly detected 94% of the time, the number of false alarms was quite low (less than 13%), and deviations in the placement of transition boundaries averaged no more than $\pm \frac{1}{10}$ of a second.

While reaction transitions were detected only 50% of the time, the identification of reaction transitions which were detected was correct 100% of the time for all reaction types. There were no false alarms. This last point is extremely important. Since the infant's facial expression may have changed briefly in the course of some vocalizations, it might have been the case that the coder would have erred by falsely detecting as Reactions the facial changes which accompany vocalizations. In the reliability data there were no cases in which such a confusion occurred. As with place coding, the placement of reaction boundaries was quite accurate with placement of the onset and offset boundaries deviating by less than $\pm \frac{1}{15}$ of a second on average.

More detailed information concerning coding procedures is available in Hilke (1985).

Data Reduction Techniques

The top diagram in Table 5.2 represents a sample segment of the session videotape. Along its length are moments where transitions or vocalizations were identified by the coder. At the bottom of Table 5.2 are representations of tape with transition periods assigned for each of the three analyses.

Each transition period consisted of all and only those video fields during which an index of experience change was coded as ongoing. Flanking each transition period was a brief (one sec) Pretransition and (one sec) Posttransition period. All other portions of the tape were considered unrelated to the transitions and were divided into Outside segments of a length equal to the average duration of transition segments characteristic of that analysis.

In the case of the reaction analysis, the location and duration of place transitions was completely ignored. Thus, place transitions could and did occur in any of the four reaction-defined periods (transition, pretransition, posttransition, outside). Similarly, reaction transitions had no effect on the segments defined in the place analysis. In the overall analysis, either type of transition was sufficient to define a transition-related period, and the outside segments never contained an instance of either index.

By taking the moment of vocal onset as the moment of vocal occurrence, each vocalization was assigned to one and only one transitionally defined segment for each analysis.

From these data, the cumulative time corresponding to each region of the tape and the cumulative number of vocalizations with onsets in these regions could be obtained. Separate subtotals were kept for each child, for each toy, and for each transition analysis. From these data, rates of vocalizing for each region in each analysis could be determined.

The hypothesis predicts that vocalization will be more prevalent in the transition periods because of the high concentration of potentially significant events

TABLE 5.2

Infant Vocalizations and Changes in Experience
Three Sample Analyses (Overall, Place, Reaction)
for the Same Hypothetical Segment Tape

Measures		*Sample Information on Tape*		
		Time—		
Place	Attend Here	————————		——— ——
	There	——	———	
Reaction	Reaction		-	-
	No Reaction	———	——— ——	—— ——
Vocalization		~	~ ~ ~	~

Sample Overall Analysis

	Place		Joint	Place	Reaction
Transition Defined Segments	--||*||------------------||*||-----||*||-------||*||--
Observed Vocalizations	~		~ ~	~	~

Transitions with voc.	2	Outside segments with voc.	1
Transitions without voc.	2	Outside segments without voc.	33

Sample Place Analysis

	Place		Place	Place
Transition Defined Segments	--||*||------------------||*||-----||*||------------ ----
Observed Vocalizations	~		~ ~	~ ~

Transitions with voc.	1	Outside segments with voc.	2
Transitions without voc.	2	Outside segments without voc.	37

Sample Reaction Analysis

	Reaction	Reaction
Transition Defined Segments	-----------------------||*||----------------||*||--
Observed Vocalizations	~	~ ~ ~ ~

Transitions with voc.	2	Outside segments with voc.	2
Transitions without voc.	0	Outside segments without voc.	42

Key: *Transition period; -- Outside segments; ~ Vocalization; || one second immediately preceding or following Transition period.

Note: The duration of Outside segments "-", is constant within each analysis and equals the average duration of transition segments for that analysis (½ sec for Overall and Place transitions, ¾ sec for Reaction transitions). In this example, the average number of Outside segments occurring between transitions is underestimated.

in these regions. Conversely, vocalizations should be less prevalent in the outside region due to the absence of these potentially significant events.

RESULTS

Vocalizations

198 vocalizations were recorded during the 43 minutes of usable tape coded. The typical vocalization in the corpus was a marginally intelligible, language-like (CV or V) utterance with little or no audible affective charge. The actual distribution of vocal forms in the corpus consisted of consonant–vowel vocalizations (40%), vocalic vocalizations (33%), consonantal vocalizations (10%), and other vocalizations (17%). Other vocalizations included laughs, sobs, grunts, and sighs. The average duration of a vocalization was three quarters of a second with over 72% lasting less than 1 second.

Transitions

426 place transitions, 90 reaction transitions, and 493 overall transitions were coded from the session tapes. Included in each of these transition sets were 21 transitions which encompassed both reaction and place transitions (Joint Transitions).

The average durations for place and overall transitions approximated slightly less than and slightly more than one-half second respectively. Reaction transitions were noticeably longer (approximately ¾ sec in duration).

Vocal Behavior: Transition vs. Outside Segments

For brevity, this report focuses on the simplest tests of the hypothesis, i.e. comparisons of the likelihood of a vocalization occurring during the transition period versus more than a second away from the period (e.g., in outside segments). 132 vocalizations comprise this subsample which subsumed approximately 30 minutes of tape segments.

The principal statistical method used for these analyses was a $2 \times 2\chi^2$ analysis comparing the proportion of transitions which evidenced a concurrent vocalization with the proportion of similarly sized outside periods which evidenced a concurrent vocalization. These proportions along with their corresponding rates of vocalizing are given in Table 5.3.

Chi-squared calculations confirm that the proportion of vocalizations associated with the transition periods is significantly higher than that associated with the outside periods. This relationship between vocal occurrence is signifi-

TABLE 5.3
Vocalization Occurrence in Transition and Outside Segments

Analysis Segtype	# Vocs	# Segs	V/Seg	V/Min	ZZ	Prob.
Overall (all toys)						
Transition	36	493	0.0730	8.7	20.3	<0.001
Outside	96	3079	0.0312	3.7		
Reaction (all toys)						
Transition	14	87	0.1610	12.8	18.1	<0.001
Outside	167	3107	0.0540	4.3		
Place (all toys)						
Transition	26	426	0.0610	8.2	11.7	<0.001
Outside	113	3746	0.0320	4.0		
Pyramid only (All Transitions)						
Transition	16	270	0.0590	7.1	11.1	<0.001
Outside	44	1876	0.0230	2.8		
Balls only (All transitions)						
Transition	12	178	0.0670	8.1	3.07	<0.05
Outside	32	844	0.0380	4.5		
Blocks only (All transitions)						
Transition	8	65	0.1230	14.6	3.42	<0.05
Outside	20	341	0.0590	7.0		

Note: All probabilities are dervied using one tailed χ^2 tests. In the case of Transition segments, "# Segs" refers to the actual number of transitions observed. In the case of Outside segements, "# Segs" refers to the number of transition-sized segments occurring in the outside region. "V/Segs" is the probability that a segment will have a vocalization co-occurring with it. "V/Min" is the quotient derived by dividing the total number of vocalizations co-occurring with a particular segment type by the total amount of time subsumed by that segment type.

cant in analyses of reaction transitions, place transitions, and all analyses based on both types of transitions. These later analyses included analyses for each toy and for all toys taken together (Overall Analysis). Separate analyses for each child in the sample confirmed increased vocalizing during transition periods for every child (binomial 7/7 $p < 0.01$, one-tailed).

Thus, the null hypothesis that the occurrence of infant vocal behavior is unrelated to the occurrence of the behavioral indices must be rejected. Similarly, hypotheses attributing this effect to a particular subject or to a particular situation must also be rejected.

Conversely, the data are highly consistent with the predictions of the hypothesis. Infant vocalizations were more prevalent during periods where significant changes in experience were assumed to occur more frequently; i.e., during transition segments.

Additional Analyses

Additional analyses which examined vocal behavior during the pretransition and posttransition segments, vocal behavior during joint transitions, and the relationship between transitions and "runs" of vocalizations are reported in Hilke (1985). While a detailed exposition of these analyses is beyond the scope of this report, a brief overview of the findings is warranted as it provides a more complete picture of the robustness of the relationship observed between infant vocal behavior and the indices of experience change coded.

For example, increased vocalizing was also predicted both immediately preceding and immediately following place transitions, since these pretransition and posttransition periods corresponded to moments when the potentially significant events of activity termination and activity initiation had an increased likelihood of occurring. As predicted, distinct peaks in vocal behavior were evident in both the pretransition and posttransition periods, although the significance of the pretransition peak was questionable. In the reaction analysis, where no pretransition or posttransition effects were predicted, none were found. However, results from the reaction analysis did suggest a relationship between reaction transitions and "runs" of vocalizations.

A reanalysis of the data was undertaken to determine the probability of a transition given "vocal runs" of various lengths. A vocal run was defined as a series of one or more consecutive vocalizations occurring within 2 seconds of each other (offset to onset). These analyses revealed that the onset of a vocal run, like the onset of an individual vocalization, was positively related to each index of changing experience. The association between the occurrence of a vocal run and the occurrence of a transition was strongest for the longer vocal runs, and most dramatic for the reaction index where the presence of a vocal run of three or more vocalizations increased the probability of observing a reaction transition by more than 600%.

Finally, the relationship between infant vocalizations and joint transitions was examined. When the proportion of transitions accompanied by a concurrent vocalization was calculated for each transition type, joint transitions, which bear double evidence of the presence of a potentially significant moment, had the highest percentage of transitions accompanied by a vocalization of any index studied (Joint 24%, Reaction 16%, Place 6%). These results suggest that the pattern of vocalizing observed is a function of the relative significance of changes in the infant's subjective experience. This is precisely the pattern predicted by the hypothesis.

In sum, the predicted relationship between infant vocal behavior and indices of changing experience persists throughout all analyses undertaken. Whether evaluated subject by subject, toy by toy, index by index, by unitary vocal behaviors or in terms of vocal runs, the infants observed in this study vocalized more often during periods when a concurrent significant change in experience was likely, and less frequently during periods when no external cues for these particular changes in experience were observed.

DISCUSSION

While this study limited its focus to infants aged 0;8, reports of related findings by other researchers suggest that infant vocalizations may accompany significant changes in experience both before and after this particular age. If, as Papoušek & Papoušek (1975) suggested, infants as young as 3 or 4 weeks will vocalize selectively given different experimental situations, it may be that the relationship between vocal occurrence and significant experiences is a part of the infant's natural endowment, perhaps functioning from birth. Given the observations of Watson (1972) with 8-week-olds, Shultz and Zigler (1970) with 2- to 4-month-olds, and Clark and Hilke (1980) with an infant from 0;4 to 1;8, it is reasonable to speculate that a relationship between vocal occurrence and significant changes in experience may be a general characteristic of infancy.

The presence of such a constraint on infant vocal occurrence could be a powerful asset to the infant in the course of day-to-day interactions with caregivers. The infant's responsiveness in these relationships, and the ultimate success of both partners, will depend on the infant's ability to express his own, personal reaction to the interactive context. The proposed relationship between verbal occurrence and changes in subjective experience is one means by which the infant could successfully express something of his or her current experiences in these interactions, allowing the infant to contribute to the information structure of the interaction.

However, much of the literature concerning infants' capacities to selectively vocalize in social interactions has assumed that the interaction, itself, is ontogenetically primary (Bullowa, 1975; Bruner, 1977; Ratner & Bruner, 1978; Schaffer, 1977), and that the capacity to use vocalizations systematically is learned within these interactions. Under this alternative interpretation, the mother's manipulation of the interactional context is seen initially to produce proper correspondences between the vocal productions of the participants and the interactive context. The systematic vocal contributions of the infant are seen as resulting from repeated instances of these maternally controlled interactions which have either modelled or reinforced the behavior that the infant eventually acquires.

This alternative perspective is elaborated in detail by Bruner (1983) who traces the developmental course of many aspects of infant vocal behavior through the same sequence of developments: from externally modelled conventions (formats), to the mastery of rule-governed behavior (conventional participation), to the generalizations of these rules into novel situations (generative rule use).

Unlike Bruner's theory in which vocalizations begin as accompaniments to action and acquire meaning through their association with conventionalized action patterns, the present hypothesis suggests that many infant vocalizations are initially meaningful from the *infant's* perspective. Vocalizations are produced in conjunction with significant moments in the infant's existence; they are from the outset expressive of that experience. While not excluding the possibility that some patterns of vocal occurrence may originate in highly routinized social conventions, the hypothesis supports an ontogenetic sequence that traces vocal occurrence from the personally expressive into the more conventional. This perspective need not account, as Bruner must, for how or when vocalizations become meaningful (vis-à-vis the infant's own personal experience as differentiated from the social interchange in which it is embedded).

Infant vocalizations, like the utterances of adult speakers of language, vary in the degree to which they are personally expressive or conventionally appropriate. Infant vocalizations can be so routinized that they appear to have little meaning outside of the social situations in which they are learned and used. At the other extreme, infant vocalizations can be so purely personal that they are little more than grunts or squeaks or screams. As infants mature, however, most of their vocalizations, like our own, convey a personal message through more or less conventional means. To be truly informative, such vocalizations must be true not only to conventional patterns of linguistic exchange but to the infant's current subjective experiences as well.

The hypothesis assures that infant vocalizations are, from the outset, tied to important aspects of subjective experience. Thus there is the possibility that the infant's evolving capacity to structure vocal behavior can be intimately related to a similarly evolving capacity to structure subjective experiences.

Vygotsky (1962) proposed that vocal communication begins as entirely social/emotive and that the child, over time, learns to relate his vocalizations to his more intellectual activities. The preceding discussion diverges sharply from Vygotsky's view. Infant vocalizations are viewed as being intimately tied to the infant's cognition of experience from the beginning. While any conclusions must, at present, be considered tentative, the systematic occurrence of vocalizations observed in this study may well be precursors to the egocentric speech Vygotsky reported in older children; and, like the vocalizations which Vygotsky observed, may herald the union of language and thought.

ACKNOWLEDGMENTS

This article has been reprinted, with stylistic changes only, with permission from the *Journal of Child Language* 15. The research reported in this article was supported in part by the National Institute of Mental Health which funded substantial portions of the author's graduate training and research at Cornell

University. Address for correspondence: D. D. Hilke, Department of Public Programs, Room MBB66, National Museum of American History, Smithsonian Institution, Washington, D.C. 20560, USA.

REFERENCES

Berlyne, D. (1974). Information and motivation. In A. Silverstein (Ed.), *Human communications: Theoretical explorations* (pp. 19-45). Hillsdale, NJ: Lawrence Erlbaum Associates.

Bloom, K. (1977). Patterning of infant vocal behaviour. *Journal of Experimental Child Psychology, 23,* 367-77.

Brazelton, T., Tronick, E., Adamson, L., Als, H., & Wise, S. (1975). Early mother-infant reciprocity. In M. O'Conner (Ed.), *Parent-infant interaction.* Amsterdam: Elsevatt.

Bruner, J. S. (1977). Early social interaction and language acquisition. In H. Schaffer (Ed.), *Studies in mother-infant interaction* (pp. 271-289). New York: Academic Press.

Bruner, J. (1983). *Child's talk: learning to use language.* New York: Norton.

Bullowa, M. (1975). When infants and adults communicate, how do they synchronize their behaviors? In A. Kendon, R. Harris, & M. Key (Eds.), *Organization of behavior in face-to-face interaction* (pp. 95-129). The Hague: Mouton.

Clark, D., & Hilke, D. (1980). *Cognition related vocalizations in infancy: a case study.* Paper presented to the International Conference on Infant Studies, New Haven, Connecticut.

Fogel, A. (1977). Temporal organization in mother-infant interaction. In H. Schaffer (Ed.), *Studies in mother-infant interaction* (pp. 119-151). New York: Academic Press.

Furrow, D., & James, P. (1985). Attentional change and vocalization: Evidence for a relation. *Child Development, 56,* 1179-1183.

Greenfield, P. (1978). Informativeness, presupposition, and semantic choice in single-word utterances. In N. Waterson & C. E. Snow (Eds.). *The development of communication* (pp. 443-452). Chichester: Wiley.

Greenfield, P. (1982). The role of perceived variability in the transition to language. *Journal of Child Language, 5,* 1-12.

Greenfield, P., & Zukow, P. (1978). Why do children say what they say when they say it?: an experimental approach to the psychogenesis of presupposition. In K. Nelson (Ed.), *Children's language* (Vol. 1, pp. 287-336). New York: Gardner Press.

Hilke, D. (1983). Predicting the occurrence of infant vocalizations: a cognitive perspective. Paper presented to the Society for Research in Child Development.

Hilke, D. (1985). The systematic occurrence of infant vocalizations prior to language (Doctoral dissertation, Cornell University). *Dissertation Abstracts International, 46,* 325B.

Kagan, J. (1971). *Change and continuity in infancy.* New York: Wiley.

Kay, K. (1977). Toward the origin of dialogue. In H. Schaffer (Ed.), *Studies in mother-infant interaction* (pp. 89-117). London: Academic Press.

Lempert, H., & Kinsbourne, M. (1985). Possible origin of speech in selective orienting. *Psychological Bulletin, 97,* 62-73.

McCall, R. B. (1972). Smiling and vocalization in infants as indices of perceptual-cognitive processes. *Merrill-Palmer Quarterly, 18,* 341–347.

Ninio, A., & Bruner, J. (1978). The achievement and antecedents of labelling. *Journal of Child Language, 5,* 1–15.

O'Conner, M. (Ed.) (1975). *Parent–infant interaction.* Amsterdam: Elsevatt.

Papoušek, H., & Papoušek, M. (1975). Cognitive aspects of pre-verbal social interaction between human infants and adults. In M. O'Conner (Ed.), *Parent–infant interaction.* Amsterdam: Elsevatt.

Ratner, N., & Bruner, J. (1978). Games, social exchange and the acquisition of language. *Journal of Child Language, 5,* 391–401.

Schaffer, H. (Ed.) (1977). Early interactive development. In *Studies in mother–infant interaction* (pp. 3–16). London: Academic Press.

Schaffer, H. (Ed.) (1977). *Studies in mother–infant interaction.* London: Academic Press.

Schaffer, H., Collis, G., & Parsons, G. (1977). Vocal interchange and visual regard in verbal and pre-verbal children. In H. Schaffer (Ed.), *Studies in mother–infant interaction* (pp. 291–324). London: Academic Press.

Shultz, T., & Zigler, E. (1970). Emotional concomitants of visual mastery in infants: The effects of stimulus movement on smiling and vocalizing. *Journal of Experimental Child Psychology, 10,* 390–402.

Stern, D., Beebe, R., Jaffe, J., & Bennett, S. (1977). The infant's stimulus world during social interaction: A study of caregiver behaviors with particular reference to repetition and timing. In H. Schaffer (Ed.), *Studies in mother–infant interaction* (pp. 177–202). New York: Academic Press.

Vygotsky, L. (1962). *Thought and language.* Cambridge, MA: MIT Press.

Vygotsky, L. (1978). *Mind in society: The development of higher psychological processes.* Cambridge, MA: Harvard University Press.

Watson, J. (1972). Smiling, cooing and "the game." *Merrill-Palmer Quarterly, 18,* 323–339.

Zelazo, P. R., Hopkins, R., Jacobson, S., & Kagan, J. (1974). Psychological reactivity to discrepent events: support for the curvilinear hypothesis. *Cognition, 2,* 385–393.

Mechanisms for Listener-Adaptation in Language Production: Limiting the Role of the "Model of the Listener"

Gary S. Dell
University of Illinois
Paula M. Brown
*National Technical Institute for the Deaf
at Rochester Institute of Technology*

One speaks in order to be understood by one's listener. Although there are many useful cognitive functions that are served by talking to yourself, there can be little doubt that the language production system's primary mission is to create utterances comprehensible to others. Because of this mission, speakers will, when faced with a choice about what to say or how to say it, choose a way that helps their listeners comprehend.

Observations of everyday interactions indicate that speakers adapt to their listeners' comprehension needs in a variety of ways. For example, they avoid syntactic structures that are difficult to parse (e.g., Bever & Langendoen, 1971) and they honor the listener's need for structural and informational features in a text, such as the marking of given and new information (Bock & Mazzella, 1983; MacWhinney & Bates, 1978). Speakers also do such things as: adjust the complexity of an utterance according to a listener's age (Shatz & Gelman, 1973); revise the content of a message when a listener does not understand (Garvey, 1975); and choose a language code appropriate to the listener's socioeconomic or linguistic status. Speakers also adjust the specificity of a message based on the listener's informational needs (Asher, 1979). In particular, they do not state information that they assume their listener already knows.

The issue of how production is adapted to comprehension is the focus of our paper. By what mechanism is adaptation achieved? A common explanation, grounded in the belief that communication is an interactive and cooperative process (Clark & Marshall, 1981; Grice, 1975; van Dyke, 1977), is that speakers produce comprehensible utterances because they take their listeners into account. Speakers have a set of beliefs about what their listeners know and can do, a "model of the listener," and this model is consulted whenever the production system has an option. This model includes exceptional characteristics of the listener such as age and cognitive abilities, assumptions about the listener's knowledge and experience, and assumptions about shared contextual information, including what has already been said. Via consultation of this model, speakers can adapt to their listener's needs.

The position that we consider in this paper is that, although many adaptations are achieved by the speaker consulting a model of the listener, some are not. It seems to us that there are two broad classes of adaptations, *particular-listener* and *generic-listener* adaptations, and that one must consider these separately when addressing this position.

Particular-listener adaptations occur when the adaptive variation in production is associated with variation in the circumstances or characteristics of the listener(s) being addressed. For example, when the listener is far away the speaker shouts, or if he[1] is taking notes the speaker talks more slowly. Moreover, there is a great deal of sensitivity on the part of the speaker to her listener's linguistic competence, the most compelling examples of which are associated with "motherese," changes in the physical and linguistic features of speech directed at young children (e.g., Newport, Gleitman, & Gleitman, 1977; Snow, 1972; Snow & Ferguson, 1977). Particular-listener adaptations such as these are produced by the speaker using some kind of model of listener essentially by definition.

Generic-listener adaptations exist when production decisions exhibit a bias toward content, structure, or a manner of production that is, *in general,* easy to comprehend. That is, such an adaptation would be said to exist when speakers choose option A over option B and the "average" listener would comprehend the message more easily if it manifested option A. For example, Lieberman (1963) showed that the word "nine" is articulated more carefully in the context "The number that you will hear is _____" than in the more redundant context "A stitch in time saves _____." Although this difference in articulation serves as an adaptation to the listener's ability to recognize words in context, adapting to a particular listener's need does not appear to motivate the decision.

Another example of what could be termed a generic-listener adaptation occurs in the use of anaphoric expressions. Marslen-Wilson, Levy, and Tyler (1982) showed that speakers refer to discourse objects in a fashion that is sensitive to the listener's ability to determine what is being referred to. When the discourse structure severely limits possible antecedents, speakers use less informative anaphors such as null anaphors or pronouns. When the structure is less limiting, speakers are more explicit. A third instance of a generic-listener adaptation can be seen in the way that speakers inform their listeners about

---

[1]The pronoun for the generic speaker in this chapter will be feminine, and the one for the generic listener will be masculine.

mistakes in their (the speaker's) speech. Levelt (1983) showed that speakers repair their errors in a way that is suited to their listener's comprehension needs. A speaker might say, for example, "It's the blue one, I mean, the *red* one." The use of the editing term *I mean,* the presence of contrastive stress on *red,* and the retracing of the noun phrase "the _____ one", all help the listener make the proper substitution of *red* for *blue.*

Are generic-listener adaptations like these produced through the speaker's consideration of a model of the listener? It could be that they are, although this is certainly not true by definition as it is for the case of particular-listener adaptations. Let us consider how generic adaptation could be effected through a model of the listener. The model might include features of the average listener by default (or perhaps the speaker's own knowledge could serve as the default), but these features would then be subject to amendment when knowledge of the particular listener is available. On this view, the knowledge that regulates both types of adaptations is to be found in this model. An advantage of this arrangement is that a bias toward the generic listener could be flexibly altered. A disadvantage is that the model of the listener becomes a large and unwieldy data structure.

Next let us consider the other possibility, that generic-listener adaptations come from mechanisms that have nothing to do with the speaker's beliefs about the listener. Perhaps the production system, by itself, exhibits biases to produce messages that are adapted to the average listener. The mechanism for this adaptation might be simply the need for both the production and comprehension systems to make use of similar conceptual and linguistic knowledge. Consider a somewhat trivial example of how this might work. Let us stipulate that speakers tend to use common words over uncommon ones (e.g., *lie* for *prevaricate*) and that this bias is adaptive to the average listener for whom common words are easier to recognize. Does the speaker exhibit this bias because she consults a model of the listener? Possibly in some cases, but in general one would not think so. Rather, it is simply that frequency-of-usage is a property of words in the mental lexicon that is relevant to both recognition and selection during production. The words that speakers naturally choose are easy to comprehend as well. The adaptation is achieved automatically because the variation in the usage of the relevant knowledge (lexical knowledge in this case) turns out to be similar for production and comprehension.

Our concern is with the mechanism behind generic-listener adaptations. The view that they result from the speaker accessing a model of the listener will be termed the *listener-knowledge hypothesis.* The opposing view, that they are automatic products of the production system, will be called the *modularity hypothesis.* The term "modularity," popularized by Fodor (1983), captures what we feel is the central idea behind this hypothesis, namely that one part of the mind, the language production system, is hypothesized *not* to use some particular kind of knowledge (beliefs about the listener) that could, in principle, be very helpful to that part's decision making. Instead, the production system is hypothe-sized to have its own devices, whose operations may roughly approximate that of consultation with listener-knowledge but are distinct from it. Fodor had made an analogous proposal in discussing the mechanism for context effects in lexi-cal processing. The language processing system was hypothesized not to use pragmatic knowledge to constrain the access of the sense of ambiguous words. However, for contexts in which access did seem to be constrained, such as the "priming context" in Seidenberg, Tanenhaus, Leiman, and Bienkowski (1982), it was proposed that a simple automatic aspect of the language processing sys-tem itself, intra-lexical priming, created the effect (see also Forster, 1979). Although recent research has questioned the efficacy of intralexical priming (O'Seaghdha, 1989; Simpson, Peterson, Casteel, & Burgess, 1989), the point remains that it is theoretically possible that a module-internal process could roughly approximate the effect of an appeal to knowledge that is to be unavail-able to the module. However, the internal process would have the disadvan-tage of being "dumb" or inflexible (Fodor, 1983). So, in the case of our own modularity hypothesis, we would expect that generic-listener adaptations would prove to be stubbornly resistant to change. If the facts about a particular listener dictated that some adaptive bias was counteradaptive in this one case, the production system would not accommodate to it. True knowledge of the listener is not available.

The listener-knowledge and modularity hypotheses are competing accounts of generic-listener adaptations. Our goal is to determine which is correct. Here we initially focus on a particular adaptation. The phenomenon is that speak-ers are more explicit about the instruments of actions when they are atypically associated with that action than when they are typical. For example, speakers are less explicit about the instrument used in a stabbing incident if it is a knife than if it is an ice pick. On the assumption that listeners can infer that the instrument is a knife more easily given the discussion of a stabbing, the varia-tion in explicitness can be seen as a case of production adapting to compre-hension. In our two experiments described in the next section we establish that this effect occurs and directly test the competing listener-knowledge and modularity hypotheses. These experiments are presented in detail in Brown and Dell (1987).

AN EXPERIMENTAL ANALYSIS
OF ADAPTATION IN PRODUCTION

In both of our experiments subjects read and then retold 20 short stories. For the first experiment, the stories, each of which contained three sentences, could appear in four versions shown by the example in Table 6.1. The first sentence, which was the same for all the versions, mentioned a critical action (such as a stabbing in the example story) in which the instrument was left unspecified. The second sentence both introduced one or more new actions and made the instrument of the critical action known (He wiped blood off the knife). However, it made the instrument known in an indirect fashion. That is, the reader must infer that the knife mentioned was what was used in the stabbing. Two of the versions mentioned an instrument typically associated with the action *(knife)* and two had an atypical, but not implausible, instrument *(ice pick)*. Typicality was assessed by giving 23 subjects the first sentence of each story and allowing them to fill in an instrument. Instruments designated as typical were filled in 74.8% of the time and those designated as atypical were filled in much less often (12.2%). The third and final sentence either referred to the instrument again ("investigators found fingerprints all over the knife") or did not ("investigators found fingerprints all over the drawers"). Thus we manipulated the typicality of the instrument and its importance or salience in the story. We expected to find that, when the stories were retold, atypical instruments would be mentioned explicitly as the instrument of the action more often than typical ones, and that importance would increase overall probability of instrument mention.

The procedure for the first experiment was quite simple. Subjects read silently each story and retold the story "in their own words" to the experimenter. For a given subject, each story was presented in only one of the four versions and the version associated with a story was counterbalanced, thus treating instrument typicality and instrument importance as within-subject as well as within-story variables.

The second experiment only used the two versions of the story in which the instrument was important. Thus only the typicality variable was manipu-

TABLE 6.1
An Example of a Story and Its Four Versions

A. Typical important instrument: knife

The robber hid behind the door and when the man entered the kitchen he stabbed him in the back. He wiped the blood off the knife and rummaged through the drawers. Later police investigators found his fingerprints all over the knife and had no trouble catching him.

B. Typical unimportant instrument: knife

The robber hid behind the door and when the man entered the kitchen he stabbed him in the back. He wiped the blood off the knife and rummaged through the drawers. Later police investigators found his fingerprints all over the drawers and had no trouble catching him.

C. Atypical important instrument: ice pick

The robber hid behind the door and when the man entered the kitchen he stabbed him in the back. He wiped the blood off the ice pick and rummaged through the drawers. Later police investigators found his fingerprints all over the ice pick and had no trouble catching him.

D. Atypical unimportant instrument: ice pick

The robber hid behind the door and when the man entered the kitchen he stabbed him in the back. He wiped the blood off the ice pick and rummaged through the drawers. Later police investigators found his fingerprints all over the drawers and had no trouble catching him.

---

lated in the stories. However, other manipulations were introduced to test directly the listener-knowledge hypothesis. Speakers told the stories to a confederate they believed was another subject and who they believed needed to know the stories for a subsequent test. In addition, each story was accompanied by a picture that was either informative about the instrument (e.g., showed the robber with a knife) or not (e.g., showed the robber with his hand behind his back). Furthermore, for half the subjects, the listener (the confederate) saw the picture as well and the subjects were made aware of the listener's knowledge of the picture. Yet another manipulation was that half the subjects saw the picture before they read the story to be told and the remaining half saw it after reading the story but before speaking. This latter manipulation had no effect on the retellings and so it will not be further discussed.

The manipulations of picture informativeness and whether or not the listener knows the content of the picture are relevant to the listener-knowledge hypothesis. Are effects of instrument typicality (greater explicitness about atypical instruments) attenuated when the speaker knows that the listener has a picture that is informative about the instrument? The listener-knowledge hypothesis would predict that such an attenuation would occur. The speaker's model of the listener should include what the listener knows from the picture. A pictured atypical instrument is already known to the listener and thus is no longer atypical and in need of explicit mention. In contrast, the modularity view would predict no attenuation of the typicality effect. Beliefs about listener knowledge are hypothesized not to be the cause of the effect, and thus should not be able to modify it. Instead the effect is assumed to be brought about by some feature of the language production system itself.

Thus, considering both experiments, we are concerned with the effect of instrument typicality (Experiments 1 and 2), instrument importance (Experiment 1) and the speaker's beliefs about instrument-relevant knowledge possessed by the listener (Experiment 2). Twenty subjects were run in the first experiment and 80 in the second. Each retelling of a story was taped, transcribed, and coded with respect to the way in which the instrument was mentioned, if at all.

Before we turn to the results of the experiments, there are two concerns that need to be addressed. First, a basic assumption of the experiment is that variations in the retelling as a function of instrument typicality can serve as adaptations to listeners. In particular, we are assuming that atypical instruments are, in some way, more difficult for comprehenders to deal with, and, in the second experiment, we are further assuming that the informative pictures eliminate this difficulty. These assumptions require verification. So, we ran two preliminary comprehension experiments. In the first, subjects read the stories presented sentence-by-sentence on a CRT and we collected the reading times for each sentence. As expected, the second sentence was read significantly more slowly (*42* msec slower per word) when it contained the atypical instrument. In a second experiment the comprehenders saw either the informative or uninformative pictures before reading the stories. When the pictures were uninformative, there were significantly slower reading times for the second sentence with the atypical instrument than for those with the typical instrument (30 msec slower per word). With informative pictures, however, there was no difference as a function of typicality (1 msec slower per word). Given these results, we can be confident that there is some comprehension difficulty associated with the atypical instruments in our materials and that our informative pictures eliminate this difficulty. What is the nature of the difficulty? It is hard to say. It may be that when reading the first sentence, the comprehender infers that the instrument of the critical action is the one most typically associated with it. There is some evidence that such "forward" or "elaborative" inferences are made for typical instruments (O'Brien, Shank, Myers, & Rayner, 1988). However, there is also evidence that this does not occur (Dosher & Corbett, 1982; McKoon & Ratcliff, 1986). If the typical instrument had been inferred when reading the first sentence, there is naturally difficulty when the second sentence comes along mentioning an atypical instrument. An alternate explanation for the difficulty is that the inference for both typical and atypical cases is made only when the instrument is mentioned (i.e., in the second sentence) but the inference is simply more difficult to establish for the atypical case. Regardless of which of these is the correct account of the difficulty with atypical instruments, however, it is clear that difficulty exists. Because of this, retellings of the stories making atypical instruments more explicit can be seen as adaptations.

The second methodological concern is the possibility that differences in instrument mention would be due to speakers failing to encode the instruments rather than choosing not to mention them. To check for this, we gave a cued-recall test for the instruments (using the first sentence of each story as the cue) to the subjects in the second experiment after they retold the stories. Recall was nearly perfect (97%). Thus, variations in instrument mentioning do not reflect failure to encode the instruments.

Now we are ready to consider the results. As expected, speakers were more explicit about atypical than typical instruments. In Experiment 1 the typical instrument was explicitly stated to be the instrument of the critical action on 81 of 200 retellings, in contrast to only 45 of 200 for the typical instrument. For Experiment 2, this effect was of similar magnitude, 392 out of 800 for atypical instruments versus 238 out of 800 for typical instruments. However, this result by itself does not reveal the mechanism of this typicality effect, whether it is mediated by expectations about what the listener knows or by some mechanism that is insulated from this knowledge. As we turn to a detailed analysis of the data we shall see that both positions are true, but that it depends on the manner in which instruments are specified. For some forms of specification, the language production system rigidly adheres to its tendency to mention atypical over typical instruments, but for other forms there is sensitivity to pragmatic information, including knowledge of the listener. We shall first go over the various ways that the speakers in our experiments tended to specify instruments and then isolate the influence of our manipulations on the particular forms of specification.

Table 6.2 presents the five categories that we used to code an instance of a subject explicitly mentioning the instrument as the instrument of the critical action. The two key dimensions behind these categories are, first, whether or not the instrument was mentioned in the same clause as the verb coding the action and, second, whether or not the instrument was mentioned before or after the verb (or during the action in the case of incorporation, use of the instrument as the verb describing the action).

The effect of typicality was surprisingly not uniformly present on all of these categories. Table 6.3 shows the percentage of specifications of typical and atypical instruments for the five categories averaged over both experiments. Specifications in a separate clause before the verb failed to show the expected predominance of atypical over typical mentioned. In fact, there was a nonsignificant tendency in both experiments for typical mentions to outnumber atypical ones for this category of mention. Similarly, the effect of instrument importance varied across categories (Table 6.4). For within-clause specifications there was no difference. However, for separate clause specifications there was a significant tendency to mention explicitly instruments that are important later in the story. It appears that any account of the instrument specification process must take into account the formal options open to the production system as well as the pragmatic factors of instrument typicality and importance.

The manipulation of listener knowledge (whether the listener is known to have a picture and whether that picture is informative about the instrument) had no significant effect on either within-clause or separate-clause—before-the-verb specifications (see Table 6.5). Only in the separate-clause—after-the-verb

TABLE 6.2
Categories of Explicit Mention of Instruments

Within-clause Categories
    (1) After the verb
        e.g., The robber stabbed the man with a knife.
    (2) Before the verb
        e.g., The robber used a knife to stab the man.
    (3) Incorporation
        e.g., The robber knifed the man.

Separate Clause Categories
    (4) After the verb
        e.g., The robber stabbed the man. He used an ice pick.
    (5) Before the verb
        e.g., The robber had a knife. He stabbed the man.

TABLE 6.3

Percentages of Explicit Mention of Instruments as a Function of Category
of Mention and Instrument Typicality.

| Category | Instrument Typicality | |
	Typical	Atypical
Within-Clause		
After	7.7	19.1
Before	1.1	4.1
Incorporation	0.6	2.8
Separate Clause		
After	2.9	8.4
Before	16.0	12.9

Note: Averaged over Experiments 1 and 2. Each percentage is based on 1000 opportunities.

category was there any indication of speakers' sensitivity to what the listener
knows from the picture. Here there were significantly fewer explicit mentions
when the listener had a picture. This was particularly true when the picture
was informative about the instrument and the instrument was atypical. (Compare 14.5% when listener is not known to have a picture to 6.5% when the
listener is known to have a picture.)

So, to sum up, there were large consistent effects of instrument typicality,
with atypical instruments mentioned explicitly much more often than typical
ones in all categories with the exception of the separate-clause—before-verb
category in which the effect was slightly reversed. The greater mentioning of
atypical instruments was, for the most part, not affected by manipulating the
listener's knowledge about the instruments by giving him a picture. However,
there were effects of contextual variables on instrument mention, notably in
the separate-clause—after-verb category, in which the listener's having a pic-

TABLE 6.4

Percentages of Explicit Mention of Instrument as a Function of Category
of Mention and Instrument Importance, Experiment 1.

| Category | Instrument Importance | |
	Important	Unimportant
Within-Clause		
After	13.5	12.5
Before	2.5	2.0
Incorporation	2.5	2.5
Separate Clause		
After	4.5	1.0
Before	13.0	9.0

Note: Each percentage is based on 200 opportunities.

TABLE 6.5
Percentages of Explicit Mention of Instruments as a Function of Category
of Mention and Experimental Conditions From Experiment 2.

	Listener known to have picture				Listener not known to have picture			
	Informative Picture		Uninformative Picture		Informative Picture		Uninformative Picture	
	T	A	T	A	T	A	T	A
Within-Clause	10.0	24.0	10.0	22.0	9.5	28.0	9.5	28.5
Separate Clause Before	16.0	16.0	16.5	11.5	18.5	14.0	16.5	13.5
Separate Clause After	2.0	6.5	1.5	9.5	4.5	14.5	4.5	8.0

Note: Each percentage is based on 200 opportunities. T = Typical; A = Atypical.

ture that is informative about an atypical instrument reduced explicit mentions. Also this category had a greater number of explicit mentions of important instruments.

Our conclusion is that, at least in this experimental paradigm, the modularity hypothesis is correct for within-clause specifications of instruments. In this case, the production system rigidly adheres to its tendency to mention atypical instruments regardless of their importance or their status vis-à-vis the listener. For separate clause specifications the picture is more complex, and to develop a complete account of the data we will have to consider the language production system as a whole. So, in the next section we present a model of some of the processes involved in constructing an utterance. In particular, the model identifies what options are open to speakers for specifying instruments. As will be seen, it provides an effective method of summarizing the data, and it makes some claims about the modularity issue, particularly about the availability of certain types of pragmatic information during production.

LANGUAGE PRODUCTION AND
INSTRUMENT SPECIFICATION MODEL

The model was derived from a general characterization of language production that has emerged over the last 10 years from the work of a number of researchers (e.g., Bock, 1982, 1987; Butterworth, 1981; Garrett, 1975, 1980; Kempen & Huijbers, 1983; Lapointe, 1985; Lapointe & Dell, 1989; Levelt, 1983, 1989; Saffran, 1982; Schwartz, 1987; Shattuck-Hufnagel, 1979; Stemberger, 1985). We can only provide a brief summary of this work here. See Levelt (1989) for more details.

On the standard view of production there are four stages: conceptual, linguistic, motoric-articulatory, and post-articulatory monitoring and repair. In the conceptual stage a "message" or semantic-pragmatic representation of the utterance is formed. Although a message is conceptual rather than linguistic, it can be distinguished from thoughts that are not messages in one, and possibly two, respects. First, although all conceptual structures can be viewed as organized sets of prepositions, a message's propositional content must stand in some relation to a speech act (inform, request, etc.). That is, messages are thoughts that are uttered to achieve some end. They participate in a planning process much as any action does. Another aspect of messages that might distinguish them from general cognitions is the possibility that they may be tuned to the linguistic encoding process; they may be specially prepared for the particular rules of language that the speaker will be employing. This possibility, which has been suggested by Levelt (1989), requires that messages contain all the semantic information that is necessarily coded by the language being spoken. For example, information that can be used to compute verb tense and aspect would be required of messages to be conveyed in English, but information about the shape of concrete objects, which is not grammaticized in English, would not necessarily be present.

The goal of the second stage, linguistic encoding, is to turn the message into the form of a sentence. Current theory divides linguistic encoding into three components or levels: a functional level, a positional level, and a sound level. The distinction between the functional and positional level was motivated primarily by differences in the patterning of speech errors involving whole lexical units and those involving sublexical units (Garrett, 1975). At the functional level, a grammatical representation of the sentence is formed in which major-class lexical items are retrieved and assigned to "slots" in a functional "frame." The lexical items are not actual sound strings but instead are abstract symbols for the items as wholes. These were termed "lemmas" by Kempen and Huijbers (1983). The exact nature of the relations that the lemmas participate in is controversial. According to Garrett (1975), who originally characterized this level, "underlying grammatical relations" are the domain of the functional representation. More recently, theorists have argued that thematic roles (e.g., agent, instrument) should be coded (Saffran, 1982; Schwartz, 1987) and Bock (1987) has presented evidence that relations such as surface subject and object are present.

The positional level representation resembles that of the functional level in that it consists of a frame with slots for lexical items. However, it differs in three respects. First, the phonological forms of lexical items, rather than lemmas, are what is assigned to slots. Second, unlike the functional level, the positional level directly represents the serial order of the morphemes in the utterance. Function words and grammatical affixes are present and the actual order of phrases is identified. The functional level only represents the order of items to the extent that it codes grammatical relations, which tend to occur in certain positions. Also, grammatical morphemes are not specified at all in the functional level representation. Third, the two levels are assumed to differ on the extent of their window of computation. The functional level is said to deal with large sections of utterances simultaneously, possibly clause- or sentence-sized chunks (Butterworth, 1989), whereas the positional level has been associated with smaller chunks such as major phrases (e.g., Lapointe, 1985).

Sometimes a separate sound level component of linguistic encoding that is responsible for specifying phonetic detail is distinguished from the positional level (e.g., Fromkin, 1971; Garrett, 1975). Evidence for this level comes from the fact that positional level errors, such as the movement of sounds or groups of sounds, are associated with morphophonemic adjustments. Thus, an error such as *an early period* → *a pearly period* shows both the movement of the sound /p/ and the accommodation of the indefinite article *a/an* to the error (Fromkin, 1971). This suggests that the specification of the phonetic shape of morphemes occurs after the processes responsible for retrieving and ordering their sounds.

The eventual output of the linguistic encoding process has been characterized as internal speech (Levelt, 1983; MacKay, 1982). It is fully specified linguistically and lacks only a mapping into the motoric domain to produce overt speech (see Dell, 1978, and Dell & Repka, in press, for some experimental analyses of errors in internal speech or "slips of the mind").

We will have little to say here about the third major stage in production, the motor-programming-articulatory stage. Although there has been much work done here (see Levelt, 1989, for a review), it is not directly relevant to the instrument adaptation issue. (It may, however, be relevant to other kinds of production adaptation, as we will discuss later.) Of more immediate concern is the fourth stage, post-articulatory monitoring. Levelt (1983) provided a detailed model of how speakers monitor what they have just said for correctness and appropriateness, and then produce an utterance that repairs any faults that are found. The monitoring is supposed to make use of the language comprehension system, and this is presumed to be sensitive to the entire range of linguistic and pragmatic knowledge that is used in comprehension.

In our model of instrument mention, we focus on three parts of the production process: (a) conceptual planning, (b) the initial phases of linguistic encoding associated with the functional representation, and (c) the monitoring and repair stage. In the conceptual planning stage, we distinguish between the creation of a macroproposition, or main idea, and other propositions that elaborate on that idea (e.g., Kinstch & van Dyck, 1978). Thus, the first step in the conceptual planning for the story presented in Table 6.1 might be to encode the first major idea in the story as the robber stabbing the man. This could then be augmented by additional propositions expressing where the event took place, where the robber was hiding, how vicious the stabbing was, and so on.

According to the model, the stabbing instrument could be specified during conceptual planning either within the message macroproposition itself, or in an elaborating proposition. Or it may not be included in the message at all.

Inclusion of the instrument in the macroproposition means, in the model, that the instrument is indispensible for a proper characterization of the action. To see what we mean here, consider how the initial macroproposition for the robber story would be constructed. Assume that there is some prior representation of the story derived from reading the text of it—subjects tell us that they often experience this as an image—and that it is this that guides the construction of the propositions of the message. This prior representation is assumed to specify the instrument of the critical action, because we found that when we asked them to recall the instrument, subjects did so nearly perfectly. We further assume that the prior representation is organized such that an initial main event, the stabbing, can be identified.

To build the message macroproposition, the speaker compares this initial main event with an inventory of verbal concepts (e.g., *hit, stab, fight with*) and selects a concept that best matches the event. A verbal concept is the concept or word-sense behind a verb or other relational construction (e.g., prepositions, verb–particle combinations). In our view of these concepts, they have two important characteristics. First, they have an argument structure, a set of associated slots providing information about components of events such as the manner of the activity, its location, and the participants in the event such as the agent, patient, instrument, and so on. This list is a bit more general than the list of thematic roles associated with a verb (e.g., Tanenhaus & Carlson, 1989) in that it contains slots for information other than necessary participants. The second important characteristic is that, like any concept, a verbal concept can be profitably described as a prototype, that is, as a central tendency in a space of possible exemplars (Rosch, 1975; Smith & Medin, 1981). The prototype would be a point, or perhaps a volume, in this space that is (by some metric) minimally distant from the set of events experienced as instances of the concept, and maximally distant from other conceptually labelled points or volumes.

Because of the assumed prototypical structure of verbal concepts, the associated argument slots will tend to be linked to information about typical fillers for the slots. Thus, each verbal concept's volume in the event space is not indifferent to dimensions of the space that code aspects of the associated arguments. For example, if most stabbing events involve bad, male, human agents stabbing human patients, with knives, the conceptual structure will reflect this.

Selecting a verbal concept for a message proposition involves choosing the closest concept to the event. However, if there is no very close concept, we assume that the concept is modified or temporarily "shifted" in event space along one or (less desirably) more dimensions. Each shift is assumed to be noted and marked in the proposition being constructed. Again considering the *stab* concept, if a stabbing occurs in a slow, gentle manner, the event may not match the *stab* concept. A shift along the manner dimension from "violent" to "gentle" might then produce a good match, and if the concept is then chosen, its manner slot would have to be marked "gentle." Similarly, a stabbing with a less typical instrument such as an ice pick may require that the *stab* concept be shifted to achieve a match, and this shift will be marked in the proposition by specifying ice pick as the instrument.

After the creation of the macroproposition, other elaborating propositions may be added to the message. Here there is another chance to specify the instrument. We assume that if the instrument is not specified in the macroproposition, it may appear in a proposition subordinate to the macroproposition. If the macroproposition for the robber paragraph was *stab (robber, man, . . .)* and did not identify the instrument, the elaborating proposition *instrument (macroprop, knife)* could be added.

There are two senses in which specification in elaborating propositions differs from specification in the macroproposition. One is that the purposes of specification are assumed to differ. As we mentioned earlier, specification in the macroproposition has the function of achieving a match between the event and a verbal concept. As such, the decision whether or not to specify in this way should be sensitive to the typicality of the information with respect to the experienced verbal concept. However, other factors such as the information's discourse function, its salience, or its status in the model of the listener, are not operative here. Thus we are assuming that specification in the macroproposition is modular. The decision is based simply on the structure of concepts. In contrast, specification through an elaborating proposition is not assumed to be modular in this way and therefore could reflect other factors which we will identify later.

The second difference between specification in macropropositions and in elaborating propositions is in the form that the information takes during linguistic encoding. If the information is present in the macroproposition then we assume that it is linguistically encoded at the same time as the verbal concept forming the basis of this proposition. Given that the initial selection of syntactic structure occurs during the construction of the functional level of representation and that this process is assumed to work in clause-sized chunks, then information present in the macroproposition should appear in the same clause as the verb encoding the critical action. Thus, instruments that are explicitly mentioned in the same-clause categories (1–3 in Table 6.2) are there, according to the model, because they were included in the macropropositions for the critical actions.

When an instrument (or any other argument of a verbal concept) appears in an elaborating proposition, the model asserts that it will appear in a separate clause from the action. Its linguistic encoding at the functional level is assumed to be distinct from that of the macroproposition. Whether the clause bearing the instrument appears before or after that of the critical action depends on when the elaborating proposition was created. By its very nature, an elaborating proposition must be created after its superordinate macroproposition.

However, there are two distinct times that such a proposition can be constructed. First, it may be constructed right after the macroproposition and before the macroproposition is linguistically encoded and articulated. Or, it may be created after the macroproposition is linguistically encoded and articulated. In the latter case, the elaborating macroproposition will necessarily come after the clause encoding the macroproposition. In the former case, the elaborating proposition could come either before or after the macroproposition clause, but for the sake of conciseness in the model, we will stipulate that it comes before.

These two options for specifying an instrument in a separate clause from the critical action should have different functions, given their different points of creation. In particular, one might expect specification in the clause after the verb to be the result of the speaker's monitoring of the already uttered clause encoding the macroproposition. Thus, specification in this way may serve the function of an appropriateness repair (Levelt, 1983), or some other form of clarification that the speaker initiates in response to listening to herself. Specification in a clause before might, in contrast, be expected to serve more of a planned discourse function. With these ideas in mind, we now turn to the presentation of the quantitative aspect of the model. Using this model and the interpretation of it based on the present discussion, we shall be able to identify the kinds of information that guide the decision making.

A QUANTITATIVE TREATMENT OF THE MODEL

The choices for specifying instruments and the parameters associated with those choices are presented in Fig. 6.1. The model's basic structure is that of a decision tree. Each branch represents an option open to the production process, and each parameter identifies the probability of choosing a particular branch given that the decision process has arrived at that point. The terminal points correspond to the five categories of explicit mention for instruments together with a sixth category for the case in which the instrument is not explicitly mentioned. We used the data from the two instrument specification experiments to estimate these parameters as a function of instrument typicality, importance, and the speaker's beliefs about listener knowledge. If an estimated parameter value is found to differ as a function of one of these manipulations, then we can conclude that the process corresponding to the parameter is affected by the kind of information varied in that manipulation. Details about the model and the parameter estimation can be found in Brown and Dell (1987).

The first option in the model is whether or not to include the instrument in the macroproposition. Parameter p represents the probability that it is included. In our discussion of this decision we hypothesized that it is modular, specifically that it would be affected by instrument typicality and not by any other pragmatic knowledge. This is exactly what the data showed. Parameter p was strongly influenced by typicality (see Table 6.6 for estimates values) such

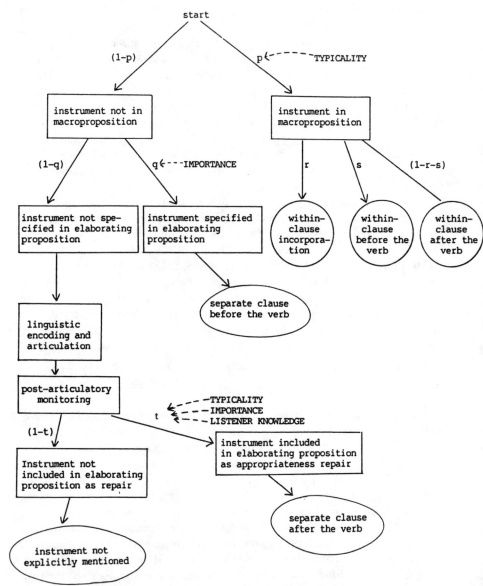

FIG. 6.1. Decision-tree model showing location of model parameters in relation to production options (boxes). The categories of explicit mention of instruments appear at the branches of the tree as circles. The hypothesized influence of experimental variables is indicated by dashed-line arrows.

TABLE 6.6
Model Parameters as a Function of Experimental Conditions

Parameter	Typicality		Importance		Listener	
	Typ	Atyp	Imp	Unimp	L-Yes	L-No
Experiment 1						
p	.08 (200)	.27 (200)*	.18 (200)	.17 (200)		
q	.14 (184)	.13 (145)	.16 (163)	.11 (166)		
r	.19 (16)	.13 (55)	.14 (37)	.15 (34)		
s	.19 (16)	.11 (55)	.14 (37)	.12 (34)		
t	.03 (159)	.06 (126)	.07 (137)	.01 (148)*		
Experiment 2						
p	.10 (800)	.26 (800)*			.17 (800)	.19 (800)
q	.19 (722)	.18 (595)			.18 (668)	.19 (649)
r	.04 (78)	.10 (205)			.08 (132)	.09 (151)
s	.10 (78)	.17 (205)			.18 (132)	.13 (151)
t	.04 (587)	.16 (485)*			.07 (548)	.12 (524)*

*Significant difference < .05, n is shown in parentheses.

that typical instruments were about three times less likely to be chosen for the macroproposition. This parameter was affected by neither the importance manipulation from the first experiment nor the manipulation of listener knowledge through pictures.

When the instrument is included in the macroproposition it is linguistically encoded in the same clause as the critical action. Parameter r represents the probability that the instrument is encoded as a verb incorporation (e.g., *he vacuumed the floor*), and s is the probability that it is specified before the verb in the same clause. The remaining option, specification in the same clause after the verb, does not require an additional parameter because these three options are mutually exclusive and exhaustive at this point in the tree. These syntactic encoding parameters were not affected significantly by any of our manipulations (see Table 6.6). The results with parameters s and r therefore provide some support, albeit negative support, for the modularity of linguistic encoding vis-à-vis conceptual encoding. The strong effect of typicality on the three within-clause forms of specification reflects only the earlier decision in the creation of the macroproposition. The linguistic encoding process itself does not matter. Rather, we can assume that selection among the within-clause encoding options is governed by factors internal to linguistic encoding, in particular, the syntactic and lexical information available to the functional level of processing. For example, whether an instrument is explicitly mentioned through incorporation will undoubtedly be related to the information present in the lexicon. Instruments that have previously been used this way may be listed as potential verbs. If an instrument that is present in the macroproposition does not have an associated verb (e.g., *broom*), a different syntactic option must be found (e.g., *with a broom*). Another linguistic-internal factor that may affect the form of within-clause specification is syntactic persistence. Levelt and Kelter (1982) and Bock (1986) found that the structure of a preceding utterance often persists into subsequent utterances. Thus, the decision regarding how to specify the instrument may be made simply by choosing the syntactic structure that was most recently used.

Now let us turn to the other side of the decision tree and consider what happens when the instrument is not encoded in the macroproposition. The first option at this point is whether or not to create a separate elaborating proposition expressing the instrument before the linguistic encoding of the macroproposition. Parameter q is the probability that such a proposition is created here. The estimates of q from the experiments reveal a marginal tendency for q to be larger when the instrument is important in the story: .11 for unimportant instruments from experiment 1, .16 for important instruments from experiment 1, and .19 from experiment 2 which only had important instruments. If we view the function of an elaborating proposition at this stage to be one of putting important information in the foreground, this tendency makes sense. However, it appears that foregrounding in this way is not sensitive to instrument typicality, nor to the listener's knowledge of instruments obtained through a picture, because the values of q were nearly identical for typical and atypical instruments and for conditions in which the listener did and did not have a picture. Thus, we have another instance in which a model component is modular, in the sense that it has limited access to pragmatic knowledge. In the case of the process associated with q, only discourse structure knowledge may be relevant. One should note as well that the effects of typicality on p and q together provide an account of the puzzling tendency found in both experiments for the typicality effect to be reversed with the category of separate clause before the verb specifications. The probability of specification in this category is estimated by $q(1-p)$. Given that p for atypical instruments is greater than for typical ones, and that q is indifferent to typicality, it follows that $q(1-p)$ is greater for typical than atypical cases.

The final choice point in the model occurs after the linguistic encoding and articulation of the material encoded in the macroproposition. The speaker evaluates what she has said and if it is found to be inappropriate in some way, a new elaborating proposition is created to repair the utterance, in this case because the utterance was found not to be specific enough. Instruments specified in this way necessarily appear in the separate-clause—after-the-verb category. The parameter associated with this process, t, was significantly sensitive to everything (typicality, importance, and whether or not the listener has a picture). Hence, the process associated with t, in contrast to all the other model components, is nonmodular. The other components had only limited access to pragmatic information. The decision coded by parameter p was influenced only by typicality, the parameters associated with syntactic encoding, r and *s,* were sensitive to none of the manipulations, and the process associated with *q* was only sensitive to instrument importance, if at all. Why is *t* so different? We suspect that it is because the monitoring and repair function of production, as discussed by Levelt (1983, 1989), really involves all the pieces of the language processing system. The comprehension system is known to be sensitive to all kinds of grammatical and pragmatic information (see, e.g., papers in Carlson & Tanenhaus, 1989). Conceivably, all of these information sources would come into play when the speaker monitors her own speech for communicative appropriateness. If a repair is needed, the entire production system may be engaged in its creation. Considering the multifaceted nature of the monitor/repair function, it is therefore not surprising that the process that we have collapsed to a single parameter, *t,* is sensitive to a variety of information types.

Let us summarize the conclusions that can be drawn from the modelling efforts. The model shows the senses in which the data from the experiments support the modularity hypothesis. First, listener knowledge, represented by the listener-picture variable, only affected the monitor/repair component of the model, not any of the other encoding processes. Second, each of these other decision points was found to be quite specific with respect to the kind of knowledge that was used. Third, the general tendency to mention atypical instruments was, for the most part, attributed to a decision process that does not have access to knowledge of the listener. Although the typicality effect serves as an adaptation to the listener, it is produced by a mechanism that is unaware of the listener.

The model was stated to be one of instrument specification. There is no reason, however, why it could not represent decisions about other types of arguments of verbal concepts, such as other participants in events, or their manner or location specifications. The syntactic encoding options would have to be different, but we feel that the basic structure could be preserved. At least, such a generalized model would make further predictions. For example, it is predicted that the specification of any argument information in the same clause as the associated verb should be sensitive to the typicality of the argument filler, and not sensitive to other pragmatic variables. These other variables should have their influence on specification in separate clauses.

In summary, our analysis of instrument specification has supported the claim that production can adapt to comprehension without the intervention of a model of the listener. Our claim for instruments is that the way that instrument information is represented and retrieved "automatically" results in a tendency for instruments that are more difficult to infer to be explicitly stated. In the final section of the paper we explore the more general claim that generic-listener adaptations are achieved through the production system's own devices without consulting beliefs about listener knowledge.

Generic-Listener Adaptations in Other Components of the Production System

In this section we examine three production phenomena from different components of the system: (a) syntactic persistence, (b) lexical accessibility effects on the order of phrasal conjuncts, and (c) semantic priming and anaphoric effects on production duration. For each we suggest that the effect can be viewed as an adaptation to the comprehension needs of the typical listener, but the effect is not produced as a result of an evaluation of the particular listener's needs.

Syntactic Persistence.   As discussed earlier, syntactic persistence is a tendency for speakers to use the structure of a previous utterance for the current one. Bock (1986) gave subjects a mixed list of sentences and pictures, ostensibly for a memory experiment. Subjects were to read aloud the sentences and describe each picture in a sentence. Whether a picture was described using the active or passive, or a double-object construction or a *to*-dative, was affected by the structure of the sentence read immediately before the picture. Specifically, the structure contained in the sentence persisted to that of the picture description. Levelt and Kelter (1982) found that a question's surface form can affect the format of the answer given, the answer repeating the structure of the question. The persistence phenomenon is very likely of some benefit to the listener. One can see this for oneself by observing that it is relatively easier to understand a reduced relative sentence such as "The horse raced past the barn fell" (Bever, 1970) after parsing the structurally similar sentence "The child given the ice cream cone smiled." Thus, duplication of syntactic structures can be seen as adaptation to comprehension. However, both Levelt and Kelter (1982) and Bock (1986) claimed that using previous structure is simply due to persistence within the syntactic system. It is not due to the speaker's decision that the listener would benefit by using the same structure again. Although no one has actually manipulated the speaker's beliefs about the listener in an attempt to ascertain whether the listener plays a role in the phenomenon, the very fact that the effect occurs in noncommunicative settings, such as Bock's "memory" experiment, suggests to us that the effect is not related to speaker–listener cooperation.

Lexical Accessibility Effects on Order.   Bock (1982) suggested that the tendency for shorter, more common words to come first in phrasal conjuncts (e.g., *salt and pepper, bread and butter*) is due to the ease of retrieving these words. Later Bock (1986) showed that by manipulating the accessibility of the phonological forms of words by phonological priming, one can influence the produced order. The more accessible forms tend to appear first in the conjunct. In addition, Kelly, Bock, and Keil (1986) found that the more prototypical (and hence

more accessible) instances of categories tended to be produced before nonproto-
typical instances in phrasal conjuncts. We suggest that phrasal ordering serves
as an adaptation to the listener by helping him comprehend and retain the conjoined phrase. Kelly and colleagues showed that the conjuncts with the prototypical instances early were judged to be more natural than those with the prototypical instance late. A standard finding in the memory literature is that the
memory span is greater for sequences in which the more accessible high frequency items are first rather than last in the sequence. One explanation for
this is that the less frequent items late in the sequence receive the benefit of
recency (often attributed to short-term store), thus eliminating their difficulty.
High frequency items are easier to recall from long-term store and thus do
not need to be recent. Whatever the explanation, however, the production system's tendency to put the difficult words last appears to benefit the listener.
We also claim that this is another case in which the listener is benefited by
properties of the production system, namely its lexical retrieval processes, not
by a decision that occurs through the intercession of the speaker's cognitions
about the listener's abilities and knowledge.

Semantic Priming Effects on Production Duration.   Earlier we discussed
the finding by Lieberman (1963) that words produced in a highly constraining
context *(A stitch in time saves NINE)* are produced more sloppily than those in
less constrained contexts. A closely related effect has recently been demonstrated
by Balota, Boland, and Shields (1989). The effect is that speakers produce two-
word sequences faster if the words are semantically related (dog–cat). Specifically, the duration of a related two-word sequence is faster than that of matched
unrelated sequences. The procedure used is one in which subjects see the sequence to be produced and then after a variable period of time, are signalled
to produce it as fast as possible. Thus the effect is purely one of production
and probably one associated with motor rather than linguistic encoding. Balota and colleagues interpreted the priming effect as the result of automatic spreading activation between related lexical items. The rate of production is assumed
to be related to the activation level of the items, and thus an item receiving
extra activation from a related one in the same sequence can be produced faster.
Balota and colleagues also argued that the effect is "cooperative," that is, it
serves as an adaptation to the listener. A cooperative speaker should vary her
speech rate as a function of the listener's ability to understand. When words
in context are primed by related preceding words, they are easier to understand. Hence, a speed-up in production duration for primed words is cooperative. However, the proposed automatic spreading activation mechanism for
the effect is not intended as a listener-sensitive mechanism. Thus this phenomenon could be another case of adaptation to the listener's needs that is effected
by the production system independently from the speaker's beliefs about the
listener.

Another case of a cooperative adaptation in the way that words are produced was discovered by Fowler and Housum (1987). They found that words produced for the first time in a passage were articulated in such a way that listeners could more easily identify them. The second mention of a word was shorter in duration and segmental information was often missing. Even more striking, though, Fowler and Housum found that listeners made use of this variation in deciding whether or not to interpret noun phrases anaphorically. Reduction of a word by the speaker is a valid cue that the discourse object referred to by the word has already been introduced. Does the speaker decide to reduce anaphoric words by actively consulting a model of the listener? Fowler and Housum's experiments do not tell us. Our view would attribute this effect, like the other adaptation effects discussed, to basic properties of the production system. For example, the reduced duration of previously mentioned words could reflect a kind of repetition priming analogous to the semantic priming effects of Balota et al. (1989).

CONCLUSIONS

Language production is a highly specialized skill, one that is designed to meet a specific goal, communication. It is therefore not surprising to find that the system is biased toward constructing and articulating speech that is comprehensible and informative. Some of these adaptations to the listener's comprehension needs are created by consulting a model of the listener, the speaker's beliefs about what the listener knows and is likely to know, and beliefs about the listener's competence. However, for some adaptations, those that we termed generic-listener adaptations, we suggest that the production system often adapts simply through its own devices. The result turns out to be adaptive essentially because the information processing that occurs during production and during comprehension are intimately related.

ACKNOWLEDGMENTS

Preparation of this manuscript was supported by National Institute for Deafness and Other Communication Disorders grant DC00435-03. The experiments reported in the manuscript were originally presented in Brown and Dell (1987) and other content is based on a talk given at the Center for the Study of Language and Information Workshop on Language Processing in June, 1985. The authors wish to thank Rosa Thompson for her contributions.

REFERENCES

Asher, S. R. (1979). Referential communication. In G. J. Whitehurst (Ed.), *The functions of language and cognition*. San Francisco: Academic Press.

Balota, D. A., Boland, J. E., & Shields (1989). Priming in pronunciation: Beyond pattern recognition and onset latency. *Journal of Memory and Language, 28,* 14–36.

Bever, T. G. (1970) The cognitive basis for linguistic structures. In J. R. Hayes (Ed.), *Cognition and the development of language.* New York: Wiley.

Bever, T. G., & Langendoen, D. T. (1971). A dynamic model for the evolution of language. *Linguistic Inquiry, 2,* 433–463.

Bock, J. K. (1982). Towards a cognitive psychology of syntax: Information processing contributions to sentence formulation. *Psychological Review, 89,* 1–47.

Bock, J. K. (1986). Syntactic persistence in language production. *Cognitive Psychology, 18,* 355–387.

Bock, J. K. (1987). An effect of accessibility of word forms on sentence structures. *Journal of Memory and Language, 26,* 119–137.

Bock, J. K., & Mazzella, J. R. (1983). Intonational marking of given and new information: Some consequences for comprehension. *Memory and Cognition, 11,* 64–76.

Brown, P. M., & Dell, G. S. (1987). Adapting production to comprehension: The explicit mention of instruments. *Cognitive Psychology, 19,* 441–472.

Butterworth, B. (1981). Speech errors: Old data in search of new theories. *Linguistics, 19,* 627–662.

Butterworth, B. (1989). Lexical access in speech production. In W. Marslen-Wilson (Ed.), *Lexical representation and process* (pp. 108–135). London: MIT Press.

Carlson, G. N., & Tanenhaus, M. K. (1989). *Linguistic structure in language processing.* Dordrecht: Kluwer.

Clark, H. H., & Marshall, C. R. (1981). Definite reference and mutual knowledge. In A. K. Joshi, B. L. Webber, & I. A. Sag (Eds.), *Elements of discourse understanding.* Cambridge: Cambridge University Press.

Dell, G. S. (1978). Slips of the mind. In M. Paradis (Ed.), *The Fourth LACUS Forum* (pp. 69–75). Columbia, SC: Hornbeam Press.

Dell, G. S., & Repka, R. (in press). Errors in inner speech. In B. Baars (Ed.), *Speech errors: A window on the mind.*

Dosher, B. A., & Corbett, A. T. (1982). Instrument inferences and verb schemata. *Memory & Cognition, 10,* 531–539.

Fodor, J. A. (1983). *The modularity of mind.* Cambridge, MA: MIT Press.

Forster, K. I. (1979). Levels of processing and the structure of the language processor. In W. E. Cooper & E. C. T. Walker (Eds.), *Sentence processing: Psycholinguistic experiments presented to Merrill Garrett.* Hillsdale, NJ: Lawrence Erlbaum Associates.

Fowler, C. A., & Housum, J. (1987). Talkers' signalling of "new" and "old" words in speech and listeners' perception and use of the distinction. *Journal of Memory and Language, 26,* 489–504.

Fromkin, V. A. (1971). The nonanomalous nature of anomalous utterances. *Language, 47,* 27–52.

Garrett, M. F. (1975). The analysis of sentence production. In G. H. Bower (Ed.), *The psychology of learning and motivation* (pp. 133–177). New York: Academic Press.

Garrett, M. F. (1980). Levels of processing in language production. In B. Butterworth (Ed.), *Language production, Vol 1* (pp. 177–220). London: Academic Press.

Garvey, C. (1975). Requests and responses in children's speech. *Journal of Child Language, 2,* 41–63.

Grice, H. P. (1975). Logic and conversation. In P. Coles & J. L. Morgan (Eds.), *Syntax and semantics, Vol. 3: Speech acts.* New York: Academic Press.

Kelly, M. H., Bock, J. K., & Keil, F. C. (1986). Prototypicality in a linguistic context: Effects on sentence structure. *Journal of Memory and Language, 25,* 59–74.

Kempen, G., & Huijbers, P. (1983). The lexicalization process in sentence production and naming: Indirect election of words. *Cognition, 14,* 185–209.

Kintsch, W., & van Dyke, T. A. (1978). Toward a model of text comprehension and production. *Psychological Review, 85,* 363–394.

Lapointe, S. (1985). A theory of verb form use in the speech of agrammatic aphasics. *Brain and Language, 24,* 100–155.

Lapointe, S., & Dell, G. S. (1989). A synthesis of some recent work in sentence production. In G. Carlson & M. K. Tanenhaus (Eds.), *Linguistic structure in language processing* (pp. 107–156). Dordrecht: Kluwer.

Levelt, W. J. M. (1983). Monitoring and self-repair in speech. *Cognition, 14,* 41–104.

Levelt, W. J. M. (1989). *Speaking: From intention to articulation.* Cambridge, MA: MIT Press.

Levelt, W. J. M., & Kelter, S. (1982). Surface form and memory in question answering. *Cognitive Psychology, 14,* 78–106.

Lieberman, P. (1963). Some effects of semantic and grammatical context on the production and perception of speech. *Language and Speech, 6,* 172–187.

MacKay, D. G. (1982). The problems of flexibility, fluency, and speed-accuracy trade-off in skilled behavior. *Psychological Review, 89,* 483–506.

MacWhinney, B., & Bates, E. (1978). Sentential devices for conveying givenness and newness: A cross-cultural developmental study. *Journal of Verbal Learning and Verbal Behavior, 17,* 539–558.

Marslen-Wilson, W., Levy, E., & Tyler, L. (1982). Producing interpretable discourse: The establishment and maintenance of reference. In R. J. Jarvella & W. Klein, (Eds.), *Speech, place, and action: Studies in deixis and related topics.* Chichester: John Wiley.

McKoon, G., & Ratcliff, R. (1986). Inferences about predictable events. *Journal of Experimental Psychology: Learning, Memory, and Cognition, 12,* 82–91.

Newport, E. L., Gleitman, H., & Gleitman, L. R. (1977). Mother, I'd rather do it myself: Some effects and non-effects of maternal speech style. In C. E. Snow & C. A. Ferguson (Eds.), *Talking to children: Language input and language acquisition.* Cambridge: Cambridge University Press.

O'Brien, E. J., Shank, D. M., Myers, J. L., & Rayner, K. (1988). Elaborative inferences during reading: Do they occur on-line? *Journal of Experimental Psychology: Learning, Memory and Cognition, 14,* 410–420.

O'Seaghdha, P. G. (1989). The dependence of lexical relatedness effects on syntactic connectedness. *Journal of Experimental Psychology: Learning, Memory, and Cognition, 15,* 73–87.

Rosch, E. (1975). Cognitive representation of semantic categories. *Journal of Experimental Psychology: General, 104,* 192–233.

Saffran, E. M. (1982). Neuropsychological approaches to the study of language. *British Journal of Psychology, 73,* 317–337.

Schwartz, M. F. (1987). Patterns of speech production deficit within and across aphasia syndromes: Applications of a psycholinguistic model. In M. Coltheart, R. Job, & G. Sartori (Eds.), *The cognitive neuropsychology of language.* Hillsdale, NJ: Lawrence Erlbaum Associates.

Seidenberg, M. S., Tanenhaus, M. K., Leiman, J. M., & Bienkowski, M. A. (1982). Automatic activation of ambiguous words in context: Some limitations of knowledge-based processing. *Cognitive Psychology, 14,* 489–537.

Shattuck-Hufnagel, S. (1979). Speech errors as evidence for serial-ordering mechanism in sentence production. In W. E. Cooper & E. C. T. Walker (Eds.), *Sentence processing: Psycholinguistic studies presented to Merrill Garrett* (pp. 295–342). Hillsdale, NJ: Lawrence Erlbaum Associates.

Shatz, M., & Gelman, R. (1973). The development of communication skills: Modification in the speech of young children as a function of listener. *Monographs for Society for Research in Child Development, 38* (Serial No. 152).

Simpson, G. B., Peterson, R. R., Casteel, M. A., & Burgess, C. (1989). Lexical and sentence context effects in word recognition. *Journal of Experimental Psychology: Learning, Memory and Cognition, 15,* 88–97.

Smith, E. E., & Medin, D. L. (1981). *Categories and concepts.* Cambridge, MA: Harvard University Press.

Snow, C. E. (1972). Mothers' speech to children learning language. *Child Development, 43,* 549–565.

Snow, C. E., & Ferguson, C. A. (Eds.). (1977). *Talking to children: Language input and acquisition.* Cambridge: Cambridge University Press.

Stemberger, J. P. (1985). An interactive activation model of language production. In A. Ellis (Ed.), *Progress in the psychology of language, (Vol. 1,* pp. 143–186). London: Lawrence Erlbaum Associates.

Tanenhaus, M. K., & Carlson, G. N. (1989). Lexical structure and language comprehension. In W. Marslen-Wilson (Ed.), *Lexical representation and process* (pp. 527–561). Cambridge, MA: MIT Press.

van Dyke, T. A. (1977). Semantic macro-structures and knowledge frames in discourse comprehension. In P. Carpenter & M. Just (Eds.), *Cognitive processes in comprehension.* Hillsdale, NJ: Lawrence Erlbaum Associates.

Linguistics and Dyslexia in Language Acquisition

Margaret B. Rawson
The Orton Dyslexia Society
Baltimore, MD

How appropriate it is to use a Festschrift to bring written tokens of celebratory honor and personal appreciation to the distinguished writer and the founding professor of linguistic studies at Swarthmore College, Lila Gleitman. In the spirit of such an occasion, each contributor brings not only words of thankful praise, but a verbally expressed part of himself or herself that has some connection with the interests of the person celebrated, yet the message will inevitably reflect each author's perspectives on whatever is his or her subject. I have, for instance, long been trying to figure out the connections between certain aspects of linguistics and the study of dyslexia, and so I have taken pleasure in focusing here on some of the interrelationships I have been seeing between these fields as they converge upon the processes and problems of the learning of one's first language, or exposure language.

I have been professionally active in the dyslexia field for many years. I have also been a serious amateur student of language, its anthropology and linguistics, for even longer. Two publications representing this double involvement and an effort to relate the fields appeared in 1970 (Rawson, 1970a, 1970b). Much has happened in both fields since that time, so it should be interesting to review their relationship in the light of 1990.

One of the major tasks of human development is the acquisition of each newborn individual of language, especially the verbal language of the culture in which he[1] grows up. Who is this newcomer? Where in his world is he and from what standpoints are we going to look at him? In the olds days of Biology

---

[1]And, of course, equally importantly *she,* though for simplicity I shall use the *non*sexist (I assure you) conventional *common gender* of old-fashioned "grammar."

101 we located him in the animal kingdom thus: "Man is a vertebrate animal of the class *Mammalia,* etc. . . ," bringing him out in the end as *Homo sapiens.* Our newcomer may turn out to be no more *"wise"* than most of us, yet the designations *Homo faber*— man, the maker—and *Homo symbolicus*—man, the symbol-user—(Kinget, 1975), will do well in further specifying his *humanity,* for that classification includes both. As far as I can, I want here to look at man and his language-acquisition task in the light of his symbol-using capacity as seen by scientists in the 1990s.

Although the use of verbal language is a distinguishing characteristic of the human species, it is not man's only route to independent, high-level, rational symbolic thinking, as it is often mistakenly claimed to be. Ask any design engineer, physicist, ingenious mechanic, or many an other, including neuropsychologist Howard Gardner (1983). It is, however, the verbal modality that concerns us just now.

The Word goes far back. "In the beginning [of man] was the word." *Homo sapiens* is, as far as we know, the first and so far the only terrestrial animal to use words as symbols (that is, as an arbitrary sign, representing meaning, an abstraction representing reality or idea) leaving room for cetaceans and perhaps other animals to put in limited claims (Griffin, 1984). The first carrier of the word may have been gesture, a valid medium for symbolic transmission based on motion, the essential element of animal life. But the spoken word has won out in terms of general usage. For us, "the word" is, first of all, the *spoken word,* primarily using auditory and kinesthetic senses—the ear and voiced kinesics of audition and speech—to carry coded symbols on sound waves. It is this system that is so venerable as to be ingrained in our species. And yet it is the mind that has the symbolic power for which the language of speech exists. Whatever the authority of Holy Writ (notice that it *is* WRIT), it seems that it was the *logos* in the human mind that was, not only mythically but perhaps biologically, "in *[its]* beginning."

They say, and it seems to be true, that "not [primarily] the eye but the brain learns to read." We can take that back a long step farther, and say "not the ear nor the tongue but the mind is at the root of spoken language." Yet (leaving gesture aside for now) it is the capacity for elaboration of the symbol base, through listening and speaking, in developmental "parity," that the child both develops and assimilates spoken language expertly in his first 5 to 6 years. As Orton, and no doubt others, conjectured and linguists have explored, the Child, the world over, has traversed the mental history of the Race by the time he is 5, 6, or 7. Then he is, if science is right, ready to take the next symbol-using leap into associating print with speech in alphabetic cultures. (There is much to say about the nonalphabetic cultures, but not just now.)

As we consider the linguistic mode, we all know that no one is born with a verbal language ready for use, and yet, no matter where he lives, each child does learn to understand and speak, and perhaps to read and write, the language to which he is exposed in the culture in which he grows up. How does he perform—and sometimes fall short of performing—this prodigious feat? The scientific evidence has become convincing that he has an inborn capacity so ancient of origin that it is below the level of awareness and generally taken for granted. Despite its recognition of the ages-long growth of human language, the scientific research community has been quite astonished by the discoveries in the past 20 years, of the high degree of built-in linguistic sophistication that lies behind the infant's first audible vocalization. The genetically blueprinted root system at the base of his individual intrauterine and infant development has turned out to be far deeper and imprinted in more specific detail than had been anticipated by even well-informed and thoughtful scientists of the earlier part of the century. Even here, we discern individual differences in learners. Although we may have marveled before, we are only in this century coming to realize how complicated and durably remarkable is the dependable inevitability of human speech and to comprehend the something of how it has contributed to the species' survival and evolution.

We realize, too, all the while, that perhaps most remarkable of all is the fact that it is with our own human brains that we are able to comprehend some part of what is now known of our own nature to which we hold the mirror. Truly, in Einstein's words, "The most incomprehensible thing about the universe is that it is comprehensible."

LINGUISTICS AND LANGUAGE DISORDERS

The study of linguistics is one way of getting to know ourselves more fully. The basic language learning process usually takes place with comparatively little effort, considering the magnitude of the task. However, in a variety of ways it can go astray. If all goes well, most of us accept mastery of speech as part of "the way we are," but some people also, because of natural curiosity or particular need, are impelled to find out how it has come about that we *are* "that way." Prominent among these searchers are the linguists who, if I understand correctly, look particularly at the nature and history of the language itself, which includes the ways in which we humans get hold of and use the verbal symbolic processes. Here is the field of *linguistics*.

What, then, constitutes the specialty of *dyslexia?* Look at it this way: If the language development system is working as expected we usually just accept it. Otherwise, in our culture, we feel some obligation to "fix it," and, contrary to much "received" opinion, this is usually possible, though often not achieved or, in fact, even undertaken. It is important to make the effort primarily because the failure causes individual and social problems in going on with life. Besides, we are puzzled and curious, and humanely concerned. Nowadays we turn selectively to workers in the life sciences, including pedagogy, to find reasons and remedies. This may lead us to focus on ''dyslexia''—a collective descriptor of inadequacy *(dys)*, in language (*-lex-*, from *legein,* to speak), especially the acquisition and use of verbal language skills at all levels.

In the literature of linguistics, Lila Gleitman and her associates (Gleitman, Gleitman, Landau, and Wanner, 1989) have recently done a full and scholarly review analysis, with copious references, of their own and other linguists' findings on the deep roots, early acquisition, demonstrable antiquity, and sophisticated structure of the language to which man is heir. A. M. and I. Y. Liberman, also, have each made a substantial recent contribution (both in 1989) to which I shall refer later. Their three excellent chapters in forthcoming books fortunately came my way as I was writing this paper; they have been invaluable, and delightful as well.

Psycholinguists like these, and people in several other disciplines, all share our concern with the understanding and treatment of dyslexia. Our ways are overlapping and complementary, rather than identical. Our perspectives are deepened by the different angles of vision.

For me to recapitulate, or even review, the developments in the field of linguistics for those likely to read this book would be carrying the proverbial coals to Newcastle. The cited authorities themselves are a far better resource of both information and reference literature. I have, however, been working for over half a century with dyslexia, which by its nature has involved me in more than casual touch with many relevant fields, including linguistics and anthropology. For a developing specialization as the field of dyslexia was when I entered it, ''wisdom is where you find it,'' and I have continued to garner rewarding harvests in linguistics, as we have all been growing. As a sampler of dyslexia-oriented contributions to the common effort, linguists and others may find of use the reference list included in my recent collection (Rawson, 1988) covering the same twenty-some years as the recent linguistic publications just mentioned or cited. Mine is by no means a complete bibliography, but rather a selective guide to the field. For myself I relish diversified involvement and opportunity to think further here about some of its implications, both philosophic and practical.

The Nature of the Problem

Each Newcomer, as a living being, from his genesis on, as he meets the world in which he is to live is under two kinds of existential constraint that shape his being. One is initiated at his start in the forms—the potentialities and limitations—determined by his genetic endowment, including its evolutionarily established blueprints and timetables of developmental stages. Here we have the growth principle that accompanies and signifies the existence of life as organized in its human-species form. The genetically ''given'' material is then acted upon and reacts to forces and materials in its pre- and postnatal environment. From his very start, then, the human being grows according to plan, modified by adaptation to his needs and purposes. Language development is the basic human need on which we focus.

It is here that we face the questions at issue in this paper: Where and how do the disciplines of linguistics, on the one hand, and of the understanding and treatment of dyslexia, on the other, come together? What results, if any, ensure from this connection? The answer to the first question lies, to being with, in the parallel but separate histories of the two lines of endeavor and, in retrospect, where they have joined in common purposes.

Parallel Histories

Historically, between about 1910 and 1960, Jespersen, Sapir and Whorf, Harris, Chomsky and their fellows in linguistics were contributing substantially to knowledge and thinking about language and its structure and development *as language.* During the same period Samuel T. Orton (1925, 1937) was beginning to identify the ''specific development language disability'' and Anna Gillingham (1921) soon, in 1928, to join him, was working on teaching children who had difficulty in learning to read, write, and spell—the then salient aspect of the problem that was later, greatly extended, to be called dyslexia. (See especially Gillingham & Stillman, 1936, the first of a series of editions of the same title[2]).

By the middle 1960s both of the groups we are looking at here were well established in their respective adjacent fields, known to each other, and, as we look back, both about to experience significant growth.

Early on, each group of workers had begun, naturally, with questions emanating from what was currently most relevant to its interests: the status of linguistic knowledge; the neurobiology of the language function; the psychology of learning; school reading failure, or related subjects. All, however, were in some way concerned with the acquisition of language by the human learner. Although at first mostly not yet associated with each other, they were moving on somewhat parallel courses, with individuals from each clan feeling pretty much at home in the others' campgrounds, where the disciplinary interfaces were initially ill-defined and are still overlapping.

The presenting problems for the linguists, then as now, had to do with what the phenomenon of language was about, how languages represented thought, how they differed from one another and what were their deep similarities. How did these phenomena persist and how were they passed down through the ages and, finally, how should today's elders initiate their juniors into the language skills in ways consistent with new linguistic insights?

---

[2]Only the revisions of 1956 and 1959 are still in print.

The ongoing focus of the dyslexia-oriented group, rooted, as already referred to, in the multidisciplinary personnel, research, and practice of the original Orton/Gillingham period, was like the linguists in consistently pursuing its own directions of interest. In about the mid-60s each group entered an era of growth in understanding, research, educational practice, and expansion. The historical events and personal and ideational changes are at least partially treated in my "The Orton Trail: 1896 to 1986" (Rawson, 1987) and in works by Gleitman and colleagues and I. Y. Liberman, to mention only those already cited. The changes in both groups have brought them closer together in understanding the nature of language as it redounds to their respective purposes.

Orton and Gillingham and the linguists had begun, as most people do, with their then-presenting problems, such as school-age reading disability, or how children manage to acquire speech or stumble in doing so. The questions they addressed, however, were by no means new ones, but a new era of understanding had begun, even in the 1920s. It was already apparent, or soon became so, that each question was part of a much larger one the working groups had in common—the whole of the language function, throughout the lifespan. With its branching particulars the pioneers, their associates and, in turn, their professional descendants became increasingly engaged. Publication in their respective literatures continued to mark broadening and productive innovations. In what is now known as the dyslexia world there were considerable, though not very widely spread, advances in clinical and educational practices. Early applications in linguistics, too, were more promising than well known.

The years since about 1970 are also rich with history. Intricate, yet ultimately unifying and simplifying, patterns and content in interdisciplinary parallels, junctures and fusions have moved both groups forward. It is now increasingly recognized that the universality of both human linguistic inheritance and language learning differences are of worldwide significance, central to us all. Conferences recently have been widespread—Italy, England, or Greece; San Francisco, Delhi, or Prague, and more—almost everywhere! The participants at each meeting have also represented many countries and cultures and not only a profusion but often a *fusion*, of interests. Even adequate listing of publications relevant just to our restricted topic would far exceed this paper's space limitations.

As I review my years of struggle with the complicated subject represented in the title of this paper, I find myself thinking of the Mississippi River and all its many confluences. We might picture Samuel Orton and Anna Gillingham as rather like the Allegheny and the Monongahela together forming the Ohio, joined by linguistic waters of the Missouri. Right now I think we as professions, and two parts of my life, are together, somewhere south of St. Louis but with a lot of insufficiently explored and mapped territory, both upstream and down.

Common Path

Recognition of the fields' commonalities as discussed previously, brought me in the early 1970s to the formulation of an agenda for teaching language that seemed to me to enwrap the subject. *"Teach the language as it is to the person as he is."* People have liked the maxim; it is easy take hold of and assent to. Simply and without jargon, it focuses on four neat components: "Teach"—"the language as it is"—"to the person"—"as he is." As we reflect, of course, we know that right here the simplicity ends, for the implications are so manifold—a judgment underscored by experience, whichever our particular field. From the text sentence there could easily grow a four-section lecture, or four volumes, or a challenge that could more than fill four related lifetime careers, but for the present, perhaps four brief statements may serve to put the case in 1990.

To "teach," in the present context, has requisites in the teacher's knowledge, philosophy, and personal wholeness—*for understanding*—and in his or her high-level, technically competent training in the relevant skills in language—*for mastery*—both permeated by all that goes into the *pedagogical relationship*. To "teach" to these criteria should most effectively open the newcomer's way into his language and his culture.

To teach "the language as it is" we need first of all to *know it*, and then we can talk about how to share the knowledge with a novice. Obviously, to us, but not, alas, to far too many of our confreres in pedagogy, one needs to know much more about this "language as it is"—both in the ordinary sense as it is now and under the deep linguistic and metalinguistic analysis that points to how it has been functioning for every newcomer through the eons. We have to be able to take off many (but not all) the linguistic wraps, and some of the metalinguistic ones. Here the knowing and the teaching are warp and woof, as they often *must* be in the dyslexia case—and *should* be in *all* of education.

"The person"—"as he is" we must see simultaneously from two sides. He is, first, "the person," *homo generis* (who learns to manage symbols the *human* way). At the same time, the pupil/student "as he is" is individual, unique. He shares his humanity with all others of his species; for its purposes his culture may put him in a group with certain similarities, *but it is as an individual that he learns*.

This is "the person as he is" to whom we propose to "teach the language as it is." The subject of study and the object of treatment of both of our professional groups, he is worthy and needful of all that, singly or together, we can supply. This is our four-part mission—and an outline for "the rest of the lecture."

Some of us have initially a consuming interest in *language*, a system that man can use to convey thought; others begin with *man* as an animal that can use language as a symbol system to convey thought. In this case it really matters which is subject and which object or agent, for that influences, when it does not dominate, our field of study. MAN, who has a special ability to use language, or LANGUAGE, a function especially useful to man; it is not so much contrast as angles of vision. There are times when one needs, like a simultaneous translator, to be at home in both worlds at once, not a simple task but, I think, worth considerable effort.

Let us look briefly at a few common issues of the two views.

Take man's equipment for becoming a language user. All he has to work with are some second-hand tools from Evolution's for-survival shop, but man is adaptable over the long as well as the short haul; he is so vulnerable he has to be. So he uses breathing, eating, and noise-making equipment to make himself into a speaker. The tools are not perfectly suitable, but they are "good enough" to serve his mind's overriding unconsciously felt need for a vehicle for transmission of symbolic thought. His auditory equipment, devised for protection and used for a start-up model, was skillfully grown into an intricate, usable system for speech reception. The two processes had to develop in synchrony, in *parity*, to use Mattingly and A. Liberman's concept (as quoted in A. Liberman, 1989), if they were to work. That took a long, long evolutionary time, as Mind made Man and Man made Language (and I make mythology, perhaps), pursuing a system to serve Mind's needs. We say Mind is the Master; so it used what it had to work with and a human speaker using symbolic language is the, to us prodigious, result.

As with any R&D project, in the evolutionary process of establishing language, there must have been many glitches, bugs, and failures, through amazingly few in proportion to all of mankind's existence. Some imperfect but usable models survived to serve their ingenious individual owners' determined purposes. Moses had his Aaron, Demosthenes his pebbles, and we, today, have specialists, informed in linguistics and speech therapy, prepared to identify and treat early speech/language problems.

For another example, take "first language." An individual's language *as acquired by him,* from *his unique* birth onward, is the language that will become as all-pervadingly important to him as is the air he breathes. "First language" to most of us initially means the child's acquisition of his own mother tongue, his "learning to speak as his elders do," but thanks to the developments in linguistics, we now have an evolutionary stage-set of increasingly convincing realism. We can view a first language *itself* as the linguists do—a deep-rooted capacity for symbolic thought that can be coded into verbal forms, a capacity ready to be triggered into use by hearing the speech of the culture that surrounds the child, whatever his ethnic origin. Far more complicated than it sounds, basic language comes into the human being's life long before he is ready to utter his first word, which is itself but a milestone to be followed rapidly by the mastery of speech in his "exposure language." Always this will be *his* "first language"—what, basically, "language" will mean to him. We see him becoming more adept in the management of his exposure language than almost anyone starting with another mother tongue can ever become. The characteristic identity it has taken in his personal repertoire by about age 5 will still be in some basic ways shaping his thought, intentions and expression in old age.

By about age 5 or 6 the child has the spoken language, or Code I, department of his phylogenetically programmed first language filled out ontogenetically to match his exposure culture. There has always been a wide range of individual language learning facility but for practical purposes the built-in program is so strong that it seems in due course to override all but the most extreme sets of risk factors. In spite of everything, the symbolic urge will somehow find expression!

We think of the language learning (call it -*lexic*-) facility dimension as ranging from top-talented, where learning is quick and easy. (*eu*- means good, so cal it *eulexia*) through many shades of aptness that call for appropriate, but not inordinate, effort (*lexia*, if it needs a name at all), to being so slow to speak that the would-be learners are "at risk" or are failing, (call it: *dyslexia, dyslexic, Dyslexia I* [pre-literate], all having to do with *dys*, poor, and *lexia*, language, as learned and managed). The more clinically careful our observations, the clearer and more significant are the early traits and patterns that seem to relate to the "dyslexic constitution."

Left to themselves, practically all children will come to adequate terms with the spoken language, but the culture owes them the degree of help they need to become fully competent in it as nearly on-schedule as their other development permits. The best way to lend a hand to a novice not yet able to "go it alone" is a perennial problem of nurturance that can sometimes require a high degree of expertise, as when a professional therapist temporarily lends a segment of skills to a learner who will, given time and help, build its replacement into his own repertoire.

A learner thrives on the *right* challenges. The feeling of having "invented a wheel" now and then is part of the good life, but the alphabet is not everybody's "wheel." Literacy is, I believe, almost universally *achievable*, but not, like speech, *inevitable*. The rudiments of literacy have a phylogenetic, Johnny-come-lately toehold, albeit a variable, somewhat undependable one. Still, what man has done once, like driving a car or catching a trout, people will come to do more and more as a matter of course. But talents differ and so dyslexic people, for instance, have especial need to know that the alphabet is no secret but a friend and often they must be given step-by-step tuition, as is now increasingly possible. To rely on "discovery" here is, in a different metaphor, to expect "bricks without straw." To let students in on the cipher and teach them to use it is good strategy for all learners; *for dyslexics it is essential.*

Here, near the end of this paper, I think we find the heart or core of the literacy problem for ourselves, and to some extent for all language communities. To keep our global village functioning increasingly requires verbal communication in visual form—reading and writing. A universal requirement for carrying out this practice is a system for representing the time sequence of audible speech in visible writing, two-dimensional graphic sequential arrays. Tempting as it is to explore alternative graphic forms, for the present we must ignore them and confine ourselves to the alphabetic code. This Code II is actually a cipher on the speech code, Code I. As with listening and speaking, parity between reading and writing, in both development and use, makes communication possible.

The variability in language acquisition talent has given rise to problems in what Klasen (1972) called the "syndrome of dyslexia," with what I think of as its "many faces." The essence of the *alphabetic principle* on which are based the written forms of a dominant group of languages, including our own, lies in the stable relationship in each one of that language's phonemes (distinguishable sounds that matter) and the graphemes (visible alphabetic characters that represent them at least well enough for their users' mutual understanding).

Figure 7.1 represents the domain of verbal language; Fig. 7.2 is a suggested overlay depicting intersensory pathways subserving language learning. These diagrams, together, organize the coverage of the range of diagnostic assessment and the Orton/Gillingham approach to teaching. For fuller discussion see Rawson 1970a, and 1970b, 1988).

I know intimately only the English language, as it is heard and spoken, written and read, but there are some worldwide language family resemblances. To make full use of the tremendous advantages of an alphabet, the representational principle must be understood, the sounds distinguished and articulated, the letter shapes remembered and reproduced. This is only a part of the problem but is the *essential alphabetic principle*. There can be difficulties in all these components, or faces, of dyslexia, but two factors are responsible for most significant problems: a) the awareness of the principle and b) the distinguishing as separate entities of the phonemes that are phonetically wrapped together in the syllables of the words that carry semantic meanings.

In what Sheldon White called "the matrix of developmental changes [in the child] between 5 and 7 years" (White, 1970), the most important for us, and quite likely for the child himself, is the development of this capacity for phoneme segmentation in speech, for it leads, we think, more directly than any other to his ability to learn to read and write. This is, of course, not the "whole answer," for it seems to me that there is none, or at least none available to man in his present state of knowledge and power of comprehension. Still, what the linguists have brought into focus as "metalinguistic awareness" does seem to be at the core of catching onto, or acquiring at some slower speed, the skills necessary to handle not only the phonology of one's language but also, if it be an alphabetic one, the literal cipher in which it is encoded into written form. This is true for the beginner with written language, no matter what his natural aptitude, but it seems crucial for the inept learner of language—the one most likely to engage our interest as dyslexic.

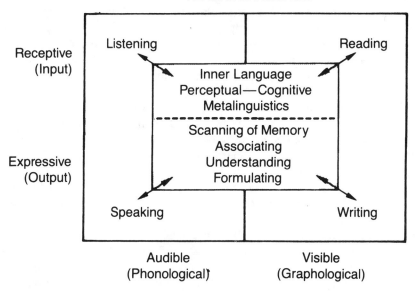

FIG. 7.1.   Analysis of verbal language. (After Rawson, 1968). See Rawson 1988.

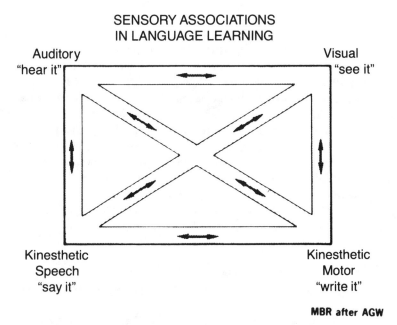

MBR after AGW

FIG. 7.2.   Sensory associations in language learning. (After A. G. Wolff, 1970).
See Rawson 1988.

The ideas themselves are not new; they rest comfortably in minds nurtured in the Orton/Gillingham approach to dyslexia.[3] It is the setting of the concepts in the scientific matrix of linguistics, the recognition of their crucial importance in educational thinking and practice, and their application in classroom experiments that, in my opinion, give them highly significant value. It has been stimulating and deeply satisfying to watch the ideas of the Liberman partnership and like-minded others productively explore this subject area and to see them and their students putting findings into schoolroom practice at all ages and in individual cases. Concurrently in the dyslexia field, theorists like Galaburda (1989), Galaburda, Rosen and Sherman (1989), and practitioners like Henry (1988) have contributed to the common resource fund for everyone's use. The people mentioned, however carefully chosen as examples, can hardly begin to represent the range covered by those who try to understand and deal with dyslexia. They work on differing dimensions and at many levels of functioning, "from reading to neurons," said Galaburda (1989), and at the several developmental stages beyond primary school and into full language competence.

There are, of course, many more areas of important interaction and collaboration, even sometimes double-identity, in our specialized common corner of the human language field. Still further beyond our particular approaches to language acquisition, there is a growing public consciousness of need for drastic educational change that gives hope for more ample support for educational initiatives. Some of the ideas from our areas are young like the formulations for pedagogy of "multisensory approaches" or "metalinguistic awareness," some as old as Bloomfield/Barnhart or Orton/Gillingham, and some as hoary as evolution, like the alphabetic principle whose return to the schoolroom I think we may now rather safely predict. I like to think our *combined* efforts are helping substantially in clearing away a few major, as well as many minor, roadblocks in the way of language education, re-education, and, indeed, in meeting the lifelong recurrence of needs in the ongoing acquisition of what is still one's first language. In the light of all this, I feel encouraged about movement toward our common goals. I like to think that what is particularly important to this paper is that it contains a positive message to the Festschrift's honoree from the world of dyslexia—that now we can "teach the language as it is to the person as he is." Her work has contributed so considerably to justifying that optimism as to be cause for celebration.

REFERENCES

Galaburda, A. M. (Ed.). (1989). *From reading to neurons*. Cambridge, MA: MIT Press.

---

[3]The Orton/Gillingham approach is a phrase introduced by June L. Orton in 1966 to represent not a doctrine or a specific method, but an approach, rational and systematic in nature, based upon the reality of language and the nature of man, open to and welcoming growth in the light of increasing knowledge and understanding.

Galaburda, A. M., Rosen, G. D., and Sherman, G. F. (1989). The neural origin of developmental dyslexia: Implications for medicine, neurology, and cognition. In A. M. Galaburda (Ed.), *From reading to neurons* (pp. 377–404). Cambridge, MA: MIT Press.

Gardner, H. (1983). *Frames of mind: The theory of multiple intelligences.* New York: Basic Books.

Gillingham, A. (1921). Experimental methods—tests. *School and Home.* Spring, 1921. New York City: Parents and Teachers Association, Ethical Culture School.

Gillingham, A., & Stillman, B. W. (1936). *Remedial training for children with specific disability in reading, spelling and penmanship* (rev. ed.). New York: Author.

Gillingham, A., & Stillman, B. (1956, 1970). *Remedial training for children with specific disability in reading, spelling and penmanship* (rev. eds.). Cambridge, MA: Educators Publishers Service.

Gleitman, L., Gleitman, H., Landau, B., & Wanner, E. (1989). Great expectations. In A. M. Galaburda (Ed.), *From reading to neurons* (pp. 91–132). Cambridge, MA: MIT Press.

Griffin, D. R. (1984). *Animal thinking.* Cambridge, MA: Harvard University Press.

Henry, M. K. (1988). Beyond phonics: Integrated decoding and spelling instruction based on word order and structure. *Annals of Dyslexia, 38,* 258–275.

Kinget, G. M. (1975). *On being human: A systematic view.* New York: Harcourt, Brace, Jovanovich.

Klasen, E. (1972). *The syndrome of dyslexia.* Baltimore: University Park Press.

Liberman, A. M. (1989). Reading is hard just because listening is easy. In C. von Euler (Ed.), *Wenner-Gren International Symposium Series: Brain and Reading.* (pp. 197–205). Hampshire, England: Macmillan.

Liberman, I. Y. (1971). Speech and the lateralization of language. *Bulletin of the Orton Society, 21,* 71–87.

Liberman, I. Y. (1989). Phonology and beginning reading revisited. In C. von Euler (Ed.), *Wenner-Gren International Symposium Series: Brain and Reading,* (pp. 207–220). Hampshire, England: Macmillan.

Orton, S. T. (1937). *Reading, writing and speech problems in children.* New York: W. W. Norton. Also in S. T. Orton, *reading, writing and speech problems in children and selected papers.* Austin, Texas; Pro-Ed. (1989).

Rawson, M. B. (1970a). The structure of English: The language to be learned. *Bulletin of the Orton Society, 20,* 103–123.

Rawson, M. B. (1970b). Semantics-1970: An essay-review. *Bulletin of the Orton Society, 20,* 128–131.

Rawson, M. B. (1987). The Orton Trail: 1896–1986. *Annals of Dyslexia, 37,* 36–50.

Rawson, M. B. (1988). *The many faces of dyslexia.* (Monograph No. 5, 1988.) Baltimore, MD: The Orton Dyslexia Society.

White, S. H. (1970). Some general outlines of the matrix of developmental changes between 5 and 7 years. *Bulletin of the Orton Society, 20,* 41–57.

Spatial Language
and Spatial Cognition

Ray Jackendoff
Brandeis University
Barbara Landau
Columbia University and
University of California, Irvine

Fundamental to spatial knowledge in all species are the representations underlying object recognition, object search, and navigation through space. What sets us aside from other species is the ability to use these representations to express our spatial experience, talking about what things are, where they are, and how we might get to them. In this paper, we address two questions crucial to understanding how this is accomplished. First, how does language draw on spatial cognition so that we can manage to talk about what we perceive? Second, how does spatial language thereby provide a window on the nature of spatial cognition?

Our goal here is to explore how language encodes objects and spatial relationships, and to do this in a way that is compatible with constraints on nonlinguistic spatial understanding. At the same time, we will use evidence from language to provide boundary conditions on a satisfactory theory of spatial cognition: Our premise is that any aspect of spatial understanding that can be expressed in language must also be present in spatial representations.

The general context of our approach assumes that the representations underlying spatial knowledge coordinate the representations specific to each of the perceptual modalities, and translate them into a common format which is neither visual nor haptic nor aural, but *spatial*. We also assume that these spatial representations must be translatable into another form of representation specific to the motor system, in order to initiate and guide behavior: We can touch what we see, look at what we hear, and avoid obstacles as we navigate through space. Finally, in order to account for the language of space, there must be a translation between the spatial format and the representations proprietary to language.

Our discussion of spatial language is in three parts. First, we discuss language pertaining to object identification and its bearing on some current theories of the encoding of object shape. Second, we discuss language pertaining to the locations of objects. Differences in these two aspects of language lead us to the third issue: How the identification and location of objects are integrated in spatial cognition and in language.

1. TALKING ABOUT OBJECTS

In the average adult vocabulary, there are roughly 10,000–15,000 names for things: count nouns that label different kinds of objects. For a large proportion of object categories, one important criterion for identification is shape (Landau, Smith, & Jones, 1988). This means that the spatial representations that are linked to object names must provide enough different shape descriptions, configured in the proper way, to be able to distinguish all the kinds of objects we linguistically categorize on the basis of appearance.

From the nonlinguistic side, a promising approach to the problem of shape description takes object shapes to be represented componentially, as in Marr (1982) and Biederman (1987). In Marr's approach, what corresponds most closely to our notion of spatial representation is his 3D model level, the format in which objects are encoded in object-centered format, independent of viewer's perspective. The representational levels closer to the retinal array correspond to what we are calling the specifically visual representations; even though Marr speaks of the 3D model as part of vision, our framework suggests that it should in fact be capable of accepting inputs derived from haptic/kinesthetic sources as well. In addition, Jackendoff (1987a, 1987b) shows that 3D model representations can be translated in part into representations suitable for linguistic expression.

The primitives for object description in the 3D model are:

1. A set of principles for describing "generalized cones" in terms of an axis and a cross-section.
2. A principle for elaborating a main axis with a subsidiary axis of a particular size and orientation relative to the main axis.

Principle 2 applies recursively, so that objects in the 3D model representation are composed of parts, each of which may have a further decomposition. As a result, highly detailed shapes can emerge, making the representations in principle rich enough to support the extensive vocabulary of object names seen in language.

Biederman's (1987) approach to object description can be viewed as an extension of the 3D model system. Like Marr, Biederman proposes that object shapes decompose into parts, but he further suggests that the parts can be represented by a small specific set of generalized cones (N = 36), which he calls "geons." Given even a very small set of attachment relationships among the cones—such as "end-to-end" or "top-to-side"—and only a few iterations, the system can generate at least as many object shapes as there are object names.

Each of these systems is capable of generating a wide range of particular object shapes from primitives. For example, Marr describes schemata for the human figure and various animals, and Biederman additionally describes such objects as airplanes and cameras. In principle, these systems should be able to generate a sufficient number of descriptions to cover all named objects (and, with a suitable similarity metric, could even account for differences among named categories such as *person* vs. *gorilla*, whose shapes are quite similar). We believe, however, that evidence from language suggests the need for additional kinds of descriptions.

We therefore wish to make a few elementary observations about spatial and linguistic descriptions of objects that point to gaps in the Marr and Biederman machinery. In each case we suggest appropriate enrichments of spatial representations that remain within the spirit of the Marr/Biederman approach.

1.1 Names for Spatial Parts: Orienting Axes

In Marr's representation of the human figure, there is a major vertical axis that defines the orientation of the torso; the limbs and head are attached in terms of position and angle along this axis. However, neither Marr nor Biederman provides a means for identifying the orientation of principal or subsidiary axes, such that one can linguistically describe an object as having an inherent *top, bottom, front, back*, and *sides*, based on features of its own shape.[1] For instance, the fact that the nose, the feet, and the belly button point in the same direction (hence are on the *front* of the body) or that the arms are attached opposite one another and orthogonal to the front (hence are on the *sides*) does not emerge as a principled aspect of the description.

A way to express these regularities is to extend the theory of axes in two ways. First, in addition to axes that are expanded into generalized cones (or geons), we introduce the possibility of auxiliary axes that serve to orient the geon radially. Let us call the main axis of the geon its *generating axis* and the other axes its *orienting axes*. In the case of the human body, the principal generating axis defines the generalized cone of the torso; there are two orienting axes, defining the front-to-back direction and the side-to-side direction.

Second, an axis can optionally be marked as intrinsically *directed* or *symmetrical*. A directed axis indicates inherent regularities dependent on distinguishing one end from the other. For example, the directed front-to-back axis of the human

---

[1]We are speaking here specifically of inherent top, bottom, front, back, and sides, based on the object's shape. There are also contextually imposed uses of these terms; see section 2.3.2.

figure establishes the regularity of alignment for the nose, feet, and belly button. A symmetric axis indicates regularities dependent on equivalent elaborations at both ends. For example, the side-to-side axis of the human figure establishes the symmetry of the limbs and face parts.

These markings can be carried by the generating axis of a geon as well as by the orienting axes. In the human figure, for example, the main generating axis is a directed axis that distinguishes top from bottom. In Biederman's camera, if the long side-to-side dimension is the generating axis for the geon, it is a symmetric generating axis.

The combination of generating and orienting axes found in the human figure is not the only possibility. For example, an arrow has a directed generating axis but no significant orienting axes. The human hand has an oriented generating axis (wrist-to-fingers, following Marr), and two directed orienting axes (back-to-palm and pinky-to-thumb). In each case, linguistic requirements—the need to label spatial parts—motivate an augmentation of the expressive power of the spatial representations.

1.2 Names for Objects Best Described as Surfaces

What kinds of things can have an edge? Examples that come to mind are sheets of paper, phonograph records, crackers, table tops, blackboards, rugs, roads, and lakes. What these have in common is that they are principally extended in two dimensions, with a relatively negligible thickness (at least in the relevant context); the edge can then be defined as the linear boundary of this surface.

How are such objects to be encoded in spatial representation? It seems intuitively odd to treat a phonograph record as a very fat cylinder with a very short main axis passing through the hole. However, this is the most natural way to formally generate it in the Marr/Biederman framework of volumetric primitives. Furthermore, a lake hardly lends itself at all to such descriptions. For instance, if its generating axis is taken as perpendicular to the surface, the description is entirely counterintuitive. If its generating axis is taken as parallel to the surface (as it might be if the lake is relatively long and narrow), it seems odd to have it fall in the interior of the geon, as in Biederman's repertoire: That would put the axis underwater.

The problem in these cases is that the Marr/Biederman volumetric primitives require one to generate a volume directly from a linear axis. A more intuitively satisfying analysis of these objects is that they are schematized as *surfaces*, elaborated into a volume by adding a *thickness*. The surface in turn may perhaps be generated by a suitable extension of the theory of generalized cones to the two-dimensional case, as Biederman suggests in passing. On this analysis, the phonograph record is schematized as basically a disk; the lake is schematized basically as its surface. It seems to be that an object can be said to have an edge just in case it has such a spatial representation.

In addition to object names for surface-like objects, there are other words that benefit from having such analysis available in spatial representation. Two classes come to mind: (a) two-dimensional shape terms like *square, circle, oval, trapezoid*, and so on, and (b) general terms for "thickened surfaces" such as *slab, sheet, layer, slice, lamina*, and *stratum*. Generalizing beyond nouns, the adjectives *thick* and *thin* can also be seen to place a metric on the elaboration of a surface into a volume, indicating further the general usefulness of this analysis.

1.3 Names for "Negative" Object Parts

Some entities may be best conceptualized as "negative parts" of objects, as alluded to by Hoffman and Richards (1984) and Herskovits (1986). Compare a *ridge* and a *groove*. A ridge is conceptualized as a protrusion from the surface of an object, with an extended linear generating axis parallel to the surface of the object. It has a directed orienting axis that projects into the surface of the object, giving the ridge a top and a bottom, plus a (roughly) symmetrical orienting axis that defines its sides. It therefore can be easily described as a part of the object within the geonic system as elaborated so far.

Now consider a groove. It is conceptualized as a depression in the surface of an object, with an extended linear generating axis parallel to the surface of the object. It has a directed orienting axis that projects into the surface of the object, giving the groove a top and a bottom, plus a (roughly) symmetrical axis that defines its sides. But it cannot be described within the geonic system, because it is not possible to conceive of it as attached to the object.

A natural way to think of a groove is as a "negative part," a shaped volume scooped out of the object instead of added to it. That is, it is a shape defined by "lack of substance" rather than substance, as in the case of normal parts. Other than that, a negative part evidently has shape descriptors—and a linguistic description—essentially parallel to those of ordinary parts. Notice, for example, that a groove not only has a top, bottom, and sides; it can be described as long or short, broad or narrow, deep or shallow.

Other negative part names are *hole, pit* (a "negative" *bump*), *notch, slot, scratch, depression, cavity*, and possibly *dent*. Words that name "negative objects" are *valley, cave, well*, and *door* and *window* (in the sense of "opening in a wall" rather than the object used to close off such an opening). Thus again a simple enrichment of spatial representation affords revealing analysis for a wide variety of things we can name (though they are not strictly speaking objects this time).

1.4 Names for Containers and Related Objects

Objects like cups, bowls, boxes, jars, tanks, and so forth are all *containers*. What is their spatial representation? One possibility, consistent with what has gone so far, is that a cup, for instance, is a cylinder out of which a large coaxial negative cylinder has been scooped. However, an alternative that has a certain intuitive appeal is that a cup is basically a thickened surface that encloses a cylindrical space—that is, the sides and bottom of the cup are not the residue of extensive scooping but rather basically surfaces.

We are not certain which of these analyses is correct, but there is some evidence that language distinguishes containers from solid objects; roughly, containers are objects that can hold things inside them (see section 2.2.1). Should one want to encode a class of containers in spatial representation, one could distinguish ''solid'' from ''hollow'' geons. Solid geons would be encoded as uniformly substantial; hollow geons would be shapes whose substance is distributed only over their surfaces, leaving a shaped empty space inside. (The openings in containers, say the top of a cup, might further be described as negative parts in an otherwise unbroken surface.) In addition to the containers mentioned above, hollow geons would nicely describe cars and other closed vehicles, houses and other buildings, stomachs, eggshells, balloons, bubbles, violins, and drums. Again, a simple parameter added to spatial representation affords an intuitively natural encoding of a significant new class of objects.

1.5 Other Cases

In addition to these factors, spatial representation needs descriptors for surface features like *dots, stripes*, and *marks*. Names for textural features, another aspect of the surface, shade imperceptibly from purely visual terms like *red* and *shiny*, through terms available to both vision and touch like *jagged, bumpy*, and *flat*, to those that seem more specifically haptic, such as *rough, smooth, hard, soft*, and *slippery*. These require further extensions to the theory that do not concern us here.

In addition to our proposed additions to the descriptive power of the Marr/Biederman framework, it remains to be shown that the whole system of decomposition into parts, each composed of a generalized cone, can be adapted to the tolerances necessary for object category discrimination. For instance, descriptions must be potentially fine-grained enough that one can decide which objects are to be named *horse* and which *donkey*, or which *dog* and which *wolf*. On the other hand, they must be potentially indeterminate enough to allow all the variation in shape allowable within each of these named categories, for example, the differences between Dalmatians and Pekinese dogs, and to allow the variation in number, placement, size, and shape of arms on a saguaro cactus. How these tolerances for discrimination are to be formalized is beyond the scope of this study.

In short, the spatial representation of objects by shape is a rich combinatorial system, involving as basic units at least generalized cones and surfaces, schematized in terms of generating axes and orienting axes. Each of these units may be "solid," "hollow," or "negative." They are combined hierarchically to form complex object descriptions, in the fashion described by Marr and Biederman. In addition, they are detailed in terms of surface and textural features. All of this is encoded within a framework that can specify tolerances acceptable for category membership.

2. TALKING ABOUT SPATIAL RELATIONS

The Marr/Biederman framework and all the amplifications discussed so far concern object recognition and categorization, that is, *what* an object is. None of this addresses *where* the object is or, if in motion, its path of movement. But of course that is an essential part of spatial cognition—and an essential part of what we talk about in spatial language.

Here we are on much less firm ground on the nonlinguistic side of the investigation. We know of no theory of visually based object location that is comparable to the Marr object shape theory and its relatives, in which one can begin to trace the representational pathways all the way from the retinal array to a multimodal representation that can justifiably be called spatial. So in this section we rely more heavily on linguistic analysis to suggest what components of spatial representations need to be encoded in a nonlinguistic theory of spatial location. We draw especially on work of Talmy (1978, 1983), Jackendoff (1983), and Herskovits (1986).

The canonical English expression of a spatial relation between two objects does not relate them directly. Rather, one object (the *reference object*) is used to define a *region* in which the other object (the *figural object* or *figure*) is located. For example, in the sentence *The cat is sitting on the mat*, the prepositional phrase *on the mat* defines a region in terms of the reference object (the mat), and the figure (the cat) is in turn located in that region. Within this complex, the preposition *on* is the linguistic element that expresses the spatial relation, in this case "contact with the surface of the reference object." In addition to prepositions, there are many verbs that incorporate spatial relations; these can (almost invariably) be paraphrased by a simpler verb plus a preposition. For instance, *enter* can be paraphrased by *go into*, *approach* by *go toward*, and *cross* by *go across*. (See Jackendoff 1983, 1990 for formalization of these relations.) Here we focus on only spatial prepositions, a fairly complete list of which appears in Table 8.1.

One of the most salient facts about prepositions is that there seem to be surprisingly few of them in comparison to the number of names for different kinds of objects. (In fact, there are few enough prepositions that they are usually considered part of the "closed-class" vocabulary, along with auxiliaries, determiners, and inflections.) We can get an idea of the order of magnitude of different spatial relations expressed in English by counting the prepositions (see Table 8.1). There is something on the order of 80 to 100, depending on how

TABLE 8.1
Prepositions of English

about	*Compounds*
above	in back of
across	in between
after	in front of
against	on top of
along	to the left of
alongside	to the right of
amid(st)	to the side of
among(st)	
around	
at	*Intransitive prepositions*
atop	afterward(s)
before	apart
behind	away
below	back
beneath	backward
beside	downstairs
between	downward
betwixt	east
beyond	forward
by	here
down	inward
from	left
in	N-ward (homeward, shoreward, etc.)
inside	north
into	outward
near	right
nearby	sideways
off	south
on	straight
onto	there
opposite	together
out	upstairs
outside	upward
over	west
past	
through	
throughout	*Nonspatial prepositions*
to	ago
toward	as
under	because of
underneath	during
up	for
upon	like
via	of
with	since
within	until
without	

one counts. Of course, many of these are polysemous, and quite a few are nonspatial (*during*, for instance, is purely temporal), so this count gives us only a ballpark figure. But compare it to the number of count nouns in English—some tens of thousands. Again, many of these are polysemous, and many are not object names, so the count is only rough. But even supposing the count is drastically biased, there is a difference between the two of approximately two orders of magnitude: For every spatial relation expressible in English, there are perhaps a hundred object names. This qualitative difference is reproduced in ever language we know of. (If there were a language with even a thousand prepositions, someone would certainly have raised a big hue and cry about it.)

Given the small number of prepositions, it is not surprising that they exhibit considerable constraint in how they express spatial relationships. The following subsections will present what we believe to be a rather comprehensive enumeration of the factors involved in defining the spatial relations expressed in English. The factors divide rather naturally into three parts: (a) asymmetries between the figural and reference objects, (b) constraints on geometries of the figural and reference objects, and (c) constraints on the relation of the figural object to the reference object.

2.1 Asymmetry Between Figure and Reference Object

Due to the distinction between reference object and figure, the standard expression of spatial location is strikingly asymmetrical. To illustrate, we have annotated the figure and reference objects in the sentences in (1):

(1) a. The book [figure] is lying on the table [reference object].
    b. The train [figure] reached the station [reference object].
    c. The star [figure] is inside the circle [reference object].
    d. The circle [figure] lies around (surrounds) the star [reference object].

Note that (1c) and (1d) can describe the very same physical stimulus. However, they organize it differently, reversing figure and reference object. These different organizations appear to reflect differences in the encoding of the stimulus in spatial representation, corresponding to reversals of figure and ground shown in classical studies of perception (Hochberg, 1978).

As has been noted by Talmy, not every pair of objects creates such an ambiguous stimulus: If the objects are unequal in size and/or mobility, the larger and more stable invariably takes the role of reference object. Consider (2):

(2) a. The book is on the table.
    b. ??The table is under the book.

It does not seem to follow from any fact specifically pertaining to language that the table is a more plausible reference object and the book a more plausible figure in this context. Rather, we believe, it is more likely to follow from principles of spatial organization, which require that an object be located relative to some other object—presumably one that will facilitate successful search.

Even what would seem to be a symmetrical spatial relation—adjacency—is subject to the asymmetry of figure–reference object dyads, as shown in (3):

(3) a.   The bicycle is next to the house.
    b. ??The house is next to the bicycle.

These asymmetries in linguistic expression suggest that a fundamental component of spatial representation is an asymmetrical marking of located and reference objects. Consistent with this hunch, such an asymmetry has been found in psychological studies of distance estimation between key landmarks and various located objects (e.g., Rosch, 1975; Sadalla, Burroughs, & Staplin, 1980).

2.2 Constraints on the Geometry of the Reference Object

Let us examine how the objects being related play a role in the system of spatial relation. Having just discussed the intricate shape descriptors required for object naming, it is worth considering whether the same descriptors are used when describing an object's place. What is striking is in fact how sparsely both the figure and reference objects appear to be represented. This section deals with constraints on the reference object; the even looser constraints on the figure are described in sections 2.3.5 and 2.3.6.

Taking a simple case, there seem to be no prepositions whose reference object must be analyzed in terms of a particular geon. A hypothetical example would be the preposition *sprough*, "reaching from end to end of a cigar-shaped object," appearing in sentences like (4a) but not (4b):

(4) a.   The rug extended sprough the airplane.
         The weevil bored sprough the cigar.
         The major axis of an ellipse goes right sprough it.
    b. *The rug extended sprough my dining room.
        *The weevil bored sprough the chair.
        *The major axis of a cup handle goes right sprough it.

Similarly, there are no prepositions that refer to the reference object's analysis into parts. An example might be the hypothetical preposition *betwaft* in (5), which requires the reference object to have a protruding part.

(5) a. The bug crawled betwaft my face.
             "The bug crawled down the junction between my nose and the main body of my face."

    b. The water ran betwaft the airplane.
       "The water ran down the junction between the wing and the fuselage."
    c. A stripe extended betwaft the cup.
       "A stripe extended along/down the junction between the body of the cup and the handle."

This seems a perfectly plausible spatial relation, but a perfectly horrible preposition.

About the most complicated cases we have found—in which some elements of object shape are relevant to the preposition's meaning—are the terms *along* and *across*. *Along* requires its reference object to have a principal axis of significant elongation, so that one can travel *along a road* or *along a beach* but not *along a chair* or *along a round table*. One can travel *along the edge of a round table*, but then the linear edge, not the table as a whole, is serving as reference object. In addition, this principal linear axis must be (more or less) horizontal: A bug can be said to crawl *along a flagpole* only if the flagpole is lying down. (We treat *across* and some further wrinkles in *along* shortly.)

And that is more or less it, in terms of specific shape requirements. However, there do seem to be certain general constraints on the range of geometries exhibited by reference objects. We now describe three such constraints.

2.2.1 Volumes, Surfaces, and Lines

For something to be *in X, X* must have an interior, but nothing more is necessary. There is no requirement on axes, for example. In other words, the reference object for *in* needs a form descriptor even coarser than Marr's basic cylinder, something like a "lump" (or, if a 2D region, a "blob"). *On* requires that its reference object be a line, a surface, or an object whose boundary is a line or a surface. *Near* and *at* require that the reference object is bounded in extent.

Inside is somewhat more specific than *in*. It seems to require that its reference object be or contain a bounded enclosure (a negative part or the interior of a hollow geon). Thus, as pointed out by Talmy, one can be either *in* or *inside* a cave or a bottle, but one can be only *in*, not *inside*, a swimming pool or lake.

2.2.2 Axes

A sizable number of prepositions, such as *on top of, in front of, in back of*, and *beside*, make reference to an axis. In the case of an object that lacks inherent axes, such as a sphere, these axes are contextually imposed (see section 2.3.2). But these prepositions can also make use of the reference object's inherent axes. *On top of* projects a region from the directed axis that in the object's normal orientation goes up and down. *In front of, in back of,* and *behind* make use of the directed horizontal front-to-back axis; *beside* and *alongside* make use of a horizontal axis perpendicular to the front-to-back axis. For the purposes of these prepositions, it does not matter whether the axes in question are generating axes or orienting axes.

As mentioned earlier, *along* requires its reference object to be basically linear and horizontal. Its partner, *across*, appears to require its reference object to be or to have a surface with sides, so that one can go across, ''from one side to the other.'' Just in case the reference object has a significant linear elonga-tion, the *sides* are distinguished from the *ends*: A square table has four sides, but a long rectangular table has two sides and two ends. In such a case, *across* pertains specifically to the sides and not to the ends, so that *across the rectangular table* describes a region that traverses the table's shorter dimension.[2] Non-rectilinear objects in this framework tend to be idealized as though they were rectilinear, so that, with respect to *across*, a round table behaves like a square table and an oval table like a rectangular one.

A further restriction on *across* is that, like *along*, it describes a horizontal trajec-tory. For instance, one draws a line *across a blackboard* in the horizontal direc-tion, not the vertical. This follows from the stipulation that *across* pertains to the sides of the object, which are normally the boundaries of a horizontal axis.

2.2.3 Quantity of Reference Object

A different sort of restriction on the reference object appears in the preposi-tions *between, among,* and *amidst.* For *between,* the reference object is not a single object but rather a pair. In the case of *among,* it is an aggregate (or collection of objects). In the case of *amidst,* it is either an aggregate or a substance.

To sum up, the restrictions placed on the form of the reference object by expressions for spatial relations are not at all severe, compared to the potential complexity of objects themselves. At most, these restrictions appeal to the very gross geometry of the coarsest level of representation of the object—whether it is a container, whether it is relatively elongated, and whether it has sides.[3]

2.3 Constraints on Spatial Relations Defining Regions

The spatial relations expressed in English factor into a number of independent features which combine to produce some of the complexity of the system.

---

[2]Going across a bridge is a special case, in that one goes from one *end* of the bridge to the other. Presumably this is motivated by the fact that the bridge itself extends from one side to the other of something else, such as a road or a river.

[3]There are a few exceptions to this overall generalization. Nautical terms like *port* and *starboard* require a boat as reference object. *Upstairs* and *downstairs* involve levels in a building (though not necessarily stairs, as one can go upstairs in a building with only elevators). And the compounds with *-ward* such as *homeward* and *shoreward* involve reference to the object named by the initial noun.

2.3.1 Relative Distance

This concerns how close the figural object is to the reference object. The closest possibility is being located in the interior of the reference object (*in, inside*); the next closest is exterior to the reference object but in contact with it (*on, against*); the next is being proximate to the reference object (*near*). Some languages provide additional values for this feature beyond proximate, for instance "not near but within reach" or "not near but visible." One such language is Korean (Soo-Won Kim, personal communication), in which the expressions *yup* and *kiyut* both translate as "near," but *yup* is confined to more immediately proximate cases. (Other examples are cited by Anderson and Keenan (1985) in connection with systems of spatial deixis corresponding to English *here* and *there*.)

Each of the degrees of relative distance found in English has a corresponding "negative," which actually means "farther away from the reference object than." The three cases are "farther away than the interior" (*out of, outside*), "farther away than in contact" (*off of*), and "farther away than proximate" (*far from*).

The prepositions *among* and *between* also involve the distance feature. As mentioned previously, the reference object for *among* is an aggregation of objects, which together define a group or virtual object that contains them all. The figural object is then specified as interior to this virtual object. The case of *between* is similar, except that the virtual object is the minimal space bounded by the pair of reference objects.

2.3.2 Direction

Direction of the figural object from the reference object provides a second parameter in specifying spatial relations. For the simplest case, gravitation supplies a vertical orientation necessary to define *over, above, under, below*, and *beneath*.

Orthogonal to gravitation is the horizontal direction that helps define *beside, by, alongside*, and *next to*. Notice that if a bird is beside, by, alongside, or next to a house, it must not be on the roof or flying overhead: It must be in proximity to the house and no higher than the house. Thus these prepositions designate the relation "proximate to the reference object in the horizontal direction." In addition, if the reference object has inherent axes that distinguish front and back from sides, these four prepositions tend to mean "horizontally proximate to the *sides* of the reference object." For instance, Bill is not *beside* me if I am facing him.

Similarly, if the reference object has an inherent front and back, *in front of* can mean "horizontally proximate to the inherent front of the reference object," and *in back of* can mean "horizontally proximate to the inherent back of the reference object." However, an alternative interpretation of these prepositions results from *contextually* assigning a front-to-back axis to the reference object: The front is the surface facing the speaker (or addressee), and the back is the surface opposite. In this case *in front of* and *in back of* mean "horizontally proximate to the contextual front/back of the reference object." A parallel ambiguity occurs with *on top of*: If a flagpole is lying on its side, one can paint the ball on top of it (referring to the inherent top), or sit on top of it (referring to the contextually determined top, in this case a long horizontal surface).

Not all spatial expressions involving axes leave this choice of reference system open. *On the top of*, by contrast with *on top of*, refers only to the inherent top of the reference object (presumably because it contains the full noun phrase *the top*). *Beyond*, in contrast to *behind*, refers only to the region projected to the contextually determined rear of the reference object.

2.3.3 Combinations of Distance and Direction

Distance and direction interact to provide further distinctions among prepositions. For instance, compare *over, above,* and *on top of. Over* is indifferent to contact versus noncontact: a cloth may be put over a table (contact), and clouds may fly over a city (noncontact). *Above*, however, specifies noncontact: Though clouds may fly above a city, one can only put a cloth above a table by putting it on a higher shelf. Finally, *on top of* strongly favors a contact reading.

In back of and *behind*, which share directionality, also differ in distance. A tree may be *right behind* (proximal), *way behind* (distal), or *right in back of* a house; but *The tree is way in back of the house* sounds odd or colloquial. Evidently the standard use of *in back of* is restricted to proximal distance (and possibly contact), whereas *behind* and colloquial *in back of* are unrestricted.

For a somewhat different case, to move *up* or *down* a mountain, tree, or wall is to move in an upward/downward direction while maintaining contact with (or, marginally, proximity to) to the surface of the reference object.

2.3.4 Visibility and Occlusion

A subsidiary use of some of the directional prepositions invokes the distinction "visible" versus "occluded." For instance, Vandeloise (1986) argues that occlusion of the reference object is the main relation expressed by French *devant* ("in front of"). Although we would not go quite so far, we believe this criterion does play a secondary role, possibly forming a preference rule system (Jackendoff, 1983) with the directional criteria. A case in English where this distinction is evident is in speaking of paint on a wall being *on top of* or *underneath* the wallpaper. Here *on top of* evidently means "in contact with visible surface," whatever its orientation, and *underneath* means "in contact with the surface opposite the visible surface." (Notice, by the way, that one cannot speak of *the bottom of the wallpaper* in this context; not all the words of vertical orientation generalize to this use.)

2.3.5 Relationships Involving Linear Axis of Figural Object

None of the spatial relations cited so far make any specification at all of the form of the figural object. However, three prepositions, *along, across*, and *around*, express spatial relations between the reference object and the linear axis of the figural object. For instance, consider *The road is along the river*. This specifies that the main axis of the road is colinear with (as well as horizontally proximate to) the main axis of the river. However, this is not the only use of *along*. If the figural object has no main horizontal axis, as in *The tree is along the river*, the condition of colinearity does not apply. If the figural object is in motion, as in *The dog loped along the river*, the trajectory of the figure rather than the figure itself is colinear with the main axis of the river. Finally, if the figural object is an aggregate, as in *The trees are along the river*, this aggregate is preferentially understood as forming a virtual object whose axis is colinear with the main axis of the river. (The adjectival form *parallel to* places constraints similar to those of *along*.)

Across, as mentioned earlier, involves a linear region or trajectory that goes from one side to the other of the reference object. Two separate senses of *across* locate the figural object differently with respect to this region. One places it on the other side of the region in relation to the observer or a secondary reference object, as in *Bill is across the road (from Harry)*. The other places the figural object within the region, where it is either coaxial with this region (*The stick lay across the road*), moving along the axis of the region (*Bill ran across the road*), or distributed along the axis of the region (*The trees extend across the field*). (The adjectival form *perpendicular to* places constraints similar to *across*. *Opposite* used as a preposition (*Bill is opposite Harry*) means about the same as the first reading of *across*, except that it leaves unexpressed the object that Bill and Harry are on opposite sides of.)

Around also has a number of variants. Ignoring the one that means roughly *near* (*There are lots of trees around here*), it designates a hollow region whose interior contains the reference object. The figure is specified as occupying the region, either as a linear object surrounding a two-dimensional reference object (*The road goes around the city*) or as a shell or thickened surface surrounding a three-dimensional reference object (*There is chocolate around the core of the candy*). A distributed figure object is again acceptable (*There are trees around the house*). A moving figure may either circumnavigate the reference object (*go all the way around*) or *detour around* it.

2.3.6 Distributed Figural Object

In *along, across*, and *around* the figure object may be specified as being linear or (in the case of *around*) a surface. A different class of prepositions requires the figural object to be distributed, either as a substance or an aggregate. Consider *There was water all over the floor*. *All over* specifies a figural object distributed over and in contact with the entire extent of the surface of the reference object.

In *There were raisins throughout the pudding, throughout* specifies an aggregate figural object more or less evenly distributed in the volume of the reference object. Thus *all over* and *throughout* are "distributive" forms of the spatial relations normally expressed as *on* and *in* respectively. *All along, all around,* and *all across* are similar distributive forms corresponding to the prepositions *along, around,* and *across.*

2.4 Spatial Relations Defining Trajectories

English uses the conceptual category of trajectories or paths to specify the figure's motion (*The bird flew to the house*) or orientation (*The sign points to New York*). There are a few simple ways of constructing trajectories, none of which draw any further on the geometry of the figural or reference objects than we already have.

The simplest class of trajectories are the environmentally oriented directions *up, down, north, south, east,* and *west.* Another class specifies the figure's motion in terms of its own inherent horizontal axes: *frontwards, backwards, sideways.* Another specifies change of the figural object's orientation in terms of its own axes: turn *around,* turn *over,* turn *left,* and turn *right.*

The largest class of trajectories, however, is constructed from the class of regions by attaching one of five operators (Jackendoff, 1983). One operator, "via," creates a trajectory that passes through the region in question. For example, to *run by the house* is to traverse a trajectory that at some point involves being *near the house*; to *walk under a bridge* is to traverse a trajectory that at some point involves being under the bridge; to *go through a room* involves a trajectory that at some point is *in the room.* If the region in question is linear, as in *along, across,* and *around,* the "via" trajectory is coaxial with the region, so that *going along X* involves moving parallel to the axis of X, for instance.

Another kind of trajectory is constructed from a region by attaching the operator "to," creating a trajectory that terminates at the region in question. For instance, *to X* expresses a trajectory that terminates *at X. Into X* and *onto X* express trajectories that terminate *in X* and *on X* respectively. Similarly, the operator "toward" constructs a trajectory that would terminate at the region if extended, but that does not in fact reach the region. So to *go toward X* is to undergo a motion that if extended would terminate *at X.*

The operator "from" is just the reverse of "to": It constructs a trajectory that begins at the region in question. Examples are *The bird emerged from under the table* and *The train came from inside the Soviet Union.* The operator "away from" is the reverse of "toward": *Bill ran away from the explosion* describes him as traversing a trajectory which if extended backward would begin at the explosion.[4]

---

[4]"Toward" and "away from" are more restricted than "to" and "from," in that the region they are constructed from is always "at X." There are no expressions *toward on X* or *away from under X,* parallel to *onto X* and *from under X,* for instance.

2.5 Other Factors

The preceding discussion presented not just a sample of the spatial relations expressed by English prepositions; it contains essentially all the spatial relations we have been able to find. This section briefly lists some of the complications that remain, none of which involve geometric properties per se.

First, there are uses that involve special situations. Herskovits (1986) points out that to be *at a desk* or *at a sink* usually implies more than being located close to it; one is probably performing characteristic actions, such as writing at the desk or washing at the sink. For another case, to *throw a ball at X* involves more more than *throwing it toward X*—roughly an intention to hit X. This difference accounts for the contrasts in (6):

(6) a. Bill threw the ball toward/?at Harry without meaning to hit him.
    b. Bill shot at/?toward Harry.

Other special situations involve conventionalized conceptualization of the reference object. For instance, when traveling, one is *in a bus* or *on a bus* but only *in*, not *on, a car*. It seems that in English, large vehicles (buses, yachts, trains, large airplanes) are conceptualized either as containers or sorts of platforms, but small vehicles (cars, rowboats, small airplanes) are only conceptualized as containers. This is just an idiosyncratic fact of English, as far as we can tell, having little to do with principles of spatial representation. For a somewhat different case, a container can be conceptualized either in terms of the volume it surrounds or in terms of the body of its substance, so we can speak of either *the water in the cup* or *the crack in the cup*.

Some special uses appear to involve forces exerted between the figure and the reference object. For example, the preposition *on* is frequently said to involve support by the reference object (Cienki, 1988; Herskovits, 1986). This is not always the case, as we can speak of *the fly on the ceiling*; but it may be a default interpretation. According to Bowerman (1989), the Dutch preposition *aan* also involves support or attachment, specifically a figural object hanging or projecting from a reference object that is something other than a horizontal surface (for example leaves *aan* a twig, a coat hook *aan* a wall, clothes *aan* a line). The English preposition *against*, as in *Bill leaned against the wall* or *The tree fell against the house*, describes contact with exertion of force, usually in a horizontal or oblique direction. Among expressions of path, there is a special reading of *into* found in *The car ran into the pole*, which means not traversal to the interior of the reference object but rather coming into contact with the reference object with considerable force.

Bowerman (1989) cites a further complex case from the verbal system of Korean. It appears that the verb *kki-ta*, roughly "put in, put together," applies to situations in which the figural object fits fairly tightly into or around the reference object, for instance a ring on a finger, a hand in a glove, a lid on a jar, and a button in a buttonhole. (The English verb *insert* appears to cover part but not all of the same semantic territory.) The verb *ppay-ta* describes the removal of the figure from a reference object with which it has been configured in this fashion. This configuration appears to involve both spatial relations and exertion of force. However, it again makes little reference to the detailed geometry of the figure and the reference object, beyond the fact that there is a match between a positive part of one and a negative part of the other.

Beyond this sort of complication, most of the complexity of English prepositions appears to involve (a) how nonstereotypical and ambiguous spatial configurations are forced into the expressions available in the language, (b) how particular prepositions are extended from core place meanings to different sorts of related paths and places (for example, the variants of *across* mentioned earlier), (c) how preposition meanings are extended to nonspatial domains such as time and possession, and (d) how prepositions are used as purely grammatical markers (for instance, *Bill believes in capitalism, The letter was received by Bill, a picture of Bill*). Extended discussions appear in Brugman, 1981; Cienki, 1988; Herskovits, 1986; Jackendoff, 1983, 1990; Lakoff, 1987, chapter II.2; Miller & Johnson-Laird, 1976; Vandeloise, 1986.[5]

3. WHY IS IT THIS WAY?

The picture that emerges from this brief overview is that, if we are anywhere near being complete (as we believe we are), the total class of spatial relations expressed in English is unexpectedly small, especially compared with the class of object names. To get a feel for the difference, compare the number of nouns mentioned in section 1 with the number of prepositions mentioned in section 2. Moreover, the ways in which spatial relations can make use of object shape descriptors are themselves even more constrained. This disparity cries out for explanation. We see two possible lines of attack, which we will call the Poverty of Language Hypothesis and the Poverty of Spatial Representations Hypothesis.

3.1 Poverty of Language Hypothesis

The disparity is a fact about language. The design of language is such that expressions of spatial relations are relegated to a minimal class, relative to names

---

[5]Pinxten, van Dooren, and Harvey (1983) make an exhaustive exploration of Navajo spatial terms. Though they emphasize how different the Navajo spatial framework is from that of English, there are few surprises with respect to the parameters discussed here (insofar as we can follow their discussion without competence in Navajo). About the only case that involves a shape descriptor for an object, the issue with which we are most concerned, is *biniká*, a postposition meaning roughly "passing through a hole," as in the eye of a needle. Thus, although we do not want to claim that English exhausts the spatial relations expressible in language, it does appear to provide a substantial and representative sampling.

for objects. Perhaps, for example, we can manage to communicate effectively while expressing only a small range of spatial relations, so language has evolved (biologically and/or diachronically) to have no more such expressions than necessary. According to this hypothesis, spatial representation itself may be considerably richer in the range of spatial relations it specifies; however, the distinctions it can encode are to a great extent invisible to the language faculty, and therefore are neutralized or leveled out in the translation into linguistic format.

There is abundant evidence that language does indeed filter representations of spatial relationships. For example, when inserting one's hand through a narrow slot, one must predict the hand's exact angle of orientation relative to the slot in order to be successful. Similarly, throwing a ball to someone involves a sensitive translation of perceived distance and angle into muscular force. And in general, all acts of navigation based on either visual or haptic–kinesthetic perception require delicate judgments of distance and angle. Even 2-year-old children appreciate these metric properties, and can use them in navigating through the world (Landau, Spelke, & Gleitman, 1984).

Yet language is crude at expressing such metric information, which plays no role at all in the relationships discussed in section 2. To be precise in expressing distances and orientations, one must invoke a culturally stipulated system of measurement, which operates by counting units such as meters or degrees (go 30 meters, turn 30 degrees). Such units have no special psychological priority; in fact, it is hard to believe that metrical precision in the human spatial system is accomplished at all in terms of counting up unit measures. Thus the translation from spatial representation to linguistic representation evidently involves a certain amount of filtering, such that significant aspects of spatial relations go unexpressed. (The nonmetric characteristics of spatial language are stressed by Talmy, 1978, 1983).

Similar filtering takes place in translating object shape descriptions into language. One can recognize with great accuracy complicated contours and surface patterns, but they are very hard to describe to someone else. Imagine, for example, trying to describe the Shepard–Metzler objects or the Attneave figures used in visual rotation experiments (Shepard & Cooper, 1982)—or the pattern of stripes on a particular zebra, or the shape of a violin, or your mother's chin. These difficulties are augmented by the relative lack of linguistic terms for describing exact sizes of objects, outside of again using a culturally stipulated system of measurement.

So language clearly does not convey all the richness of spatial representation. However, by itself, this leveling out of metric information does not explain the striking disparity between the richness of object shape expressions and the poverty of spatial relation expressions, because both domains are subject to similar leveling. What remains a puzzle is why objects that are being named seem to have relatively complex geometries (hence relatively small shape changes lead to new named categories), whereas objects that are being *located* and the regions in which they are located are treated in terms of a relatively simple geometric description. Why are objects and places represented so differently?

3.2 Poverty of Spatial Representations Hypothesis

An alternative possibility is that the disparity may be inherent in spatial representation. According to this hypothesis, spatial representation is relatively rich in its possibilities for object shape description by relatively impoverished in its possibilities for description of spatial relations. The disparity observed in language is then a relatively accurate reflection of the underlying spatial concepts that language expresses.

We believe that both of these hypotheses are partly right. On one hand, language does fail to express the full richness of spatial representation (that's why a picture is worth a thousand words); but on the other hand, there still seems to remain this disparity in the representations encoding object shapes and spatial relations.

3.3 The "What" and "Where" Systems

We conjecture that a significant proportion of the disparity reflects a functional bifurcation of the system of spatial representation (perhaps into "submodules" in the sense of Fodor, 1983, as refined by Jackendoff, 1987b, chapter 12). One part of the system is devoted primarily to object shape identification; the other, to locating objects in space relative to each other and to the observer. The expressive power of the noun system is linked to the shape identification submodule; the expressive power of the preposition system is linked to the spatial relation submodule.

This conjecture finds an interesting kind of support in the evidence that the brain contains separate areas specialized for object identification and object location. Ungerleider and Mishkin (1982), building on previous work, show that damage to the inferior temporal cortex in monkeys produces deficits in pattern and shape recognition, whereas damage to the posterior parietal cortex impairs following routes, reaching for objects, and using landmarks to locate objects. They distinguish these two systems as the "what" and "where" systems. Farah, Hammond, Levine, and Calvanio (1988) document a human case in which bilateral damage to inferior temporal areas with sparing of parietal regions has produced a deficit in a wide range of tasks involving shape recognition but has preserved normal performance in tasks involving object localization and spatial relations.[6] In a different sort of study, Rueckl, Cave, and

---

[6]Farah et al. call the difference one between "visual" and "spatial" capacities. One of us (R. J.) has a somewhat different interpretation: that we should think of both as subsystems of the multimodal spatial capacity. Because all the tasks tested by Farah et al. were exclusively visual—there were no haptic or motor tasks—the evidence so far does not distinguish the two possible interpretations.

Kosslyn (1988) found that in a PDP model of a very simple visual system, a certain degree of extra efficiency accrues to a system that strongly separates computation of the "what" and "where" functions, as long as both subsystems have sufficient computational resources.

In order to see how these observations bear on the Poverty of Spatial Representation Hypothesis, let us consider for a moment the logic of a representation that separates "what" from "where." What information does the "where" system have to encode? At the very least, it must have a space of possible locations and a way to mark which ones are occupied. But this is obviously not enough. It would not do just for the "what" system to know that one is seeing a cat and a dog, and for the "where" system to know that positions A and B are occupied: Is the cat at A and the dog at B, or vice versa? In order to keep track of which objects are where, there must be a liaison between the two representations.

A simple way to accomplish this liaison formally is by co-indexing or linking the object representations in the two systems. The "where" system could then encode very rudimentary representations of the objects being located, perhaps as simple as "thing here." Such extremely schematized objects would place only minimal demands on information-bearing capacity within the "where" system. However, they would in addition be linked to or associated with representations in the "what" system that encode the objects' detailed shapes. In other words, the "where" system can get by with including just a little object information, as long as it can link its object tokens to those in the "what" system.[7]

Our guess is that the relatively simple shape specifications observed in the prepositional system are revealing the extent of detail possible in object descriptions within the "where" system. These details go somewhat beyond "thing here," but not much. In particular, as we have seen, the way the system works is not in terms of absolute locations of objects, but rather by locating one object in terms of another. Most of the detail in the system's shape descriptions is concentrated on the reference object, which defines the space in which the figure is located—and even that is highly restricted. The geometry of the figure goes beyond "thing here" only in the small class of cases in which the issue is its orientation (*along, across, around*) or its distribution through a region (*all over, throughout*).

An ordinary-life analogy to the situation in the "where" system is the conventionalized representation in maps. What is at issue in a map is how to navigate through a region. A map cannot just specify "wheres": It has to have something to stand in for the objects being located. Typically these stand-

---

[7]Of course, formal indexing does not answer the psychological or neurological question of how the link is effected. But this is altogether parallel to the well-known problem within language of how multiple representations are psychologically or neurologically linked—for example, what it means neurologically for the representation of the sound of a word to be linked to the encoding of its meaning.

ins are points and lines, with some conventionalized symbols to distinguish different sorts of objects from each other (big cities vs. small cities, main roads vs. subsidiary roads, churches vs. hospitals, etc.). If a map had to distinguish all the objects by their shape, it would be much more complex and quite possibly unusable. We are not suggesting that the "where" system necessarily encodes something like an internalized map. The point is only that many of the same design criteria are applicable—in particular the need to represent objects as tokens in the representation and the need to compress their encoding by eliminating most information about their form.

A last point on the disparity between the expressive power of the two systems: Rueckl, Cave, and Kosslyn's (1988) study involved a stimulus space containing only nine different shapes, each of which could occur in nine partially overlapping locations. Within this tiny system, it was found that the optimal allocation of resources between the "what" and "where" systems used over three times as many "what" units as "where" units. Although it is hard to know how this case generalizes to a more realistic system, the disparity is reminiscent of that found between the noun and the preposition system. However, Rueckl, Cave, and Kosslyn argue that the disparity can only increase as one moves to a more realistic system. Thus our conjecture of the Poverty of Spatial Representation is suggestively supported on computational grounds.

3.4 Directions for Research

If our conjecture is correct, we have found a bifurcation in the expressive power of language that corresponds to a bifurcation in the functional and anatomical systems of the brain. This is, to our knowledge, the first time within cognitive science that a correlation has been made between a property of grammar and a property of a nonlinguistic part of the brain. What is exciting about this correlation is that, where previous studies have documented the tasks performed by the two systems, linguistic evidence can now provide a window on the actual forms of information the systems encode.

This possibility has suggested two programs of research currently being conducted by one of us (B.L.). The first stems from the asymmetry of spatial relations. According to the linguistic evidence, a spatial relation defines a *region* in terms of a reference object; the figural object is then located in the region. The implication is that regions are in some sense psychologically real—that one can investigate their properties experimentally. Studies currently under way suggest that adults and children as young as 3 years old make systematic judgments that reveal highly structured regions surrounding reference objects. For example, when asked to make repeated judgments as to whether one object is *near* a reference object, subjects accept all positions within a well-defined region surrounding the landmark. Moreover, the structure (shape) of the region is determined in part by the structure of the landmark: If the landmark is square or round, subjects accept positions within a roughly round region; if the landmark is rectangular, they accept positions within a roughly oblong region. We believe that systematic manipulation of the configuration of the landmark will therefore reveal how people geometrically represent regions, and how they level out particular geometric features from the reference object in doing so.

The second program of research concerns children's acquisition of nouns vs. prepositions. According to our approach, a child learning a new object word ought to generalize its use based on properties of the "what" system: The particulars of object shape should matter, but the object's position should not. In contrast, a child learning a new spatial preposition ought to generalize based on properties of the "where" system: The particulars of object shape should not matter, but the object's position should. Landau and Stecker (1990) achieved just this set of results with children as young as 3 years old.

4. CONCLUSIONS

We have shown significant constraints on the kinds of spatial relationships that are represented by language. Some of these limits do not appear to be due to absolute limits on the spatial representational system itself, but rather they partially reflect a property of language design: leveling of metric information.

However, we have spent most of our effort here reviewing linguistic evidence that suggests there are very different spatial-representational bases for objects and places. This evidence shows a striking asymmetry between the way that object shapes are represented when they are being named and the way they are represented when they play the role of figure or ground object in a locational expression. We have conjectured that these differences in how objects and places are represented reflect a property of neurological design: a separation of spatial cognition into "what" and "where." This rather surprising convergence between linguistic and nonlinguistic evidence for the two subsystems suggests that language can provide a new source of insight into the nature of spatial representation.

ACKNOWLEDGMENTS

The first author was a student at Swarthmore but did not have the privilege of studying with Lila Gleitman. It was therefore necessary to complete the gestalt by collaborating with the second author, who did not go to Swarthmore but did study with Lila Gleitman. Both of us are grateful for this opportunity to honor Lila, who through many years of association has been a constant source of inspiration, wisdom, and good jokes.

This research was supported in part by NSF Grant IRI 88-08286 to Brandeis University and by Social and Behavioral Sciences Research Grant #12-214 from the March of Dimes Birth Defects Foundation to Barbara Landau. We are grateful to Edgar Zurif and David Murray for essential references used in this study.

REFERENCES

Anderson, S., & Keenan, E. (1985). Deixis. In T. Shopen (Ed.), *Language typology and syntactic description*. Cambridge: Cambridge University Press.

Biederman, I. (1987). Recognition-by-components: A theory of human image understanding. *Psychological Review, 94*(2), 115–147.

Bowerman, M. (1989). Learning a semantic system: What role do cognitive predispositions play? In M. L. Rice & R. C. Schiefenbusch (Eds.), *The teachability of language* (pp. 133–169). Baltimore: Paul H. Brooks.

Brugman, C. (1981). Story of *Over*. Bloomington, IN: Indiana University Linguistics Club.

Cienki, A. (1988). Spatial cognition and the semantics of prepositions in English, Polish, and Russian. Ph.D. thesis. Providence, RI: Brown University.

Farah, M., Hammond, K., Levine, D., & Calvanio, R. (1988). Visual and spatial mental imagery: Dissociable systems of representation. *Cognitive Psychology, 20*, 439–462.

Fodor, J. (1983). *Modularity of mind*. Cambridge, MA: MIT Press.

Herskovits, A. (1986) *Language and spatial cognition: An interdisciplinary study of the prepositions in English*. Cambridge: Cambridge University Press.

Hochberg, J. (1978). *Perception*. Englewood Cliffs, NJ: Prentice-Hall.

Hoffman, D., & Richards, W. (1984). Parts of recognition. *Cognition, 18*, 65–96.

Jackendoff, R. (1983). *Semantics and cognition*. Cambridge, MA: MIT Press.

Jackendoff, R. (1987a). On beyond zebra: The relation of linguistic and visual information. *Cognition, 26*, 89–114.

Jackendoff, R. (1987b). *Consciousness and the computational mind*. Cambridge, MA: MIT Press.

Jackendoff, R. (1990). *Semantic structures*. Cambridge, MA: MIT Press.

Lakoff, G. (1987). *Women, fire, and dangerous things*. Chicago: University of Chicago Press.

Landau, B., Smith, L., & Jones, S. (1988). The importance of shape in early lexical learning. *Cognitive Development, 3*, 299–321.

Landau, B., Spelke, E., & Gleitman, H. (1984). Spatial knowledge in a young blind child. *Cognition, 16*, 225–260.

Landau, B., & Stecker, D. (1990). Objects and places: Syntactic geometric representations in early lexical learning. *Cognitive Development 5*, 287–312.

Marr, D. (1982). *Vision*. San Francisco: W. H. Freeman.

Miller, G. A., & Johnson-Laird, P. (1976) *Language and perception*. Cambridge, MA: Harvard University Press.

Pinxten, R., van Dooren, I., & Harvey, K. (1983). *The anthropology of space: Explorations into natural philosophy and semantics of the Navajo*. Philadelphia: University of Pennsylvania Press.

Rosch, E. (1975). Cognitive reference points. *Cognitive Psychology, 7*(4), 532–547.

Rueckl, J., Cave, K., & Kosslyn, S. (1988). Why are "what" and "where" processed by separate cortical visual systems? A computational investigation. *Journal of Cognitive Neuroscience, 1*(2), 171–186.

Sadalla, E., Burroughs, W. J., & Staplin, L. J. (1980). Reference points in spatial cognition. *Journal of Experimental Psychology: Human Learning and Memory, 6*(5), 516–528.

Shepard, R. N., & Cooper, L. (1982). *Mental images and their transformations*. Cambridge, MA: MIT Press.

Talmy, L. (1978). The relation of grammar to cognition. In D. Waltz, (Ed.), *Proceedings of TINLAP-2: Theoretical issues in natural language processing* (pp. 14–24). Urbana, IL: University of Illinois.

Talmy, L. (1983). How language structures space. In H. Pick & L. Acredolo (Eds.), *Spatial orientation: Theory, research, and application*. New York: Plenum Press.

Ungerleider, L. G., & Mishkin, M. (1982). Two cortical visual systems. In D. J. Ingle, M. A. Goodale, & R. J. W. Mansfield (Eds.), *Analysis of visual behavior* (pp. 549–586). Cambridge, MA: MIT Press.

Vandeloise, C. (1986). *L'espace en français*. Paris: Éditions du Seuil.

9

Farewell to "Thee"

Elizabeth F. Shipley
University of Pennsylvania

Ten years after I left Swarthmore I was puttering with psychophysical models when my firstborn began to talk. This was clearly an amazing accomplishment, but the psychology I knew had little to say about it. Around this time I met Lila Gleitman, then a new mother also, and learned from her a greater appreciation of the magnitude of this accomplishment.

In our family the Quaker Plain Language, with second person singular familiar pronouns *thee, thy*, and *thine*, was used by the parents to address the children, each other, and a few other relatives. All others we addressed with the standard *you, your*, and *yours*. However, the children never used the familiar with anyone. My husband and I were puzzled by our children's failure to imitate what we thought were their most obvious models, ourselves, so we interviewed other families with young children in which the Plain Language was used. We found the pattern of use in our family to be the norm: Children tended to use the forms used in the wider community, not the forms used with them by their parents (Shipley & Shipley, 1969). This paper reconsiders and follows up the earlier work, and speculates about the role of children in changes over time in the Plain Language.

In the 17th century, when the Quaker religion was founded, English, like other European languages, had two forms of pronouns of address: the plural which was also used as the formal, *ye, you, your*, and *yours*, and the familiar singular, *thou, thee, thy*, and *thine*. The abbreviation V (for the Latin *vos*) will be used to refer to formal pronouns and T (for the Latin *tu*) will be used to refer to familiar pronouns. The use of the abreviations T and V, as well as the following brief summary of the history of pronouns of address, is based primarily upon Roger Brown's work (1965; Brown & Gilman, 1960).

European languages, like many other languages, have familiar and formal modes of address of single persons. The distinction between V and T in European languages began in the 4th century when the plural V was used to address the Roman emperor. The use of the plural may have reflected the existence of two emperors at the time or it may have reflected a general tendency to equate power and status with plurality. From this beginning the distinction between V and T spread throughout the European languages, moving from the French court to the English court in the 13th century. Initially, in England as in other countries, the nobility used V among themselves and T with inferiors, whereas others used V with the nobility and T among themselves. The nonreciprocal use of V and T indicated relative status, higher status people used T and received V.

Over time, V and T were used to signify a second dimension of social relations, solidarity. The nobility began to use T with close peers as well as inferiors; commoners began to use V with older family members. Thus, V was used to signify both higher status and distance, T was used to signify both inferiority and familiarity. Brown and Gilman (1960) provided extensive data on the existence of these norms in pronouns of address in many languages. Subsequent work has confirmed their conclusions (Kroger, Wood, & Kim, 1984; Paulson, 1976).

One consequence of the existence of a social norm is that its violation is meaningful. In most languages it has been an insult to use T with someone who merits V by status unless the speaker has been invited by the higher status person to use T. Similarly, the use of V with someone who merits T by status can be a compliment or sign of respect. However, V can also be used negatively, for instance, as a way of indicating someone is a snob (Paulson, 1976), to insult, or to distance the addressor from the addressee. See Brown and Gilman (1960) and references there for instances of such use by Shakespeare and other writers.

The Quakers in the 17th century as a matter of religious principle refused to use the V form with anyone, thereby denying differences of status. Likewise they refused to remove their hats for any person. These actions were insults to those who expected deference, such as parents and nobility. As the Quakers persisted in their use of T with everyone, it slowly disappeared from other dialects of English. It has been suggested that the disappearance of T from English is due, at least in part, to a distaste for the Quakers' use of T (Brown, 1965).

In contrast to English, in other languages the use of T has increased as a sign of egalitarian beliefs (Brown, 1965; Fang & Heng, 1983; Paulson, 1976).

As T forms disappeared from other dialects of English, their use by Quakers has been primarily to signify family and religious solidarity. Rather than expressing solidarity with all people, its use has been seen by some to express exclusivity. When we first examined the use of T within Quaker families,

Philadelphia was one of the few places in this country, perhaps in the world, where a T form was used by any English speakers.

A RECONSIDERATION OF
QUAKER CHILDREN'S USE OF *THEE*

In the 1969 paper the use of T in 16 families where both parents consistently used T with the children was examined (Shipley & Shipley, 1969). In only 2 of the 16 families did the children reciprocate and consistently use T with the parents. In 3 more families the children used T intermittently or rarely with the parents. In the other 11 families the children never used T with the parents.

The use of T with siblings was slightly more prevalent than with parents. In two families siblings used T consistently among themselves; in five other families there was some use of T with some siblings by some children.

The use of T by the children varied with the extent of the parents' use of T. Specifically, in the two families where the children consistently used T with their parents, as well as in two of the three families with intermittent use of T by the children, the parents used T reciprocally with friends (usually Friends) and neighbors, as well as with more distant relatives. In the fifth family with some use of T with siblings, the parents used T reciprocally with relatives beyond the immediate family. However, in families where the use of T by parents was restricted to the immediate family, there was no use of T by the children.

In the 1969 paper we presented a relational account of the children's patterns of use of T. We assumed that children come to understand the appropriate use of first and second person pronouns by observation of other people addressing one another, and that in these dyads they interpret the pronouns with respect to addressee and addressor, not with respect to individual A and individual B. Thus, when a speaker says "I" in speaking to another person, *I* is registered as referring to whomever is speaking, not to the specific individual saying "I." By attending to the speaker, no matter who that is, the child should be protected from the false beliefs that one person's name is "I" and another person's name is "you" or ("thee"), or that one person has several different names, including "I" and "you" (or "thee"). By this assumption the child is also spared the task of translating "I" and "you" (or "thee") into "you" and "I" respectively when engaged in a dialogue (Macnamara, 1982).

This assumption accounts for the finding that the families in which the children used T were families with the widest use of T by the parents. Such families offer children the most opportunities to observe different dyads using T reciprocally.

There is, of course, an obvious fault in this account. The most available model for use of first and second person pronouns in our sample would seem to be the parents who used T with each other. Therefore, all children should have used T as their initial pronouns of address. To explain the children's failure to model their pronouns of address on those used between their parents, we credited the children with a sensitivity to social roles. The children were assumed to ignore the parents' use of T with each other as a model for pronouns of address because they, the children, were not parents addressing spouses.

A second possible model for pronouns of address was provided by a parent's speech to other children in the family. Again, this should have led children in multichild families to adopt T. Again, the failure to find many children using T was attributed to an unwillingness of children to adopt the role of the user of T, namely the role of parent addressing a child.

A finer analysis of the patterns of children's use of T provided some support for these conjectures about the influence of perceived social roles in the determination of children's use of T. In a family with 6 children the 2 oldest girls, when 4- or 5 years old, began an intermittent use of T with their younger siblings. Perhaps these little girls were assuming the role of mother and adopting the pronouns of address of their mother with her children.

Other patterns within families can also be explained by an appeal to perceived social roles, although not necessarily the roles of parent or child. In two families, the children, all teenagers at the time of our interviews, were using T more consistently with their parents and grandparents than they had when younger. In addition, the older children used T more consistently with parents, grandparents, and siblings, than did the younger children. Thus, as the children in these families grew up they assumed the role of adults and adopted the adult way of speaking.

Perceived sex roles could have accounted for the anomalous pattern in a family in which the father had a reciprocal use of T with many of his relatives, as well as with his wife. However, the mother received T only from her husband. Although both parents used T when addressing their two sons and infant daughter, the sons used T only with the father and rejected the suggestion that they use T with their mother and little sister. In the latter case one boy refused with "Oh no, she's a girl." For these children T belonged to the male role. In retrospect it would have been nice to know which pronouns, T or V, these boys used first, as well as the age at which they began to discriminate recipients on the basis of sex.

Finally, in a family in which the children consistently used T with each other and a close cousin, but never with their parents, the children could have perceived T as the appropriate way for everyone to address same-aged peers.

This somewhat elaborate ad hoc account of children's usage of pronouns of address seemed plausible at the time it was offered. However, subsequent study of bilingual children in families in which each parent speaks a different language in the home make this account more questionable (Volterra & Taeschner, 1978). Bilingual children go through three stages of language mastery.

In the first stage the children apparently fail to distinguish the two languages in any way. Their two-word utterances sometimes include words from different languages. Two of the 3 children studied had a second person pronoun in their lexicon in this first stage. In the second stage the children distinguish two lexicons but use the same syntactic constructions in both languages. Not until the third stage, which evidently begins around the third birthday, does the child distinguish the two language with respect to both syntax and speakers. At the beginning of this stage violations of language–speaker pairings, such as one parent using the language of the other parent, were upsetting. For example, children cried or vehemently objected when told that a known speaker of one language also spoke a second language.

Such findings indicate that children do not distinguish between their parents as speakers of different languages until after they begin to use second person pronouns. Hence, it seems very unlikely that children could make the more subtle distinction between those who use T and those who use V before the children themselves use any second person pronouns. Further, little understanding of social role (dyads) is found before the third year (Watson & Fischer, 1980). Consequently, it seems implausible to attribute children's initial use of T or V to a sensitivity to differences in the social roles of those who use T and those who use V.

In brief, the assumption made in the original paper that children master pronouns of address and first person pronouns by observation of conversations between others still seems necessary to account for the finding that children's initial pronouns of address frequently are not the pronouns used by the parents with the children. However, an appeal to children's sensitivity to a variety of social roles to account for initial pronoun use seems dubious now.

If children cannot rely on an understanding of social roles to decide what pronouns to use, the question remains: Why do children fail to use the pronouns of address used by their parents to one another and to their siblings?

I propose that young language learners ignore the pronouns used by their parents within the family and attend only to pronoun use outside the immediate family. Young children could use other clues, which they are known to be sensitive to at an early age, such as prosody (Mehler et al, 1988), simplified locutions called "motherese" (Fernald, 1984), direction of parental gaze (Butterworth, 1979), and mention of proper names (Macnamara, 1982), to detect the addressee of parental speech within the immediate family.

The assumption that young children ignore pronoun use within the family implies that children learn to use T by listening to conversations between parents and persons outside the immediate family, as well as between two or more persons outside the immediate family. This assumption accounts for some of the original data. For instance, it explains why the consistent initial use of T by children with their parents is found only in families where T is used reciprocally by the parents with friends and members of the extended family. It also explains why in the family where only the father received T from outsiders, the children used T with the father but not with the mother who received T only from the father.

Perception of social roles would be a factor only in cases where children's initial use of pronouns of address changed as they grew older.

Obviously, further data are necessary if this conjecture that children ignore pronoun use within the immediate family is to be taken seriously. However, it is supported by Volterra and Taeschner's (1978) finding that the initial second person pronouns of bilingual children are the pronouns of the language spoken in the surrounding community—the language of the father (Italian) in one case, the language of the mother (English) in the other case. Further, the inability of some 4-year-olds to report who used T (Shipley & Shipley, 1969) is consistent with this conjecture. Although weakly supported, this account suggests that in studies of the effect of the linguistic environment upon a child's first language mastery, the interactions between family members and nonfamily members should be examined. See Macnamara (1982) for a similar argument.

A FOLLOW-UP OF THE ORIGINAL STUDY

Given that children do not use the pronouns used by their parents within the family and may not register the details of parental speech when mastering pronouns, the question arises: Does the child who has never used the parental form T have any knowledge of it? To answer this question a limited follow-up of the original study was carried out. This follow-up had two parts: (a) interviews to determine pronoun use as adults of children in the original study, and (b) evaluation of knowledge of the Plain Language by people exposed to it as children who never used it.

Parents from 5 families in the original study were asked about their children's subsequent use of T. In each of these families T was used by both parents with each other and with their immediate family. These families contained a total of 19 children. Table 9.1 summarizes the results. The findings are clear: All individuals who used T forms as adults also used them when young. However, most individuals who used T forms as children did not use them as adults.

What knowledge did the children who never used T retain of the Plain Language? Obviously, as adults they knew their parents used T, just as visitors to the families knew T was used within the families. Further, most literate English speakers know something about T forms in English from the King James Standard Version of the Bible and Shakespeare's plays. The interest was in seeing if the children exposed to T when learning their first language retained some competency with that dialect, even though they never used it. To phrase the question very generally, is production necessary for competency?

TABLE 9.1.

Use of T as Children and as Adults by 19 Individuals Who Were Raised
in Families Where Both Parents Used T With Each Other and With the Children

	Use as Children		
Use as Adults	Consistent with parents and siblings	Intermittent with siblings	No use
With parents & children	1	0	0
With parents only	1 a	0	0
With children only	0	1	0
No use	6	1 a	9

Note. Cell entries are number of individuals.
a. These individuals have no children.

To answer this question a crude measure of competency in the Plain Language was devised and used with 4 adults in the follow-up sample who had never used T, with 6 adults who were close friends and frequent visitors of Quaker families in which T was used, and with a control group of 6 adults with no exposure to the Plain Language. The first group will be referred to as Family, the second group as Visitors, and the third group as Controls.

The subjects' task was to read aloud the dialogue in a brief excerpt from a play and to change the pronouns as instructed as they read. For the first excerpt, from *All My Sons* (Arthur Miller, 1956), the reader was asked to replace third person singular pronouns with so-called "neutral" nonsense pronouns which had no gender. For instance, the nonsense pronoun *per* was to replace the possessive *his* and *her*. The subjects could look at printed examples of appropriate changes whenever they wished as they read.

For the second excerpt, from *Mrs. Warren's Profession* (George Bernard Shaw, 1956), the subjects were asked to change second person pronouns to a singular form when appropriate and to change the verb when the subject was changed. Nonsense pronouns that rhymed with the Quaker pronouns were provided, *see* for the nominative and objective case, *sye* for the possessive case. For the third excerpt, again from *Mrs. Warren's Profession*, the subjects were asked to use *thee* and *thy*. Again in each case, whenever they wished, the subjects could look at printed examples of pronoun replacement, with examples of verb number change where appropriate.

The expectation was that residual competency with the Plain Language would reveal itself when the Quaker pronouns were used, and might even be apparent when nonsense pronouns that merely rhymed with the Quaker forms were used. On the other hand, if the Family subjects were oblivious of pronoun use within the family as children, their performance was expected to be similar to that of Visitors, but perhaps better than Controls.

As can be seen in Table 9.2, all subjects did equally well in replacing pronouns correctly in all three excerpts. However, the Family subjects evidently had greater knowledge of the Plain Language than the others because they were significantly better in making the appropriate change in the verbs. An analysis of variance on the percent of verbs correctly changed with Groups (Family, Visitor, or Control) and Type of Pronoun (nonsense or Quaker) as factors yields a significant effect of Groups $F(2,13) = 7.45$, $p < .01$. (Although the factor Type of Pronoun was significant also, no conclusions are possible about the effect of different kinds of pronouns, because Type of Pronoun was confounded with order of presentation of the tasks.) Thus, children exposed to T from infancy retained a sensitivity to the syntactic requirement of T.

A language with T forms permits the speaker to indicate economically and clearly whether one or more than one person is addressed. A variety of ways have developed to indicate the plural when using a pronoun of address, for instance *y'all* and *youse* (Stevick, 1968). I thought that adults exposed to T as children might be more sensitive to the need to make such a distinction in number, and hence might have developed distinctive forms to indicate number. Therefore, upon completing their reading tasks, all subjects were asked what they would say to ask one person within a group a specific question and what they would say to ask everyone present the same question. In their question to a single person, all subjects used "you" and a proper name to indicate the addressee. In their question to an entire group, the Family subjects never mentioned "you"; they used "we" or "everyone" or "everybody" instead. In contrast, most of the other subjects included "you" in their questions; they used phrases such as "you all" or "you guys" or "all of you." (The difference was significant, Fisher's exact test $p < .05$.) It is tempting to think that

TABLE 9.2
On-line Replacement of Pronouns and Change of Verb Number

Subjects	Requested Pronoun Replacement		
	Nonsense 3rd person	*Nonsense 2nd person*	*Quaker 2nd person*
	Pronoun Replacement		
Family	79	91	85
Visitor	89	75	81
Control	77	83	80
	Verb Change of Number		
Family	--a	65	91
Visitor	--	19	44
Control	--	33	17

Note. Cell entries are percent correct.

a. Verb change was not required in this task.

exposure to T as children had led to an unambiguous interpretion of *you* as the singular.

In spite of the limited samples in this preliminary study, it is apparent that nonusers of the Plain Language exposed to it from birth differ from other native speakers of English in knowledge of T and perhaps even in the use' of pronouns of address. Other differences may exist but not appear with such limited tasks and small groups. At a minimum this study indicates that limited competence with T was acquired without production.

CHANGES IN THE PLAIN LANGUAGE OVER TIME

When the Quakers adopted T for use with everyone, the T pronouns in English were *thou, thee, thy* and *thine* and the V pronouns were *ye, you, your,* and *yours*.

In the late 16th century both *ye* and *you* were used in both the nominative and objective case. By the 18th century *you* was used for both cases (Strang, 1970). In Quaker speech *thee* eventually replaced *thou* in nominative case. However, this change in T forms lagged far behind the similar change in the V forms. The use of *thou art* by some contemporary Quakers is mentioned in an article on Quaker speech written in 1926 (Tibbals, 1926) and by a parent informant in the follow-up study described earlier.

Why should the same change occur in the use of T by Quakers that had occurred much earlier in the use of V? Given the discrepancy between children and parents in their use of T, perhaps children were the instrument of change. Suppose that in earlier generations, as is the case for children in more contemporary Quaker families, some Quaker children initially used V. Suppose further that in earlier generations parents corrected those aspects of their children's speech that they correct today, the truth of the child's utterance (Brown & Hanlon, 1970) and " 'naughty' words" (Brown, 1973, p. 412). For Quaker parents with a strong commitment to the Plain Language based upon religious principles, the use of V forms by their children would merit correction. Thus when a child said "you," the parent would prescribe "thou" or "thee" depending upon the case. For a child who was told sometimes that "you" should be "thee" and other times that "you" should be "thou," the easy solution would be to use the same pronoun to replace all instances of "you." With *thee* and *thou* as the two candidates, *thee* would seem to have the advantage as a consequence of rhyming with *he, she,* and *we*.

SUMMARY AND CONCLUSIONS

Historically, the use of T in English has all but ended, even among linguistically conservative Quakers. The Shipley and Shipley (1969) study, together with the follow-up study, indicate the community of T speakers is too small to support the continued use of T, even with consistent use by a few parents to their children.

Developmentally, observations of the patterns of use of pronouns of address within these few Quaker families indicates that analysis of children's initial mastery of pronouns in communities where both T and V are used may provide information on how the first language learner uses the available linguistic input. In addition, such observations may contribute to the growing knowledge on children's role in language change.

ACKNOWLEDGMENTS

Preparation of this chapter was supported in part by the Spencer Foundation. I am grateful to Thomas E. Shipley for helpful discussions, to Geoff Hall and Amy Pierce for useful suggestions, and to Jim Shah for assistance with the follow-up study.

REFERENCES

Brown, R. (1965). *Social psychology* (First edition). New York: The Free Press.

Brown, R. (1973). *A first language*. Cambridge: Harvard University Press.

Brown, R., & Gilman, A. (1960). The pronouns of power and solidarity. In T. Seboek (Ed.), *Aspects of style in language*. Cambridge: MIT Press.

Brown, R., & Hanlon, C. (1970). Derivational complexity and order of acquisition in child speech. In J. R. Hayes (Ed.), *Cognition and the development of language*. New York: Wiley.

Butterworth, G. (1979). What minds have in common is space: a perceptual mechanism for joint reference in infancy. Paper presented to the Annual Conference of the Developmental Psychology Section, British Psychological Society, Southampton.

Fang, H., & Heng, J. H. (1983). Social changes and changing address norms in China. *Language in Society, 12*, 495–507.

Fernald, A. (1984). The perceptual and affective saliency of mothers' speech to infants. In L. Feagans, C. Garvey, & R. Golinkoff (Eds.), *The origins and growth of communication*. Norwood, NJ: Ablex.

Kroger, R. O., Wood, L.A., & Kim, U. (1984). Are the rules of address universal? III. Comparison of Chinese, Greek, and Korean usage. *Journal of Cross-Cultural Psychology, 15*, 273–284.

Macnamara, J. (1982). *Names for things*. Cambridge: MIT Press.

Mehler, J., Jusczyk, P., Lambertz, G., Halsted, N., Bertoncini, J., & Amiel-Tison, C. (1988). A precursor of language acquisition in young infants. *Cognition, 29*, 143–178.

Miller, A. (1956). All my sons. In *Six Great Modern Plays*. New York: Dell.

Paulson, C. B. (1976). Pronouns of address in Swedish: Social class semantics and a changing system. *Language in Society, 5*, 359–386.

Shaw, G. B. (1956). Mrs. Warren's Profession. In *Six Great Modern Plays*. New York: Dell.

Shipley, E. F., & Shipley, T. E., Jr. (1969). Quaker children's use of *thee*: A relational analysis. *Journal of Verbal Learning and Verbal Behavior, 8*, 112–117.

Stevick, R. D. (1968). *English and its history*. Boston: Allyn & Bacon.

Strang, B. M. H. (1970). *History of English*. London: Methuen & Co.

Tibbals, K. W. (1926). The speech of plain Friends. *American Speech, 1*, 193–208.

Volterra, V., & Taeschner, T. (1978). The acquisition and development of language by bilingual children. *Journal of Child Language, 5*, 311–326.

Watson, M. W., & Fischer, K. W. (1980). Development of social roles in elicited and spontaneous behavior during the preschool years. *Developmental Psychology, 16*, 483–494.

10

Linearity as a Scope Principle for Chinese: The Evidence from First Language Acquisition

Thomas Hun-tak Lee
The Chinese University of Hong Kong

INTRODUCTION

In the linguistics and philosophy literature, it has long been observed that a salient property of quantifier noun phrases (QNP) such as *a babysitter, two strings, every child* lies in their ability to exhibit relative scope (cf. e.g., Keenan, 1971, Lakoff, 1971, Quine, 1960).[1] This can be illustrated by the English sentence (1), which contains two QNPs—*a babysitter* and *every child*. Depending on which QNP falls within the scope of the other, (1) can have two interpretations, given in (2a) and (2b).

(1) *A babysitter* looks after *every child*.
(2) a. There is a x = babysitter such that for all y = child, x looks after y.
    b. For all y = child, there is a x = babysitter such that x looks after y.

In the interpretation (2a), *every child* is within the scope of *a babysitter*; the former is said to have narrow scope, whereas the latter has wide scope: It is the same babysitter who looks after every child. In the reading represented by (2b), where *a babysitter* has narrow scope, the choice of referent depends on the choice of the child: Different babysitters may look after different children.[2]

---

[1] The relative scope property is of course not restricted to QNPs. Other quantificational elements such as negators, adverbs, and modals also display relative scope. This study focuses on the relative scope of QNPs.

[2] A scope-independent reading in which the referents of the two QNPs are determined separately is also possible (see Kempson & Cormack, 1981). Given a universal quantifier and an existential quantifier, the wide scope reading of the existential QNP is indistinguishable from the scope-independent reading of the sentence. This paper is concerned with the possibilities of scope-differentiated readings.

The question of how children of various ages interpret the relative scope of quantifiers is of considerable interest from the standpoint of learnability. The representation of scope requires theoretical constructs such as operators (e.g., there is a x, for all y) and variables (e.g., x, y), as well as well-formedness conditions governing the binding of variables.[3] It seems plausible to assume that abstract constructs such as operators and variables are not learned inductively, but are part of the initial state of the child. In other words, they might be among the substantive universals of Universal Grammar (UG). Following the spirit of Fodor's (1980) argument, it is clear that children who do not possess the linguistic concepts of operators and variables would find it impossible to learn whether the language they are exposed to (e.g., English) displays scope ambiguity. This is because given a sentence like (1), children first of all need to have the means of representing the two scope interpretations of the sentence before they can detect scope ambiguity. The representation of scope possibilities presupposes the postulation of operators and variables in the first place.[4]

A further point that can be made is that even though the variable-binding property of QNPs may be endowed as part of UG,[5] it is possible that these innate properties are not available to the child at the outset. Rather, they manifest themselves at a later stage as the child matures. As Borer and Wexler (1987) observed, although children's grammar may be consistent with UG principles at all stages of its evolution, it is conceivable that some UG principles are not realized at particular stages because of maturational factors. It remains, therefore, for empirical investigations to ascertain whether children indeed grasp the scope property of QNPs early in their development.

The acquisition of quantificational scope also deserves attention because the principles determining scope interpretation differ from one language to another. Quantificational scope is an area of grammar that shows parametric variation. A striking contrast between Chinese and English is that English permits scope ambiguity much more freely than Chinese. In English, the relative scope of QNPs in a clause is generally not uniquely determined by the relative position of the QNPs at S-structure. Thus, it is not the case that in (1), the structur-

---

[3]An example of a well-formedness condition on the binding of variables is that operators must bind variables. Thus a representation with operators not associated with any variables will be ill-formed and uninterpretable, e.g. "There is a x = person such that John saw Mary".

[4]Quine (1973) suggests that variable-binding may be learned inductively from wh-questions. On empirical grounds, as our data reveals, it is doubtful whether the learning of wh-bound variables can be extended in a straightforward way to the variable-binding of QNPs. The literature shows clearly that canonical *who, what- where*-questions are understood by age 4 at least in some verbal contexts (cf. e.g., Brown, 1968, Cairns & Hsu, 1978, Tyack & Ingram, 1977). If this can be taken as an indication of acquisition of bound variables (see Roeper, 1986, for an alternative view), then the acquisition of the variable-binding property of QNPs may be very different from that of wh-questions, as the data available suggest that knowledge of the former is not clearly evidenced until after age 5 (cf. Lee, 1986).

[5]This position was adopted by Hornstein (1984), though he further assumed that the variable finding property may actually surface quite early.

ally superior subject QNP *a babysitter* always has wide scope over the object QNP *every child*. Rather, either QNP may have wide scope. In Chinese, however, as first observed by S.F. Huang (1981), a strong isomorphism exists between S-structure and Logical Form (LF).[6] A subject QNP invariably has scope over an object QNP, as shown by (3). The sentence cannot have the interpretation (3b) where the object QNP *meige xuesheng* "every student" has the subject QNP *yige jingcha* "a cop" within its scope.

> (3) a. Turan, yige jingcha zhuazou le meige xuesheng suddenly one-CL cop arrest ASP every-CL student "Suddenly, a cop arrested every student."
>
> b. There is a x = cop such that for all y = student, x arrested y.
>
> c. *For all y = student, there is a x = cop such that x arrested y.

Some languages may use linear precedence as a principle for scope interpretation, so that if QNP A precedes QNP B at S-structure, then A has scope over B at LF. As we argue later, this is an important principle for Chinese. For other languages such as English, linearity may be irrelevant. Given these cross-linguistic facts, one may assume that the parameters for the determination of scope may take on different values (e.g., different syntactic relations) across languages.

If languages vary in how quantifier scope is determined, how do children learn the scope interpretation principles of their native language? What initial principles do they adopt? Do they assume free scope order or do they regard scope order as given directly by the relative positions of the QNPs at S-structure? These are intriguing learnability issues which can only receive satisfactory answers when acquisition data are available for a variety of languages governed by different scope interpretation principles. The present research is intended to be a contribution to this line of inquiry. We demonstrate empirically that linearity must be a strong principle assumed by Mandarin-speaking children in their understanding of scope. Following is an outline of principles for determining quantifier scope in adult Mandarin Chinese before turning to the experimental study.

QUANTIFIER SCOPE IN MANDARIN CHINESE

The scope principles for Mandarin Chinese that we adopt for the experimen-

---

[6]S-structure and Logical Form refer to the levels of syntax standardly assumed in the Government Binding theory (cf. Chomsky, 1981, van Riemsdijk & Williams, 1986). For the purpose of our discussion, Logical Form can be broadly understood to be a level of representation one of whose identifying properties is that scope ambiguity is primarily represented structurally at that level (cf. May, 1977, 1986).

tal investigation are given in (4) (cf. Aoun & Li, 1989, J. Huang, 1983, for alternative analysis):[7]

(4) Suppose A and B are QNPs, then:

    a. If A asymmetrically commands B at S-structure, A has scope over B at Logical Form (LF). (A *commands* B if neither dominates the other and the first S node dominating A also dominates B.)

    b. If A and B command each other and A precedes B at S-structure, A has scope over B at LF.

The first principle captures the clause-boundedness of the effect of quantification. Intuitively, a QNP cannot escape from its own clause to have scope over another QNP in a higher clause. Figures 10.1a and 10.1b illustrate structures in which QNP_2 asymmetrically commands QNP_1. In Fig. 10.1a, QNP_1 occurs within a sentential subject; in Fig. 10.1b, QNP_1 is located within a relative clause modifying a subject NP. In both figures, QNP_2 commands QNP_1 because the first S-node dominating QNP_2 is S_0, which dominates S_1, the first S node dominating QNP_1. However, QNP_1 does not command QNP_2. Examples of these structures are given in (5) and (6).

(5) a. [xili   jinnian   qing le   sange   zhujiao]
       department-in this-year   hire ASP three-CL teaching-assistant
       dui meige   laoshi   dou you   haochu
       to every-CL teacher   all   have benefit
       "(the fact) [that the department hired three teaching assistants] this year is beneficial to every teacher"

    b. For all y = teacher, the fact that there are three x = teaching assistant such that the department hired x is beneficial to y.

    c. *There are three x = teaching assistant such that for all y = teacher, the fact that the department hired x is beneficial to y.

(6) a. [shujia   kan le yibai   ben shu] de tongxue
       summer read ASP one hundred CL book NOM classmate
       dedao meige laoshi de chengzan
       obtain every-CL teacher NOM praise
       "Students [who read a hundred books in the summer] obtained the praise of every teacher."

    b. For all y = teacher, students such that there are a hundred x = book and students read x obtained the praise of y.

    c. *There are a hundred x = book such that for all y = teacher, students who read x won the praise of y.

In (5), QNP_2 is *meige laoshi* "every teacher," and QNP_1 is *sange xuesheng* "three students." In (6), QNP_2 is also *meige laoshi* "every teacher," and QNP_1 is *yibai*

---

[7]It is generally recognized that c-command rather than command or linearity is a more descriptively adequate notion for the anaphora and quantifier facts of English (Reinhart, 1981, May, 1977, 1986). The view assumed here is that this may not hold for all languages with respect to quantifier scope. Chinese is a case in point.

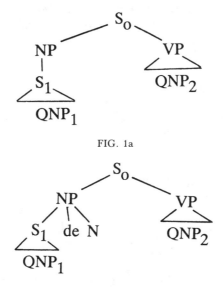

FIG. 1a

FIG. 1b

ben shu "a hundred books." By our scope principle (4a), only QNP_2 may have wide scope in both sentences. This is borne out by the data. The fact that asymmetrical command is the relevant principle for deciding the relative scope of QNPs in separate clauses can also be seen from the fact that linear order fails to play any role in these cases. Although QNP_1 precedes QNP_2 in (5) and (6) it is QNP_2 that takes wide scope.

Linear order is relevant for scope interpretation only when asymmetrical command does not obtain, as stated in (4b). If two QNPs mutually command each other, the one that precedes will have wide scope. In the following text we examine four types of structures in which the QNPs mutually command each other. For all these cases, the linearity principle makes the correct prediction. Consider Fig. 10.2, which shows a QNP in subject position (QNP_1) and another QNP in object position (QNP_2). A sentence whose core structure coincides with that in this figure was given earlier in (3).

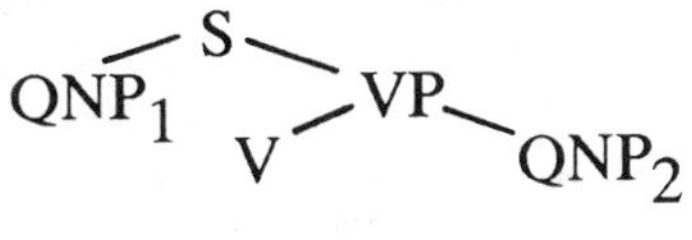

$$QNP_1 \quad\overset{\displaystyle S}{\underset{\displaystyle V}{\qquad}}\quad VP \quad QNP_2$$

FIG. 2.

The scope principle (4b) says that QNP_1 will have scope over QNP_2. This is consistent with the facts of the unambiguous sentence (3), in which only *jige jingcha* "a cop" may have wide scope. Although on the surface (4b) seems to be factually accurate, sentences such as those represented in Fig. 10.2 do not provide crucial support for it. Notice that in the figure, the two QNPs reflect two kinds of relations. QNP_1 precedes QNP_2, and at the same time the former c-commands the latter (A *c-commands* B if and only if neither dominates the other, and the first branching node dominating A also dominates B). In other words, linear order is confounded with c-command in these structures. To identify the independent contribution of linearity in scope relations, we need to turn to sentences where neither of the mutually commanding QNPs c-commands the other. Some of these cases are represented in Fig. 10.3 and 10.4. In Fig. 10.3, QNP_1 is a preverbal prepositional object and QNP_2 a postverbal object (either a direct object or a prepositional object). In Fig. 10.4, both QNPs are prepositional objects in preverbal position. The structure in Fig. 10.3 is illustrated by (7), and that of Fig. 10.4 is exemplified by (8).

(7) a. Wo changchang [dui liangge nanren] baoyuan meige nuren
       I   often   to two-CL male   complain every-CL woman
       "I often complain to two men about every woman"

    b. There are two x-man such that for all y = woman,
       I often complain to x about y.

    c. *For all y = woman, there are two x = man such that
       I often complain to x about y.

(8) a. Daoyan [gen liangge sheyingshi]   [cong meige jiaodu]
       director with two-CL cameraman   from every-CL angle
       paishe changcheng
       film   Great-Wall
       "The director filmed the Great Wall with two cameramen from every angle"

    b. There are two x = cameraman, such that for every y = angle,
       the director filmed the Great Wall with x from y.

    c. *For every y = angle, there are two x = cameraman, such that the
       director filmed the Great Wall with x from y.

In (7) and (8), on our definition of c-command, neither QNP c-commands the other. The interpretations given in (7b) and (8b) and the illformedness of the readings (7c) and (8c) show that generally, in accordance with the linearity principle (4b), the QNP that precedes has wide scope.[8]

---

[8]Alternatively, one coudl treat the preverbal PPs as merely superficially PPs and analyze them as being on a par with NPs, because both preverbal NPs and PPs can function as topics (cf. Chao, 1968, Li & Thompson, 1981). One could further assume that the first preverbal superficial PP in Fig. 10.4 is adjoined to VP and is therefore not a sister of the second PP. Once this assumption is made, QNP_1 will c-command QNP_2 in both Figs. 10.3 and 10.4. Acceptance of this line of analysis will mean that it would be virtually impossible to find unequivocal cases of mutually commanding QNPs that do not show any c-commanding relationship. This is because *[V PP PP] structures are prohibited by a well-known phrase structure constraint on verb complementation in Chinese (Huang, 1982).

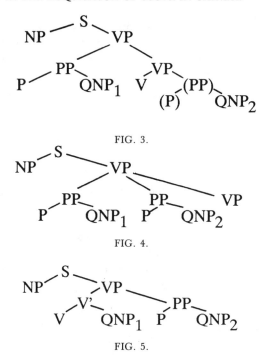

FIG. 3.

FIG. 4.

FIG. 5.

A third type of structure that reveals the role of linear order is that given in Fig. 10.5, where both QNPs occur postverbally, one as direct object and the other as prepositional object. An example of this structure is given in (9). On one analysis of the sentence, the verb and the direct object form one constituent V', which then combines with a PP to form VP (cf. Aoun & Li, 1989).[9]

   (9) a. Laoshi song le liangben shu gei meige tongxue teacher give ASP two-CL book to every-CL classmate "The teacher gave two books to every classmate"

      b. There are two x = book such that for all y = classmate the teacher gave x to y.

      c. For all y = classmate, there are two x = book, such that the teacher gave x to y.

On this constituent analysis, neither QNP c-commands the other. By (4b), QNP_1 should take wide scope. This is in fact one of the two interpretations of the sentence. However, unlike sentences such as (3), (7), (8), which are un-

---

[9]The analysis is motivated in part by the requirement of strict binary branching. If one adopts a [V NP PP]$_{VP}$ rather than a [[V NP]$_{V'}$ PP] analysis, QNP_1 will both precede and c-command QNP_2. This will render the sentence structure (our test sentence Type II) irrelevant to deciding between c-command and linearity. The acquisition results in the section titled Experiment Results reveal, however, a great deal of similarity between the children's performance on the structure of Fig 10.3 and that of Fig. 10.5

ambiguous, more than one scope reading is possible with sentences like (9), as first observed by Aoun and Li (1989). Suffice it to say at this point that the linearity principle allows us to predict some, if not all, of the scope interpretations of a clause and that the principle does not make false predictions. Further observations are made about scope ambiguity in later sections.

CHILDREN'S UNDERSTANDING OF QUANTIFIER SCOPE

An earlier study (Lee, 1986) investigated how Mandarin-speaking children aged between 3 and 8 years comprehended the relative scope of QNPs in subject and object positions, that is, sentences represented by Fig. 10.2. A major finding of the study was that Chinese children probably interpreted QNPs as inherently referential; clear evidence for the variable-binding property of QNPs was not observed among the children until after age 5. In other words, given a sentence such as (10), whose adult interpretation is represented by (10b), 3- to 5-year-olds interpreted *yige dangao* "a cake" as referring to a specific entity.

(1 0) a . Meige   xiaohai   dou zai chi   yige   dangao
              every-CL child   all ASP eat   one-CL   cake
              "Every child is eating a cake"
         b.   For all x = child, there is a y = cake such that
              x is eating a cake.

The reading according to which different children are eating different cakes was clearly evidenced only in the older age groups. The study, however, failed to establish the scope interpretation principles assumed by children once the variable-binding property of QNPs is understood. The subject QNP both precedes and c-commands the object QNP (cf. Fig. 10.2), and to the extent that children interpreted QNP_1 as having wide scope, it is unclear whether they were following linear precedence or c-command.

Test Material

To overcome the inadequacies of the earlier study, the test sentences of the present experiment include QNPs that do not show any c-command relationship, such as those illustrated in Fig. 10.3 and 10.5. The data discussed in this paper cover two of these sentence types.[10] The first sentence type shows QNP_1 in a preverbal locative phrase (a prepositional phrase headed by *zai* "at") and QNP_2 as a postverbal object. As observed earlier (cf. sentence (7) and

---

[10]The experiment included a third sentence type, the *Ba*-construction, corresponding to the structure of Fig. 10.3. See Lee (1989) for acquisition data on *Ba*-sentences.

Fig. 10.3), this type of sentence is unambiguous, with QNP_1 having scope over QNP_2.

(11) Sentence Type 1 (*zai*-sentences)

    a. X zai *yige dengzi*   shang fang *meigen shengzi*   (EA)
        at   one-CL stool on   put every-CL string
        "X puts every string on a stool"

    b. X zai *meige dengzi*   shang dou fang *yigen shengzi*   (AE)
        at every-CL stool on   all put one-CL string
        "X puts a string on every stool"

    c. X zai *yige xiaohai*   shenshang gai *meitiao maojin*   (EA)
        at   one-CL child body-on lay every-CL towel
        "X lays every towel on a child"

    d. X zai *meige xiaohai*   shenshang dou gai *yitiao maojin* (AE)
        at every-CL child body-on   all lay one-CL towel
        "X lays a towel on every child"

The second type of sentence involves QNP_1 as direct object and QNP_2 as a postverbal object of a locative phrase (a prepositional phrase headed by *zai* "at"). As discussed earlier (cf. sentence (9) and Fig. 10.5), two scope interpretations are possible for these sentences, with the linearity principle predicting only one of the two readings.

(12) Sentence Type II (V-sentences)

    a. X fang *yigen shengzi*   zai *meige*   *dengzishang*   (EA)
        put one-CL string   at every-CL stool-on
        "X puts a string on every stool"

    b. X fang *meigen shengzi*   zai *yige*   *dengzishang*   (AE)
        put every-CL string at one-CL stool-on
        "X puts every string on a stool"

    c. X gai *yitiao maojin*   zai *meige*   *xiaohai*   shenshang   (EA)
        lay one-CL towel at   every-CL child   body-on
        "X lays a towel on every child"

    d. X gai *meitiao maojin*   zai *yige xiaohai*   shenshang   (AE)
        lay every-CL towel at one-CL child body-on
        "X lays every towel on a child"

In the test sentences (11) and (12), X stands for the name of the child subject. There are two experimental settings (or prop settings) corresponding to each sentence type, one involving the placement of strings on stools, and the other requiring the positioning of towels over the bodies of dolls. The strings were long enough to span three stools, and the towels large enough to cover all three dolls. The props are illustrated in Fig. 10.6. The (a,b) sentences in (11) and (12) refer to the prop setup in Fig. 6a, whereas the (c,d) sentences correspond to the props in Fig. 10.6.

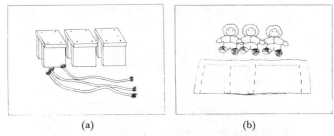

(a)   (b)

FIG. 10.6.   Arrangement of Experimental Props.
(a). Prop Setting A. (b). Prop Setting B.

For each sentence type and prop setting, two quantifier orders were used, an EA order with an existential QNP preceding a universal QNP, as well as an AE order with a universal QNP preceding an existential QNP. The (a) and (c) sentences in (11) and (12) show EA order, whereas the (b) and (d) sentences display AE order. The following data include a total of 2 (sentence type) x 2 (prop setting) x 2 (quantifier order) = 8 sentences.

Procedure

117 Mandarin-speaking children aged between 3 and 8 years were drawn from two kindergartens and two primary schools in Beijing. The subjects included sixteen 3-year-olds, twenty-one 4-year-olds, twenty-one 5-year-olds, nineteen 6-year-olds, twenty 7-year-olds, and twenty 8-year-olds. In addition, a group of adults were tested as control. The 3-to-8-year-olds were chosen because in Lee (1986) it was found that the critical point of development occurred around age 5 or 6. It was thought, therefore, that the age range selected for the present study should give a sufficient span to observe some of the critical stages of development.

The children were interviewed individually, each for about 20 minutes. They were shown the props by the writer and another researcher, who is a native speaker of Beijing Mandarin, and the test sentences were read to them. The subjects were then asked to act out the meaning of the sentences. Only act-out tasks were used, because in Lee (1986) it was found that children were much more consistent in act-out tasks than in picture identification tasks when responding to sentences containing more than one QNP. In the experiment, the prop settings and the test sentences for each prop setting were randomized and were used together with some other picture-identification items not directly related to the relative scope of QNPs (see Lee, 1989, for details).

The experimental procedure for adults differed slightly from that for children. Adult subjects were interviewed in groups of 5 to 6 rather than individually. Instead of using the subject's name in the position of X in the test sentences, the morpheme *qing* "please" was used as X. Adults were shown the props and were asked to represent their interpretation schematically with pencil and paper (e.g., using lines to represent strings and rectangular boxes to symbolize stools).

Results

Predictions Based on the Linearity Principle

If the linearity principle (4b) is correct, then one should predict that the wide scope of QNP_1 is available for all the test sentences. For unambiguous sentences such as the *zai*-sentences in (11) (Type I, cf. Fig. 10.3), one should expect QNP_1 to predominantly receive wide scope interpretation in the adult and older age groups. For sentences where ambiguity exists, such as the V-sentences of (12) (Type II, cf. Fig. 10.5), the wide scope reading of QNP_1 should show up at least as a major pattern in the adults and older subjects.

The children's performance, however, may show a task bias which will affect how they respond to sentences of the AE and EA orders. In the experiment, the subjects were shown three objects (stools or dolls) that refer to the location or goal of three other objects (strings or towels), and were asked to act according to their understanding of the test sentences. Earlier studies (cf. Donaldson & McGarrigle, 1974) suggested that in such prop settings, children are likely to put objects in one–one correspondence without really attending to the linguistic clues in the sentence.[11] This potential danger may be especially evident in the youngest groups, who may not have acquired stable knowledge of the relevant linguistic principles. In other words, given a sentence of AE order, with a universal quantifier as QNP_1, the children may place strings and stools, or towels and dolls, in one–one correpondence, giving the semblance of a wide scope reading of QNP_1. This response may be a reflection of task bias rather than an understanding of the linearity principle. If a task bias indeed exists, then one would expect the younger children to pair the two sets of props irrespective of quantifier order, that is, children's responses to the AE sentences may superficially resemble a wide scope of QNP_1 interpretation, and their responses to the EA sentences may seem to suggest a wide scope of QNP_2 reading. The predictions of our analysis are given in Table 10.1.

---

[11]An interesting fact reported in Donaldson and McGarrigle (1974) is that sentences such as "All the cars are in the garages" were judged true by their children subjects only if each garage was occupied by a car. Likewise, sentences such as "All the books are in the boxes" were judged true only if the numbers of books and boxes were equal. They suggest that "for children under five, there is something peculiarly fundamental and compelling about the notion of fullness."(p. 186) An alternative view is that the children are taking the two sets of objects separately, that is, they are giving scope-independent readings, and that there is something compelling about matching objects in one-one correspondences.

TABLE 10.1
Predicted Results Based on Linearity and Task Bias

Sentence Type	Linear Order	Task Bias	Testing Case for Linearity
zai EA	wide scope of E	wide scope of A	yes
zai AE	wide scope of a	wide scope of A	no
V EA	wide scope of E	wide scope of A	yes
V AE	wide scope of A	wide scope of A	no

According to the linearity principle, the first QNP should take wide scope irrespective of sentence type and quantifier type, as shown in the second column of Table 10.1. If subjects act only under the influence of the task bias, they will respond as though they were opting for the wide scope of the universal quantifier, irrespective of quantifier order, as shown in the third column. If the responses predicted by linearity happen to be also predicted by the task bias, as is the case with all the AE sentences, the result will not tell us the precise role of linear order in the children's interpretation. If, however, the responses based on linearity are exactly the opposite of that due to task bias, as in all the EA sentences, then evidence for the wide scope interpretation of the existential quantifier can be construed as a very strong indication that children are following linear precedence in interpreting scope. The sentences that inform us of the role of linearity are marked "yes" in the fourth column. As our results reveal, the task bias indeed influenced the younger subjects.

Experiment Results

The data reported here are concerned with the scope-differentiated interpretations of the subjects. Responses that cannot be classified as corresponding to the wide scope of one of the QNPs are excluded from our analysis.[12] Corresponding to each sentence type and quantifier order, three categories of responses are distinguished. One type of response shows subjects consistently assigning wide scope to QNP_1 on the two test sentences (cf. the two prop arrangements). Another type of response shows subjects who consistently take QNP_2 as the wide scope quantifier on the two test sentences. In the third type

---

[12]An example of a response from a subject that cannot be classified as a scope-differentiated response is one where the subject placed only one of the objects (strings or towels) on another object (stool/doll) for the AE sentences. Similar non-scope responses were also observed among the younger subjects in Lee (1986).

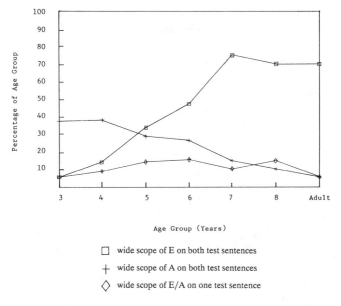

FIG. 10.7.   Children's Interpretation of *zai*-sentences
Existential Quantifier (E) precedes Universal Quantifier (A)

Type I: NP [zai QNP₁] V QNP₂
                          E   A

of response, subjects fluctuate between the wide scope of QNP₁ on one test sentence and the wide scope of QNP₂ on the other. That is, the third category consists of inconsistent responses.

Results on Zai-Sentences (Type I)

Figure 10.7 gives the results on the *zai*-sentences with EA order. The lines connected by squares represent the percentage of an age group that consistently chose the wide scope of QNP₁ (in this case the existential quantifier). The graph marked by crosses represents the percentage of an age group that consistently violated the linearity principle by choosing the wide scope reading of QNP₂ (in this case the universal quantifier). The lines joined by diamonds show the proportion of an age group that varied between the two scope interpretations. Here, a wide scope interpretation of E is one where all the strings/towels are placed on a single stool/doll. A wide scope interpretation of the universal quantifier is one where each of the strings/towels is placed on a different stool/doll.

With respect to the adult subjects, it is clear that the majority of them (70%) consistently assigned wide scope to E in accordance with the linearity principle. A small percentage (5%) consistently interpreted the universal quantifier as wide scope, violating linearity. Another 5% gave inconsistent responses. The reason the adults did not show a higher level of uniformity as one would expect may be related to a lexical idiosyncrasy of *mei* "every": quantification of postverbal theme/patient objects by *mei* often results in unnatural sentences (see Xu & Lee, 1989, for discussion).[13]

The responses of the child subjects display a clear pattern. The percentage of 3- and 4-year-olds who assigned wide scope to E was very low (6% and 14% respectively). However, this percentage increased steadily with age to a peak of 75% at age 7. The initially low level of correct responses may have been due to the task bias discussed earlier which gradually became overridden by the linguistic principles of scope interpretation.

Turning to the subjects who consistently violated linearity, 38% of the 3- and 4-year-olds assigned wide scope to the universal quantifier. The figure declined steadily after age 5 to a low of 10% at age 8. Later discussion shows that the apparent violation of linearity in the younger age groups was due to the task bias, which exerted a noticeable influence when the linearity principle had not been firmly established. It is worthy of note that the children were generally consistent in their performance: The inconsistent responses never accounted for more than 16% of an age group.

The results on the *zai*-sentences with AE order are presented in Fig. 10.8. As in Fig. 10.7, the lines marked with squares indicate the percentage of an age group that opted for the wide scope of QNP_1 (in this case A) on both test sentences. The graph with crosses represents the percentage of an age group that chose the wide scope of QNP_2 (in this case E) on both sentences. A wide scope of A response is one where the strings/towels are each placed on a different stool/doll. A wide scope of E response is one where a single string/towel is laid across all three stools/dolls. If the children were acting exclusively according to linguistic principles, the pattern of responses in the two figures should be highly similar, because the only difference between the test sentences lies in quantifier order. That is to say, one would expect the wide scope of QNP_1 reading to show similar paths of development in the two figures. However, the patterns revealed in the figures are strikingly different. First, with respect to the adult subjects, all of them consistently assigned wide scope to the universal quantifier in accordance with linearity. The unanimous adult response may be due to the fact that in the *zai*-sentences with AE order, the universal quantifier *mei* "every" no longer quantifies a postverbal patient/theme object, but rather quantifies a locative phrase. The test sentences are therefore perfectly natural.

---

[13]For some reason, 20% of the adult subjects gave at least one non-scope interpretation. This may be related to the fact that the sentence type violated lexical restrictions on the universal quantifier *mei* "every." Some adult subjects in fact reported that they found this sentence type very odd.

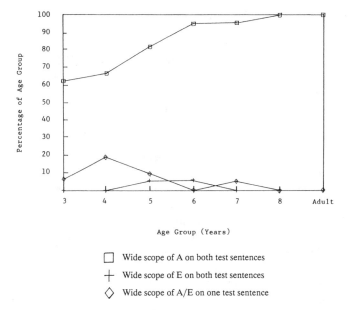

FIG. 10.8.   Children's Interpretation of *zai*-sentences
Universal Quantifier (A) precedes Existential Quantifier (E)

Type I: NP [zai QNP₁] V QNP₂
                   A   E

In contrast to the data on *zai*-sentences with EA order, the wide scope of
QNP₁ response is evidenced fairly early in the *zai*-sentences with AE order.
Sixty-three percent of the 3-year-olds and 67% of the 4-year-olds gave this
response. The figure climbed to 81% by age 5 and 95% by age 6. The surprisingly early onset of the wide scope of QNP₁ reading consistent with linearity,
as well as the relatively higher percentage of this response across all age groups,
may be attributed to the task bias.

Another difference from the patterns of the *zai*-sentences with EA order,
where some of the children (between 10% and 38%) across all ages chose the
wide scope QNP₂ reading in apparent violation of linearity (see Fig. 10.7), is
that extremely few children chose the wide scope of QNP₂ reading in the *zai*-
sentences with AE order. None of the 3-, 4-, 7-, and 8-year-olds showed this
response, and only 5% of the 5- and 6-year-olds offered this interpretation.
This suggests that when a violation of the linearity principle was not favored
by the task bias, virtually no consistent violations of linearity could be observed.

Figure 10.8 also indicates that, as in Fig. 10.7, the percentage of children
showing inconsistent responses on *zai*-sentences with AE order was small. Except for the 4-year-olds, less than 10% of the age groups showed inconsistent
interpretations.

In order to ascertain whether the younger children were acting according to linguistic principles of were mainly influenced by experimental setting, it was decided to compare the children's responses on the EA sentences with their responses on the corresponding AE sentences that involve the same props. The comparison should inform us as to whether children were sensitive to the distinction between EA and AE ordering. Tables 10.2 and 10.3 below provide information about four categories of responses for subjects who showed scope-differentiated responses. In both tables, the third column gives the number of subjects who consistently followed the linearity principle, assigning QNP_1 wide scope regardless of whether it is an existential or universal quantifier. The fourth column shows the number of subjects who consistently violated the linearity principle by assigning QNP_2 wide scope irrespective of quantifier type. The last two columns show the numbers of subjects who assigned wide scope to particular quantifiers irrespective of quantifier position. The fifth column gives the figures for those who indiscriminately assigned wide scope to the universal quantifier, and the sixth column gives the figures for those who indiscriminately interpreted the existential quantifier as having wide scope.

As can be seen from the figures in the third column of the two tables, less than 10 subjects (i.e., less than 50%) among the 3- to 5-year-olds consistently used the linearity principle when presented with a particular set of props and different quantifier orders. The relevant figure, however, climbed steadily to between 14 and 18 subjects among the 7- and 8-year-olds. Note that the number of subjects who consistently violated the linearity principle (cf. the fourth column) never exceeded 3 among the 3- to 5-year-olds, and was nil in the other age groups. This argues convincingly for the growth of linearity as a scope principle for the child subjects.

At the same time, between 7 and 10 (cf. the fifth column) of the 3- to 5-year-olds assigned wide scope to the universal quantifier irrespective of quantifier order. The number of subjects exhibiting this tendency dropped to 5 or less in the 7- and 8-year-olds. Note, however, that the figures in the sixth column

TABLE 10.2
Children's Interpretation of *Zai*-Sentences—EA Order vs. AE Order
(Prop Setting A: Strings and Stools)

Age (yr)	No. of subjects	wide sc. of E on EA / wide sc. of A on AE	wide sc. of A on EA / wide sc. of E on AE	wide sc. of A on EA / wide sc. of A on AE	wide sc. of E on EA / wide sc. of E on AE
3	10	2	0	8	0
4	17	7	0	10	0
5	18	9	1	8	0
6	18	12	0	6	0
7	20	16	0	4	0
8	19	14	0	5	0
Adult	18	17	0	1	0

TABLE 10.3
Children's Interpretation of *Zai*-Sentences—EA Order vs. AE Order
(Prop Setting B: Towels and Dolls)

Age (yr)	No. of subjects	wide sc. of E on EA wide sc. of A on AE	wide sc. of A on EA wide sc. of E on AE	wide sc. of A on EA wide sc. of A on AE	wide sc. of E on EA wide sc. of E on AE
3	9	0	0	8	1
4	14	2	3	9	0
5	17	8	1	7	1
6	17	10	0	7	0
7	19	15	0	4	1
8	20	18	0	2	0
Adult	18	16	0	2	0

show that, across all ages, at most 1 subject indiscriminately assigned wide scope to the existential quantifier irrespective of quantifier position. The data thus strongly support the existence of a task bias that favors a one–one correspondence of props, which must be taken into consideration in our analysis.

Results on V-sentences (Type II)

The data on the subjects' interpretation of the relative scope of two postverbal QNPs are given in Figs. 10.9 and 10.10. Figure 10.9 reports on the test sentences with EA order. First of all, examining the adult data, one notices that the percentage of adults who consistently assigned wide scope to QNP_1 (= E) was only 55%, whereas the percentage of adults assigning wide scope to QNP_2 (= A) was 25%, with another 15% varying between the two readings. This indicates that adults found these sentences scope-ambiguous.

Turning to the children's performance, we see that as with the *zai*-sentences, the percentage of 3- and 4-year-olds who took QNP_1 as the wide scope quantifier was very low (13% and 14% respectively). The figure for this response climbed to 38% at age 5, and reached a peak of 85% at age 7. It is plausible to believe that the initially low figure was due to interference of the task bias. As the children matured, the linearity principle became gradually established, thereby strengthening the wide scope of QNP_1 reading. It is interesting to observe that unlike the results in the *zai*-EA sentences, the linearity-based reading for the V-sentences with EA order dropped after 7 years of age to 65% at age 8. This suggests that linearity is counterbalanced by some other scope principle in the older age groups.

As for the percentage of subjects consistently choosing QNP_2 as having wide scope, the figure stood at 31% at age 3, increased to 62% among the 4-year-olds, and then steadily declined to a low of 5% at age 7. Thereafter, the figure rebounded to 20% in the 8-year-old group. Again, the general decline in this

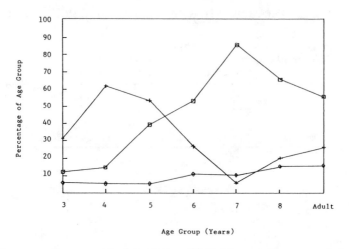

Age Group (Years)

☐ Wide scope of E on both test sentences

+ Wide scope of A on both test sentences

◇ Wide scope of E/A on one test sentence

FIG. 10.9. Children's interpretation of V-sentences. Existential Quantifier (E) precedes Universal Quantifier (A).

Type II: NP V QNP₁ [P QNP₂]
                 E   A

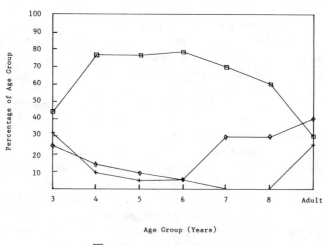

Age Group (Years)

☐ Wide scope of A on both test sentences

+ Wide scope of E on both test sentences

◇ Wide scope of A/E on one test sentence

FIG. 10.10. Children's interpretation of V-sentences. Universal Quantifier (A) precedes Existential Quantifier (E).

Type II: NP V QNP₁ [P QNP₂]
                 A   E

type of response (except for a slight increase in the 4-year-olds) alongside the growth of the linearity principle parallels what we observed in the *zai*-EA sentences. Evidently, the task bias exerted its influence mainly in the younger age groups. The slight rise in the wide scope of QNP_2 (= A) reading among the 8-year-olds, which happened concurrently with the drop in the linearity-based reading, is another indication of the ambiguity of this type of sentence. With regard to the third type of response, a very low level of inconsistency (between 5% and 15%) can be observed, corroborating the finding on *zai*-EA sentences.

The adult data for the V-sentences with AE order, given in Fig. 10.10, show considerable similarity to the corresponding data in the V-sentences with EA order (refer to Fig. 10.10). Thirty percent of the subjects consistently selected the wide scope of QNP_1 interpretation in accordance with linear precedence. Twenty-five percent of them consistently assigned wide scope to QNP_2 (= E), and 40% of them vacillated between the two readings. This confirms the ambiguity status of the sentences. It should also be observed that unlike the V-sentences with EA order, the V-sentences with AE order involve a lexical idiosyncrasy of *mei* "every" discussed earlier, because it quantifies a postverbal patient/theme object in these sentences. As a result, the V-sentences with AE order sound unnatural to native speakers of Mandarin.[14]

Just as the children's data on EA and AE orders for the *zai*-sentences show divergent patterns, so the developmental findings on V-sentences with AE order, given in Fig. 10.10, do not replicate those with EA order (cf. Fig. 10.9). First of all, a relatively higher percentage of the younger age groups chose the wide scope interpretation of QNP_1 on the AE order than on the EA order. Forty-four percent of the 3-year-olds selected this reading. The value increased to 76% at age 5 and stayed at that level until 6 years of age, then dropped to 60% among the 8-year-olds. Parallel to a similar decline after age 7 in Fig. 10.9, a decline in the wide scope of QNP_1 reading after age 6 was observed, presumably due to the emergence of ambiguity of these sentences for the children. Secondly, a small number (30%) of children opted for the wide scope of QNP_2 (= E) at the 3-year-old level, but the value dropped sharply to 5% in the 5- and 6-year-olds, and 0% after age 6. This suggests that whatever the principle is that contributes to the wide scope reading of QNP_2, it does not seem to be sufficiently strongly established in the older age groups to allow

---

[14]An additional phrase structure constraint needs to be noted. It has been pointed out by Chen (1987) that generally in sentences of the form:

$$X \text{ V } NP_1 \text{ [}zai \text{ } NP_2\text{]}$$

the NP_1 cannot be definite, as seen in the ill-formedness of

??Fang   neiben   shu   zai   zhuo   shang
    put   that-CL   book   at   table   on
"Put that book on (the) table"

The oddness of the V-sentences with AE order may also be related to the fact that universal quantifiers generally pattern with definite NPs, thus leading to violation of this phrase structure constraint.

them to go against the task bias, which favors the wide scope of QNP_1 reading in this case. Thirdly, with respect to the inconsistent responses, a fairly high level of the 3-, 4-, 7-, and 8-year olds (between 14% and 30%) assigned wide scope to QNP_1 on one sentence and to QNP_2 on another. This relative high level of inconsistency, especially among the older age groups, may be an indirect reflection of the scope ambiguity of the sentences. It may also be due to the violation of the lexical properties of *mei* "every," which prohibits quantification of postverbal theme/patient objects.

To determine whether subjects were sensitive to quantifier order for the V-sentences, comparisons of subjects' responses on AE and EA sentences were made for each prop setting. These are shown in Tables 10.4 and 10.5.

The third column of the two tables show that only one 3-year-old, four 4-year-olds, and seven 5-year-olds assigned wide scope to QNP_1 irrespective of quantifier type. This figure increased to a peak of 14–18 among the 7-year-olds, followed by a slight drop after age 7. The pattern is similar to that we found for the *zai*-sentences, showing that children did not successfully apply linear precedence as a consistent principle until after age 6. The fifth column of the two tables indicate that between 4 and 15 of the 3-, 4-, and 5-year-olds assigned wide scope to the universal quantifier irrespective of quantifier order, pointing to the influence of the prop arrangement. The number of subjects showing this type of response dropped after 6 years of age to 7 or less, demonstrating clearly that the task bias was overridden by linguistic principles beyond a certain point of development. A glance at the fourth column shows that virtually no subject consistently violated the linearity principle across all age groups.

DISCUSSION

Our data demonstrate that linear order is a strong scope interpretation principle for Chinese, and that it is firmly acquired at around age 7. This can be seen from the similarities shared by the developmental patterns of the EA sentences across the three sentence types. Comparing the graphs of Figs. 10.7 and 10.9, one observes that in both figures, the percentage of an age group that selected the consistent wide scope reading of QNP_1 (= E) began at around 10% at age 3, climbed to approximately 40% at age 5, and peaked at 70% to 80% by 7 years of age. Concurrent with the gradual strengthening of linearity, one also observes a decline in the consistent wide scope reading of QNP_2 between 4 and 7 years of age. The subjects' acquisition of the linearity principle is also reflected in their differential responses to sentences with EA and AE orders. In all sentence types (cf. Tables 10.2 through 10.5), sensitivity to quantifier order was recorded after age 5, and the adoption of the linear precedence principle was evidenced with respect to the *zai*- and V-sentences.

TABLE 10.4
Children's Interpretation of V-Sentences—EA Order vs. AE Order
(Prop Setting A: Strings and Stools)

Age (yr)	No. of subjects	wide sc. of E on EA wide sc. of A on AE	wide sc. of A on EA wide sc. of E on AE	wide sc. of A on EA wide sc. of A on AE	wide sc. of E on EA wide sc. of E on AE
3	8	1	0	7	0
4	19	4	0	15	0
5	20	7	0	11	2
6	18	8	0	7	3
7	20	18	1	0	1
8	20	14	1	3	2
Adult	18	4	2	4	7

The differences between the two sentence types point to the presence of scope ambiguity in the V-sentences. With respect to the EA order, one difference between the V- (cf. Fig. 10.9) and the *zai*-sentences (cf. Fig. 10.7) is that the wide scope interpretation of QNP_1 showed a marked decline in the former sentence types after age 7, but not in the latter. Parallel to this difference is the slight rise in the wide scope reading of QNP_2 after age 7, in the V-sentences but not in the *zai*-sentences. The presence of scope ambiguity can also be seen from the divergences among the AE sentences. Although the consistent wide scope reading of QNP_1 ($=A$) showed a steady increase in the *zai*-sentences (cf. Fig. 10.8), that of the V-sentences (cf. Fig. 10.10) indicated a steady decline after age 4. The decline of the wide scope of QNP_1 reading in a prop setting that favored such a reading is another indication of the availability of scope ambiguity.

TABLE 10.5
Children's Interpretation of V-Sentences—EA Order vs. AE Order
(Prop Setting B: Towels and Dolls)

Age (yr)	No. of subjects	wide sc. of E on EA wide sc. of A on AE	wide sc. of A on EA wide sc. of E on AE	wide sc. of A on EA wide sc. of A on AE	wide sc. of E on EA wide sc. of E on AE
3	5	1	0	4	0
4	15	4	0	11	0
5	19	7	1	10	1
6	16	9	0	6	1
7	20	14	1	2	3
8	18	10	1	5	2
Adult	20	8	3	4	5

Why is there ambiguity in the V-sentences and not in the *zai*-sentences? It was proposed by Xu and Lee (1989) that scope ambiguity in Chinese is restricted to the verb phrase, and stems from the joint effects of the linearity principle and a thematic hierarchy as follows:

Thematic Hierarchy
(Group A): Agent, Location, Source, Goal
(Group B): Theme, Patient, Factitive (Narrow Scope Thematic Roles)

The thematic roles in Group A are higher on the hierarchy than those in Group B as far as scope is concerned. In general, if a QNP bears a thematic role that is higher on the thematic hierarchy than another QNP within the same VP, then the former may have scope over the latter. In the *zai*-sentences, QNP_1 precedes QNP_2 and should therefore have scope over the latter by the linearity principle. At the same time, QNP_1 bears a location thematic role, which takes priority over the theme/patient role borne by QNP_2 according to the thematic hierarchy. Therefore by both principles, QNP_1 should take wide scope, and the sentence is unambiguous. In the V-sentences, QNP_1 should likewise have wide scope by the linearity principle. However, QNP_2 bears the location role, which is higher on the thematic hierarchy than the theme/patient role carried by QNP_1. The conflicting demands of the two scope interpretation principles give rise to ambiguity.

CONCLUSIONS

Assuming the relevance of linear precedence to the scope interpretation of adult Mandarin, we set out to investigate the development of this principle in Mandarin-speaking children, with a view to providing a basis for further study of parametric variation. Two kinds of sentences were examined, both of which contained mutually commanding QNPs that do not c-command each other. The two sentence types also differed with respect to the possibility of scope ambiguity.

The findings reveal that quantifier order is distinguished by Chinese children by age 6 and that the linearity principle for scope interpretation is firmly established by age 7. There is also evidence to suggest that if scope ambiguity is entirely due to the operation of the thematic hierarchy, the latter scope interpretation principle is acquired late, probably after age 7.

ACKNOWLEDGMENTS

This chapter is based on an experiment reported in greater detail in Lee (1989). I wish to express sincere gratitude to Chen Ping, Lin Chongde, Xie Jun, Xiong Zhenghui, without whose assistance the experiments could not have been conducted. I am indebted to Yu-Chin Chien, Nina Hyams, Xu Lie-jiong, Ken Wexler, and the editors of this volume for comments on various points in the paper. This research was supported in part by the Hsin Chong-K.N. Godfrey Yeh Educational Fund.

REFERENCES

Aoun, J., & Li, A. (1989). Scope and Constituency. *Linguistic Inquiry, 20*(2), 141–172.

Borer, H., & Wexler, K. (1987). The Maturation of Syntax. In T. Roeper & E. Williams (Eds.), *Parameter Setting* (pp. 123–172). Dordrecht: D. Reidel.

Brown, R. (1968). The development of Wh-questions in Child Speech. *Journal of Verbal Learning and Behavior, 7*, 279–290.

Cairns, H., & Hsu, J. (1978). Who, why, when, and how—a developmental study. *Journal of Child Language, 5*, 477–488.

Chao, Y. R. (1968). *A Grammar of Spoken Chinese*. Berkeley: University of California Press.

Chen, P. (1987, March). On Referentiality vs. nonreferentiality, identifiability vs. nonidentifiability, specificity vs. nonspecificity, and genericity vs. individuality in Chinese. *Zhongguo Yuwen*, pp. 81–92.

Chomsky, N. (1981). *Lectures on Government and Binding*. Dordrecht: Foris.

Donaldson, M., & McGarrigle, J. (1974). Some Clues to the Nature of Semantic Development. *Journal of Child Language, 1*, 185–194.

Fodor, J. A. (1980). On the Impossibility of Acquiring "more powerful" structures. In M. Piattelli-Palmarini (Ed.), *Languae Learning: The debate between Jean Piaget and Noam Chomsky* (pp. 142–162). Cambridge: Harvard University Press.

Hornstein, N. (1984). *Logic as Grammar*. Cambridge: MIT Press.

Huang, J. (1982). Logical Relations in Chinese and the Theory of Grammar. Unpublished doctoral dissertation, MIT.

Huang, J. (1983). On the Representation of Scope in Chinese. *Journal of Chinese Linguistics, 11*(1), 36–91.

Huang, S. (1981). On the Scope Phenomenon of Chinese Quantifiers. *Journal of Chinese Linguistics, 9*(2), 226–243.

Keenan, E. (1971). Quantifier Structures in English. *Foundations of Language, 7*, 255–284.

Kempson, R., & Cormack, A. (1981). Ambiguity and Quantification. *Linguistics and Philosophy 4*, 254–309.

Lakoff, G. (1971). On Generative Semantics. In D. Steinberg & L. Jakobovits (Eds.), *Semantics* (pp. 232–296). London: Cambridge University Press.

Lee, T. (1986). Acquisition of Quantificational Scope in Mandarin Chinese. *Papers and Reports on Child Language Development, 25*, 57–64.

Lee, T. (1989). The Role of Linear Order in the Acquisition of Quantifier Scope in Chinese. *CUHK Papers in Linguistics, 1*, 18–45.

Li, C., & Thompson, S. (1981). *Mandarin Chinese: A Functional Reference Grammar*. Los Angeles: University of California Press.

May, R. (1977). *The Grammar of Quantification*. Bloomington: IULC.

May, R. (1986). *Logical Form*. Cambridge: The MIT Press.

Quine, W. (1960). *Word and Object*. Cambridge: The MIT Press.

Quine, W. (1973). *The Roots of Reference*. La Salle: Open Court.

Reinhart, T. (1981). Definite NP Anaphora and C-command Domains. *Linguistic Inquiry, 12*(4), 605–635.

Roeper, T. (1986). How Children Acquire Bond Variables: In B. Lust (Ed), *Studies in the Acquisition of Anaphora* (pp. 191–200). Dordrecht: D. Reidel.

Tyack, D., & Ingram, D. (1977). Children's Production and Comprehension of Questions. *Journal of Child Language, 4*, 211–224.

van Riemsdijk, H., & Williams, E. (1986). *Introduction to the Theory of Grammar*. Cambridge: The MIT Press.

Xu, L., & Lee, T. (1989). Scope Ambiguity and Disambiguity in Chinese. Papers from the 25th Chicago Linguistic Society Meeting: Part One, the General Session, Chicago, IL.

11

On Interpreting Partitives

Ann M. Reed
College of William and Mary

In this paper, I propose that the interpretation of English partitive constructions like *one of the boys* depends on the particular discourse function of partitives: evoking subgroups of discourse groups.[1] The requirements of this discourse function account for several distributional idiosyncracies of partitive expressions, including the Partitive Constraint, the apparent preference for a definite NP in the embedded NP, and the Definite Head Constraint, the necessity for an explicit restrictive modifier when the determiner is *the*. These constraints stem from the discourse requirements that the full partitive NP evoke a discourse subgroup and the embedded NP access a discourse group.

In focusing on discourse reference, this analysis diverges from most work done on partitives, which has tended to be either syntactic or semantic. Selkirk (1977) and Jackendoff (1977), although noting the distributional patterns discussed in this paper, concentrated on syntactic structure. More recently, Barwise and Cooper (1981), Ladusaw (1982) and Keenan and Stavi (1986) have proposed semantic characterizations of determiners to explain such distributional patterns.

The approach taken here does, however, parallel recent studies (Fox, 1987; Hawkins, 1978; Heim, 1982; Rando & Napoli, 1978; Reed, 1982; Sidner, 1986; Webber, 1986) that have suggested that some constructions, particularly definite noun phrases and existentials, are inherently discourse-linked. These studies have shown that the interpretation of definites and existentials depends on some determination of the discourse reference of a given NP. Furthermore, they have

---

[1]An early version of this paper was presented in part at NEMLA, April 1986. I am grateful for the comments of conference participants, Ken Safir, Susan Rothstein, Lily Knesevich, Deborah Cameron, Janine Scancarelli, and anonymous reviewers.

suggested that the distributional patterns of such constructions are best explained in terms of their discourse function.

In this discussion of partitives, I first identify the general principles that control discourse reference and affect the interpretation and distribution of NPs. I then characterize partitive noun phrases in terms of discourse function and show that the same principles explain their interpretation and apparent constraints on their distribution.

DISCOURSE REFERENCE

The concept of discourse reference originates in the study of discourse anaphora, particularly with respect to the distribution of pronouns (Fox, 1987; Heim, 1982; Karttunen, 1976; Webber 1979). Discourse referents or, in Webber's (1986) terms, discourse entities, comprise a set of entities naturally evoked in a discourse.[2] The use of a definite pronoun is usually dependent on the establishment of a discourse entity, which can be evoked by a full indefinite NP earlier in the discourse or, as (2) shows, through association (Fox, 1987; Hawkins, 1978):

(1) A man came in...he pulled a gun.
(2) I went to buy a book...I went down to NYU to get it...he was handing me the book and he said it would be twenty dollars.
   (he = cashier, evoked in association with book search)
(3) Some boys came in...they started a fight.

As (3) shows, discourse entities can be groups as well as individuals; that is, the plural *they* refers to a group of boys. Ordinary plurals like *some boys* are the most obvious constructions that evoke such discourse groups. However, conjunction, as in (4), or even separate occurrence in the discourse, as in (5), can also evoke a discourse group.

(4) I took a train and a bus and they were both on time.
(5) John talked to Bill about it and then they left.

---

[2]Following Webber (1986), I use the terms *evoke/access* rather than *denote* or *refer* to reflect NP reference in context. According to Webber (1986):

> Informally, a discourse model (DM) may be described as the set of entities 'naturally evoked'...by a discourse...I have called these things 'discourse entities' and Sidner has called them "cognitive elements". In linguistics, they harken back to what [Karttunen, 1976] has called "discourse referents". The alternate terminologies that Sidner and I have adopted rest on wanting to keep 'refer' a separate term. That is, 'referring' is what people do with language. Evoking and accessing discourse entities are what texts/discourses do. A discourse entity inhabits a speaker's discourse model and represents something the speaker has referred to. A speaker refers to something by utterances that either evoke (if first reference) or access (if subsequent reference) its corresponding discourse entity. (p. 397)

Within this framework, indefinite noun phrases, as noted above, normally serve to evoke discourse entities. In contrast, definite noun phrases differ from indefinites in that, like pronouns, they normally access rather than evoke discourse entities (Hawkins, 1978; Heim, 1982). Their access of discourse entities can depend on previous mention, as in (6), or association, as in (7), where, Hawkins (1978) showed, our understanding that weddings generally have only one bride makes the definite acceptable:

(6) She hit a boy and his dog and the boy died.

(7) I went to a wedding and the bride cried.

Plural definites, like plural pronouns, access discourse groups; and, as in the case of pronouns, those groups can be evoked by a single plural indefinite noun phrase or by separately occurring NPs in the discourse.

(8) I invited Harry and Tom but the snobs wouldn't come.

(9) John talked to Bill about Mary and then the boys left.

Thus both definites and pronouns, unlike indefinites, access a previously evoked discourse entity, individual or group, which may be determined in a variety of ways.[3]

The examples of pronouns and definites so far can be described in terms of anaphora, the noun phrases accessing previously evoked discourse entities. However, in the case of nonanaphoric definites, explicit linguistic material, usually in the form of a restrictive modifier, occurs within the definite noun phrase to affect the discourse model. In the following novel definites, that is, noun phrases used as first mention of the *boy* or the *book*, the NP contains a restrictive modifier.

(10) We got to the fair on time but *the boy in the parking lot* wouldn't let us in.

---

[3]Existential sentences, of the form *there be NP*, are related to this discussion of NP use in that they make a direct assertion about discourse reference, with respect to the predicate NP (deJong, 1987; Rando & Napoli, 1978; Sidner, 1986). The predicate NP is placed within some discourse group, sometimes simply within the set of discourse entities, sometimes in a location, et cetera:

(i) There might be a solution to this problem; what would it look like?

(ii) There is a solution to this problem in this book.

Because the discourse function of existentials is thus to introduce a discourse entity into the discourse, the predicate NP in an existential is normally indefinite. However, there are many well-known counterexamples to this distribution where definite NPs are acceptable as predicate NPs. In such cases, the definite, although it accesses a discourse entity already, is asserted to belong to some subgroup of discourse entities. For example, as Rando and Napoli (1978) showed, definites in a list will be acceptable if the list as taken as a new discourse group.

(iii) *There is the boy.

(iv) Of course you have friends; there's the boy, and me, and uh...

Similarly, if the context defines a new subgroup of discourse entities, the existential can assert that even a definite belongs to that subgroup:

(v) Who will let us in?...Well, there is the boy.

(11) Just bring me *the first book you see*.

Although not anaphoric, these noun phrases share with anaphoric definites an interpretation of identifiability: The discourse entities linked to *the boy* and *the book* are identifiable within the discourse just as the discourse entities linked to *the boy* and *the bride* in examples (6) and (7) were.

In discussing these nonanaphoric definites, Webber (1986) incorporated them into her model thus: Definite noun phrases can "access entities presumed to be in the listener's discourse model" after having been evoked earlier by an indefinite "or they can be used to evoke new entities into the model" (p. 399) by the types of restrictive modification we have noted. Although definites thus appear to have two discourse functions, accessing and evoking discoursing entities, Webber proposed that they have a unitary interpretation in terms of an identifying description, that "information about an entity that can. . .be assumed to be shared (though not necessarily believed) by both speaker and hearer." (p. 397) Definites, whether accessing or evoking discourse entities, differ from indefinites in her analysis in that "the entity evoked by a singular definite noun phrase can usually be described adequately by just that description" (p. 399). The identifying description for the discourse entity in the anaphoric case (6) will be *the (just mentioned) boy she hit*, which can be accessed simply by the definite *the boy*, and in the newly evoked case (10) will be *the boy in the parking lot*; in both cases, the identifying description will serve to identify the discourse entity.

Although Webber described these nonanaphoric NPs as evoking rather than accessing entities, I suggest they evoke and access a discourse entity simultaneously. Because it is the presence of an identifying description in the discourse model that allows a definite to access the discourse entity and because that identifying description is explicit in the nonanaphoric definites, the ability to identify/access a discourse entity is present simultaneously with its being evoked.

In this regard, restrictive modifiers have a particular role in changing the discourse model, a role that restricts their distribution in discourse. For example, when a discourse entity has been previously evoked, further identification by means of a restrictive modifier is anomalous:

(12) A man and a woman were watching the dog;
    (a) the man laughed at it
    (b) the man with blue eyes laughed at it.

In (12a), the simple definite *the man* is an acceptable continuation of the discourse in that it accesses one of two possible discourse entities, which might be described as *the man watching the dog* or *the woman watching the dog*. However, in (12b), the additional restrictive *with blue eyes* is anomalous since the first conjunct has already evoked a discourse entity. (Note that information about the man's eyes might be included in the discourse, for example, *by the way, he had the clearest blue eyes I've ever seen* and would, in Webber's analysis, be added as an additional description of the discourse entity.)

On the other hand, as Clark and Haviland (1977) pointed out, when a subgroup of a discourse group has to be accessed, some explicit linguistic material, often in the form of restrictive modification, is needed to evoke it. In the following example, where the definite noun phrase accesses a subgroup of a discourse group, the (a) continuation is unacceptable because it does not contain explicit linguistic material to identify the discourse entity accessed by the definite NP, but the restrictive modifier *who were drunk* in the (b) continuation makes the definite acceptable:

(13) Some men were watching a lame dog
    (a) ...the ones watching it laughed out loud.
    (b) ...the ones who were drunk laughed out loud.

Thus, even when a discourse group has been evoked, a subgroup of that group must be explicitly evoked.

The discussion of discourse reference so far has relevance for the analysis of partitive noun phrases in several ways. The interpretation and distributional patterns of partitives are restricted by the fact that indefinite noun phrases normally evoke discourse entities, anaphoric definites access them, and nonanaphoric definites simultaneously evoke and access them. Furthermore, restrictive modification directly affects the discourse model, through its use in nonanaphoric definites and, in particular, in evoking subgroups of discourse groups.

PARTITIVE STRUCTURE AND INTERPRETATION

I define partitives as NPs of the form *Det (one) of NP* where Det = *the, this, that, every, each, all, none, any, some, a, many, few, several, much, both, neither, either, half, most,* or a numeral.[4] By this definition, all of the following expressions are partitives, although, in this paper, I only consider partitives in which the embedded NP is plural:

(14) all of your friends; one of the boys; each (one) of Harry's cats; none of five finalists; much of the snow; some of that wildlife.

For purposes of this discussion, I assume that the syntactic structure for partitives is similar to that proposed in Jackendoff (1977 pp. 106–119).[5]

---

[4] I will not discuss the pseudopartitives (Jackendoff, 1977) like a *number of men* or *two bunches of daffodils*, which have a full nominal head and which do not observe the discourse conditions discussed in this paper.

[5] For ease of exposition, I have left out the N′″ level. I have also ignored the generation and position of *of*. I assume, as argued in Jackendoff (1977, pp. 114–119), that the *one* that appears in *none, every one, each (one),* and *any (one)* in partitives and in anaphoric NPs is a result of substantivization, that is, a realization of PRO with certain lexical items.

(15)

$$N'' = \text{MATRIX NP}$$

```
              N"  =  MATRIX NP
            /     \
        DET        N'
         |        /
       MANY     N
                 |
                PRO  of  NP  =  EMBEDDED NP
```

(Note that I refer to the full partitive NP as the MATRIX NP and to the lower NP as the EMBEDDED NP.) For my purposes, the crucial feature of this partitive structure is that it contains two noun phrases, the matrix NP and the embedded NP; such a structure is easily related to the analysis of partitive interpretation that follows.[6] Other analyses, such as one postulating a Noun in place of the DET in (15) and a PP in place of the N ' in (15), could accommodate the following analysis as long as a two-nominal structure occurs. However, Jackendoff's structure, which posits an empty N (= PRO) in the N ', suggests a natural interpretation for the N ', which I pursue shortly.

As Jackendoff argued, the existence of two nominals in partitive structures receives support from modification facts: There appear to be two positions for modifiers within partitive structure. In (16), for example, *with braces* can describe either *the children* or *many (PRO) of the children*.

(16) Many of the children with braces walked to the stage.

Evidence for this ambiguity comes from the two possible preposings of elements within the NP:

(17) Of the children with braces, many walked to the stage.
(18) Of the children, many with braces walked to the stage.

In (17), *the children with braces* is a constituent and thus can occur in preposed position, but in (18), where *with braces* modifies *PRO of NP*, only *the children* is fronted. Similarly, nonrestrictives apparently have two possible positions, one modifying the matrix NP and one the embedded NP:

(19) One of the boys, who was singing in the shower, didn't hear.
(20) One of the boys, who were all singing in the shower, heard.

In these examples the differences in number agreement support the analysis of two nominals within the noun phrases; so also in (32), where the clause is restrictive:

(21) One of the boys who has/have blue eyes sang.

---

[6]Jackendoff argued for the constituent status of *of NP* from preposing and extraposition evidence and for the existence of a nominal before *of*, largely on the basis of modification and of substantivization, for example, *each one of the boys*. Keenan and Stavi (1986) proposed a structure for partitives in which *many of the* in *many of the men* is a complex determiner. As they do not develop the analysis in full, it is not clear how they could handle Jackendoff's arguments and I will not attempt to answer the arguments they do represent for complex determiners.

Partitive Interpretation

Intuitively, the interpretation of the partitive is quite straightforward: The matrix NP denotes a subset of the set referred to by the embedded NP, for example, *many of the men* denotes a subset of the men. However, the denotation of an NP is generally assumed to be a subset of the denotation of the N', in most cases a common noun but in the case of partitives *PRO of NP*. Thus, in the partitive example, the relationship between the embedded NP *the men* and the N' *PRO of the men* remains to be determined and here is where PRO appears to be a useful term. In Jackendoff's analysis, N' is the level on which the head and its arguments occur; we find under N' expressions like *leader of the men* and *criticism of the play*. Assuming a similar pattern for the partitive N', PRO, as the head under N, will take the embedded NP as an argument. This PRO is interpreted as an existential predicate, parallel either to the identity predicate as in *x is the teacher/John Smith* or to a set-membership predicate, as in *x is a doctor/a friend of mine*.[7] For the purposes of this paper, I assume that N' denotes membership in the set denoted by the embedded NP. For plural partitives, this is the most natural interpretation, as well as the one supposed in most of the literature (Aldridge, 1982; Hogg, 1972, 1977; Jackendoff, 1977; Lee, 1971, 1972).

The interpretation of the matrix NP as a subset of the embedded NP is assumed in most of the semantic accounts of partitives and fits our intuitions about this construction. However, it does not offer a direct explanation of distributional patterns in partitive noun phrases such as the preference for a definite NP in the embedded NP but not in the matrix NP. Within the semantic accounts of partitives, as noted previously, various limits on the determiners in embedded NPs have been proposed to effect these distributional patterns. Reed

---

[7]Whether identity or set membership is the more accurate interpretation will depend on how we characterize NP denotation, in particular the denotation of mass nouns. Most analyses of partitives focus on plural count NPs, where the set membership interpretation is natural. Indeed, Keenan and Stavi (1986) restricted the embedded NP to a plural. But there are many instances of apparent partitives with singular NPs; *some, a little, much, more, most, all*, and *half* can occur with singular nouns, both mass and count, in partitives (Ladusaw, 1982; McCawley, 1978). Whether or not a set-membership interpretation can extend to such mass partitives is questionable. If it does, the N' would refer to the member of a single-member set and the semantics of *much* and other mass quantifiers would have to account for the fact that the full NP has a mass interpretation. That does appear to be the case as well in nonpartitive expressions, as in (i), and in examples like (ii) and (iii), where the mass quantifier seems to apply to sets of individuals taken distributively.

    (i) There wasn't much cake left.
    (ii) I have read much of many books.
    (iii) He ate all of each cookie.

The latter group needs more study, especially because they do not observe the discourse conditions discussed in this paper.

    (iv) The archaeologists just found half of a house.
    (v) I read some of both of those books.

(1988) and later discussion in this paper argue that such accounts have so far been unable to account for all the distributional patterns and have not given a satisfactory explanation for the patterns.

Indeed these characterizations of partitive interpretation and distribution are bound to be inadequate, I claim, insofar as they ignore the special discourse function of partitives. I propose that partitives differ from simple NPs, which also denote subsets of sets, in having a particular discourse function. That function, as suggested earlier, is to evoke subgroups of previously evoked discourse groups.

In this regard, we can contrast the interpretation of simple NPs with partitives containing the same determiners, as follows:

(22) a. No unicorns appear in tapestries of that period.
     b. None of the unicorns appear in tapestries of that period.
(23) a. Matisse could have painted some pictures then.
     b. Matisse could have painted some of the pictures then.

In each of these cases, the (b) example differs from the (a) example in its supposition of a relevant discourse group. Thus, although both *no unicorns* and *none of the unicorns* both denote empty sets, they differ in that the second, but not the first, supposes a discourse-relevant group of (woven) unicorns. Similarly, in (23), although both the (a) and (b) example could be continued by *but he didn't*, the (b) example would still access a discourse-relevant group of pictures, which might well be the topic of discussion.

The need for the partitives in the (b) examples is intuitively obvious; although *some boys* may refer to a subset of the universal set of boys, we sometimes need to refer to a portion of a particular discouse-relevant group of boys, hence *some of the boys* or even *none of the boys*:

(24) We interviewed many boys and some girls but some of the boys
      quit.
(25) John talked to Bill and Fred but none of the boys called me.

Conversational implicature may account for the fact that the subgroup is normally taken to be a proper subgroup. Although partitives with *both* and *all* (to be discussed later) are universal, in all other cases the partitive is taken as referring to a proper subgroup of the embedded NP. For example, *two of the boys* implies that there are other boys in the relevant group, although *two boys* does not.

Thus partitive noun phrases, like indefinites, evoke discourse entities. But partitives differ from indefinites in that the entities they evoke are subgroups of already evoked discourse groups. It is this function, I argue, that accounts for the distributional patterns they exhibit.

DISTRIBUTIONAL PATTERNS

From the discourse function of partitives just defined, it follows that the embedded NP and the matrix NP in partitives have different discourse functions: The embedded NP must access a discourse entity, in fact, a discourse group, and the matrix NP must evoke a subgroup of that discourse group. If the embedded NP in partitives must access a discourse group, we would expect it to be definite, in accordance with the discussion of discourse reference earlier. We find that in all the examples of partitives so far, the embedded NP is a definite noun phrase, although of course it could be a pronoun, as in *John talked to Bill and Fred but none of them called me*. And, if the matrix NP must evoke a discourse entity, such as the subgroup of a discourse group, we would expect it to be indefinite, as the examples above have illustrated with determiners like *one, none, some*, and *two*.

On the other hand, we would not expect to find indefinites in the embedded NP nor definites in the matrix NP. And, in general, this is the case, with some exceptions which support the discourse-based distribution rather than a determiner-based one.

The following discussion first examines the distributional patterns of the matrix NP and then those of the embedded NP. In each case, the discourse requirements of evoking or accessing discourse entities account for the patterns we observe.

Limits on the Matrix NP: The Definite Head Constraint

As noted earlier, we expect indefinite, but not definite determiners in the matrix NP of partitives because the matrix NP must evoke a discourse entity. In general, definites are not judged acceptable in the matrix NP:

(26) *The one of the boys failed.
(27) *The two of his friends told on him.

Parallel simple NPs are acceptable, of course, because the definite only has to access a (previously-evoked) discourse entity:

(28) The two friends told on him.

However, it has been noted for some time that partitive NPs with definite heads become acceptable if the definite head is modified by an explicit restrictive (Jackendoff, 1977; Stockwell, Schachter, & Partee, 1973):

(29) The one of the boys who was/*were cheating failed.
(30) The two of his friends who saw told on him.

(The claim that the restrictive is tied to the matrix rather than to the embedded NP is supported by the number agreement facts in (29), as well as the following preposings:

(31) *Of his friends who saw, the two told on him.
(32) Of his friends, the two who saw told on him.)

If the discourse requirements on the matrix NP hold, the definite with a restrictive modifier, as in (29) and (30), must meet the requirement of evoking a discourse entity.

That is, of course, the function we noted for nonanaphoric definites, which occurred with restrictive modifiers, in (10) and (11). Following Webber, we observed that such NPs, despite being identifiable through the restrictive modifier, evoked new discourse entities. Thus in the case of a modified definite head, the partitive can still serve to evoke a new subgroup, for example, the discourse entity described by *the boy who was cheating*, of a discourse group.

Partitive Determiners

Other determiners, such as *both, all, most, either*, and *neither*, are often classified as [+ definite], usually because of their unacceptability in existentials. However, in contrast to the definite article, these determiners are acceptable in the matrix NP of partitives without restrictive modification:

(33) Both of the boys passed. (cf. *the two of the boys passed.)
(34) Most of the children were crying.

Reed 1988 and 1989 argued that these are intrinsically partitive determiners, always evoking subgroups of discourse groups. (Even a simple NP like *both boys* is partitive, equivalent to *both of the boys* and similarly dependent on a discourse group of boys.) For example, *both of the boys*, in contrast to *the two boys*, will occur in discourse to stress the (universal) subgroup of a group of two boys, often with some discourse implication—in this example, . . . *they must have studied together*.

If these determiners are intrinsically partitive, their appearance in the matrix NP of partitives is, of course, expected.

Limits on the Embedded NP: Partitive Constraint

The requirement that the embedded NP access a discourse entity explains the distribution underlying the Partitive Constraint. The need to access a discourse entity creates a preference for, but not a restriction to, definite NPs in the embedded position. In the following discussion three types of embedded NPs will be noted: NPs with definite determiners which do not access a discourse group, NPs with indefinite determiners which manage to access a discourse group, and NPs with partitive determiners like *both* which evoke subgroups of discourse groups. In each case, the question of acceptability is determined by the discourse requirement.

There is widespread agreement that in partitives, a definiteness constraint, sometimes called the Partitive Constraint, exists (Barwise & Cooper, 1981; Jackendoff, 1977; deJong, 1987; Keenan & Stavi, 1986; Ladusaw, 1982; Selkirk, 1977). For many, the following distinctions are clear-cut and suggest that the determiner of the embedded NP must be definite:

(35) *two of many men; *some of few men.

(36) one of my men; one of the men; one of you.

Indefinites (*many, some, several, no, any, few*, and numerals) usually are not acceptable in the embedded NP. Definites (*the, those, these*, and possessives), on the other hand, usually are.

Observation of this distribution has prompted varying semantic characterizations of the determiners that are allowed in partitives, generally amounting to restricting the embedded NP to [+definite] determiners. However, not all [+definite] determiners can occur in partitives. For example, the partitive determiners noted above, *both, all, most, either*, and *neither* cannot:

(37) *two of most boys, some of all children, one of both cakes, one of either boy.

In explaining this distribution, Barwise and Cooper (1981) used the concept of a proper principal filter to distinguish *the* from *all*. DeJong (1987) suggested that *most* differs from definites in having the semantic feature of cardinality, which makes it unacceptable in partitives. Ladusaw (1982), Dowty and Brodie (1984), and Keenan and Stavi (1986) proposed additional semantic criteria, for example distributiveness, to distinguish *both* from *the two*, which appears to have similar semantic characteristics but which is acceptable in partitives.

Reed (1988), arguing that such semantic criteria are not sufficient to explain the behavior of *both*, drew a distinction between semantic/lexical groups and discourse groups. It seems clear that the existence of a semantic/lexical group is not sufficient for the embedded NP of the partitive, although a discourse group is. For example, definite collectives, which are lexically plural (Hoeksema, 1983), on first mention, are not taken as discourse groups and are unacceptable with (count) partitives:

(38) *One of the crowd died.

(39) *One of the couple died.

However, once they occur in the discourse, they evoke a discourse group and a partitive can access it.

(40) A crowd gathered but most of them were quiet.

(41) A couple moved in and then one of them died.

The same argument applies to other cases of semantic groups that are not discourse groups. Critically, it is not sufficient that the plural NP contain definites; it must access a discourse group. This is clear when we consider cases of definite plurals that do not access a discourse group. Note the following examples of conjoined definite NPs which are not acceptable in partitives.

(42) *Two of the dean, the provost, and the president must have voted against it.

(43) *One of the boy and the girl must have written this.

The NPS in these examples, by any of the semantic criteria noted, are definite and plural, and yet they are impossible in the embedded NP of the partitive. Of course, in such cases, the conjoined definite NPs access separate entities, for example the boy and the girl, rather than a discourse group.[8] So the discourse-based explanation appears to account for these examples, which are problematic for all the semantic accounts. (Note, however, that once such a conjoined NP occurs, it evokes a discourse group, which can then serve as antecedent to partitives: *the dean, the provost and the president met together and two of them must have voted against it*).

The preceding examples show that definites that do not access a discourse group are not acceptable in the embedded NP of partitives, an observation that is explained, of course, by the discourse function of the embedded NP.

We now turn to the observation that some indefinites are commonly judged acceptable in partitive constructions. As noted earlier, the fact that indefinites evoke, but do not access, discourse entities accounts for their general unacceptability in partitives. However, in some long-noted cases (Ladusaw, 1982; Stockwell, Schachter, & Partee, 1973; Yotsukura, 1970), indefinites are acceptable in the embedded NP of partitives.

(44) The dog was stoned by two of some boys playing in that field.

(45) Only one of many people who saw the accident would testify.

What appears to make these partitives acceptable is the addition of descriptive material, similar to Webber's identifying description for a definite; in each case, in fact, the modifier relates directly to a particular discourse situation, the scene of the stoning or the application process. In contrast to these examples, note that when an embedded indefinite is modified by material less salient in the discourse, the partitive is much less acceptable.

(46) *The dog was stoned by two of some boys who can play baseball.

(47) *Only one of many people who sing auditioned.

---

[8]In contrast, the following partitives, which include conjoined common nouns, are acceptable.

   (i) One of the pens and pencils on his desk fell off.

   (ii) Some of the boys and girls came to the party.

   (iii) Peewee brought many of the pens and pencils he had bought.

In these cases, the conjunction of the common nouns, for example, *pens and pencils*, under the single determiner *the*, can be interpreted, like a singleton plural, as a discourse group.

These examples suggest that an indefinite within the partitive will be acceptable only with salient descriptive modifiers.

Furthermore, in some cases, an indefinite can be acceptable in a partitive when its discourse reference is determinable through context. The reference, like that of definites, may be implicitly determined by association, as in (48):

(48) Only one of many applicants passed the test.

where the full discourse group is determined by the context of the job-seeking process, that is, the many applicants must be the total number of applicants for a particular job. Similarly, Ladusaw (1982) noted (49) and (50) as counterexamples to the semantic characterization of partitive restrictions:

(49) That book could belong to one of three people.
(50) This is one of a number of counterexamples to the Partitive Constraint.

where, in Ladusaw's terms, "the user has a particular group of individuals in mind," and the NP thus denotes "an introduced discourse entity." (p. 240)

These acceptable indefinites are usually viewed in the literature as interesting exceptions to the semantic prohibition against indefinites. In this analysis, the requirement that the embedded NP access a discourse group allows us to create a more coherent explanation for their acceptability. If explicit modification or the discourse context makes the discourse entity evoked by the indefinite more accessible, the indefinite will be judged acceptable.[9]

Finally, this approach allows us to explain the idiosyncratic behavior of partitive determiners in the embedded NP. Their unacceptability stems from a more general restriction against recursive partitives, that is, partitives in the embedded NP, like those in (51) and (52) (Keenan & Stavi, 1986; Westerstahl, 1984):

(51) *One of (the) three of the eligible students was turned down.
(52) *Only one of some of his students told the truth.

According to the discourse requirement for the embedded NP, these sentences, which include a partitive within a partitive, are anomalous because the embed-

---

[9]A proposed indefinite NP can also make a partitive interpretation acceptable (Ladusaw, 1982).

(i) Of twenty semifinalists, three will go on.
(ii) Of (the) many men there, few sang.

The effect of such preposing, as noted by Gundel (1977) and Davison (1984), is discourse reference for the preposed NP.

ded partitive NP, for example *three of the eligible students*, does not access a discourse group.[10]

A similar explanation holds for *both, all, most, half, either*, and *neither*. The explanation for their unacceptability in partitives lies in their particular discourse function. Because they are used to evoke subgroups of discourse groups, they cannot access such groups and thus cannot occur in the embedded NP position of partitives.

The evidence from definites, indefinites, and partitive determiners, then, suggests a discourse-based explanation for the distributions that prompted the Partitive Constraint, in particular, the need for a discourse group rather than a definite determiner. I conclude from this that there is no formal restriction on determiners in partitives, but that the interpretation for partitives demands that the embedded NP access a discourse group.

In sum, then, for both the matrix NP and the embedded NP of partitives, we find that distributional patterns of definites, indefinites, and other determiners can be directly explained in terms of discourse function. In contrast, those semantic accounts of the distributional patterns that have appeared so far do not seem to offer a comprehensive explanation.

CONCLUSION

The results of this study parallel those of the investigations of definites and existentials noted earlier in this paper. Like partitives, definites and existentials have particular discourse functions that affect their distributional patterns. And in each case, as noted above and in the literature, either explicit linguistic material in the form of some restrictive modifier or previous discourse information is crucial.

Also like partitives, definites and existentials have had varying semantic treatments, definites being defined as markers of uniqueness or universality and existentials as assertions of existence or set membership. Such treatments,

---

[10]Similar sentences which include a restrictive, however, are acceptable:

    (i) One of *(the) three of the eligible students who applied* was turned down.

    (ii) Only one of *some of his students who testified* would talk to the press.

Note that, in these examples, the restrictive is on the (underscored) embedded partitive NP, for example, on *some of his students* and not *his students*:

    (iii) *Of his students who testified, only one of some would talk to the press.

    (iv) Of some of his students who testified, only one would talk to the press.

Thus recursive partitives are acceptable only if the embedded partitive NP is modified. (In this regard, the partitive determiners are more restricted in their discourse use than indefinites; a restrictive clause does not make them acceptable in the embedded NP.

    (v) *One of both boys who were here left.

Reed (1989) notes a general prohibition of restrictive modification on partitive determiner heads.)

however, generally cannot encompass the effects of context and are forced to treat them as counterexamples. So Reuland and ter Meulen (1987), in the introduction to a recent, primarily semantic, collection on (in) definiteness, noted:

> . . . The interpretation of an NP used to modify the conversational domain cannot be defined in terms of the hitherto current domain but must appeal to elements outside this current domain. Specifically, its interpretation cannot be a generalized quantifier in Barwise and Cooper's sense. We call such uses of NPs nonquantificational and claim that they are directly discourse-linked. Representations of nonquantificational uses of NPs may contain a new referential marker and enter into dependency relations with already available referential markers or assignment functions. It remains an open question to what extent such ideas may be formalized in a genuinely compositional framework and the state of the art does not warrant any conclusions concerning the ultimate necessity of a representational level between the natural language syntax and the purely semantic interpretation. (p. 14)

The inability of a fixed-model semantics to account for definites and existentials certainly extends to partitives, where, as we have seen, the distinction between a semantic group and a discourse group is critical.

Some recent studies (Heim, 1982; Kamp, 1984) have investigated shifting discourse models with particular attention to anaphora. In the past few years, moreover, several studies have suggested that the interpretive rules of the semantics might be extended to include not only explicit linguistic material, such as restrictive modifiers, but also the implicit contextual information that effects change in the discourse model (Rothstein, 1988; Rothstein & Reed, 1984; Westerstahl, 1984). Although such approaches remain to be worked out with regard to distributional effects, they offer the possibility of including in our interpretation of definites, partitives, and existentials those limits that appear to be created by discourse function. Whether the proper treatment of distributional effects rests in a discourse representation or in expanded interpretive rules, the evidence presented here (and elsewhere) suggests that discourse effects must be considered part of NP interpretation.

REFERENCES

Aldridge, M.V. (1982). *English Quantifiers*. Wiltshire, England: Avebury.

Barwise, J., & Cooper, R. (1981). Generalized Quantifiers and Natural Language. *Linguistics and Philosophy, 4*, 159–219.

Clark, H. H., & Haviland, S. (1977). Comprehension and the Given-New Contrast. In R. Freedle (Ed.), *Discourse Processes: Advances in Research and Theory* (pp. 1-40). Norwood, NJ: Ablex.

Davison, A. (1984). Syntactic Markedness and the Definition of Sentence Topic. *Language, 60,* 797–846.

deJong, F. (1987). The compositional nature of (In)definiteness. In E. Reuland & A. ter Meulen, (Eds.), The Representation of (In)definiteness (pp. 270-285). Cambridge, MA: MIT Press.

Dowty, D., & Brodie, B. (1984). Semantics of "Floated" Quantifiers in a Transformationless Grammar. In M. Cobler, S. Mackae, & M. Wescoat (Eds.), (pp. 75-90). Stanford: Stanford Linguistics Association.

Fox, B. (1987). *Discourse Structure and Anaphora.* Cambridge: Cambridge University Press.

Gundel, J. (1977). *Role of Topic and Comment in Linguistic Theory.* Bloomington: IULC.

Hawkins, J. (1978). *Definiteness and Indefiniteness.* London: Croom Helm.

Heim, I. (1982). *Semantics of Definite and Indefinite Noun Phrases.* Unpublished doctoral dissertation. University of Massachusetts, Amherst.

Hogg, R. M. (1972). Quantifiers and Possessives. *Lingua, 30,* 227–232.

Hogg, R. M. (1977). English Quantifier Systems. New York: Elsevier.

Jackendoff, R. (1977). $\bar{X}$ Syntax. Cambridge: MIT Press.

Kamp, H. (1984). A Theory of truth and semantic representation. In J. Groeniendijk, T. Janssen, & M. Stokhof (Eds.), *Interpretation and information.* Dordrecht: Foris. 1–41.

Karttunen, L. (1976). Discourse Referents. In J. McCawley (Ed.), *Syntax and Semantics 7: Notes from the Linguistic Underground,* (pp. 363–385). New York: Academic Press.

Keenan, E., & Stavi, J. (1986). A Semantic Characterization of English Language Determiners. *Linguistics and Philosophy, 9,* 253–327.

Ladusaw, W. (1982). Semantic Constraints on the English Partitive Construction. In D. Flickinger, M. Macken & N. Wiegand (Eds.), *WCCFL1* (pp. 231–242). Stanford: Stanford Linguistics Association.

Lee, D.A. (1971). Quantifiers and Identity in Relativization. *Lingua, 27,* 1–19.

Lee, D.A. (1972). Reply to "Quantifiers and Possessives". *Lingua, 30,* 223–242.

McCawley, J. (1978). Conversational Implicature and the Lexicon. In P. Cole (Ed.), *Syntax and Semantics 9: Pragmatics* (pp. 245–259). New York: Academic Press.

Rando, E., & Napoli, D. (1978). Definites in THERE-Sentences. *Language, 54,* 300–313.

Reed, A. (1982). Contextual Reference and Predicatives. *Linguistic Analysis, 10,* 327–359.

Reed, A. (1988). Semantic Groups vs. Pragmatic Groups. *ESCOL,* 416–427.

Reed, A. (1989). Semantic Partitives. Unpublished manuscript.

Reuland, E., & ter Meulen, A. (1987). *The Representation of (In)definiteness.* Cambridge: MIT.

Rothstein, S. (1988). Conservativity and the syntax of determiners. *Linguistics, 26,* 999–1019.

Rothstein, S., & Reed, A. (1984 June). (In)definiteness and Set Determination. Paper presented at the Fifth Groningen Round Table, Groningen, Holland.

Selkirk, E. (1977). Noun Phrase Structure. In P. Culicover, T. Wasow, & A. Akmajian (Eds.), *Formal Syntax* (pp. 285–316). New York: Academic Press.

Sidner, C. (1986). Focusing in the Comprehension of Definite Anaphora. In B. Grosz, K. Jones, & B. Webber (Eds.), *Readings in Natural Language Processing* (pp. 363–394). Los Altos, CA: Morgan Kaufman Publishers.

Stockwell, R., Schachter, P. & Partee, B. (1973). *The Major Syntactic Structures of English.* New York: Holt, Rinehart & Winston.

Webber, B. (1979). *A Formal Approach to Discourse Anaphora.* New York: Garland.

Webber, B. (1986). So What Can We Talk About Now? In B. Grosz, K. Jones, & B. Webber (Eds.), *Readings in Natural Language Processing* (pp. 395–414). Los Altos, CA: Morgan Kaufman Publishers.

Westerstahl, D. (1984). Determiners and Context Sets. In J. van Benthem & A. ter Meulen (Eds.), *Generalized Quantifiers in Natural Language* (pp. 45-71). Dordrecht: Foris.

Yotsukura, S. (1970). *The Article in English*. The Hague: Mouton.

On the Relevance of Traditional Phonological Analysis to the Abstract Patterns Found in ASL and Other Signed Languages

Geoffrey R. Coulter
University of Rochester

INTRODUCTION

American Sign Language (ASL) has developed historically in a natural way, through use by a community of signers. It is synchronically acquired by deaf children in a natural context, from parents and others who use the language in interactions with children and each other. The acquisition of ASL exhibits the same developmental milestones that characterize language development in hearing children (Newport & Meier, 1985). ASL is an SVO language (that is, a language in which the unmarked word order is subject-verb-object), topic-prominent, with relatively free word order. Verbs are optionally inflected to agree in person and/or number with the subject and/or object, and they can incorporate agent/source, theme/instrument, and patient/goal classifiers. In addition, verbs and temporal adverbs can be inflected for a large number of different temporal aspects. Topic clauses, conditional clauses, and what are functionally ''relative clauses'' are all morphologically marked. Moreover, ASL has extensive derivational morphology, both in the lexicon and in the syntax.[1]

Such characteristics have convinced most linguists that, in spite of the fact that ASL is signed rather than spoken, it should properly be considered a natural human language, not simply some sort of makeshift communication system used by deaf people who are unable to use a spoken language (Bellugi & Studdert-Kennedy, 1980; Klima & Bellugi et al., 1979; Lane & Grosjean, 1980; Siple, 1978).

But, notwithstanding its status as a natural human language, there has been some question whether it can properly be said to exhibit phonological structure. This is not because the language lacks abstract patterns of articulation.

---

[1]For example, Liddell & Johnson (1984) and Liddell (in press) used the term *hold*; Sandler (1987, in press) used the term *location*; Perlmutter (1988, 1989a, in press) used the term *position*; and Coulter (1990a, 1990b, in press) used the term *stop*.

On the contrary, many abstract, context-sensitive rules are well attested, both in historical change, and in synchronic derivation and inflection. But there have been several reasons for suspecting that the system as a whole is different from what is found in spoken languages. Foremost among these is the obvious fact that the modality of the signal differs so strikingly from that of spoken languages. It has been wondered, for example, whether signed languages can exhibit patterns of stress and intonation, since these are realized in terms of differences in sound amplitude and pitch in spoken languages, features specific to the auditory signal. (In later sections of this paper, I describe aspects of stress and intonation in ASL.)

Also, early linguistic analyses of ASL suggested that its articulatory patterns were quite different from what we would expect to find in a spoken language. For example, there appears to be much more simultaneous structure in ASL than one might expect to find in a spoken language. In fact, early descriptions of the structure of ASL suggested that whereas the phonemes of spoken languages are sequentially ordered, the "phonemes" of ASL always occur simultaneously (Friedman, 1975; Stokoe, 1960; Stokoe, Casterline, & Croneberg, 1965). Also, it has been thought that many signs are iconic or pantomimic, perhaps even universal, in contrast to the words of spoken languages which are constructed from a limited, language specific set of arbitrary, discrete phonological elements.

Although it is true that the physical characteristics of the signal differ enormously between sign and speech, it is possible that patterns at a more abstract level of analysis might have more nearly the same type of structure. We already know, for example, that in spoken languages, low level phonetic detail is not directly relevant to more abstract patterns of phonological structure. If the same is true of signed languages, then it is possible that the more abstract articulatory patterns in the two modalities have very similar form—even though the low level phonetic details are quite different.

This raises an interesting question. What evidence would we require to decide whether abstract articulatory patterns in ASL constitute phonological patterns of the usual kind? In order to answer this question, we need to identify those characteristics of a phonological system that are essential or definitional, without which we would be unwilling to call a system of articulatory patterns a phonological system. And we need to find definitional characteristics that will not, simply by fiat, bias the answer in favor of spoken languages.

Unfortunately, much of the existing terminology referring to the articulatory patterns of human languages includes reference to the modality, even where there is no particular theoretical need for it. For example, although the term "phoneme" is commonly used simply to refer to a minimal chunk of the language code, identified on the basis of morphological contrasts, many linguists balk at its application to the analysis of signed language structure. But it is not clear that there is any substantive reason why the term should not be applied to ASL. Of course, the etymology of the term "phoneme" (< Gr. phon- "sound") is not without historical interest; but there is no reason to think that the term was originally coined with the intention of excluding nonauditory phonemes, nor that this is an important part of the current usage of the term in phonological theory. It is possible, of course, that an abstract minimal chunk of a sound-based signal might differ in significant ways from an abstract chunk of a gesture-based signal. But if they should turn out to share all of the definitional characteristics of the notion "phoneme" we would want to accord them equal status within phonological theory, and use the same term for both. It would thus appear that the only reasonable way to proceed is to construct a definition that does not refer to the modality unless necessary, and then to make a detailed comparison of "minimal chunks" in the two modalities.

The problem, then, is to differentiate essential characteristics of a phonological system from those which are merely typical of the phonologies of spoken languages, while remembering that some of the trappings of traditional phonological theory accidently make reference to sound simply because, until recently, we have not seriously investigated the possibility that signed languages might exhibit abstract phonological structure of the kind typical of spoken languages.

In the present paper, it is suggested that there are three "fundamental" or "distinguishing" characteristics of a phonological system. It is then demonstrated that ASL abstract articulatory patterns exhibit each of these characteristics, and from this it is concluded that the American Signed Language of the Deaf has "phonological structure of the usual kind."

DEFINING CHARACTERISTICS OF A PHONOLOGICAL SYSTEM

I suggest that there are just three characteristics that are necessary and sufficient for identifying a system of articulatory structure as a phonological system of the usual kind. Such as system must have:

1. A limited set of arbitrary, discrete, componential units.
2. Sequential organization into segments, syllables, phonological words, and phrases.
3. A modular system (lexicon, phonology, phonetics) of context sensitive rules.

These three characteristics are described in more detail in the next section after which I turn to ASL, demonstrating the existence of each of these three characteristics in its abstract articulatory patterns.

Limited Set of Arbitrary, Discrete, Componential Units

This aspect of phonological structure can be broken down into several semi-independent aspects: the basic building blocks are (a) "combinatorial," (b) "arbitrary," and (c) "discrete."

First, it is expected that the system will involve the combination of units drawn from a limited set of basic building blocks of the phonological code. We do not expect, for example, that complex words will lack internal structure, the way in which a complex pantomime might be said to lack discrete, combinatorial subcomponents, drawn from a small set of such components.

Second, it is expected that these basic building blocks be "essentially arbitrary," and discrete (rather than analog). An important point here is that the basic building blocks should not be directly determined by genetics. (However, a genetically determined propensity for choosing building blocks of a certain kind, with certain characteristics, is expected. For example, spoken languages are all thought to have a dental stop. This fact is presumably not accidental, but derives from the various possibilities provided by oral articulation, and from the nature of acoustic perception.) A second important point is that we expect the choice of basic units to be determined by social convention. That is, any given language might in theory choose a different set of basic units.

And third, the basic building blocks of the language code are expected to be discrete rather than analog. Probably the major reason for interest in the discrete nature of the basic building blocks is that this level of structure is not directly relevant to the association of form and meaning: The basic units themselves do not vary in order to convey different meanings; instead, different combinations of basic units are used to construct different symbols (words).

It is important to note, however, that in spoken languages, neither phonemes nor words are required to lack iconic motivation. For example, there are a large number of English words having to do with nose-related phenomena, which all began with an "sn" cluster: "sneeze," "sniff," "snore," "snuff," "snout," "snort," and so forth. It is quite plausible that, historically, these particular sounds are found in these words because of the iconicity involved: the "s" for "breathiness," and the "n" for "nasality." However, we would never reject these as English words on the grounds that iconic motivation may have originally played a major role in the choice of segments found in these words. What is important is that synchronically, the iconicity is essentially incidental: (a) English words about breathy nasal things are not required to have an "sn" cluster; and (b) the "sn" cluster is not directly relevant to the meaning of the word. (Although we can expect the pattern to have been noticed by poets, and, hopefully, put to good use!) In sum, there is no requirement that the words of a language be unmotivated. In fact, motivated, iconic structure is actually a pervasive feature of the words of human language (Haiman, 1980).

Sequential Structure

We can assume that the basic building blocks of the language code will need to be linearized for output. In particular, we expect that not only will the words/signs of a language be linearly ordered, but also that the individual words/signs themselves will exhibit sequential arrangement of discrete segments. We would probably not accept a system of communication without such linear structure as a phonology of the usual kind, although it is quite conceivable that a communicative system could, at least theoretically, exist without linear structure in words and phrases.

Modular System of Context-Sensitive Rules

Phonological patterns can be divided into (a) patterns that are relatively "frozen" (exhibiting irregularities in conditioning context, in the pattern itself, and in associated meanings), (b) patterns that are relatively productive, exceptionless, and regular in form, and (c) patterns that are quite regular, but depend on rate of speaking or register (e.g., level of formality). According to contemporary linguistic theory, these different types of patterns are said to belong to different "modules." Phonetic patterns apparently serve frequently as the historical source of phonological patterns, which in turn serve as the source of lexical patterns. It is hard to see how one could have a "phonology of the usual kind" without this process of grammatical development; and it is for this reason that "modular structure" has been included as a defining characteristic of phonology.

Secondly, an important feature of phonological structure is the existence of patterns of variation which depend on the immediate articulatory context of the variable item, rather than on semantic or syntactic features. Cross-linguistically in spoken languages, such variation includes an extraordinary variety of patterns which differ greatly in detail, but which can be broadly classified as patterns of assimilation, dissimilation, segment loss (including apocophy and cluster simplification), consonant/vowel epenthesis (including cluster breakup and "intrusive consonants"), and stress-related lengthening and diphthongization (as well as shortening and monophthongization), and so forth.

Other Characteristics

What else might we include in the definition of phonology? One possibility is that a phonology exhibit phonological patterns and constraints of the traditional kind, such as assimilation, syncopy, the obligatory contour principle. But I think that this would be a mistake, for two reasons. First, I doubt very much that we would want to claim that a given language lacked phonological structure simply on the ground that it lacked one or more types of phonological patterns typically found in spoken languages. Second, if our definition of phonology is correct, then we should expect these kinds of patterns to show up. If they do, this would then provide confirmation that the language does in fact have phonoloy of the usual kind.

What is *not* included in the definition of a phonology? We might note several features: (a) the particular modality of the signal, (b) lack of iconic motivation, (c) lack of simultaneous structure, and (d) linear componential structure in each word/morpheme.

First, the modality of the signal is not included as part of the definition of phonological structure. Because phonology deals with abstract patterns of articulation, low level features of the signal are irrelevant to phonology per se.

Second, it is not required that either the basic building blocks or the words lack iconic motivation. As already pointed out, such motivation is quite common in the words of spoken languages, although this feature is often overlooked.

Third, although we expect the words/morphemes of a language to exhibit linear structure, there is no prohibition against the presence of complex simultaneous structure. In fact, phonologists currently working within the "autosegmental" framework have provided extensive descriptions of patterns in a multitude of languages that occur simultaneously within a given word. In fact, there may be little or no interaction of patterns at different levels of structure (different "autosegmental tiers").

And fourth, although we expect that words will often consist of a simultaneous and/or sequential combination of basic building blocks, there is no prohibition against having words/morphemes that consist of only a single segment, (such as the English indefinite article, *a*, and the plural suffix *s/z*), or only a single phonological feature. In fact, it is quite conceivable that a given language might have a very large number of (possibly homophonous) morphemes, each of which consists of only a single basic building block.

ABSTRACT ARTICULATORY PATTERNS IN ASL

The three characteristics that I suggest are necessary and sufficient for identifying a system of articulatory structure as a phonological system of the usual kind are:

1. A limited set of arbitrary, discrete, componential units.
2. Sequential organization into segments, syllables, phonological words and phrases.
3. A modular system (lexicon, phonology, phonetics) of context-sensitive rules.

In this section, I demonstrate the existence of each of these three characteristics in the abstract articulatory patterns of ASL.

Limited Set of Arbitrary, Discrete, Componential Units

Traditionally, the most serious reason for doubting the existence of phonological structure in ASL was the notion that signed languages are basically just pantomime, without discrete, conventional, componential structure. But the work of Stokoe (1960) and Stokoe, Casterline, and Croneberg (1965) clearly describes the conventional, discrete, componential structure of ASL signs. Simplifying somewhat, Stokoe described signs in terms of a small set of discrete handshapes, locations, and movement patterns. A full sign, then, involves the combination of a component from each of these three major categories. For example, following the approach of Stokoe, the sign GIVE.TO can be described as being made with the "flat O" handshape, in "neutral space" (roughly in front of the signer's chest), with movement of the hand away from the signer. (See Fig. 12.1.) (I have cited ASL signs with an English gloss in capital letters, as has become traditional; I use a period between words when more than one is needed for the gloss, to avoid implying a morphological analysis. The phonological notation presented here is not intended to be complete—only enough phonological features have been noted to help the reader identify the segments, and to mark important contrasts between different examples.)

Although it has long been accepted that basic items in the lexicon are constructed of discrete components, from time to time in the past it was also suggested that ASL is actually a mixed system, making use of three different types of symbols—conventionalized signs, fingerspelling, and pantomime—all of which exhibit different structural characteristics. In fact, it now appears that (a) the structure of fingerspelling is not phonologically distinct from that of signs in general, except for a tendency for certain phonological resources to be relatively more common in either the lexical signs or in fingerspelling, and (b) those aspects of ASL which have appeared to be pantomime actually involve inflectional and derivational morphology in the syntax. Just like fingerspelling, in comparison with basic lexemes, these inflectional and derivational patterns in the syntax make somewhat different use of available phonological resources.

Fingerspelling

At one point many linguists subscribed to the notion that fingerspelling in ASL is essentially extrasystemic, according to the notion that it is a way of representing an English word, where an ASL sign does not exist for a given

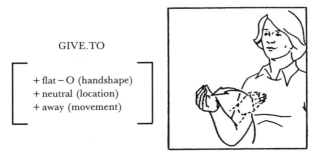

GIVE.TO

$$\begin{bmatrix} + \text{flat} - \text{O (handshape)} \\ + \text{neutral (location)} \\ + \text{away (movement)} \end{bmatrix}$$

FIG. 12.1

notion. Although this is in fact one of the functions of ASL fingerspelling, it has been argued more recently that fingerspelled sequences are not extrasystemic, but function in ASL much like the acronyms of spoken languages: In both cases, they involve pronunciation not of foreign words, but of native words for the letters of the alphabet (Johnson, 1989); also in both cases, the spelled items can be lexicalized, coming to function as regular lexical items of the language (Battison, 1978).

Inflectional Morphology

Verb agreement for first, second, and third person involves movement from a location associated with the subject (agent or source), to a location associated with the object (patient or goal). It is unlike pantomime in that only an extremely small number of distinct locations are contrastive, and some of these are lexically idiosyncratic. Moreover, transitive verbs move between two locations even when the verb is not inflected: In this case, the verb functions as an active or passive participle (depending on whether the verb moves away from, or toward the signer, respectively.) In other words, the locations used in verb agreement are discrete, conventionalized locations, not real-world locations functioning in a pantomime. To those unfamiliar with the system, however, these inflected signs look quite pantomimic. The difference between uninflected and inflected verbs is exemplified by the citation form of the verb GIVE.TO (see Fig. 12.2), the same verb inflected for first person subject and second person object (fig. 12.3); and the verb inflected for collective plural object (Fig. 12.4). [In these examples, both m ("movement") and arc (-arc = straight) are binary distinctive features; prox. and dist. stand for "proximal" and "distal"; and ð stands for "syllable" (the following section discusses ASL consonants, vowels, and syllables).]

Derivational Morphology

Derivational morphology includes morphology used in the descriptions of objects, locative relations, and movements. This morphology can easily be mis-

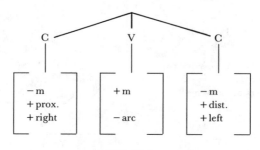

FIG. 12.2.

1p + GIVE.TO + 2p

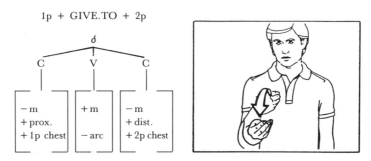

FIG. 12.3.

identified as pantomime, for several reasons. First, although the morphology is both conventional and discrete, it is also highly iconic, sometimes even transparent to the nonsigner. This iconicity can mislead the casual observer to assume that the system is pantomime.

For example, many signs include classifier affixes, which are phonologically realized as handshapes. (See Fig. 12.5.) The classifier "long thin object" is realized as the [1] handshape (with index finger extended), the classifier "narrow flat object" is realized as the [H] handshape (with index and middle fingers extended, unspread), and the classifier "large flat object" is realized by the [B] handshape (with all fingers extended, unspread).

Thus, the width of the object seems to be directly mapped onto the width shown by the hands. But these classifiers are both phonologically and morphologically discrete. For example, a handshape with three fingers extended cannot be used to indicate an object with a width in between that represented by the "narrow object" and "wide object" classifiers. And the "narrow flat object" classifier is appropriate for tongues, regardless of the size of the tongue in question (or the ratio of its width to its length). Both long, thin forked snake tongues, and large, flat, triangularly shaped elephant tongues take the "narrow flat object" classifier.

GIVE.TO + COLL.PL.

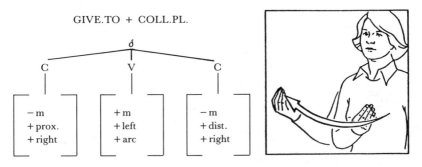

FIG. 12.4.

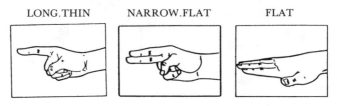

LONG.THIN   NARROW.FLAT   FLAT

FIG. 12.5.   Classifiers.

Second, verb chains may involve the same incorporated classifier, and the final location of one verb may be identical to the initial location of the following verb (Supalla, 1982). Even though the system is functioning with discrete, conventionalized morphology, it has the superficial appearance of pantomime, without sequential discrete structure. For example, consider Fig. 12.6.

This phrase consists of three verbs, each of which includes the "car/vehicle" classifier affix: CAR + GO.TO + FORWARD, CAR + TURN, and CAR + GO.TO + THE.SIDE "the car turned." But although the phrase superficially appears pantomimic, it is important to note that the three verbs are readily distinguished in ASL: Each has well defined, discrete morphological structure. And there are constraints on which morphemes can be simultaneously affixed in an ASL verb of motion, and on which verbs can follow another in a given sequence (Supalla, Newport, & Coulter, 1987).

Third, ASL has a variety of phonological contrasts which are defined in relative rather than absolute terms. In spoken languages, for example, a high tone is not defined in terms of any particular absolute pitch, but relative to other tones within the system. In ASL, differences in location are contrastive; like tones, however, the absolute location is not relevant. Instead, only the contrast between one location and another is significant. That is, just as the small set of contrasting tones in a spoken language is phonetically realized as a wide range of absolute pitches, the small number of location contrasts in ASL are phonetically realized in terms of a wide range of absolute locations. Consider the phonological contrast "under," as in the locative phrase "the animal is under the car" (Fig. 12.7).

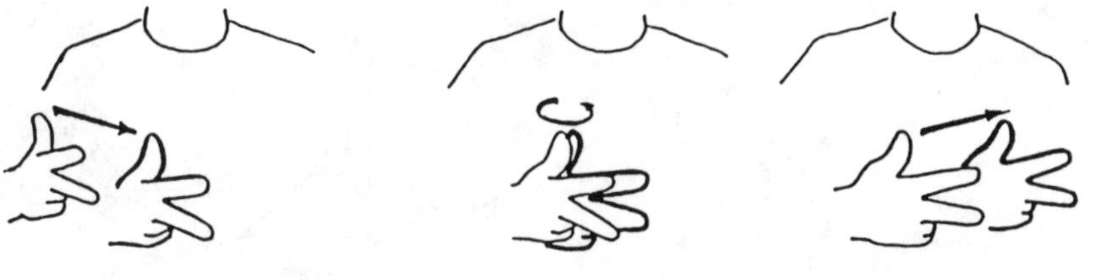

CAR + GO.TO + FORWARD   CAR + TURN   CAR + GO.TO + THE.SIDE

FIG. 12.6.   "Car turn."

CAR(CL) + THREE[i]   ANIMAL(CL) + under[i]

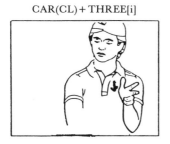 

FIG. 12.7.   "Animal is under car."

This contrast is realized by positioning one classifier under another. But the absolute location of neither classifier is relevant. In any event, the wide variation in surface form (different locations) can be misleading unless the linguist looks for a distinction between underlying phonological contrasts and surface phonetic realization.

In sum, although ASL has many iconic components, the structure of the system is discrete, arbitrary (in the relevant sense), and conventionalized. This failure to make use of analog representation even where it is theoretically available is a pervasive characteristic of ASL (Coulter, 1977), suggesting that analog representation is not possible in human language, regardless of the modality.

Sequential Structure

In the earliest work on ASL articulatory structure, it was suggested that although ASL signs are composed of "phonemes" like the words of spoken languages, in ASL these "phonemes" (or "cheremes" < Gr. CHER- "hand") are simultaneously realized, rather than sequentially ordered. For example, earlier in the paper I described the approach of Stokoe, Casterline, & Croneberg (1965), in which a sign such as GIVE would be characterized as having three, nonlinearly ordered "phonemes": /flat-O/ to describe the handshape involved, /away/ for movement away from the signer, and /neutral space/ for the general area in front of the signer's chest (see Fig. 12.1). (The transcriptions in this dictionary are intentionally underspecified; it was attempted to notate only those aspects of a sign which could not be predicted by a native signer according to general rules of the language.)

Phonological Segments

Subsequent work, however, has demonstrated that the complex patterns of derivational and inflectional morphology in ASL (which was largely ignored in the earliest linguistic analyses of ASL), can only be described by recognizing sign internal sequential structure. The sign GIVE.TO, for example, can be inflected to agree with the subject and indirect object; this inflectional system affects features at the beginning and end of the sign. The exact nature of the segmental structure of ASL signs is currently controversial. But the most widely accepted analysis to date treats signs as a sequence of "movemental" segments, and "configurational" segments (the latter are variously called "holds," "locations," "positions," and "stops").[1] Thus, the inflections just described change features associated with initial and final configurational segments, as shown in Figs. 12.2, 12.3, and 12.4.

ASL Syllables

There is growing interest in the way these segments are grouped together into syllables. It has been suggested that movemental and configurational segments differ in sonority (Coulter, 1990a), and that these differences in sonority can be used to divide ASL signs into syllables. Evidence that the units thus identified are in fact syllables comes from patterns of word-level stress and rhythm, and from sequencing and co-occurrence constraints.

The sonorous segments in spoken languages have greater acoustic energy than segments with low sonority, they are articulated with a relatively open and unobstructed vocal tract, and they are perceptually more salient. ASL movemental segments contrast in analogous ways with the configurational segments. They involve greater energy in their production, they involve a larger visual image, and they are perceptually more salient.

Because movemental and configurational segments tend to alternate in ASL signs, we find the same "waves" of increasing and decreasing sonority that characterize the syllable structure of spoken words. It is thus possible to divide signs into "syllables" according to differences in segment sonority.

In fact, the units thus identified turn out to be basic units of stress and rhythm in ASL. Figure 12.8 shows the stress pattern found in signs derived by reduplicating a monosyllabic root ("unidirectional" signs).

These units are also relevant to sequencing constraints. Simplifying somewhat, the focal fingers of the initial and final handshapes of a syllable can differ only in a single feature. Figure 12.9 shows grammatical and ungrammatical sequences. The fact that both stress and sequencing constraints have as their domain the unit identified on the basis of differences in segment sonority suggests strongly that these units are syllables in the traditional sense.

Moreover, it has been suggested that the traditional notion that ASL signs are relatively lacking in sequential structure is largely due to the fact that ASL is a monosyllabic language, like Chinese (Coulter, 1990b). Although ASL does

---

[1]For example, Liddell & Johnson (1984) and Liddell (in press) used the term "hold"; Sandler (1987, in press) used the term "location"; Perlmutter (1988, 1989a, in press) used the term "position"; and Coulter (1990a, 1990b, in press) used the term "stop."

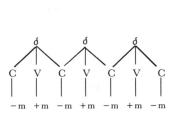

FIG. 12.8.   Stress pattern found in WORK.

Grammatical: HATE

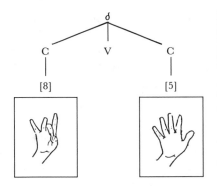
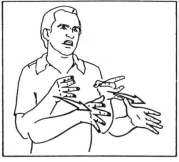

Ungrammatical:

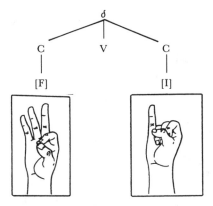

FIG. 12.9.   Handshape sequences.

237

in fact have many polysyllabic surface forms, it was argued that almost all of these are derived from monosyllabic roots through compounding and reduplication, and that for the most part, each of these underlying roots is a possible word.

For example, if we look at the lexicon, we find that the majority of items are either monosyllabic (such as GIVE.TO, shown in Fig. 12.1), or involve the reduplication of an underlying monosyllabic root (as in the sign WORK, shown in Fig. 12.8). There are also a variety of compounds such as MOTHER + FATHER "parents" (Fig. 12.10); these too are derived from monosyllabic roots.

This property of ASL is very interesting in light of the fact that ASL has rich and productive systems of derivational and inflectional morphology. However, rather than involving the addition of prefixes or suffixes, this morphology typically involves changes in the features associated with particular segments (such as the subject and object agreement shown in Figs. 12.3 and 12.4), or the addition of features to an underspecified root (Liddell & Johnson, 1984). For example, the sign FLY.TO is derived by affixing the AIRPLANE classifier to the root GO.TO (Fig. 12.11). In sum, the earlier notion that ASL signs lack sequential phonological structure is probably due in part to the failure to recognize the monosyllabic typology of ASL.

ASL Words and Phrases

As previously mentioned, ASL words exhibit "primary stress" patterns, just as do the words of spoken languages (Coulter, 1990a, 1990d). In signs involving the reduplication of an underlying monosyllabic root (e.g., WORK), primary stress is word-initial (see Fig. 12.8). Coordinate compounds such as MOTHER + FATHER "parents" (Fig. 12.10) exhibit relatively equal stress

MOTHER (root) + FATHER (root) = > MOTHER + FATHER 'parents'

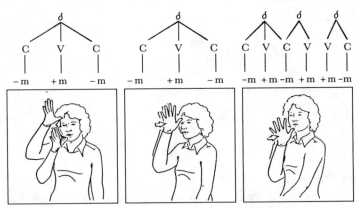

FIG. 12.10.

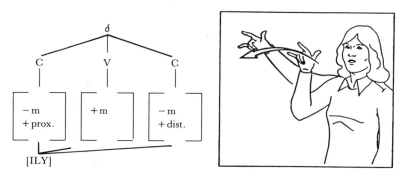

FIG. 12.11.   FLY.TO

on both members of the compound. In noncoordinate compounds such as WITCH, on the other hand, the first syllable of the second member of the compound is stressed (Fig. 12.12). Other disyllabic signs exhibit either initial or final stress. The sign ILLEGAL (which has an "excessive" suffix), and CHICAGO (which has a "city name" prefix) are examples of signs that include one of the few syllabic affixes occurring in ASL. Here, the root is stressed (see Figs. 12.13 and 12.14).

The structure of ASL phonological phrases has not yet been extensively investigated. However, it now seems clear that ASL exhibits many of the same intonational patterns found in spoken languages. For example, Grosjean (1979) found that ASL exhibits phrase-final lengthening, a feature of phonological phrases that is universal in spoken languages. And Covington (1973) noted that ASL distinguishes questions and declaratives by a difference in boundary intonation: She noted that the hands tend to fall immediately after a declarative, but are held in a stationary position briefly before falling in questions.

Modular System of Context-Sensitive Rules

Perhaps some of the most important early linguistic work on ASL phonology was that done by Frishberg (1975, 1976) and Battison (1978), who demon-

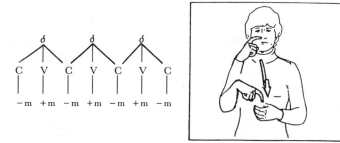

FIG. 12.12.   Stress pattern in compound WITCH.

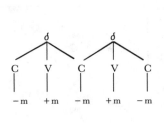
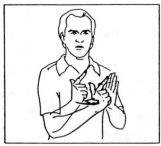

FIG. 12.13.   Stress pattern in ILLEGAL.

strated that historical change in articulation in ASL is not semantically motivated, but depends on phonological factors, just as it does in spoken languages.
Frishberg, for example, presented evidence of context-sensitive rules in historical
change. She noted that for signs articulated with one hand, those contacting
the face tend to move toward the periphery of the face, whereas signs contacting the body tended to move toward the midline. For example the sign SEE
was originally produced with finger contact under each eye, with the hand
roughly in the center of the face; the hand articulating the sign has shifted-
toward the periphery, so that contact is now only made under the ipsilateral
eye (Fig. 12.15). On the other hand, the sign LOVE was originally made over
the heart, but has shifted to a more central position (Fig. 12.16). In other words,
the historical shift in location (closer to the midline, or farther away from the
midline), is dependent on whether the sign contacts the face or the body.

Assimilation is also readily apparent in ASL. For example, anticipatory assimilation of handshape features is found in the compound EAR + YELLOW
"gold/California." In EAR, the thumb and little finger would normally be
[-extended]; however, in the compound (Fig. 12.17), they have both shifted
to [+extended], in anticipation of the way in which the second member of
the compound is articulated: in YELLOW, the thumb and little finger are both
[+extended].

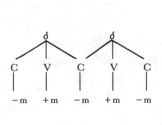

FIG. 12.14.   Stress pattern in CHICAGO.

SEE (historical)
mid face, under eyes

SEE (contemporary)
under ipsilateral eye

FIG. 12.15. Historical shift toward periphery of face.

LOVE (historical)
over heart

LOVE (contemporary)
at midline

FIG. 12.16. Historical shift toward midline.

1: [−extended / _____ [+extended]   = >   [+extended]
5: [−extended / _____ [+extended]   = >   [+extended]

EAR   YELLOW   EAR + YELLOW

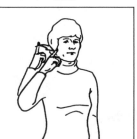  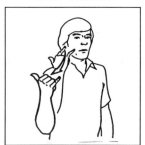

FIG. 12.17. Assimilation of extension of first and fifth fingers of EAR, to extension of first and fifth fingers of YELLOW, in compound EAR + YELLOW "California."

241

Padden and Perlmutter (1987) demonstrated the existence of modularity in ASL phonology. They showed that there are lexical rules that feed each other, and also feed post-lexical rules; but that whereas post-lexical rules feed each other, they cannot feed lexical rules. The key example involves the fact that after a post-lexical phonological rule ("Weak Drop") has applied to a sign such as QUIET, a lexical phonological rule (the "Characteristic Adjective Rule") can no longer apply. (See Figs. 12.18, 12.19, and 12.20.)

This constitutes a demonstration that ASL lexical rules and phonological rules belong to different modules of the grammar. Thus, not only do lexical rules and phonological rules belong to different modules in spoken langauge (apparently universally), they also belong to different modules in ASL (and presumably in other signed languages as well).

SUMMARY

The abstract articulatory patterns of ASL exhibit all three of the characteristics that I suggested are defining characteristics of a phonological system per se. From this, it must be concluded that ASL has "phonology of the usual kind."

There are important consequences of this conclusion. First, it makes it possible to test phonological theories that have been developed for spoken languages, in an independent context—by looking to see whether these patterns also show up in signed languages. Second, it makes it possible to begin studying which aspects of the phonological structure of a given language are influenced by the modality of the signal, something that is extremely difficult to do if the study of language is restricted to language in a single modality. And finally, as it is clear that phonological patterns are not restricted to language in the spoken modality, we need to look for the possible existence of such patterns of articulation not only in ASL and other signed languages, but also in other kinds of complex, nonlinguistic sequential human behavior.

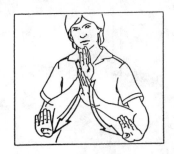

FIG. 12.18.   QUIET, basic lexical item.

FIG. 12.19.   QUIET, after application of "Weak Drop" to form in Fig. 12.18.

FIG. 12.20.   *TACITURN, after application of "Characteristic Adjective Rule" to form in Fig. 12.19.

We can expect that the study of theoretical phonology in signed languages such as ASL will continue to make important contributions to our understanding of the nature of phonological structure in human language.

ACKNOWLEDGMENTS

This paper is a revised and expanded version of a short paper presented in San Diego in 1986, at the conference "Linguistics at UCSD: The First 20 Years." This work was supported in part by NIH grant #NS16878 to E. Newport and T. Supalla, in part by NIH grant #HD07205 to the University of Illinois, and in part by NIH grant #DC00475-04 to G. Coulter.

I would like to thank all of those affiliated with the Supalla–Newport lab for the study of ASL and language acquisition, especially all of the deaf people who have served as language models and research associates; and also especially Elissa Newport, for valuable discussions and advice.

REFERENCES

Battison, R. (1978). *Lexical borrowing in American Sign Language*. Silver Spring, MD: Linstok Press.

Bellugi, U., & Studdert-Kennedy, M. (Eds.). (1980). *Signed and spoken language: Biological constraints on linguistic form.* [Dahlem Konferenzen 1980.] Weinheim, Germany: Verlag Chemie GmbH.

Coulter, G. (1977). Continuous representation in American Sign Language: In W. C. Stokoe (Ed.), *Proceedings of the First National Symposium on Sign Language Research and Teaching* (pp. 247–257). Silver Spring, MD: National Association of the Deaf.

Coulter, G. (1990a). *ASL sonority and syllable structure.* Unpublished manuscript, Department of Psychology, University of Rochester.

Coulter, G. (1990b). *Evidence that ASL is a monosyllabic language.* Unpublished manuscript, Department of Psychology, University of Rochester.

Coulter, G. (in press). Introduction: G. Coulter (Ed.), *Phonological Structure in ASL, the American Signed Language of the Deaf: Current issues.* Phonetics and Phonology 3. New York: Academic Press.

Coulter, G. (1990d). *Primary stress in ASL, the American Signed Language of the Deaf.* Unpublished manuscript, Department of Psychology, University of Rochester.

Covington, V. (1973). Juncture in American Sign Language. *Sign Language Studies, 32,* 221–238.

Friedman, L. (1975). Space, time, and person reference in American Sign Language. *Language, 51,* 940–961.

Frishberg, N. (1975). Arbitrariness and Iconicity: Historical change in American Sign Language. *Language, 51,* 676–710.

Frishberg, N. (1976). *Some aspects of the historical development of signs in American Sign Language.* Doctoral dissertation, University of California, San Diego.

Grosjean, F. (1979). A study of timing in a manual and a spoken language: American Sign Language and English. *Journal of Psycholinguistic Research, 8*(4), 379–405.

Haiman, J. (1980). The iconicity of grammar. *Language, 56*(3), 515–540.

Johnson, R. (1989). *ASL Phonological Rules.* Colloquium presentation, Rochester, NY: Department of Psychology, University of Rochester.

Klima, E., & Bellugi, U., Battison, R., Boyes-Braem, P., Fischer, S., Frishberg, N., Lane, H., Lentz, E.M., Newkirk, D., Newport, E., Pedersen, C.C., & Siple, P. (1979). *The Signs of Language.* Cambridge, MA: Harvard University Press.

Lane, H., & Grosjean, F. (Eds.). (1980). *Recent perspectives on American Sign Language.* Hillsdale, NJ: Lawrence Erlbaum Associates.

Liddell, S. (1984). Think and Believe: Sequentiality in American Sign Language. *Language, 60*(2), 372–399.

Liddell, S. (in press). Holds and positions: Comparing two models of segmentation in ASL: In G. Coulter (Ed.), *Phonological Structure in ASL, the American Signed Language of the Deaf: Current issues,* Phonetics and Phonology 3. New York: Academic Press.

Liddell, S., & Johnson, R. (1984). Structural diversity in the American Sign Language lexicon. In D. Testen, V. Mishra, & J. Drogo (Eds.), *Papers from the parasession on lexical semantics* (pp. 173–186). Chicago IL: Chicago Linguistic Society.

Newport, E. L., & Meier, R. (1985). The acquisition of American Sign Language: In D. Slobin (Ed.), *The Crosslinguistic study of language acquisition; Volume 1: The data* (pp. 881–938). Hillsdale, NJ: Lawrence Erlbaum Associates.

Padden, C., & Perlmutter, D. (1987). American Sign Language and the architecture of phonological theory. *Natural Language and Linguistic Theory, 5*(3), 335–375.

Perlmutter, D. (1988). Skeleton–Feature relations in American Sign Language: Problems of phonological representation and phonetic interpretation. Unpublished manuscript, UCSD, LaJolla, CA.

Perlmutter, D. (1989a). A moraic theory of American Sign Language syllable structure. Unpublished manuscript, UCSD, La Jolla, CA.

Perlmutter, D. (in press). Nucleus vs. satellite in ASL syllable structure: In G. Coulter (Ed.), *Phonological Structure in ASL, the American Signed Language of the Deaf: Current issues*. Phonetics and Phonology 3. New York: Academic Press.

Sandler, W. (1987). Sequentiality and simultaneity in American Sign Language phonology. Doctoral dissertation, University of Texas, Austin, TX.

Sandler, W. (in press). Linearization of phonological tiers in ASL. In Geoffrey Coulter (Ed.), *Phonological Structure in ASL, the American Signed Language of the Deaf: Current issues*. Phonetics and Phonology 3. New York: Academic Press.

Siple, P. (Ed.). (1978). *Understanding language through Sign Language research*. New York, NY: Academic Press.

Stokoe, W.C., Jr. (1960). Sign Language structure. *Studies in Linguistics, Occasional Paper 8*. [Series editor George L. Trager.] Buffalo, NY: University of Buffalo Press.

Stokoe, W.C., Jr., Casterline, D., & Croneberg, C. (1965). *A dictionary of American Sign Language on linguistic principles*. Washington, DC: Gallaudet College Press.

Supalla, T. (1982). *Structure and acquisition of verbs of motion and location in American Sign Language*. Doctoral dissertation, University of California, San Diego.

13

Phonology as an Intelligent System

John Goldsmith
The University of Chicago

-Par où on commence? demanda Viale. Par le haut ou par le bas?
-Il n'y a pas de règles, observa Dumont.
Il retira ses lunettes, les astiqua.
-En général, par le haut, quand même, dit Dumont.

(La mort dans une voiture solitaire, p. 46 Hugues Pagan)

INTRODUCTION

The phrase "phonology as an intelligent system" suggests a contrast: a contrast with other views such as "phonology as an articulatory system," "phonology as a communicative system," "phonology as a social system," and "phonology as a mechanical system." Each of these views has something important to contribute to the study of phonology, but there is an important side of the matter that has been underplayed, and which today we should bring out and to the fore. The most interesting aspect of language is its role in the expression of human thought and intelligence, and yet until recently it seemed that there was a serious rift between those aspects of syntax and semantics that reflect thought, on the one hand, and the principles that govern phonology, on the other.[1]

---

[1]A recent perspective on this subject, but one taking a very different point of view, may be found in Bromberger and Halle, 1989. They suggested that phonology is fundamentally different from syntax in certain respects—which it indeed may be—but among the differences Bromberger and Halle suggested is the need for strict rule ordering in phonology. They offered one example, the well-known case involving the choice of the allophones of the diphthong [ay] in front of a voiced

This rift no longer gives the impression of being quite so immense and un-bridgeable. This is not to say that phonology encodes propositional material; rather, the principles that govern the structure of the phonological components of a grammar, it is becoming clear, operate in accordance with more general principles that offer some hope of being understood within the larger context of cognition; and this is the possibility that I wish to consider. Thus we may emphasize here phonology as a cognitive system, one that organizes informa-tion first and foremost, one in which what is important is not the accidental outer form, the sound, associated with the elements of the phonological sys-tem, nor the social or communicative context, but rather the system of con-trasts and constructs which is the essence of the phonological system within the grammar.

I focus on the goal-directedness of phonological processes in the following discussion, because there is a close connection between goal-directedness and intelligence. If we were to find a system that displayed no goal-directedness in its behavior, no matter how broadly construed, we would be hard-pressed to imagine a reason for calling the system intelligent. If, on the other hand, it did manifest some goal-directed behavior, then to that extent we would like-ly be willing to grant it a rudimentary portion of intelligence. Intelligence, for our purposes, we may take to be the ability to consider alternatives to being where one presently is, and to select the alternative that best suits one's cur-

---

and a voiceless consonant in North American English: The diphthong in *write* is more central than it is in *ride*. The distinction between these two vowels is governed by rules, but is not lost when the consonant following (*t* or *d*) has been turned into a flap. They observed that *if* rules responsible for these processes are ordered, then the vowel-allophony rule must not be ordered after the flap-formation rule. This observation fails to make their point, though, for at least three reasons. First, it provides no argument that rules need to be linearly ordered; the two rules in question (ay-raising and flap-formation) could be unordered, applying simultaneously, and the correct result would result (see, for example, Lakoff [in press] for a long discussion of this point, or Kenstowicz & Kis-seberth, 1979). Second, the context within which the rule of ay-raising applies is not, in fact, lost on the surface, that is, after flap-formation applies; again, crucial rule-ordering is not necessary, because there is a clear difference of phonetic vowel length in the syllable nuclei of the first syllable of *riding* and that of *writing*. From the point of view of Bromberger and Halle's argument, one could as well posit that length-difference is what determines the vowel quality of the diphthong. Third, as a development of the second point, the most important process involved in this area is not restricted to the diphthong *ay*, but holds more generally for all vowels, and involves the rela-tive length of the vowel on the one hand, and the consonant following (*t, d*) on the other; we may say that the phonological feature of voicing is realized prominently in the determination of the ratio of the length of these two segments (vowel, consonant). How this calculation and realization is carried out will govern the distribution of the central versus noncentral allphones of *ay*. But this phonetic calculation is simply not the sort of process that is feasible within current phonological theory. The only representation for length within current phonological theory allows for integral units of length (1,2, perhaps 3; cf. Hayes, 1989, for example), and the differences at play in Brom-berger and Halle's case are below these threshold differences; that is, the allophones of *ay* are both phonologically long, that is, associated with two moras. Hence current phonological theory would not even allow this rule to be a phonological rule, regardless of whether such rules could be ordered.

rent requirements. Phonological systems, in their own primitive way, I shall suggest, illustrate that kind of operation.

RULES IN CLASSICAL GENERATIVE PHONOLOGY

Phonological rules in classical generative phonology act, in each instance, as rules that modify a representation just in case their structural description is met (with further external conditions placed as well involving, for the most part, questions of rule ordering that we may comfortably leave aside for our present purposes). These rules' ability to effect a change in a representation comes, so to speak, from within; our conception of these rules is based on an implicit metaphor according to which these rules are internally powered—battery-operated, so to speak. Nothing further need be true for a rule to apply but that its structural description be satisfied. This conception of rules applying to representations is the generative inheritance from two sources: first, from logicians' formalization of logical derivation—in particular, Post's notion of a production system, and second, from historical linguistics' notion of regular sound change, in which ordered sequences of rules correspond simply and directly to stages in the evolution of a language.

I hope to show that this conception of rule application—which is by now thoroughly established in our modes of thinking—is both unnecessary and unsatisfactory, and that its rejection in no way entails a retreat or return to the static modes of thinking associated with structuralist conceptions. We can (and, as I will suggest, we have already begun to) establish a conception of phonology that largely (though not in every detail, to be sure) rejects this earlier governing metaphor, and replaces it with one that is more congenial to the modes of analyzing intelligence that have arisen in other disciplines.

CURRENT WORK IN PHONOLOGICAL THEORY

Work in autosegmental, metrical, and syllable phonology over the past 15 years has led us to a picture of phonology that is quite different in a number of ways from the image established in the classical period of generative phonology, the period influenced by *The Sound Pattern of English* (Chomsky & Halle, 1968). The most striking differences have been in the relative importance and articulation of the nature of phonological representations, on the one hand, and the class of phonological rules, on the other. In the classical period of generative phonology, representations consisted simply of linearly ordered strings of segments, themselves bundles of distinctive features. Today, complex multitiered structures are routinely explored to account more satisfactorily for phenomena from tone spreading to intrusive consonant insertion. In early generative phonology, the syllable not only played no role, it had no way to be expressed; today it would be unthinkable to analyze a phonological system without something corresponding to the syllable, and both the internal and the external structure of the syllable are areas of ongoing research.

Phonological rules, in early generative grammar, were of considerable complexity, and problems of abbreviatory convention, of intrinsic and extrinsic ordering, and cyclic reapplication were of great importance. Now only the last, the problem of cyclic application, remains with us, and even it has been reformulated so as to help us come to grips with larger issues regarding the relationship between phonology and morphology.

In short, the balance of attention has shifted away from rules to problems of representation. Some have gone so far, in fact, as to deny the significance, or even the existence, of language-particular phonological rules. I shall explain some of my reasons for rejecting this later, but the tendency illustrates, by its extreme position, the shift that we are currently seeing in phonology.

Going hand in hand with the shift in emphasis towards problems of representation has been another shift which has by and large gone unnoticed up to now—or rather, it has been noticed only in bits and pieces, and the significance of the shift as a whole has not been apparent. With an articulated theory, or vocabulary, of phonological representations, it now becomes possible to make generalizations about phonological structures, and ask whether the phonological modifications that our phonological rules create are all pointing in a common direction or set of directions. Put simply, we may ask whether phonological rules uniformly modify phonological representations towards certain patterns, patterns at various different levels (using the term in a nontechnical sense for the moment): patterns regarding possible segments, possible syllables, possible feet, possible phonological words, and perhaps possible sequences of segments. To put it yet another way, we may ask whether there is not a sense in which phonological rules do more pulling (in particular directions) than pushing (away from the structural descriptions specified by a given rule); and whether even when they are pushing away from the structural description it is typically because of a more general property of the sound pattern of the language.

The answer to this question is, I believe, positive. Such an answer finds support in my own work, and draws together the work of many others currently working in phonological theory who have made less sweeping generalizations pointing in the same direction. Two brief examples might be helpful now, and we return to the matter in more detail later.

A growing (and by now overwhelming) body of literature on vowel epenthesis and deletion, beginning perhaps with Kisseberth's influential work (1970) on conspiracies, has established that the bulk of vowel epenthesis and deletion rules are sensitive to the syllable structure of the representation derived by the rule. A rule of epenthesis will typically apply just in case two conditions hold: its output contains sequences of well-formed syllables and its input is not properly syllabified—to put it simply, just in case its output is better than its input. To put the matter in such terms, of course, we need a general vocabulary and theory of syllabification, and as I have noted, we have taken many steps towards such an account in the last decade (for a recent discussion, see Itô, 1989). But the classical theory of generative phonology has no room at all for such notions; this theory is based on the notion of a rewrite rule that applies just in case its input conditions, or structural description, are met by a representation. A classical generative rule does not aim at any output or target structure; it is not, we may say, operating teleologically, with an eye to the structure that it is creating, and there is no sense in which we should understand it as aiming at a target schema. But that is just the property of vowel insertion and deletion rules that has emerged out of phonological research over the past two decades.

For example, Kisseberth (1970) pointed out that the epenthesis of the vowel *i* in Yawelmani Yokuts is the response of the phonological grammar to a situation where not all the phonological material is properly syllabified. Syllables in Yokuts may contain no more than one consonant in the onset and one in the coda, so sequences of three consonants can never be properly syllabified. In (1d), for example, the sequence of three consonants *gwh* is not syllabifiable as such, and the epenthetic vowel *i* is inserted in order to achieve proper syllabification of all of the phonological material. The hyphenation in the underlying and surface forms indicates breaks between morphemes; syllabification is not marked as such, but may be inferred from the generalizations just given.

(1)

surface	underlying	surface	underlying
a. xat-hin	/xat-hin/	xat-al	/xat-al/
b. bok '-hin	/bok '-hin/	bok '-ol	/bok '-al/
c. dos-hin	/do:s-hin/	do:s-ol	/do:s-al/
d. logiw-hin	/logw-hin/	logw-ol	/logw-al/

Similarly, early work in autosegmental phonology (Goldsmith, 1976) emphasized the importance of processes that spread autosegmental association over unbounded distance, up to (but not including) an already present association line. A good deal of controversy has attended the question of whether these automatic spreading processes can be uniformly universal, or whether they are to some extent language-particular. Regardless of the matter of universality, what is clear about such processes is that they are active processes aiming at a simple, particular target structure: one in which each vowel (for example) is associated with at least one tone, in the case of tone spreading, or one vowel harmony autosegment, in the case of vowel harmony, and so on. Spreading rules spread, in short, in order to create structures that are as saturated as possible—each vowel getting a tone, for example, when circumstances permit (and it is the rules that define whether the circumstances do in fact permit).

HARMONIC APPLICATION

The picture that emerges from examples like these, and many others, is one in which both target structures (or equivalently, phonotactics, or again, well-formedness conditions) and phonological rules play an important role, in a mutually supportive fashion, in a way that we may summarize as follows: All phonological rules apply in a harmonic fashion,[2] which is to say, they apply just in case their output is better than their input with respect to some criteria specified by a phonotactic (of the relevant level). In a word, then, rules apply for a good reason: in order to make a representation better match a pattern, or template, or phonotactic.[3] This is crudely put, to be sure; many of the most important operations involve patterns that are quite intricate, and other patterns involve structuration. For example, the single most important template towards which phonological rules move a representation is that according to which all segments are well integrated into a pattern of syllables. Thus, the erection of syllable structure, as well as of metrical structure, on a word is part of the pattern of a well-formed word that the phonological rules are pushing the representation toward. Patterns need not be merely at the level of overt sequences of phonetic segments; they may involve any item in the phonological vocabulary.

Such a notion smacks of the commonplace from the point of view of psychology, for example, where notions such as schemata—not to mention pattern recognition—are perfectly familiar. Such notions presuppose a global construction in which a number of properties are expected by the system to occur together. In the absence of reason to the contrary, a system utilizing schemata may use the information inherent to a given schema to increase the information available in a given situation, or even to modify information presently available. For example, believing that someone is a parent may lead us to further assume that they are adult, though that need not necessarily be true; and believing that someone has applied for a particular job and that he has not yet begun his dissertation may lead us to revise that second belief, on higher-order grounds: one would hardly be applying for such a job (we may reason) if one's dissertation were not done, or nearly done; we revise our assumptions in the light of our global knowledge. Phonological operations operate in certain parallel respects: Default specifications may be filled in, in accordance with both language-particular and universal principles, and phonological information may actually be changed on the basis of calculating the simplifications that would be achieved by modifying the representation in a derived environment (see the following discussion of lexical phonology for more on this).

---

[2] I allude here to Smolensky's harmony theory; see Smolensky, 1986.

[3] This notion has been discussed in similar contexts by Goldsmith (1989, in press a), Paradis (1988), Singh (1987, in press), Sommerstein (1974).

One thing that makes a system that understands special is that it shifts its representations in preestablished (or already definable) directions. That is, modifications of one's belief structures are made both in order to satisfy additional external information, of course, and in order to meet various internal conditions of coherence and simplicity: Defining and establishing such notions in formal and explicit ways is, to be sure, a difficult task, but to the extent that we succeed in doing it, what we expect of an intelligent system is that it should modify its representations in such a way that the structures better satisfy conditions of maximal coherence and simplicity.[4]

Each of these aspects of an intelligent system finds corresponding elements in phonology, I would suggest. The bulk of phonological rules apply in order to arrive at representations that maximally satisfy constraints (or, equivalently, schemata) that involve structuring phonological information.

If we may speak of harmonic application of phonological rules, we may also then consider speaking of a harmonic phonology, one in which this mode of rule application is central and essential, in ways that we will now clarify.

LEVELS IN HARMONIC PHONOLOGY

The picture that has emerged at this point may be described in the following way. A phonological description must include at least two things: a set of rules which describe the transitions that a given language permits, and a set of statements regarding relative well-formedness of various phonological structures. We may refer to this latter set of statements as phonotactics, and their role is to interact with the rules as described previously in relation to harmonic application: Rules apply just in case their output is better formed—better satisfies the phonotactics—than the input.

We may revise our mental image of this model in the following way. Rules specify permitted (and unordered) transitions between pairs of states (a word with and without a final consonant, for example, or with and without stress on the first syllable); these are language-particular statements, and can be conceived of as linking points on a large map that represents all possible phonological representations of a given language. The purpose of the phonotactics is to give a sense of peaks and valleys to that map, in such a way that the higher a representation is, the more poorly-formed (or less in step with the phonotac-

---

[4]This has nothing—or virtually nothing—to do with evaluation metrics of the sort considered and often discussed in generative grammar, which involve the issue of selecting a grammar on the basis of a given corpus of data—specifically, of selecting from a class of possible grammars which all satisfy the boundary conditions set by the observed data. On such a view of grammar selection (either as a methodology or as a theory of language acquisition), grammars are compared on the basis of simplicity; the matter discussed in the text involves the modification of representations within a grammar on the basis of simplicity considerations, broadly construed.

tics) it is, whereas the lower a representation is, the better it satisfies the phonotactics of the language. In such a picture, then, a representation will always seek the lowest position available to it through a sequence of permitted transitions on what we may call the *landscape* of that phonology.

Such an image is strikingly different from the image we have of traditional generative grammars, in part becaues of the much more lowly role played by rules in this picture, which goes so far as to virtually suggest that rules can be conceived of as being replaced by representations, though in this case the representation is not of any particular form, but rather is a representation of the sound pattern of the entire language.

This picture is useful for some aspects of phonological analysis, and not useful for others. It is especially useful for understanding those aspects of phonological analysis that involve considerable feeding orders, for example, and in which there are no counterfeeding orders. Syllabification, for example, typically involves an interaction of a large number of processes, such as coda formation, onset formation, epenthesis, vowel deletion, and foot formation (i.e., stress assignment); a similar observation holds for the process of foot formation as well. In most cases, these processes can be reformulated as involving constraints whose simultaneous solution represents the correct or observed pattern.[5,6]

However, wha makes phonology strikingly different from other aspects of grammatical theory is that one simply cannot establish a set of phonotactics, or constraints, for the phonology of a given language, and leave it at that; put in a more traditional way, there are significant rule interactions not of the sort just mentioned, and there are rules whose effects are not harmonic.

Consider, for example, some well-known facts from Lardil, an Australian language analyzed by Hale (1973), and discussed as well by Kenstowicz and Kisseberth (1979). In Lardil, a word may end with an open syllable (i.e., with a vowel), as in (2a), or with an apical consonant (2b), but with no other consonant. If a word ends underlyingly with one or more nonapical consonants, the consonant(s) are deleted, so as to satisfy the condition on how the Lardil word may end. This is illustrated by the examples in (2c), in which a stem

---

[5]The insufficiency of Lamb's (1962 and elsewhere) stratificational models was argued by Postal (1968) on the grounds of the commonness of feeding orders in natural languages. A revised and updated version of this argument was made by Lachter and Bever (1988, pp. 201-03) against connectionist views of phonology. These arguments do not transfer to the present framework, where feeding orders, or their equivalent (cf. footnote 5), are permitted; cf. also footnote 1.

[6]From a more radical perspective, adumbrated in the section on cyclicity below and discussed in more detail in Goldsmith(in press b), the effects of harmonic rule application result not from an algorithmic procedure that applies discrete rules in a linear sequence, but rather would result from the phonological model itself being implemented in a network where the presence or absence of a given feature or structural relation can be assigned a real number with a value from -1 to + 1. In such a scheme, the rules of the level may be replaced by statements of local connections between neighboring elements, and the "output" of the level is the equilibrium value that the network settles into. This approach is developed in Goldsmith (in press b) for some cases involving the metrical grid and stress patterns.

such as *ngalu* (underlyingly *ngaluk*) loses its final consonant in the uninflected form, surfacing then as *ngalu*. (*th* represents a single, laminal dental consonant, and *ng* represents a velar nasal throughout, *ṭ* is an apicodomal stop, and *r* is apicodomal as well.)

(2) a.

tipiti	species of rock cod
mela	sea
wanka	arm
kungka	groin
nguka	water
kaṭa	child
ngawa	wife
ngalu	story
putu	short
murkuni	nullah
ngawunga	termite

b.

yalul	flame
mayar	rainbow
wiwal	bush mango
karikar	butter-fish
yiliyil	species of oyster
yukar	husband
wulun	species of fruit
wuṭal	meat
kantukan	red
karwakar	species of wattle

c.

underlying form of stem	uninflected	non-future	future	gloss
thurarang	thurara	thurarang-in	thurarang-kur	shark
ngaluk	ngalu	ngaluk-in	ngaluk-ur	story

If a word with three or more syllables ends in a vowel underlyingly, however, it loses that vowel, as in the uninflected (first column) forms in (3a), and if this vowel loss leads to a situation in which a nonapical consonant is now[7] word-final, then these nonapical consonants are lost, just as before; this is illustrated in (3b). The crucial point for us is that the loss of the vowel is not motivated by a need to satisfy a phonotactic, for word-final vowels are perfectly satisfactory, and the shift from (e.g.) *munkumunku* to *munkumunk* (which is then followed by the deletion of the word-final consonants; cf. footnote 4) is one that

---

[7]We slip here into derivational idiom, but only for a moment, and it should be taken as a touch of irony.

moves away from satisfaction of the phonotactics. Hence there are at least some rules with this nonharmonic property, and we must deal with that fact. (*tj* represents a single, laminal alveopalatal consonant, and *th* a single laminal dental consonant).

(3) a.

stem	*uninflected*	*nonfuture*	*future*	*Gloss*
yalulu	yalul	yalulu-n	yalulu-r	flame
mayara	mayar	mayara-n	mayara-r	rainbow
wiwala	wiwal	wiwala-n	wiwala-r	bush mango
karikari	karikar	karikari-n	karikari-wur	butter-fish
yiliyili	yiliyil	yiliyili-n	yiliyili-wur	species of oyster

b.

putuka	putu	putuka-n	putuka-r	short
murkunima	murkuni	murkunima-n	murkunima-r	nullah
ngawungawu	ngawunga	ngawungawu-n	ngawungawu-r	termite
tipitipi	tipiti	tipitipi-n	tipitipi-wur	species of rock-cod
thaputji	thapu	thaputji-n	thaputji-wur	older brother
munkumunku	munkumu	munkumunku-n	munkumunku-r	wooden axe

These hard, unpleasant facts of phonological life force us to recognize that the image of rules as transitions on a phonological landscape is only a part of a larger picture, and that that part corresponds to the traditional notion of levels in linguistic theory. That is, what constitutes a level, in traditional terms, is a set of generalizations regarding the linguistic representation; these generalizations may be restated in their entirety as phonotactics (or, in our metaphor, as statements regarding what is higher than what, and what is lower than what, on the landscape). A level is not, then, one stage in a derivation; it is not even a single representation: It is (and this is the point of this paper) a set of phonotactics, and a representation of a given utterance U on a level L is a path from a starting point R_1 to a final resting point R_n. The final resting point R_n is that representation which is the best-formed (i.e., the lowest on the landscape) of all points accessible to R_1 via the paths made available by the rules of the language on that level.

Each level, then, contains a set of rules, which we may refer to as intralevel rules, and these rules will necessarily apply in a harmonic fashion. But as we have just suggested, there is more than one level in a phonology of a natural language. A fair amount of exploration suggests that although two phonological levels is inadequate, a model with three levels is sufficiently rich to deal with the phenomena that have come to light. Such a model will contain three levels—which we will refer to as M-level (essentially the underlying, or morphophonemic, level), the W-level (the level at which pure syllable structure is established), and P-level (phonetic level). Each level consists of the statement of tactics at its level, plus a set of intralevel rules. The three phonological levels, we may assume, relate to each other in much the same way that the other linguistic levels relate to one another (I draw heavily here on Sadock 1985, 1990). That is, the relation between the W-level and the M-level is logically parallel to that between the syntax and the morphology: the two tend to line up, in general, in a natural way, but do not need to do so in any particular case. The rules that relate levels (whether they be M-level or syntactic) are interface rules, in Sadock's terminology (or cross-level rules). In principle, then, there should be six classes of phonological rules: three intralevel rule sets—M-level, W-level, and P-level intralevel rules: (M,M); (W,W); (P,P), and three cross-level rule sets: (M,W); (W,P); and (M,P). If there is a hierarchization of levels in phonology, the last one—(M,P)—may not exist (as I shall assume for expository reasons), and we would arrive at a picture as follows:

(4)

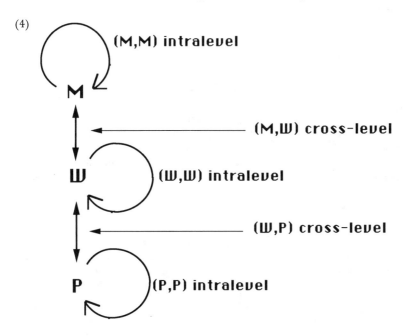

M/W/P model

FIG. 13.1.

Ultimately, the three levels of phonological theory should be viewed as not different in kind from the other levels of grammatical theory, such as the morphological[8], the (two) syntactic levels, an argument-structure level, and so forth.

This perspective requires us to consider all nonharmonic rule effects as cross-level (or interface) rules; this has as a consequence that there can be no more than two such rule applications in any given phonological derivation. The rule deleting a word-final vowel in Lardil is thus a cross-level (M,W) rule, and the rule that eliminates illicit word-final consonants (i.e., nonapical word-final consonants) operates as a (W,W) rule.

Although rules applying within a level give rise to what appear to be quite transparent rule interactions, the system as a whole need not have that property, no more than any familiar generative system. The constraints and the rules on the W-level and the P-level may be sufficiently different that the effect of having both levels (with their rules) is one of a reasonable degree of complexity. Consider the case of Yup'ik, for example, as discussed by Jacobson (1985).[9] Although there is a good deal of variation among the various dialects of Yup'ik in Siberia and Alaska, in Central Alaskan Yup'ik, stress is assigned to all bimoraic syllables, as well as to certain other syllables: to word-initial closed syllables, and to every other syllable (the even-numbered syllable) in sequences of light syllables (excluding the case of closed plus open light syllables), as illustrated in (5), where italicized syllables are stressed; word-final syllables are never stressed.

(5) a. *aang* qagh *llagh* llang *yug* tuq   "he wants to make a big ball"
   b. ang *yagh* llagh *llang* yug tuq   "he wants to make a big boat"
   c. qa *ya* ni   "his own kayak"
   d. qa *yaa* ni   "in his (another's) kayak"
   e. sa *qu yaa* ni   "in his (another's) drum"
   f. qa *ya* pig *ka* ni   "his own future authentic kayak"
   g. qa *ya* pig *kaa* ni   "in his (another's) future authentic kayak"
   h. a *te* pik   "real name"
   i. ang *yagh* lla ka   "my big boat"
   j. ang *yagh* lla kaa   "it is his big boat"

---

[8]There is occasionally a confusion between the morphological level and the M-level. The M-level consists of elements that are essentially phonological: The utterance *the dog is asleep* consists of twelve phonological segments on that level. On the morphological level of analysis, this expression has five units present, including the copula, the Present tense morpheme, and the single, atomic morpheme *dog*.

[9]The examples given here are from Jacobson (1985), and are discussed as well in Goldsmith (1990), where I unfortunately failed to cite Jacobson directly, giving only the name of the volume in which his work appears (Krauss, 1985). This example is discussed in the text in essentially the terms used by Jeff Leer, to whom I am indebted, in unpublished work. In addition to the Jacobson paper and others in Krauss (1985), see especially Leer (1985). Anyone who has looked at the prosodic systems of Yup'ik and related languages will know full well that any single, simple statement risks being an unfortunate oversimplification; I trust I have not oversimplified to the point of inaccuracy, and Leer is not to be taken as responsible for any oversimplifications that I have brought into the picture.

These patterns are established at the W-level, and involve reference to two types of conditions at this level. First, and quite generally across languages, there is a preference for bimoraic syllables to be stressed, rather than unstressed (a condition referred to by Prince, 1983, as Quantity–Sensitivity). Stress is assigned to satisfy this requirement. In addition, syllables must be organized into feet, and these are iambic in Yupik (i.e., weak–strong).[10] In short, at this level, stress is assigned to match inherent quantity of the syllables. At P-level, a rather different process occurs, by which syllable weight is modified to match the stress pattern that was established at the other level. In essence, what happens is that if a syllable is stressed, it must be heavy; if it is already— inherently—heavy by virtue of having a long vowel or being closed, that is sufficient; otherwise, the syllable is made heavy by one means or another (essentially, lengthening the vowel of the syllable unless that vowel is a schwa, in which case the consonant of the following onset is geminated, creating a

---

[10]Although there is a relationship between these two principles, it is not one that needs to be conceived of in terms of derivational rule ordering. What is crucial is that the grammar capture the fact that the first generalization—Quantity-Sensitivity—is a stricter generalization than the second (that syllables are organized into iambic (weak–strong) groupings). That is, if a grouping of syllables into weak–strong/weak–strong/. . .should attempt to put a long-voweled syllable in a weak position of a foot, an inappropriate structure would result. This can be conceived of in several ways, one of which is ordering quantity–sensitivity first (others include: making the algorithm that assigns iambic feet directly relevant to the inherent quantity of the first part of the foot; or treating the long voweled syllable as composed of two units over which an iambic foot must be erected without going any further. I ignore these various possibilities for expositional reasons; see Goldsmith (1990, chapter 4), and Krauss (1985) for further discussion). But nonderivational conceptions of this relationship are possible as well. It goes beyond the scope of this paper to go into the question in the detail it deserves, but we may address it informally here. As suggested in the text, we must consider that the addition of metrical structure (here, at W-level) to a series of syllables that does not have metrical structure is a "descent" on the energy landscape, that is, a decrease in total complexity. If there were no long syllables in a word to worry about, then from the point of view of an energy landscape, the establishment of binary feet throughout would be analyzed as the result of our assigning a certain cost C_1 (i.e., a height in energy space) to a syllable *not* being part of a foot, and also of assigning a cost C_2 to the establishment of each foot. Thus it is better for each syllable to be in a foot than not to be in one; but feet do not come free. Only if C_2 is greater than zero can we be sure that we will not simply assign foothood (i.e., stress) to each and every syllable: There must be a "cost" assigned to setting up such feet. (Clearly, C_2 must be less than two times C_1 as well—that is, the cost of setting up the foot must be no greater than the reward we get for act, which is a savings of amount C_1, twice over, once for each syllable that is placed in the foot.) Now, to ensure that Quantity–Sensitivity as a generalization has precedence over the assignment of iambic feet, in a framework without derivations and the ordering that they assume, it is sufficient to consider the difference D in energy height between that assigned to a long-vowel syllable that is the head of its foot and that assigned to a long-vowel syllable that is not the head of its foot. If we establish D as being greater than C_2 (the "cost" of establishing a new foot), then we will get the desired result. Put another way, the only thing that blocks setting up a new foot for each syllable is that feet "cost" something (C_2, by definition); but if we make sure that the profit derived from assigning a foot to a heavy syllable is positive (i.e., the proceeds exceed the necessary costs [D > C_2]), then we will get the desired result.

closed syllable, except in Central Siberian). This is illustrated in (6). Thus the effect of the generalizations on the two distinct levels is to make the effects of each level less than obvious, even though the effects within each individual level are simple and direct. Each level—W and P—strives to achieve a simple matching between the accent and the weight of the syllables, though the two levels achieve this (to the extent that they succeed) in opposite directions.

(6) a. W-level: qa *ya* pig *ka* ni   "his own future authentic
        surface: [qa *ya:* pix *ka:* ni]   kayak"
    b. W-level: ang *yagh* lla ka   "my big boat"
        surface: [ang *yax̱* la ka]

LEXICAL PHONOLOGY

Lexical phonology (Kiparksy, 1982) makes a particular suggestion that has not been especially pursued by most phonologists endorsing that research program, one that is relevant to our discussion (see also Goldsmith, 1990, chapter 5). The suggestion is that the class of lexical phonological rules is coextensive with the set of rules that establishes markedness for lexical entries. For example, if the rule of trisyllabic shortening (7) is a lexical phonological of English, operative in such hoary examples as *divine/divinity* to shorten the first vowel of the suffixed, derived nominal, it also functions to express the generalization that any vowel followed by an unstressed syllable and another syllable ought to be short, and will be long only under marked conditions; in that sense, *Canada*, with its short first vowel, is better than *rudiment*, with its long first vowel.

(7) $V \rightarrow$ [-long] / — C_0 [V,-stress] C_0 V

Lexical phonology unfortunately offers no explicit means for the language learner to figure out what the lexical redundancy rules of his or her language are, but it does suggest that once such rules have been established, they are now operative in analyzing morphophonemic alternations, or in lexical phonology's terminology, they function as lexical phonological rules. Put another way, if we take statements of markedness with regard to lexical redundancy to be contributions to the statements of relative wellformedness on either M-level or W-level, with better formed (i.e., less marked) representations being lower on the landscape then minimally different, but marked, representations, then lexical phonological rules will always make a representation move downhill, that is, harmonically. Repeating the last example, if a short vowel if less marked than a long vowel in the position / — c [v, -stress] c v, then when a long vowel becomes short (in *divin-ity*) during the derivational process that is responsible for the deadjectival nominal, the shift involved is one that simplifies the representation, or pushes the representation downhill. Thus even the rules of lexical phonology, understood in this way, have the harmonic property that we are focusing upon.

CYCLICITY

The simple model described earlier in (4), Fig. 13.1, with its three levels, appears to say nothing about the concept of cyclicity, a notion central to lexical phonology and a good deal of recent work in phonology. The present model does offer an interesting and attractive reanalysis of some of the fundamental properties of a cyclic account however.

On most accounts, the notion of cyclicity involves particular details of rule application and reapplication. For lexical phonology, which is heavily committed to a processual and derivational conception of phonological analysis, cyclic strata are organized in such a fashion that after each successive affix is attached, a sequence of phonological rules is applied, as their individual structural descriptions are met; there will be as many opportunities for the entire set of rules to apply as there are affixes attached.

This notion of cyclicity has no place in the present model, because the overwhelmingly derivational model that is assumed by lexical phonology has no place here. Let us take the opportunity to step back and observe what is involved in considerations of cyclicity. We find in general two schools of thought of the subject. On the one hand, there is the word-based school of cyclicity, discussed in Brame (1972a, 1974), Aronoff (1976), Harris (1983), Kiparksy (1982), and Goldsmith (1990), according to which the word is the unit to which further operations may be performed to yield derived words: schematically, as in (8); the domains marked "W[ord]", and no units smaller, are subject to cyclic reapplication. On the other hand, there is another view of cyclicity according to which cyclicity has nothing to do with the phonological word, but devolves rather from the dynamic process of word formation, as discussed in (for example) Chomsky and Halle (1968), and more recently, Poser (1989).[11] The last example is useful in establishing a contrast between these conceptions.

(8) [w [w a] b];

Poser (1989), based on work of Peter Austin, discussed the case of Diyari, a language in which stress is assigned to alternate syllables, starting on the left, within each morpheme of a word, as illustrated in (9), with morpheme-final syllables not receiving stress in any event. Rather than allow a grammar

---

[11]Poser cited lexical phonology throughout, seemingly unaware that Kiparsky's (1982) statement of lexical phonology requires that cyclic domains be minimally words.

the ability to say such a thing directly, Poser suggested that the effect should be derived indirectly, in the following way: A cyclic analysis, as he described it, will leave visible only the root on the first cycle, and on each successive cycle the grammar will find one more affix than it did on the cycle before. Therefore, he suggested, a cyclic account may assign alternating (left to right) stress to the root, and again on each successive cycle, just so long as the stress assignment done on an earlier cycle is left untouched on the later cycle(s). In such a way, each cycle will affect only the material that is new on that cycle, and by the way things have been set up, each affix will have exactly one cycle during which it is the new affix to which no stress has yet been assigned. Crucial to Poser's account is that the morphemes in question are in no way and in no sense words.

(9) a. ŋádawàlka-tádi   "to close + passive"
    b. yákalka-yìrpa-màli-na   "ask-benefactive-recipient-partative"

Such a view of cyclicity has little or nothing in its favor in this case (or others), as far as I can see, except that it permits one an indirect fashion of saying what one might as well say directly, which is that the relationship established between syllables and the metrical grid may be sensitive to morphemic identity—just as tone–syllable initial association may be, in many tone language (e.g., in Llogoori; Leung, 1986; Goldsmith, in press c), where the initial tone association of each tone must be to the leftmost vowel of the morpheme that is logically associated with that tone; the process is thus a morpheme-by-morpheme process, not a word-level process.[12]

The real significance of cyclicity, as Brame and the others cited earlier argued, is that there are phonological cases in which one can argue that there is a nested bracketing of phonological words, as in $[_{w-1} [_{w-2} \text{ a }] \text{ b }]$; cf. (8). Cyclicity then enters into the analysis in two ways: first, phonological processes may be effected within W_2 because it is a phonological word, processes that would not occur otherwise (i.e., processes that would not occur if the material marked as ''a'' were not treated as a word); and second, effects that we otherwise expect to take place within a phonological word may be blocked across the boundary separating W-1 and W-2, that is, between the base and the suffix. The first case is exemplified in Selayarese (as discussed by Mithun & Basri,

---

[12]This point was first made, I believe, in Clements (1983). In general, cyclicity will not help in cases of the following sort: where on a "new cycle," both suffixal material on the skeletal tier and suffixal material on the tonal tier is added, and where the final vowel of the base (i.e., the material already present on the previous cycle) was not associated with a tone. If the tonal material associates with the suffixal skeletal material, rather than with the leftmost available vowel in the base, as is the case, for example, in Llogoori, then it is simply necessary to allow tone-to-skeleton association to be directly sensitive to morphemic identity—the very possibility that Poser's discussion presumes should not be allowed.

1986),where we find that stems that end in *s*, *l*, or *r* must have an epenthetic vowel (identical to the preceding vowel) added to them if they are to serve as full phonological words; /lamber/ "long" therefore surfaces as [lambere], for example. When a suffix such as *-ang* "comparative" is added, the base is not treated as a separate word, and we find no epenthetic vowel, as in /lamberang/ "longer." However, there are other suffixes which attach to units that must be analyzed as full phonological words; the first person possessive suffix *ku*, for example, attaches to the word *sahala* "profit" (from underlying /sahal/), to give the complex form /sahalakku/, which has the structure [w [w sahala] ku].

Concerning the second effect of cyclicity—or, as we may equally refer to it, recursive phonological word-structure—we find cases as in, for example, English *Indianaism* (a speech pattern peculiar to Indiana) in which phonotactic regularities that otherwise hold for English are blocked across a boundary. Here, we have a sequence of schwa plus high vowel, which can otherwise be found in English only across full word boundaries, but never inside a single phonological word. When the suffix *-ism* is attached to a base without the recursive word structure of (8), the schwa is deleted (as in *buddha* + *ism* > *buddhism*); but this process of deletion does not happen to the schwa at the end of the inner cycle in [[indiana]ism], an example of the second type of cyclicity effect.[13]

These two effects are, I believe, the only robust effects that can be attributed to cyclicity, and both can be reconstructed from a point of view that reconstructs derivations in the way I have suggested in this paper.[14] Regarding the first point, if a subpart of a larger phonological word is itself a phonological word, as in (8), then it must satisfy the language's tactics for being a well-formed word, just as an embedded clause must satisfy all the grammatical conditions for being a clause, even though it may well be (irrelevantly) embedded within a larger, matrix clause. Regarding the second point, we must observe that it is still an open question as to which word-level phonological rules are blocked from applying across word-boundary (so to speak) as in a structure like (8). The simplest account would be one according to which no word-level rules apply strictly across such boundaries; in those cases where rules appear to, one of two alternatives may be the case: (a) in the case of rules such as

---

[13]A similar case can be found in Hall, 1989, where the distribution of German [ç] and [x] is explored from the point of view of lexical phonology. As Hall pointed out, [x] appears after a back vowel, and [ç] essentially elsewhere, but this generalization must be restricted to take the phonological word as an absolute barrier, as seen in a form such as the classic *Kuhchen* "cow (diminutive)," which has the form [[ku] çən]. As Hall observed, attempts to formulate this observation in derivational terms consistent with the principles of lexical phonology regarding the interleaving of phonological and morphology leads ineluctably to violations of other principles that are equally central to lexical phonology.

[14]From one point of view, this should hardly be surprising: The two cyclicity effects that I have reviewed in the text have precise analogs in syntax, and the claim has been established that the syntactic cycle can be reinterpreted in (or rather, reduced to) nonderivational terms.

Trisyllabic Shortening, applying to *divin-ity* to form *divinity* with a short second vowel, the phonological structure is not as in (8), but simply [divinity]: that is, phonological structure need not match morphological structure (or, to put it another way, word-based morphology need not always give rise to nested phonological word-structure); (b) in the case of stress rules, as Halle and Vergnaud (1988) demonstrated, each word-cycle may construct its own metrical grid, independent of the grid associated with the embedded phonological word; this gives the appearance of the grid constructed with outer word cycle overriding that constructed on an embedded cycle.

DISCUSSION AND CONCLUSION

The picture that emerges of the phonological system, then, is one in which rules serve as a means for getting representations to maximally satisfy phonotactics of the individual phonological levels of the grammar. How, we may ask, does this picture fit in with other conceptions of grammar and of cognition?

Recent work on connectionism speaks in a kindred fashion. Rumelhart and McClelland, for example, offered the following observation,

> Imagine a computational system that has as a primitive, "Relax into a state that represents an optimal global interpretation of the current input." This would be, of course, an extremely powerful place to begin building up a theory of higher level computations... These sort of primitives... are the kind of emergent properties that PDP mechanisms give us, and it seems very likely that the availability of such primitives will change the shape of higher level theory considerably. (Rumelhart & McClelland, 1986, pp. 126–127)

This appears to be exactly the sort of higher-level vocabulary that is required by the type of phonology—harmonic phonology—that I have adumbrated in this paper. Various discussions in the current literature have raised questions regarding the relevance of connectionist modeling to linguistic problems (for example, Lachter & Bever, 1988; Pinker & Prince, 1988). I interpret the difference between their pessimism and my optimism as based largely on how satisfied one is that the current models of phonology (or grammar, more generally) are within shouting distance of the final truth. If our current derivational models are—minor details aside—essentially correct models of the truth, then connectionist revisions are neither welcome nor helpful. If, on the other hand, serious reconsideration of even the most basic questions of the organization of phonological derivations and rule application are the order of the day, as I have suggested here, then it is certainly within the realm of the conceivable that the types of generalizations that emerge from connectionist models may be closer to the sort that we need in the newer model of phonology.[15]

---

[15]I have made some concrete proposals along these lines for the treatment of stress in Goldsmith, in press c, and with Gary Larson, for syllabification in Goldsmith and Larson, 1990. See also Larson, 1990.

I have mentioned several possibilities in this paper that concern what comes close to being a nonderivational phonology. The possibilities of a nonderivational syntax have been discussed and explored considerably over the past decade or more; few serious candidates for anything parallel have arisen in phonology, precisely because a static conception seems so unappealing in the face of all that we know about phonological systems in natural languages. What I have suggested in this paper amounts to a proposal to factor the dynamic character of phonological analyses into a number of subsections, corresponding to individual linguistic levels, in such a way that we can identify the phonological dynamic in each case as an instance of maximally satisfying the constraints of that particular level. If this program can be satisfactorily extended to the whole of phonology (and then, presumably, grammar as a whole), we may well find ourselves in a position in which our linguistic model satisfies simultaneously the requirements of a psychologically real model and those of a linguistically complete model.

ACKNOWLEDGMENTS

I am very happy to offer this paper to this volume for Lila Gleitman, my first linguistics teacher. She has often insisted on the importance of bringing together considerations of linguistic evidence and of psychological reality, and it may go without saying that the considerations discussed in this paper arose largely out of the psychological implausibility of current generative accounts of phonology. This is an abbreviated version of a longer work (Goldsmith, in press) to be published in a collection edited by myself, and also reflects some suggestions made in Goldsmith 1989a and 1990. I am grateful to many people for discussions or suggestions that led to the conclusions here, including Anna Bosch, Diane Brentari, Morris Halle, Gary Larson, Jeff Leer, John McCarthy, K.P. Mohanan, Carole Paradis, Jerry Sadock, Ivan Sag, Raj Singh, and Caroline Wiltshire.

REFERENCES

Aronoff, M. (1976). *Word-formation in generative grammar*. Linguistic Inquiry Monograph Series 1. Cambridge, MA: MIT Press.

Brame, M. (1972a). The segmental cycle. In M. Brame (Ed.), *Contributions to generative phonology*. Austin: University of Texas Press.

Brame, M. (Ed.). (1972b). *Contributions to generative phonology*. Austin: University of Texas Press.

Brame, M. (1974). The cycle in phonology: Stress in Palestinian, Maltese, and Spanish. *Linguistic Inquiry, 5*, 39–60.

Bromberger, S. & Halle, M. (1989). Why phonology is different. *Linguistic Inquiry, 20*, 51–70.

Chomsky, N. & Halle, M. (1968). *The sound pattern of English*. New York: Harper and Row.

Clements, G. N. (1983). *Some parameters of variation in tone languages*. Paper presented at the Conference on Hierarchy and Constituency in Phonology, University of Massachusetts at Amherst.

Goldsmith, J. (1976). *Autosegmental phonology*. PhD dissertation, MIT.

Goldsmith, J. (1989). Licensing, inalterability, and harmonic rule application. In R. Graczyk, B. Music, & C. Wiltshire (Eds.), *Papers from the 25th Annual Regional Meeting of the Chicago Linguistic Society*. Chicago: Chicago Linguistic Society.

Goldsmith, J. (1990). *Autosegmental and metrical phonology*. Oxford, England and Cambridge, MA: Basil Blackwell.

Goldsmith, J. (in press a). Harmonic phonology. In J. Goldsmith (Ed.), *The last phonological rule: Reflections on constraints and derivations*.

Goldsmith, J. (in press b). Local modeling in phonology. In S. Davis, (Ed.), *Connectionism: Theory and practice*. Vancouver: University of British Columbia Press.

Goldsmith, J. (in press c). Tone and accent in Llogoori. In D. Brentari, G. Larson, & L. Macleod (Eds.), *The joy of syntax: Papers in honor of James McCawley*. Amsterdam: Benjamins.

Goldsmith, J. and Larson, G. (1990). Local modeling and syllabification. In K. Deaton, M. Naske, & M. Ziolkowski, *Papers from the 26th Annual Regional Meeting of the Chicago Linguistic Society, Part Two: Parasession on the Syllable in Phonetics and Phonology*.

Hale, K. (1973). Deep and surface canonical disparities in relation to analysis and change: An Australian example. *Current Trends in Linguistics* 11, 401–458.

Hall, T. A. (1989). Lexical Phonology and the distribution of German [ç] and [x]. *Phonology*, 6(1): 1–17.

Halle, M. & Vergnaud, J. R. (1988). *An essay on stress*. Cambridge, MA: MIT press.

Harris, J. W. (1983). *Spanish syllable structure and stress: A nonlinear analysis*. Linguistic Inquiry Monograph 8. Cambridge, MA: MIT Press.

Hayes, B. (1989). Compensatory lengthening in moraic phonology. *Linguistic Inquiry*, *20*, 253–306.

Itô, J. (1989). Prosodic theory of epenthesis. *Natural Language and Linguistic Theory*, 7, 217–260.

Jacobson, S.A. (1985). Siberian Yupik and Central Yupik Prosody. In M. Krauss (Ed.), *Yupik eskimo prosodic systems: Descriptive and comparative studies*.

Kenstowicz, M. & Kisseberth, C. (1979). *Generative phonology*. New York: Academic Press.

Kiparsky, P. (1982). Lexical morphology and phonology. In I.-S. Yang (Ed.), *Linguistics in the morning calm* (pp. 3–91). Seoul: Hanshin.

Kisseberth, C. (1970). Vowel elision in Tonkawa and derivational constraints. In J. M. Sadock & A.L. Vanek (Eds.), *Studies presented to Robert B. Lees by his students* (pp. 109–137). Champaign: Linguistic Research Inc.

Krauss, M. (Ed.). (1985). *Yupik eskimo prosodic systems: Descriptive and comparative studies*. Alaska Native Language Center Research Papers Number 7. Fairbanks: Alaska Native Language Center.

Lachter, J. & Bever, T.G. (1988). The relation between linguistic structure and associative theories of language learning: A constructive critique of some connectionist learning models. In S. Pinker & J. Mehler (Eds.), *Connections and symbols*. Cambridge, MA: MIT Press.

Lakoff, G. (in press). Cognitive phonology. In J. Goldsmith (Ed.), *The last phonological rule*.

Lamb, S. (1962). *Outline of stratificational grammar*. Berkeley: University of California.

Larson, G. (1990). Local computation networks and the distribution segments in the Spanish syllable. In K. Deaton, M. Noske, & M. Ziolkowski, *Papers from the 26th Annual Regional Meeting of the Chicago Linguistic Society, Part Two: Parasession on the Syllable in Phonetics and Phonology.*

Leer, J. (1985). Toward a metrical interpretation of Yupik prosody. In M. Krauss (Ed.), *Yupik eskimo prosodic systems: Descriptive and comparative studies.*

Leung, E. (1986). *The tonal phonology of Llogoori: A study of Llogoori verbs.* Unpublished master's thesis; Cornell University.

Mithun, M. & Basri, H. (1986). The phonology of Selayarese. *Oceanic Linguistics, 25,* 210–254.

Paradis, C. (1988). On constraints and repair strategies. *The Linguistic Review, 6,* 71–97.

Pinker, S. & Prince, A. S. (1988). On language and connectionism: Analysis of a parallel distributed processing model of language acquisition. In S. Pinker & J. Mehler (Eds.), *Connections and symbols*. Cambridge, MA: MIT Press.

Poser, W. (1989). The metrical foot in Diyari. *Phonology, 6,* 117–148.

Prince, A.S. (1983). Relating to the Grid. *Linguistic Inquiry, 14,* 19–100.

Rumelhart, D. & McClelland, J. (1986). PDP models and general issues in cognitive science. In D.E. Rumelhart, J.L. McClelland, & the PDP Research Group, *Parallel distributed processing: Explorations in the microstructure of cognition. Vol. 1: Foundations.* Cambridge, MA: MIT Press.

Sadock, J. (1985). Autolexical syntax: A proposal for the treatment of noun incorporation and similar phenomena. *Natural Language and Linguistic Theory, 3,* 379–440.

Sadock, J. (1990). *Autolexical syntax.* Chicago: University of Chicago Press.

Singh, R. (1987). Well-formedness conditions and phonological theory. In Dressler et al 1987.

Singh, R. (in press). On repair strategies and constraints: A reply to Paradis. *Linguistic Review, 6.*

Smolensky, Paul. 1986. Information processing in dynamical systems: Foundations of harmony theory. In D.E. Rumelhart, J.L. McClelland, & the PDP Research Group. *Parallel distributed processing: Explorations in the microstructure of cognition. Vol. 1: Foundations.* Cambridge, MA: MIT Press.

Sommerstein, A.H. (1974). On phonotactically motivated rules. *Journal of Linguistics, 10,* 71–94.

Linguistic Theory and the Naturalist Approach to Semantics

Robert May
University of California, Irvine

ON SEMANTIC NATURALISM

A number of years ago, I was having a discussion with the philosopher and logician Wilfried Sieg. During our conversation, I was describing some research I was doing at the time, to which he was dutifully and patiently listening. After awhile Wilfried stopped me, and asked, regarding a central notion I was using, "Why do you call it logical form?" Although I of course gave his question something of an answer at the time, it was clear that he was not satisfied, and this lack of satisfaction got me to thinking about just why he was asking that question. In my ponderings, the first thought that came to mind was that we were perhaps talking about different things. For the linguist, the term Logical Form is a proper name. Thus, when we write it we capitalize it, and take it to name some definite, theoretical object. For the philosopher, on the other hand, this term is a common noun, not capitalized, picking out some property of formal systems. Thus, my initial conclusion was that Wilfried had every right to look at me quizzically during our discussion, since he perhaps thought, and perhaps rightly, that I was making a category mistake.

Having reached this state of affairs, however, my reflections on Seig's question did not abate, and this further cogitation led me to a second thought. Does what is dubbed "Logical Form" have the property of being a logical form? To answer this, however, it was necessary to arrive at some insight about two obviously more fundamental and antecedent questions. One we may call the philosopher's question—What is logical form?—the other the linguist's question—What is Logical Form? Now the mistake one wants to avoid in providing responses is thinking that the linguist's question and the philosopher's question are one and the same. If one were hearing this, rather than reading it, this might be an easy mistake to make, as after all their homophony could be very misleading. The reader, however, has the aid of the use of minuscules and majuscules as cues to their divergent parses, and hence can avoid being led astray. Now, of course, these two questions could have the same *answers*, some might hold even that they *must* have the same answers. If this is so, however, then the answer to our first question is trivial, as Logical Form and logical form would be identical, in that the former would have exactly the properties of the latter, and no others. On the other hand, if the answers to the linguist's question and the philosopher's question are different, then matters become considerably more interesting, and the initial question becomes one whose answer potentially has content. Indeed, the matter would conceivably become an empirical issue, on which various matters of evidence would weigh.

The answers I want to explore here to the linguist's and philosopher's questions are as follows: *Logical Form* (or LF) is a level of linguistic representation, closed under defined transformational mappings and conditions on structural well-formedness; *logical form* is a representation of the structure relevant for the truth-definition of the logical terms of the language. Then, to rephrase our initial question, we are now in the position to ask whether the linguistic structure is the structure relevant for the truth-definition. What research over the past decade and a half has shown is that there is an affirmative answer to be had. The nature of the answer can be seen clearly through examination of the general treatment of quantification in natural language. For quantification, the semantic rules are the clauses via which they are integrated into the recursive definition of truth. These rules apply just in case the quantifiers occur in a specified formal arrangement, from which it is possible to distinguish open and closed sentences, and hence free from bound occurrences of variables. The syntactic rules involved with quantification are occurrences of QR, so that representations at Logical Form are structures derived transformationally, containing occurrences of traces. Equating these traces with variables, we can utilize basic structural notions such as c-command, to define domains in which these elements are free and bound, and hence to define open and closed sentences. These latter definitions are known sufficient to allow for the proper application of the semantic rules to Logical Form representations, so that the logical structure can literally be read off the syntactic structure (May 1977, 1985, 1989, 1991). We therefore conclude that Logical Form indeed has the property of being a logical form: It specifies the grammatical structure relevant to the proper characterization of the truth-definition. In this regard, we can say that Logical Form is, or perhaps more accurately, embeds, a logical form.[1]

---

[1]The point here can be generated by consideration of other semantic properties besides quantification; see Heim (1982), Higginbotham (1985), Larson (1985) among other references. Note that we say "embeds" because there may be aspects of LF which are strictly of syntactic importance; see May (1991).

It is possible to distinguish between two approaches to logical form, the "naturalist" and "constructionist." The terms are due to Sommers (1982). The naturalist identifies semantic structure with some form of syntactic structure, so that, as Sommers quite nicely put it, "Logical syntax is implicit in the grammar of natural language and...the structure attributed by grammarians to sentences of natural language is in close correspondence to their logical form." (p. 2) The constructionist, on the other hand, rejects this position, maintaining rather that if a natural language is associated with a logical form, it is an aspect of its *semantic*, not its *synatactic*, structure. For the constructionist, the relation of syntax and semantics is translational, so that expressions of natural language pick out expressions of a formal language, with the meanings of the former identified with those of the latter. In contrast, for the naturalist, logical form is an aspect of the syntax of natural language itself; there is no translation. Thus, for the naturalist the syntax *represents* a logical form, whereas for the constructionist, the syntax *denotes* a logical form.

Between the naturalist and the constructionist, there is a debate to be had regarding in which component the structure relevant to logical form is located, the syntax or the semantics. Proponents of both positions would agree about certain things of couse, such as that there is syntactic structure per se, or that it must be possible to derive, from appropriate semantic axioms, the truth-definition for the language. The question that arises is whether anything more than this is needed for an adequate semantics? For the constructionist the answer is affirmative: For semantic adequacy, lingusitic theory must countenance an additional kind of structure—semantic structure—distinct from the syntactic structure of the language. Thus, this view comes intuitively attached to a greater theoretical cost than the naturalist alternative, which provides a negative answer: Nothing further is required, because the semantic structure is part of the syntactic structure itself. Accordingly, arguments for constructionist theories of semantics have the burden of having to demonstrate the necessity of extending linguistic theory in the manner described. In contemporary linguistics, such theories have found vocal expression in work deriving from Montague. A hallmark of this approach is that it standardly involves a translation into a functionally typed intensional logic through which the semantic structure of the language is represented. In this context, a well-known argument has been presented for the constructionist position arising from the treatment of sloppy identity in VP-ellipsis offered by Sag (1976). Sag's view is that the strict/sloppy ambiguity of *John loves his mother, and Bill does too* turns, in essence, on whether the elided VP is taken as a copy of the antecedent verb phrase or of the predication this verb phrase expresses, so that the analysis of the strict reading refers to identity of *syntactic* structure, that of the sloppy, identity of *semantic* structure. This semantic identity condition, note, refers to the *formal* structure of predication: Two predicates are semantically identical if and only if they differ in at most the *alphabetic* values of the variables they contain.

Thus, in (1) the λ-expressions are semantically identical in that they express the same predicate, differing only in their mere formal representation:

(1) John$_i$ λx$_i$ (x$_i$ saw x$_i$'s mother), and Bill$_j$ λx$_j$ (x$_j$ saw x$_j$'s mother)

It is in this sense that the analysis involves logical *form*, understood here crucially as an aspect of the *semantic* structure. This semantic structure is distinct from the *syntactic* structure of the language, so it is necessary to map from the syntax onto the semantic representation which reveals the structure of predication needed for the identity condition. It is because there is this translational step that we have an argument for the constructionist position.

The approach to ellipsis just sketched is a mixed theory, in that it is partially syntactic, partially semantic. Note that because the syntax and the semantics are distinct components of grammar, there can be no interdependencies between their rules. For VP-ellipsis, this means that there can be no dependencies between strict and sloppy readings, so that if many pronouns were involved, rather than just one, each could be understood freely, one way or the other. But consider (2):

(2) Dulles$_i$ said he$_i$ thought he$_i$ saw Philby pass secrets, and Angleton$_i$ did too

This sentence allows of two construals: Either the pronouns are both read strictly ("...*and Angleton thought Dulles said Dulles saw Philby pass secrets*"), or both sloppily ("...*and Angleton thought Angleton said Angleton saw Philby pass secrets*"). That is, there is an "across-the-board" effect—there are no readings where one pronoun is understood as strict, the other as sloppy. But this is contrary to the expectations raised by our previous discussion of the constructionist view, as the prediction is that independent, mixed readings ought to exist. This is because "λx$_j$ (...he$_j$...x$_j$ ...)," for instance, expresses the same predication as "λx$_i$ (...he$_i$...x$_i$ ...)," of which it is an alphabetic variant.

What these considerations show us is that although the analysis of ellipsis involves logical form, it must do so in a way that allows a proper statement of the dependencies between readings. But to do so the theory can not be mixed between components. Unification is not possible in the semantics, however, because the strict reading is known to be syntactically determined. Hence it must be in the syntax, and accordingly it must be in this component that logical form is to be found. A syntactically unified theory of ellipsis is presented in Fiengo and May (1991). Their central premise is that reconstruction of anaphora in ellipsis requires the preservation of indexical types found in the antecedent verb phrase. Briefly, the germ of the idea developed there is that indices may have either dependent or independent occurrences, and that the theory of ellipsis requires that reconstruction respect this distinction. The sloppy/strict ambiguity of sentences such as *John loves his mother, and Bill does, too* then reduces to whether the pronoun's index depends upon that of its antecedent, in which case reconstruction must recapitulate the same pattern of dependency, or does not, in which case reconstruction copies over the pronoun with an occurrence of the index it bears. Now reconsider (2). Example (3) displays the available indexings; reconstructed material is in boldface for clarity:

(3) a Dulles$_i$ said he$_i$ thought he$_i$ saw Philby pass secrets,and Angleton$_j$ **said he$_i$ thought he$_i$ saw Philby pass secrets**

b Dulles$_i$ said he$_i$ thought he$_i$ saw Philby pass secrets, and Angleton$_j$ **said he$_j$ thought he$_j$ saw Philby pass secrets**

c *Dulles$_i$ said he$_i$ thought he$_i$ saw Philby pass secrets, and Angleton$_j$ **said he$_i$ thought he$_j$ saw Philby pass secrets**

d *Dulles$_i$ said he$_i$ thought he$_i$ saw Philby pass secrets, and Angleton$_j$ **said he$_j$ thought he$_i$ saw Philby pass secrets**

It is just the (a) and (b) representations that are well-formed; these are the across-the-board strict and sloppy readings, respectively. The other two representations copy neither the pattern of indexical dependency—both pronouns having the same index as the subject—nor the actual values of the indices themselves. We thus capture the dependency effects in a theory which presumes a syntactically unified analysis; see Fiengo and May (1991) for a detailed discussion.

Now, in what sense is this analysis of ellipsis dependent upon logical form? Rephrasing this, we more properly ask in what sense is there a dependency on the level that represents logical form, namely LF? One answer to this question is that LF is implicated because it is at this level that the elided material is reconstructed. There is, however, a much more general answer to this question, arising from consideration of antecedent contained constructions (May, 1985):

(4) Dulles suspected everyone that Angleton did

The problem here is that the elided VP is contained within its antecedent, so that any reconstruction based on its surface form will immediately lead to a reconstructive regress. At LF, however, the structure of (4) is altered in a fundamental way. Because it contains a quantified phrase—the restrictive relative—it is subject to QR, deriving the following:

(5) [everyone that Angleton did[$_{VP}$e]$_i$ [Dulles [$_{VP}$ suspected e$_i$]]]

But now, the elided VP is no longer contained within its antecedent, so that reconstruction can proceed apace:

(6) [everyone that Angleton [$_{VP}$ **suspected** e$_i$]$_i$ [Dulles [$_{VP}$ suspected e$_i$]]]

What this shows is that it is in a strong sense that logical form plays a role in the analysis of ellipsis, as the logical aspects of the structure of LF play a central role in articulating the structure required for reconstruction. Bear in mind that logical form as we have it here is an aspect of the *syntactic* structure of the language. Thus, if our analysis is along the right lines, considerations of ellipsis argue not for the constructionist view, but rather for the naturalist.

The lesson to be learned from the naturalist perspective on the semantics of natural language is to "listen to the grammar." What we have heard is that the syntax manifests, at Logical Form, a logical syntax built on the theoretical nomenclature independently associated with syntactic movement and binding. Now this thesis brings along with it as a corollary the notion that grammatical constraints that define the well-formedness of representations at this level determine logical structure. There is now an extensive literature devoted to the investigation of the roles of various constraints, especially as they interact with matters such as quantificational binding (including *wh*) and its relation to anaphora.[2] Pereira (1989), however, expressed reservations about this thesis. His view is of interest not so much because it calls into question the empirical content of the theory, but rather because he believes that such theories are in principle noncompositional. Taking as his example a constraint that proscribes unbound occurrences of variables (traces), he noted that "the constraint is formulated in terms of restrictions on formal objects (logical forms)" but that "compositionality as it is commonly understood requires meanings of phrases to be functions of the *meanings* rather than the forms of their constituents." (p. 153) Although it is certainly true that compositionality is the notion that the meaning of an expression is a function of the meanings of its parts, what the syntax determines is what are the *parts* and their mode of combination. It is because a verb and a noun phrase, say, are *syntactic* parts of a verb phrase that we say that the meaning of a VP is a composition of the meaning of the V and the meaning of the NP. Without an antecedent formal characterization, we can have no notion of what is being composed. We are certainly within our rights to speak of LF as being compositional insofar as it properly specifies the structure via which the composition of meaning, by such semantic operations as predication and quantification, is determined. It is certainly fair to accuse the theory of Logical Form of being wrong, and appropriate evidence may show that to be so, but not that it is not compositional.

For the naturalist the shape logical form can have is wholly determined by the possibilities of syntactic well-formedness. In May (1990), I distinguished such "intrinsic" constraints from the "extrinsic" constraints placed by the interpretation, constraints that effectively allow us to recognize the syntax as in fact representing a logical form. The extrinsic constraints determine the "fit" of the syntax and the semantics, determining whether the formal factors required for the proper application of the semantic rules are satisfied by the syntax. The semantic interpretation plays no role beyond this in the characterization of Logical Form, so, for instance, we would not want to hold that the shape

---

[2] For just some of the most recent discussion, see Fiengo and May (1991), Nishigauchi (1990), and the papers in Huang and May (1991).

of logical form is constrained by some preconceived notion of expressability of natural language. Some have mistakenly thought this. Hintikka (1989) maintained that "Logical forms are for a GB theorist essentially like the logical formulas of quantification theory (extensional first-order logic, lower predicate calculus, or whatever your favorite term for this basic type of logical language is)." (p. 43) Logical Form, in and of itself, however, could not possibly have such a property, as it is just part of the formal theory of syntax. It can only make available certain structural patterns, which are otherwise motivated within the grammar, to which the semantic rules are sensitive. What it represents relevant to quantification is that a moved, adjoined phrase properly binds a trace. Traces are empty categories; although they may be *interpreted* as individual variables, identifying them as such is not part of the syntactic induction of the language. Here language diverges from logic; whether the semantic rules determine a first-order interpretation for Logical Form is an ancillary issue, in part empirical, in part ontological and metaphysical. In my opinion, the first-order core of natural language is extensive, covering most, but not all, of the quantificational aspects of natural language.[3] But be that as it may, whether this is the case or not does not derive from any requirments imposed by our definition of Logical Form that it must be a first-order predicate logic.

Hintikka's objections to the Theory of Logical Form, it turns out, are somewhat more general, and are not limited to its purported first-order character alone, but also to the devices used to implement it: "It is the use of certain notions, such as scope and binding (coreference), as the key explanatory concepts that bothers me in linguists' reliance on first-order languages." (p. 44) Hintikka's bother arose from what he saw as empirical shortcomings, and he presented arguments in support of this contention. According to Hintikka, these arguments are of importance because they show that " . . . the usual quantificational notation is (at least if we try to apply it dirctly) useless for the purpose of exhibiting the 'logical form' . . . " (p. 47), and that theories employing it are "misguided," as they are "trying to accomplish something which is not on the agenda of a satisfactory theory." (p. 53). In fact, all the arguments appear to show is an ignorance of the relevant literature. One claim of Hintikka's is that the theory of Logical Form is not up to the demands of crossed binding "Bach-Peters" sentences. But Hintikka made no mention of the discussion in Higginbotham and May (1981), and its development in May (1985, 1989), (although he did cite May, 1985, elsewhere in his paper.) I will not rehearse the "absorption" analysis presented there other than to say the obvious, that Hintikka has not presented any arguments against it. A second, potentially

---

[3]See May (1989). It is shown there that many cases of independent construals of quantifiers are first-order expressible. Other cases, however, are not, but those which are not can be determined compositionally from their structure. Typically, they contain floated occurrences of quantifier words like *all* or *each*, or other sorts of quantificational adverbs. For an enlightening discussion, see Sher (1989).

more interesting argument of Hintikka's centers around properties of reciprocal constructions which he believed show "The inadequacy of the concept of
coreference (at least in the form in which it has been used recently in GB-type
theorizing) for the purpose of uncovering the logical form of an English sentence..." (p. 48). The purportedly problematic cases are the following four
sentences (= Hintikka (1989), examples (11)-(14)):

(7) a   Tom and Dick admired each other's gift to him
    b   Tom and Dick admired each other's gift to himself
    c   Tom and Dick admired each other's gift to them
    d *Tom and Dick admired each other's gift to themselves

The well-formed sentences are to be understood with the readings expressed
by the following paraphrases:

(8) a   Tom admired Dick's gift to Tom, and Dick admired Tom's gift
        to Dick
    b   Tom admired Dick's gift to Dick,and Dick admired Tom's gift
        to Tom
    c   Tom admired Dick's gift to Tom and Dick, and Dick admired
        Tom's gift to Tom and Dick

The problem, according to Hintikka, is that there is no notion of "coreference" sufficient to cover the three types of anaphoric connections exhibited
by (7a–c) and also account for the deviance of (7d): "As Wittgenstein might
have said, the surface forms of [(7)] do not have the sufficient "logical multiplicity" to create satisfactory semantic representations for themselves if they
are dealt with by means of notions like coreference and scope applied to their
logical forms." (Hintikka, 1989, p. 49)

    This judgment, it turns out, is quite a bit too hasty, as work by Heim, Las-
nik, and May (1991), again uncited by Hintikka, shows that at LF examples
like those in (7) in fact *do* show exactly the logical multiplicity required. Briefly, on the theory presented there, deriving the LF representation of a reciprocal sentence involves movement of the *each* part of the reciprocal pronoun, with
attachment to the "antecedent" noun phrase. So, for example, *Oscar and Max
saw each other* would have the following representation:[4]

(9) [[Oscar and Max$_1$] each$_2$] saw [e_2 other]$_3$

A variety of arguments are presented for the indexing displayed by (9) and
how it interacts with principles of syntactic binding. In particular, it is shown
that the trace of the moved *each* is an anaphor, and must be locally bound by

---

[4]In fact, there are further derivational steps involved, moving the *each*-phrase and the *other*-
phrase, and attaching them to S and VP, respectively. I ignore this here, as it is immaterial to
the point at hand.

the composite LF-derived subject, as per the strictures of Principle A of the Binding Theory. The interpretation that (9) projects is as in (10), where we read "$\bullet\Pi$" as "is-an-atomic-part-of," or, more colloquially, "is-one-of":

(10) $\forall x_2 \ (x_2\bullet\Pi \ \text{Oscar and Max}_1) \ \exists x_3 \ (x_3\bullet\Pi \ \text{Oscar and Max}_1 \wedge x_2{\neq}x_3) \ x_2$
        saw x_3

Given the indexing indicated, Heim, Lasnik and May pointed out that there are three possible loci for anaphoric connections, but that these connections are of two different types. As can be seen from (10), in the interpretation of representations such as (9), *each* and *other* introduce quantificational conditions into the semantics, as opposed to the NP *Oscar and Max*. Thus, anaphoric connections indicated by co-indexing with the two former expressions would constitute instances of *bound variable anaphora*, with the latter expression, *coreference anaphora*. As such, the former are cases of singular anaphora, the latter of plural. Now reconsider Hintikka's cases. Their representations at LF are as follows:

(11) a [[Tom and Dick]$_1$ each$_2$] admired [e_2 other$_3$'s gift to him$_2$]
       b [[Tom and Dick]$_1$ each $_2$] admired [e_2 other$_3$'s gift to himself$_3$]
       c [[Tom and Dick]$_1$ each$_2$] admired [e_2 other$_3$'s gift to them$_1$]
       d *[[Tom and Dick]$_1$ each$_2$] admired [e_2 other$_3$'s gift to themselves$_1$]

The inner bracketed phrase indicates the governing categories of the pronouns and reflexives which stand as the objects of the prepositions. The pronoun in (11a) must be free in this domain, but can be bound outside it. As it is singular, it can be bound by *each*, and it will be construed as a variable bound by the quantifier it introduces.[5] In contrast, the reflexive in (11b) must be bound in this category, which it can only be if it is bound by *other*. It will be construed as a variable bound by the quantifier *other* introduces. The plural pronoun *them* in (11c) can only take an outside antecedent, and only one is available, the NP *Tom and Dick*. As this expression does not in itself introduce a quantifier, this is a case of coreference anaphora—the pronoun picks up the reference introduced by this NP. In (11d), on the other hand, the plural reflexive cannot be connected to this NP, as it must be bound within its governing category. Thus, this last case stands in violation of the Binding Theory. For each of these cases, given these structures, these are the only anaphoric indexings possible. The interpretations that these structures project are as follows:

(12) a $\forall x_2 \ (x_2\bullet\Pi \ \text{Tom and Dick}\ _1) \ \exists x_3 (x_3\bullet\Pi \ \text{Tom and Dick}_1 \wedge x_2 \neq x_3)$
         x_2 admired x_3's gift to x_2
       b $\forall x_2 \ (x_2\bullet\Pi \ \text{Tom and Dick}\ _1) \ \exists x_3 (x_3\bullet\Pi \ \text{Tom and Dick}_1 \wedge x_2 \neq x_3)$
         x_2 admired x_3's gift to x_3

---

[5]Note that the trace of *each* does not bind this pronoun. As it is the determiner of the NP, its c-command domain is limited to that phrase.

c $\forall x_2 (x_2 \cdot \Pi \text{ Tom and Dick }_1) \exists x_3 (x_3 \cdot \Pi \text{ Tom and Dick}_1 \wedge x_2 \neq x_3)$
x_2 admired x_3's gift to them$_1$

This makes clear that the structures in (11a–c) represent just the three readings given by Hintikka's (1989) paraphrases—a result contrary to Hintikka's claim that this "...is a case in which the logical form of an English sentence is not derivable directly from its surface form." (p. 50)

The problem with Hintikka's criticism is that he presumed that the treatment of anaphora makes use of an unanalyzed notion of coreference. This is not so, as we have just seen, for the proper treatment of the cases at hand involves distinguishing bound variable from coreference anaphora. It is well-known that these two types of anaphora are subject to differential constraints; thus, consider the examples in (13) and (14):

(13) a   Oscar and Max criticized John after he had left the room
     b   After he had left the room, Oscar and Max criticized John

(14) a   Oscar and Max criticized everybody after he had left the room
     b   *After he had left the room, Oscar and Max criticized everybody

In (13), regardless of whether the adjunct clause has been preposed or not, an anaphoric construal of the pronoun is possible. But in (14), where a quantifier has been substituted, this structural difference effects the possibility of anaphora: Although it is possible in (14a), it is precluded in (14b). Now, examples such as (15) are presented in Heim, Lasnik, and May (1991):[6]

(15) Oscar and Max criticized each other after they had left the room

This sentence is (at least) three ways ambiguous, with the pronoun understood as anaphoric. These construals can be paraphrased as in (16):

(16) a   Oscar criticized Max after Oscar had left the room
     b   Oscar criticized Max after Max had left the room
     c   Oscar criticized Max after Oscar and Max had left the room

Comparison with Hintikka's examples shows that in (15) we have the types of readings found in (7a–c) collapsed into one sentence. We represent these readings as in (17):

(17) a   [[Oscar and Max$_1$] each]$_2$ criticized [e_2 other]$_3$ after they$_2$ had left the room
     b   [[Oscar and Max$_1$] each]$_2$ criticized [e_2 other]$_3$ after they$_3$ had left the room
     c   [[Oscar and Max$_1$] each]$_2$ criticized [e_2 other]$_3$ after they$_1$ had left the room

---

[6]These examples are patterned after cases initially discussed in Higginbotham (1985). See Heim, Lasnik, and May (1991) for discussion, particularly in relation to Higginbotham's "linking" theory of anaphora.

Recall that of these structures, (a) and (b) represent bound variable anaphora, whereas (c) represents coreference anaphora, as above. Thus, our expectation is that the former two should be sensitive to constraints on bound variable anaphora, as opposed to the third. So, consider (18):

(18) After they had left the room, Oscar and Max criticized each other

What is of interest about this sentence is that it only has the reading comparable to the paraphrase in (16c), that is, the coreference reading. Excluded, as expected, are the bound variable readings, comparable to (16a) and (16b), consistent with the constraints on this type of anaphora shown by (14). It thus appears, contrary to Hintikka's assertions, that the theory of Logical Form is appropriately articulated, relative to its notions of scope and anaphora, to account for the data at hand.

In viewing the theory of Logical Form, the mistake that Hintikka made is in assuming that it is based on the constructionist conception of the relation of syntax and semantics. Hintikka himself held a variant of the constructionist position, what he called "game-theoretical semantics." Although for him there is no representation of logical form, its properties are nonetheless manifest in the semantic rules. Logical form on this view is a metaproperty of the semantics, derived by generalization over the functioning of the semantic rules. As Hintikka (1989) said: "In my game-theoretical semantics what in effect is the logical form of a sentence S is not determined by its surface form directly, but by the entire structure of the semantical game G(S) associated with S." (p. 43) Natural language, therefore, need not, and in Hintikka's view, ought not, have a logical form. Hintikka committed here what we might call the "constructionist's fallacy" of maintaining that the form of natural languages is determined by the structure of its interpretation, so that if you have the wrong semantics, then you have the wrong syntax. Thus, if first-order logic is incorrect for natural language, then so are the formal devices projecting it into the syntax. In making this "appeal to meaning," however, it remains completely opaque how the resulting, impoverished syntax is going to be up to the empirical demands placed on it. It is highly problematic that syntactic theories are ever, or can be, wholly constrained by the semantic structure, if they are to reach appropriate levels of empirical adequacy.[7] Thus, not only has Hintikka not demonstrated the advantage of his semantical approach, but also leaves us with yawning questions about the nature of syntactic inquiry. To the naturalist such matters are moot, naturally.

---

[7]For further discussion of this unfilled promissory note of constructionist theories, see May (1986), where this matter is discussed in the context of "storage" theories of quantification and anaphora.

ON AMBIGUITY IN LOGICAL FORM

The brief that I am presenting for the naturalist position is an empirical one. For the naturalist, the role of the semantics is to specify a theory of truth for the language that interprets its syntactically represented logical form. This logical form has certain properties, of binding and scope, through which it represents quantification. Bear in mind, however, that it is by no means a given of linguistic theory that the syntax of a natural language should be sufficiently expressive intrinsically, while remaining appropriately constrained, to be able to satisfy the extrinsic constraints imposed by the formal requirements of the semantics. After all, why should we expect that a formal system designed to meet the empirical demands of representing syntactic structure would also be up to the task of representing semantic structure, and it is certainly not a *requirement* on the grammar that it have this ability. That it is at all constitutes an empirical insight, a discovery. We could easily imagine the contrary, a syntax too weak, so that operations within the semantics itself would be required to induce the proper formal configurations. At what point does the syntax cease to express a logical form, becoming so weak as to be unable to represent the appropriate properties? This may very well not be an all or nothing affair but rather a matter of degree. The syntax might partially express a logical form, representing structural information necessary for the semantic rules, but not all that is sufficient. So long as the syntax—in the guise of Logical Form—provides the structural information required by the truth-definition, it has a logical form.

One of the structural properties most intimate to our understanding of logical form is that of scope, the domain of binding. Its role comes into play in precisely distinguishing open from closed sentences, the central distinction in the statement of the semantic clauses for the quantifiers. In the grammar, scope can be directly defined on the basis of c-command: The scope of an element is its c-command domain. This notion of scope is necessary for the application of the quantifier rules. But there is another notion of scope which serves a rather different purpose. It pertains to the determination of the *order* of application when more than one rule is applicable. So, suppose we have a simple sentence of multiple generalization: *Every spy suspects some mole.* The question immediately arises: Which rule applies first, the rule for *every* or the rule for *some*? The answer is straightforward, if we allow one or the other quantifier to have scope over the other, to have a binding domain that includes (but is not included in) the other's. The order of application of the rules then just follows the scope order of the quantifiers. A theory in which multiple quantifiers are structually distinguished as to their scope *relations* is said to have a logical form which is disambiguated.

The desirability of a general thesis of disambiguation of logical form has been broadly commented upon. Thomason (1974), in the context of reflections on the work of Montague, put the rationale as follows:

> Human languages are rich in syntactic ambiguities, and disambiguated languages must be regarded as theoretical constructs. But both logicians and linguists have been interested in such languages: logicians because logical consequence can only be defined as a relation among syntactically disambiguated sentences, linguists because one of the traditional tasks of syntax is the exposure of syntactic ambiguity. (Thomason, 1974, p. 4)

Higginbotham (1985) further elucidated this theme; for him, disambiguation is part and parcel of providing a definition of the notion "sentence," so that under a proper analysis natural languages would be seen to be rife with homonymity, but not with ambiguity:

> Chomsky...has emphasized that, in his view, the *objects* of linguistic theory are best taken to be the grammatical structures, not their spoken forms...For this reason, to speak of "structurally ambiguous sentences" can be misleading, as though the grammar were merely a device for classifying sentences; it would be better to talk of homonymous syntactic structures...If we used the word *sentence* in the way that we customarily use *word*, then we would say of the classic examples, such as *Flying planes can be dangerous*, not that they are single sentences that are ambiguous, but rather that they constitute two sentences that happen to sound alike. (Higginbotham, 1985, p. 552)

And so too with quantification. From the standpoint of the grammar, we would view the ambiguities of quantification as a matter of *constructional homonymity*, in the sense put forth by Chomsky (1957), early on in *Syntactic Structures*.

Returning to the specific thesis regarding quantification, a disambiguated theory of logical form embedded within an overall theory of natural language syntax was presented in May (1977). On that view, multiply quantified sentences mapped onto two structures, distinct in their relative c-command, and hence scope, domains. Thus, our sentence earlier would have dual representations at LF:

(19) a $[_S$ some mole$_j$ $[_S$ every spy$_i$ $[_S$ e_i suspects $e_j]]]$
     b $[_S$ every spy$_i$ $[_S$ some mole$_j$ $[_S$ e_i suspects $e_j]]]$

In (19a), the universal phrase asymmetrically c-commands the existential, whereas in (19b), it is the existential that asymmetrically c-commands the universal. This in turn corresponds to their relative scopes—in the former, the universal has broader scope, in the latter, the existential—and hence they map onto two distinct interpretations.

A large part of the attractiveness of this approach to quantification is that it turns on an inherent property of the grammatical rules involved in the derivation of the structures representing quantification. QR, the rule involved, is by hypothesis transformational, and effects an adjunction. Formally, an adjunction of an element α to a category β results in a structure of the form $[\beta \; \alpha \; \beta]$; that is, in the derivation of a "copy" of β. If a rule effects an adjunction to β, then after each adjunction there will be an additional occurrence of β to which further adjunction can occur. For QR, this means that after an initial adjunction, standardly to S as illustrated in (19), there will be two occurrences of S to which subsequent applications of QR can adjoin. Depending upon to which one the adjunction is made, the variant scope orders will be derived. So, for instance, if in the derivation of the structures in (19), the initial movement was of the universal phrase, subsequent adjunction to the lower S would give the universal broader scope, to the higher S, narrower scope. In this way, the theory affords an account of the scope ambiguities of multiple quantification via disambiguation; the account is explanatory as it turns on prior syntactic principles.

Now, because the account does turn on the nature of syntactic structure, it follows that advances in our understanding of syntax may lead us to quite different views of how it incorporates logical structure. This has been the case for quantification. In May (1985, 1989), I argued that there are good reasons to believe that, contrary to my earlier views, it is not the case that both structures in (19) are well-formed. In part, this was based on well-known observations regarding multiple *wh*-constructions, so-called "superiority" effects. The basic contrast is as in (20):

(20) a   Who admires what
      b *What does who admire

The analysis of this difference turns on assuming that they differ in their structures at Logical Form:

(21) a $[_S,$ who$_j$ what$_i$ $[_S$ e_i admires $e_j]]$
      b *$[_S,$ what$_i$ who$_j$ $[_S$ e_i admires $e_j]]$

(21b) is ruled out, it has been argued, as it contravenes a grammatical principle, the Empty Category Principle (ECP), which in such contexts requires structural contiguity between a trace and the category that binds it (Aoun, Hornstein, & Sportiche, 1981). By parity of reasoning, it follows that (19b) is also ruled out, as it too fails to display the required configuration. But if (19a) is the only structure we have, then we are apparently left without a representation in which the universal phrase has broader scope.

There is an inadequacy here only if we persist in taking the structures in (19) as being configurations of asymmetric c-command. It is possible, however, to view these structures in a different way, as configurations of *symmetric* c-command. Our initial calculation of the c-command relations in (19) was based on the definition offered by Reinhart (1976, 1983), which turns on domination by branching nodes. More recently, Aoun and Sportiche (1983) gave a definition based on domination by maximal categorial projections: α c-commands β if and only if every maximal projection dominating the former also dominates the latter, (and the former does not contain the latter). In May

(1985), an articulation of these concepts was provided. Suppose that categories can be complex, made up of parts, or segments, so that an element is dominated by a category just in case it is dominated by all its parts. Then it follows that an adjunct α is not dominated by the category β to which it is adjoined, but only by those categories that dominate β. (The notion of command that incorporates the theory of adjunction is often referred to as m-command.) Applying these definitions to (19) now results in a calculation under which the adjoined quantified expressions *symmetrically c-command each other*. This is because they are both adjuncts of the same category. In May (1985) such groupings of quantifiers are called Σ-sequences. Thus, at Logical Form what we have for a multiply quantified sentence is one representation—for only one satisfies the grammatical constraints—and it is a representation in which the quantifiers mutually c-command. The theory is that this single representation is compatible with both possible construals: Because the c-command relations are symmetrical, we can read this structure as expressing either order of scope dependencies.

In May (1985), a range of arguments were presented for this approach to multiple quantification, and a formal semantics for LF was given in May (1989).[8] Observations regarding the sentences in (22) provide another:

(22) a Some man admires everyone, and Mary does too
     b Some man admires everyone, and some woman does too

Example (22a), initially discussed by Sag (1976) and Williams (1977), has the curious property that although the first clause in isolation can be ambiguous, when placed in this sort of ellipsis context it becomes unambiguous, only having a reading under which the subject existential phrase is understood to have broader scope. Hirschbühler (1982) subsequently pointed out that the very similar (22b) allows for the other scope possibility, so that this sentence also allows for a construal under which the universal phrase is understood with wider scope. Consequently, it is adjudged as true if everyone is admired by a man and a woman. This difference in the construal of these minimally differing examples is particularly perplexing, as Hirschbühler pointed out, because the Sag/Williams theory of ellipsis is constrained to exclude this latter interpretation. There is no reason in their theory why substituting a quantified expression for a nonquantified one in the second clause should lead to the observed contrast.

In the theory of Fiengo and May (1991) described earlier, coincidence of indices plays a central role in conditioning reconstruction. The notion of an indexical pattern employed there is perfectly general; it covers various types of binding, including both A and $\overline{\text{A}}$-binding patterns. I discussed a case of the former type in the beginning of the chapter. (23) is an example of the latter:

---

[8]One general set of arguments presented there concerned the scope interactions of quantifiers and *wh*-phrases. For recent discussion of interest on this matter, see May (1988), Jaeggli (1990), Larson and Kim (1989), and Pritchett (1990).

(23) I know which book Mary read, and which book Bill didn't

The reconstructed form of this example, at Logical Form, is shown in (24):

(24) I know which book$_i$ Mary read e_i and which book$_j$ Bill didn't **read
e_j**

This is a well-formed structure because the pattern of indexing is the same, even though the actual indices themselves are not.

Now suppose that reconstruction of ellipsis requires not only that the properties of indices be recapitulated, but also the relations these indices enter into. One relation in which indices can stand is that of forming a Σ-sequence, so that we would expect that if in the antecedent a quantifier that binds a variable in the VP occurs in a Σ-sequence, then this must be recapitulated in the reconstruction of the elided VP. With this extension, we can account for the puzzling contrast of scope possibilities exhibited in (22) by examining their LF-representations. Taking (22a) first, consider (25), derived by copying the antecedent verb phrase, and then applying QR in each clause:

(25) *[everyone$_i$ [some man$_j$ [e_j admires e_i]]], and [**everyone$_i$** [Mary **admires e_i**]]

This structure is ill-formed. The reason is that in the antecedent there is a relation between the quantifiers that is not present in the second conjunct. (26), however, exists as an alternative, differing from (25) in that the quantifiers have been adjoined to VP, not S, a possibility for QR adjunction (May, 1985; Williams, 1977):

(26) [some man$_j$ [e_j [everyone$_i$ [admires e_i]]]], and [Mary [**everyone$_k$**
[**admires e_k**]]]

Here the two quantifiers do not c-command one another; rather, one asymmetrically c-commands the other. As such, their scope relations are fixed, with the existential phrase having broader scope. But as there is no relation between the quantifiers here—no Σ-sequence—there is nothing to be recapitulated in the second clause aside from the structure of the VP. Thus this structure is well-formed, but only with a univocal reading.

Now we turn to (22b). Here, adjunction to S does give a well-formed structure:

(27) [everyone$_i$ [some man$_j$ [e_j admires e_i]]], and [**everyone$_k$** [some
woman$_m$ [e_m **admires e_k**]]]

Because there is a quantifier already in the second clause, a proper reconstruction can be effected, because in both clauses we find parallel Σ-sequences. In this structure, both the properties and relations of the antecedent are properly reconstructed. And, because the quantifiers occur in Σ-sequences, we can interpret this structure under both possible scope orderings of the quantifiers.

On the theory we are considering LF expresses a domain of interpretability for quantification just in case the quantifiers form a Σ-sequence, resulting in structures compatible with a range of construals. Thus, structures of multiple quantification such as (19a) are ambiguous in a strong sense—they represent two distinct interpretations. Ergo, Logical Form is not disambiguated. Now it may appear that to hold this position is to give up effectively the notion that Logical Form is a representation of logical form. But before making such a rash judgment, we need to consider more carefully how Logical Form is mated with its semantic interpretation. On the standard view, unambiguous representations of quantification are generated through a recursive procedure in the syntax. There is, however, also a recursive procedure built into the semantics which comes into play with sentences to which more than one quantifier clause applies. The central semantic notion in the statement of these clauses is that of *satisfaction by a sequence* of individuals. Formally, we say that a sequence σ satisfies a sentence of the form $Qx_i\varphi x_i$ iff for Q-many sequences σ', where σ' differs from σ in at most the ith-place, σ' satisfies φx_i. Now, suppose that we have a multiply quantified sentence of the form $Qx_iQx_j\psi x_ix_j$. The way we proceed is to apply the rule for Qx_i first, for sequences σ' which differ from σ in the ith place, and then the rule for Qx_j, for sequences σ'' which differ from σ' in at most the jth place. To take a concrete example, applying the semantic rules for *every* and *some*, we would evaluate the truth of *Everyone loves someone* relative to a sequence σ by determining that for every sequence σ' that varies from σ in at most the ith place, there is some sequence σ'', that varies from σ' in at most the jth place, such that the relation x_i *loves* x_j holds between the ith and j^{th} individuals. On the other hand, these rules could equally well apply in the opposite order, so that relative to some σ' that varies in the ith place, we consider every σ'' that differs from σ' in no more than the jth. This iterative procedure of rule application can be applied quite generally to multiple quantifiers, and in doing so it induces an ordered dependency among the quantifiers. Thus, the scope ambiguity of *Everyone loves someone* will correspond to whether the semantic clause of the universal phrase precedes that of the existential, or vice versa.[9]

Now, if logical form is disambiguated, it is plain, in virtue of compositionality, that the order of application of the quantifier rules mirrors the scope order of the quantifiers, as represented at Logical Form. But then there is a redundancy between the syntactic and semantic descriptions of quantification, because particular dependency relations between quantifiers are characterized both in their logical structure, via scope, and in their semantic structure, by the ordering of application of the quantifier clauses. On the revised theory of Logical Form, however, this redundancy is eliminated, as there is no representation of any scope dependencies which hold *between* the quantifiers. But observe that because the statements of these dependencies is truly redundant,

---

[9]This argument can be restated in terms of the application of binary absorbed quantifiers, a derived type of generalized quantifier; see May (1989).

eliminating them syntactically will not affect the overall expressiveness of the theory, as the dependencies will still be induced semantically. The only issue at hand, then, is whether our "ambiguous" representations are correctly structured to allow for proper truth definitions for quantified sentences to be derived, so that associated with "ambiguous" sentences will be multiple truth definitions.

For the syntax to be correctly structured, it need be that it deterministically provides for the following sorts of information: (a) that certain quantifier rules are properly applicable and (b) how many of them apply relative to a given structural domain. Clearly this information is represented in structures such as (19a) under our "ambiguous" interpretation—it allows just the same definitions of open and closed sentence, free and bound occurrence of variables, et cetera as before, and from them we can determine that the quantifiers in the initial cluster all have the same sentential domain. The information that is missing from such representations is what ordering relations hold between the quantifiers. But whatever dependencies there are among them will arise simply from the ordering combinatorics of the semantic clauses that interpret them.

In saying that Logical Form is not disambiguated, what we are saying is that it does not support a "relative" notion of scope, one which holds among the quantifiers themselves. This notion of scope has a rather different status semantically than an "absolute" notion of scope. The absolute notion is necessary to the determination of whether the semantic rules are applicable at all, whether their "structural description" is satisfied. The relative notion only comes into play to keep straight the precise ordering of these rules, given that more than one is antecedently applicable. *Any syntax that provides an absolute notion has a logical form.* It does not follow, however, that a syntax that does not support a relative notion is not a logical form. The relative notion provides sufficiency only. A syntax that failed to support a relative notion of scope would only not determine any precise ordering of semantic rules; it would not fail to determine that the rules apply. The search for necessary and sufficient conditions applies to our *overall* theory of the semantics of natural language. There is no reason why the syntax should be required to carry the entire burden.

On our view, then, it is a proper description of the linguistic level of Logical Form to say of it that it embeds a logical form, a representation of the form of the logical terms of the language. In giving this characterization, we have distinguished two parts of the project: the syntactic one of specifying the logical form and the semantic one of specifying its truth definition. We can also distinguish a third part, the logical part of the project, concerned with specifying inference. A traditional view of the logical project was that it falls in with the syntactic project: Inference, on this view, is a formal relation between sentences of the language itself. But if the language, in the guise of its logical form, is not disambiguated then this is clearly not viable, as we could not insure that we were inferring truths from truths. But if ambiguity is fully resolved only with respect to the truth definition, that is, in the semantics relative to the interpretation of the language, then it follows that the logical project must be aligned with the semantic one. Thus, the notion of logical consequence of sentences in the language is to be characterized indirectly, relative to a notion of valid entailment determined by the logic of the semantic meta-language. This is because it is only with respect to the meta-language that we will find the disambiguation necessary for a theory of inference. Disambiguation, therefore, is a constraint on the *logical* enterprise; it is not a constraint on the syntactic enterprise. The latter's semantic task is just to characterize a level of representation that supports the truth definition for the language, and nothing in that inherently requires disambiguation.

To conclude, to the semantic naturalist language has a logical syntax because it reflects deep properties of language itself. If natural language has a structure which looks very much like what we see in logic it is not because we have imposed upon it some ultimately artificial notions of logic, but rather because this is what the grammar of natural language itself determines its structure to be.

ACKNOWLEDGMENTS

I am most pleased to contribute this paper to a volume for Lila Gleitman, especially one that celebrates her brief, but highly successful, tenure in linguistics at Swarthmore College. I had the pleasure of being one of Lila's students during that time, and as my first teacher of linguistics, it was she who initially sparked my interest and set me down the road I follow today. Although our particular research interests are quite divergent, I believe that the scholarly standards she set, the vigor with which she undertook her research, and her love of the study of language have been part of my inspiration for linguistics from those very first days. I hope they will remain so for the rest.

REFERENCES

Aoun, J., Hornstein, N. & Sportiche, D. (1981). Some aspects of wide scope quantification. *Journal of Linguistic Research*, *1*, 69–95.

Aoun, J., & Sportiche, D. (1983). On the formal theory of government. *Linguistic Review*, *2*, 211–236.

Chomsky, N. (1957). *Syntactic structures*. The Hague: Mouton.

Fiengo, R., & May, R. (1991). *Indexing and Identity*. Manuscript in preparation.

Heim, I. (1982). *The semantics of definite and indefinite noun phrases*. Unpublished doctoral dissertation, University of Massachusetts, Amherst.

Heim, I., Lasnik, H. & May, R. (1991). Reciprocity and plurality. *Linguistic Inquiry*, *21*, 63–101.

Higginbotham, J. (1985). On semantics, *Linguistic Inquiry*, *16*, 547–594.

Higginbotham, J. & May, R. (1981). Questions, quantifiers and crossing, *Linguistic Review*, *1*, 41–79.

Hintikka, J. (1989). Logical form and linguistic theory. In A. George (Ed.), *Approaches to Chomsky*. Oxford: Basil Blackwell.

Hirschbühler, P. (1982). VP-deletion and across-the-board quantifier scope. In J. Pustejovsky & P. Sells, (Eds.), *Proceedings of NELS 12*, GLSA, University of Massachusetts, Amherst, MA. University of Massachusetts, Amherst, MA: Graduate Student Linguistics Association.

Huang, J., & May, R. (Eds.). (1991). *Logical structure and linguistic structure*. Dordrecht: Kluwer.

Jaeggli, O. (1990). Head government in LF-representations. In J. Huang & R. May (Eds.), *Logical structure and linguistic structure*. Dordrecht: Kluwer.

Larson, R. (1985). On the syntax of disjunction scope. *Natural Language and Linguistic Theory*, *3*, 217–264.

Larson, R., & Kim, Y. (1989). Scope interpretation and the syntax of psych-verbs. *Linguistic Inquiry*, *20*, 681–688.

May, R. (1977). *The grammar of quantification*. Unpublished doctoral dissertation, MIT, Cambridge, MA.

May, R. (1985). *Logical form: Its structure and derivation*. Cambridge, MA: MIT Press.

May, R. (1986). *Review of R. Cooper "Quantification and Syntactic Theory."* Language, *62*, 902–908.

May, R. (1988). Ambiguities of quantification and *wh:* A reply to Williams. *Linguistic Inquiry*, *19*, 118–135.

May, R. (1989). Interpreting logical form. *Linguistics and Philosophy*, *12*, 387–435.

May, R. (1991). Syntax, semantics and logical form. In A. Kasher (Ed.), *The Chomskian turn*. Oxford: Basil Blackwell.

Nishigauchi, T. (1990). *Quantification in the theory of grammar*. Dordrecht: Kluwer.

Pereira, F. (1989). A calculus for semantic composition and scoping, *Proceedings of the 27th Annual Meeting of the Association of Computational Linguistics*, Vancouver, British Columbia.

Pritchett, B. (1990). A note on scope interaction with plural NPs. *Linguistic Inquiry*, *21*, 646–654.

Reinhart, T. (1976). *The syntactic domain of anaphora*. Unpublished doctoral dissertation, MIT, Cambridge, MA.

Reinhart, T. (1983). *Anaphora and semantic interpretation*. London: Croon Helm.

Sag, I. (1976). *Deletion and logical form*. Unpublished doctoral dissertation, MIT, Cambridge, MA.

Sher, G. (1989). *Generalized logic*. Unpublished doctoral dissertation, Columbia University, New York.

Sommers, F. (1982). *The logic of natural language*. Oxford: Oxford University Press.

Thomason, R. (1974). Introduction to R. Thomason (ed.), Formal *philosophy: Selected papers of Richard Montague*, New Haven: Yale University Press.

Williams, E. (1977). Discourse and logical form. *Linguistic Inquiry*, *8*, 101–139.

Author Index

A

Abraham, W. C., 6, *17*
Adamson, L., 91, *103*
Aldridge, M. V., 213, *221*
Als, H., 91, *103*
Amiel-Tison, C., 175, *180*
Andersen, G. J., 63, 81, *86*
Anderson, J. R., 30, *31*
Anderson, S., 157, *168*
Anstis, S. M., 61, *87*
Aoun, J., 189, 190, *205*, 282, *287*
Arbib, M. A., 31, *31*
Armstrong, S. L., 36, 50, *52*
Aronoff, M., 261, *265*
Asher, S. R., 105, *126*
Ashmead, D. H., 1, 6, 7, 8, *17*

B

Balota, D. A., 125, 126, *127*
Barwise, J., 207, 217, *221*
Basri, H., 262, *267*
Bates, E., 105, *128*
Battison, R., 225, 232, 239, *243*, *244*
Beck, J., 60, *87*
Beebe, R., 91, *104*
Bellugi, U., 225, *244*
Bennett, S., 91, *104*

Berlyne, D., 90, *103*
Bertoncini, J., 175, *180*
Bever, T. G., 105, 124, *127*, 254, 264, *266*
Biederman, I., 146, *168*
Bienkowski, M. A., 108, *129*
Bloom, K., 91, *103*
Bock, J. K., 105, 114, 115, 122, 124, *127*,
128
Boland, J. E., 125, 126, *127*
Borer, H., 184, *205*
Born, W. S., 85, *88*
Bower, G. H., 31, *31*
Bower, T. G. R., 1, 2, 3, 4, 5, 8, 12, *16*
Bowerman, M., 161, *168*
Boyes-Braem, P., 225, *244*
Braddick, O. J., 79, *87*
Brame, M., 261, *265*
Brazelton, T., 91, *103*
Brodie, B., 217, *221*
Bromberger, S., 247, *266*
Broughton, J. M., 1, 2, 3, 12, *16*
Brown, P. M., 108, 119, 126, *127*
Brown, R., 171, 172, 179, *180*, 184, *205*
Brugman, C., 162, *168*
Bruner, J. S., 1, 3, 6, 10, 13, 16, 91, 101,
103, *104*
Bryant, P. E., 9, *16*
Bullowa, M., 91, 101, *103*
Burgess, C., 108, *129*
Burroughs, W. J., 154, *168*
Bushnell, E. W., 1, 6, 7, 12, *16*, *17*

289

X, Y

Z

Subject Index